Pre-Marital

Counseling

Pre-Marital

Counseling

By

AARON L. RUTLEDGE

SCHENKMAN PUBLISHING COMPANY, INC.

Cambridge, Massachusetts

Copyright © 1966

SCHENKMAN PUBLISHING COMPANY, INC.

Cambridge, Massachusetts 02138

PRINTED IN THE UNITED STATES

Library of Congress Catalog Card Number: 65-25590

To My Wife With Gratitude

To My Children With Hope

CONTENTS

ix

PREFACE

A perpetual concern of educator and counselor is where to focus in order to render the two-fold service of preventing illness and stimulating healthy growth. When is it most appropriate to invest professionally in an individual's life?

The best preparation for marriage is composed of all those experiences of living so natural that they do not attract attention. But hurtful experiences occur also, and a complicated society throws a thousand blocks in the path of healthy development. By the time of marriage much of the personality structure is established, and yet a lasting human characteristic is the capacity to grow and to change. As marriage approaches, all the forces of nature—sex, love, self-fulfillment, relating—are available to be guided and utilized in renewed personality growth. This is one of the greatest teachable moments or opportunities for learning. A minimum of skilled help at this time can effect changes in personality that would take years to accomplish later, and basic ways of handling relationship problems can be developed for a life of meaningful interaction. Premarital counseling is the greatest educational and clinical opportunity in the life of a person—still time to effect adult personality changes and at the same time invest in soon-to-be-born children; a chance to influence both the chicken and the egg.

Family life educators in high school and college, ministers and other religious leaders, family service, planned parenthood, and other agency personnel, marriage counselors, physicians, psychologists, social workers and many others now are awakening to the tremendous need and challenge of preparation for marriage. Divorces will become easier to obtain in the future, but the probability is that marriage laws will be tightened progressively, perhaps even to the point of requiring pre-marital counseling, although coercion can never take the place of individual motivation.

This book may be approached in a variety of ways. As a graduate text, Part Two, which is an extensive annotated bibliography of background literature, may be studied first. The practicing clinician may wish to skim through this content, becoming familiar enough to use it as a reference when indicated, and move more directly to Part One, where principles and process are the focus.

This text is directed to those professional people who are involved in the task of preparing youth for married living, including parenthood. It would be as inappropriate to tell the professional what to do with each case as that technique would be with the clients themselves. Therefore, this is neither a "do it yourself" pre-marital construction kit nor "three easy lessons" for the aspiring counselor. Rather it is a description of principles and process out of one man's experience with hundreds of couples; through it each counselor may be stimulated to evolve his own methods of working effectively with people before they are married, with each successive couple his teacher.

Chapter 1

PREPARATION FOR MARRIAGE

The multifaceted family life of today produces an endless variety of personalities who in turn multiply the types of marriages and of family dynamics in the culture. This means that the ways of finding meaningfulness within marriage are endless; but *when* preparation for a particular marriage begins must be considered.

A. WHERE DOES PREPARATION FOR MARRIAGE BEGIN?

Ideally, preparation for marriage is a never-ending cycle in the family—from babyhood to matehood, to parenthood, to babyhood again—and in the community. The best preparation for married living is comprised of all those experiences which are so natural that they do not call special attention to themselves. As the tiny baby grows and learns through sharing and receiving, the fundamental self-image so necessary to full self-expression is being formed. As the year and a half or two year old, and the four or five year old, works out identification with parents of both sexes, he is gaining the clarity of identity that will serve him well in later stages of growth, and in man-woman relationships. As all of this continues in the older child, as he grows a value system, and builds inner guidance and control, the timbers of a future marriage are in the making. As puberty comes with its confusing internal and external transitions, and as young adulthood brings rapidly increasing freedom and responsibility, the individual is getting ready for the kind of marriage relationship he will be able to achieve in any marriage he contracts. A clear-cut realistic sense of self-identity is the cornerstone of the marital structure.

I. Maturity for Marriage

Modern marriage calls for more emotional maturity, at least in its developing form, than any other relationship. Saul [1] outlined several "levels of maturity" which are applicable here. These are not meant to be ascending steps up the ladder of growth, but rather, each affords an area in which one can check the progress of his maturing. As a scientific basis for

[1] Saul, Leon J., *Emotional Maturity*, Philadelphia: J. B. Lippincott, 1947, pp. 3-22.

morality, he considered the evil in man as the "persisting traumatic infantile," and saw good not as submissiveness to a code but as an expression of the strength of maturity. The goal of human brotherhood reflects this struggle to grow up. Social peace demands inner peace and the only path to inner peace is the path to maturity. This is especially true in the marriage relationship. Saul sees maturity in terms of movement in several critical areas:

1) *The dependence-independence scale.* Each individual proceeds at varying speeds and to varying degrees from a state of intra-uterine dependence upon the mother to complete independence from the parents. Perhaps the attraction in both directions—dependence-independence—composes the central struggle of adolescence and young adulthood.

2) *The give-get balance.* The growing person sees a gradual increase in his productive capacity and a consequent decrease in receptive needs, finding it increasingly at least as "blessed" to give as to receive. The healthier an individual is the more he enjoys the actual investment of self in his work, not merely the paycheck or status involved.

3) *Troublesome feelings.* Part of the growth process is learning to handle the constellations of inferiority feelings, egotism and competitiveness so prevalent in the culture. True, one "ought not to think more highly of himself than he ought to think," but it is equally imperative not to think too lowly of self: one's opinion of others will be colored drastically by his opinion of himself. *Undue comparison* of oneself to others is both unrealistic and unhealthy. One can never be like another and comparison either leads to feelings of superiority and contempt, or to inferiority feelings and hatred of the one considered superior. *To compete* with another, in terms of personal worth, ultimately is to resent him. If the goal is to become like the other person or better than he, failure usually ensues. The failure is projected upon the object of competition, who, in turn, catches the resultant hatred. One of the most destructive elements in the culture is neurotic competition. One lives most effectively "for the joy of living," not for the thrill of conquering. Other sources of insecurity, and thus of endless troublesome feelings, include passive-receptive-dependent desires, physical defects, real or imagined guilt, hurt pride, fear, and many regressive forces.

4) *Sexual responsibility.* Few functions have so much potential for health or for destruction as sexual drive and expression. The maturing person accepts his sexual nature and moves toward the attainment of

genital sexuality, which involves a willingness to accept responsibility for one's own sexual life and possible children.

5) *Hostility,* the most destructive force yet to be unleashed in the universe, is based primarily upon unresolved emotional problems of early childhood and later maturing. Fear, aggression, defense and atonement is the neurotic cycle. Every person responds with hostility at times, but the growing person learns to divert this energy away from destruction of self and of others into constructive, productive channels.

6) *Rose-tinted glasses* must be removed. Each person tends to see situations and people in terms of his own feelings, which often are traceable to childhood and early adult reactions which have not been outgrown. This impairs individual efficiency and happiness. Facing reality can be painful, but it is a necessary and profitable step toward emotional maturing.

7) The growing person will be *highly flexible and adaptable,* whereas the stunted individual will go through life repeating reactions which were appropriate to hurtful childhood situations, but quite inappropriate to adult living. For instance, one may tend to repeat compulsively with his spouse or children the treatment he received from his parents or siblings.

Maturity means not merely the capacity for these attitudes and functions, but also the ability to enjoy them to the fullest.

II. Barriers to Marital Readiness

An alarmingly high percentage of youth grows up with poor preparation for marriage, as evidenced by the marital break-up rate and the disruptive conflict in the marriages that survive. Being old enough to join the army or to vote does not mean that one has the emotional maturity necessary to the role of husband or wife. One can be "of age" physically and intellectually and yet be a veritable infant in handling emotions. This *emotional infantilism* reveals itself in the unpleasant temperament or disposition of one who is out of harmony with himself and his environment, in incapability for new ideas and interests, perhaps in jealousy and tantrums when disappointed. It is an immature person who *demands* that he be the "head of the house," who has to avoid having children because he would resent sharing love; or who expects marriage to be made up of a perpetual courtship based upon physical attraction alone.

Unconscious needs in the motivation for marriage add to the confusions of every couple. Marriage is a way of incorporating that which promises to make the self complete, fulfilling the unrealized side of the self. Although in external matters "like is attracted to like," at the level of deep emotional needs mate selection often tends to be on the basis of complementarity. It is as if each person seeks to marry himself, or the side of self that can be realized only through another. Often this is a side of self which is both longed for and rejected at the same time; therefore, the mate is subjected to the ambivalent feelings toward his hidden part of self-need; "damned if he does and if he doesn't." Extremely neurotic men and women are notorious for their attraction to each other on the unrealistic promise of meeting each other's unfulfilled insatiable needs.

A surprisingly large percentage of marital struggle is due to the *re-enactment of earlier unsatisfactory relationships and experiences.* Marriage is complicated by a multitude of unresolved, carry-over feelings from childhood which try to find satisfaction in the new relationship, including those growing out of parent-child and other authoritative situations, sibling and peer rivalries and unresolved love affairs. To the clinician, these can be seen as clear cut "transference" relations in which unresolved needs and issues of the past are acted out repetitiously on the new stage of engagement and marriage. Both neurotic and healthy complementarity are discussed further in Chapter 2, The Nature of Marriage.

Other barriers to adequate preparation for married living are found in the way in which *custom tends to dictate* the events prior to marriage, even push the couple into marriage. In certain lower socio-economic groups intensive dating, often characterized by a minimum of verbal communication and a maximum of sexual expression, is followed by early marriage. The decision to marry may be precipitated by a joint decision that they were meant for each other or joint decision to give a name to their unborn child or the insistence of the girl that they must marry because they have had intercourse, or by her refusing further sexual relations unless they get married, or the insistence of parents, friends, church, or the law that they should marry because of pregnancy.

In middle class America a period of regular dating, in which the field gradually is narrowed, is followed by a more or less formal engagement and a planned wedding. Any of the factors mentioned above may speed up the decision to marry in this class as well, and it is probable that this tendency is increasing. Youth of the upper class may have less to say about whom they marry than either the lower or middle class, although a great deal is made of the engagement and wedding. In most cases for all classes of society more attention by far is given to the material aspects of wedding plans than to the emotional aspects of marriage.

Much attention has been given to the fact that *sex urges* play a dominant part in pre-marital and early marital relationships. Nevertheless certain vital factors seldom are mentioned by parents or youth. Although sexual attraction within the home—to mother, father, or siblings—is seldom discussed, it can become the chief pressure that forces a youth to get out before hurt occurs. This is not limited to cases where overt sexual advances are made; in fact, anxiety may be all the stronger because the urges have been kept repressed by parent, child, or both. Emerging sex needs of the youth threaten to put desire and object together in consciousness. Thus flight from home into marriage may seem to be the healthiest of the two choices for a young person. Often the problem of growing sex need is handled by fleeing into pre-marital sex behavior, which is then legalized and made compatible with conscience by marriage.

There is another closely related factor which leads many couples to marriage before they are grown up sufficiently for the responsibility entailed. Marriage is the only ticket to adulthood for the children of many families, and no matter how old, educated, wise, and financially adequate these youths may be, these parents continue treating them as children. As a desperate bid for recognition as an emerging adult, such youths often seek to prove their maturity by rushing into marriage.

In addition to the unconscious and semi-conscious sources of marital difficulty, there are factors of which the couple are quite aware that may become the proverbial back-breaking straw, unless these are understood and made manageable prior to marriage. The most deadly is found in the magical promise of marriage today. Marriage is supposed to combine the virtues of a vacation in a tropical paradise, a successful psychoanalysis, and a religious conversion experience, all in one painless dose. Educational efforts of both religion and social science, coupled with popular communication media, have raised the expectations from marriage to an all-time high. This is seen in the kinds of personality desired in a mate, as well as in what is expected of him socially, economically, in the love life, and in terms of "happiness." Yet, there are many barriers to marital preparedness. Emotional infantilism, unconscious ambivalent needs, reenactment of early unsatisfactory relationships, the push of sex and loneliness, lack of other avenues to symbolic adulthood, all coupled with a pollyanna promise of self-fulfillment in all these areas can add up to an irresistible push toward the altar. Such a ground swell can leave little time or energy for pre-marital counseling.

The trouble is that "know how" has failed to keep pace with the rising goals for marital success. It is like being convinced of the pot of gold at the end of the rainbow, only to find the end is out of reach, or like offering the child candy on a shelf only to withhold the stepping stool which would make it possible to reach the sweets. When these high expectations are not forthcoming in a marriage, the result is further alienation and misery. The couple is torn apart inwardly as they visualize the satisfactions desired in contrast to their present static marital state. It is little wonder that many give up in despair and find divorce necessary.

But this does not mean that change cannot be made in adulthood or that all possibility of growth is ended at majority. It does indicate that youth must be sold on the advantage of preparedness before the tide of need begins to erode reason. High school and college personnel, especially counselors and family life teachers, are beginning to provide some assistance toward readiness for marriage over and above the usual course content. Churches are beginning to realize their responsibility in family life education. But these combined efforts may not be enough when the couple is approaching the beginning of a new family. Whatever has been accomplished previously, much remains to be done after the counselor is invited into the wedding plans of a couple. It is his opportunity to help them check out the degree of readiness and set about the remaining tasks for the most demanding challenge of adulthood.

III.   Readiness for Change

Much of the success of a marriage arrives ready-made in the structure of the two personalities. But this is not as fatalistic as it might seem, since each mate also brings the possibility of change. Each person grows the basic timbers of personality in the early years of life. It is equally true, however, that one of the lasting characteristics of personality is the ability to change and grow.

A good proportion of marriages occur during adolescence, a time of personality upheaval. For youth in this culture, the degree of personality disorganization and confusion can have many of the ear marks of a pre-psychotic state, as the transition from childhood to adulthood, prolonged unmercifully in the absence of "rites of passage," activates any previous doubts about self. This is accompanied by activation of past hurts, excavation of painful memories, and the kind of confusion about self-identity and worth that can make adolescence a painful period indeed. To the healthier youth this state of "flux" provides an opportunity for reintegration of personality at a more meaningful level as he steps over into adulthood.

For those who have been seriously deprived and crippled, or who do not receive sufficient guidance and assistance, the pain of the experience has to be guarded against, accounting for much of the bizarre acting-out behavior common to adolescence. The denial of the disturbing elements brought to awareness in the personality upheaval accounts for much of the stubborn refusal to accept professional help at this time.

There is something about an approaching wedding, at least for those who take the time to think at all about its seriousness, that can create the same state of individual upheaval common to adolescence. Popular humor about the insane nature of love is not without grounds. As thinking people of any age approach marriage, the emotional stage is set for personality change—regression, or stabilization by means of concretized personality defenses, or a new level of healthy integration setting the basis for continued growth—just as is true in the adolescent struggle. On the other hand, the activation of unresolved emotional needs, exacerbation of self doubts, dislodgment of defenses previously thought to be strengths, heightening of ambivalences, coupled with all the anxiety-creating personality needs outlined earlier in this chapter, can make it necessary to bring closure by moving precipitously into the marriage relationship. If means can be found to impinge upon the couple at the time of this upheaval, they can be helped to use the anxiety and energy from the turmoil as an investment in pre-marital counseling. The need is present, admitted or not. Someone must make them aware of the value and availability of professional assistance. Once the counselor is involved, the stimulus of engagement and aspirations for a good marriage can be utilized as an opportunity for renewed growth of both personality and relationship.

Every therapist knows how difficult it is to "tell" people the solution to problems or the secrets of growth. It doesn't permeate their personalities, doesn't become integrated; it is only superimposed on old conditioning. It takes time to bring about personality change and renewed growth. Yet, many young people will be particularly susceptible to guidance when approaching marriage, motivated by the emotional and sexual need for each other. The desire to establish a meaningful family life can be as strong as the need for sexual mating. Here is one of the "teachable moments" or opportunities for learning, the like of which comes only a few times after early childhood. With the total impetus of nature, tremendous growth can occur, if motivation is stimulated and direction is provided. A minimum of concentrated help here can bring about personality changes which might take years of psychotherapy to effect later.

"Delay marriage until you are more grown up," is a major plea, especially in middle class groups, and the high rate of failure among early marriages justifies the admonition. But merely waiting for more birthdays may have little to do with maturing for marriage. College *can* be an extension of adolescence which gets in the way of the kind of emotional maturing necessary to marriage. The college youth thus, in effect, puts off for four years the kind of growing up and facing of adult responsibility which those who marry upon graduating from high school must begin to handle almost imediately, whether or not they are prepared.

At any age it is evident that immaturity is a primary cause of marital friction and breakdown, but little has been written about marriage as a positive force in growing up. The young engaged couple might be the first to admit their unreadiness for all responsibilities of "pair living" and of parenthood. But it is as though all the forces for growth and health decide to cast their lot with marriage, knowing that it will call for and demand the best youth has, including continued growth. Along with the host of people who get hurt and end an early marriage, and those who have to "practice" in several marriages before being able to find one they can tolerate, the counselor must not lose sight of the tremendous challenge to growth which a marriage can provide. Such growth might never occur for some of those under the protective wings of the parental home.

This readiness for change in the engaged seems to be contradicted by the fact that most couples do not seek such help in getting ready for marriage. Such unwillingness may be based on ignorance of the value of counseling, or upon a sense of false modesty, or false pride. On the other hand, it may be fear of facing facts about oneself or about the relationship. Beneath the fears and hesitancy a genuine desire for assistance, which will assert itself once initial barriers are removed, often is found. The most frequent reason for not seeking help is the failure of homes, churches, schools, and counselors to underline its value and to make pre-marital counseling readily available. Increasingly, youth, particularly those who go to college, are seeking professional help to insure preparation for growth in their marriage, rather than risk hurt and failure.

B. A FRAME OF REFERENCE FOR PRE-MARITAL COUNSELING

The people who do pre-marital counseling will come from such professional backgrounds as pastoral counseling, psychology, social work, family life education, medicine, and marriage counseling. Those who are best prepared for pre-marital counseling have studied the basic premises and contributions from all these fields, (see Chapters 9 and 10, Prerequisite Knowledge). The virtues of eclecticism were never greater than in working with young people who are anticipating marriage. However, one can get lost unless these many approaches and accumulated data can be assimilated, synthesized, and begin to emerge as a unified approach to personal and marital development and function. The pre-marital counselor who has made extensive and intensive excursions into the world of professional literature and clinical practice begins to need a simplified reference point which will be functional, stable, and yet modifiable through experience.

I. An Individual Frame of Reference

While recognizing that some kinds of results, often helpful, can be obtained through any approach to counseling and from within any possible frame of reference (this in itself is a tribute to human potential), a brief statement of the philosophy underlying the writing of this text may challenge others to grow their own functional frame of reference.

1. A Philosophy of Man

This viewpoint rejects the concept of "total depravity" wherein man by nature is wholly inclined to evil and has no good in him, a position held today by about as many scientists, although described in different terminology, as theologians. Likewise it rejects the good-bad, flesh-spirit dichotomy, a view which is popular among certain churchmen and which was secularized into Freud's basic instincts of *Thanatos* and *Eros,* and the Americanized version of "love against hate." It refuses to believe that man is *tabula rasa* or "psycho-physically neutral," except in that the baby is born neutral in a moral and ethical sense.

The newborn infant, the foetus for that matter, is a unified whole; actions are responses of the total person and are teleological, and within the organism, as with any energy system, is a tendency to become as nearly complete, to gain as complete self-realization, as circumstances will permit. This is true, whether one examines physical, social, or emotional aspects of growth, or total growth. This potential is not a placid, plastic substance which lies inert waiting to receive environmental imprints. To the contrary, the baby is a kicking, squirming, reacting entity, beginning instantly to make his own imprint upon the environment and to determine somewhat its effect upon him. This is potential with a push toward organismic self-realization. Environment does not act simply as a coercive field whose pressure casts the person into a certain mold; rather it provides for the raw material, the specific and general stimuli, and the opportunities for collaboration between the internal and the external forces. At the point of convergence of the inner potential and the environmental stimuli, occurs the real person.

This inner force or potential of the organism for growth has been described variously. The Gestaltists saw it as a tendency toward wholeness, a principle which is inherent in the universe. Rank described it as "will"; others, as cause and effect, resulting from efforts to meet one's needs for satisfaction. Jiminy Cricket called it "just the nature of things." This tendency toward self-development, self-realization, self-fulfillment—toward wholeness, completeness, and health—is closely related to the Judeo-Christian concept of *Imago Dei*. Man is made "in the image of God," has capacity for some of the traits attributed to the Supreme Being, including love, and wholeness, which results in spontaneous autonomy (every man is his own priest), empathy (love your fellow as yourself), creativity (co-laborers with God), and other personal competencies.[2]

2. Principles of Growth

Fundamental to any workable frame of reference is the concept of growth. What is its nature? How does it take place? The principles of personality growth can best be illustrated by focusing briefly upon the process of physical development. All growth, whether animal, mineral or vegetable, happens according to principles. A new life begins when the sperm and egg unite in conception. The nuclei merge, chromosomes and genes pair off and cellular division begins. All phases of the growth process are present and active at this early stage. One phase is *differentiation,* by which the body grows in size and shape, developing legs, liver, lungs and appendages. Another part of the growth process is *integration.* These two facets of growth must proceed concomitantly if a healthy organism is to result. Too much differentiation produces freaks or imperfect development of the organism. Cells running rampant in differentiation, with the process of integration failing to keep pace, may result in tumorous growth. The third element in growth is *assimilation.* In order to grow physically, to provide energy for growth, the organism must have the

[2] Maslow, A. H., "Self-Actualizing People, A Study of Psychological Health," Wolff, W., editor, from *Personality Symposium, No. 1,* New York: Grune and Stratton, 1950, pp. 11-34; Jahoda, Marie, *Current Concepts of Positive Mental Health,* New York: Basic Books, 1958; and Goldstein, Kurt, *The Organism, A Holistic Approach to Biology,* Boston: Beacon Press 1939, 1963.

sustenance of food, water, and oxygen. No one has to guide the growth of the prenatal organism; egg and sperm united in a nourishing environment sets nature's process into operation.

Only physical growth has been described to this point, but of course any such division is artificial. Physical growth cannot be separated from what might be called emotional growth, or social growth, or personal growth, or, to string them together, emotional-social-personal growth. Any actual separation represents a degree of "malgrowth." They can be separated only arbitrarily in discussing functions of an individual in an effort to understand the whole person. The point is that all growth occurs according to these same principles. The all-inclusive basic drive in any organism is to self-fulfillment, but self-fulfillment in man far surpasses that of even the most highly developed of other animals. Even so, such a personality grows by the joint process of simultaneous differentiation and integration, fed by assimilation. This is as true of functions—i.e., manual, intellectual, problem solving, relating—as of physical structure. Differentiation can precede integration somewhat, but integration catches up, else the result is some kind of physical or personality malformation.

3. Sustenance for Growth

This raises the question of what is the basic sustenance on which human personality grows and thrives. Solving this dilemma provides the most fundamental value next to personality itself.

The most basic of all human needs can best be described as *nearness*.[3] It is closeness; the absence of loneliness, of isolation. The human being needs to be an individual, not only in childhood and in marriage, but an individual in relationship. Just as food and oxygen are necessary to grow and maintain a body, nearness is essential to a healthy personality. This is the most basic *human* need. Nearness provides emotional-social-physical nourishment for the growth, maintenance, and smooth functioning of an individual. Nearness is fundamental to the beginning of life, and to all subsequently described as relationship, empathy, rapport, fellowship, sharing, and love. It is from the fulfilling of this need that spontaneous relationships flow.

Many child development specialists describe *the baby* as fundamentally selfish. There is no argument with this because selfishness is a healthy trait; not the crippled, insatiable kind of self-preoccupation based upon doubts about self-identity, seen in the neurotic, but a comfortable, reasonable, reality-based acceptance of self.

[3] Rutledge, Aaron L., "Missing Ingredient in Marriage: Nearness." *Social Science,* Vol. 36, No. 1, 1961, pp. 88-90.

However, this need for nearness found in the child and in all of nature is not one-sided. Nearness is mutual; always reciprocal. You cannot be near another without his having the opportunity of being close to you. You cannot give without his having a chance to receive from you, nor share without his being available to respond to you.

This too can be illustrated in terms of development. It is in the reciprocal nearness of sexual intercourse that conception occurs. At the moment when egg and sperm unite there is nearness, and the nearness is "give and receive." There is the reciprocity of the pairing of DNA filaments when, in a microscopic manner, the heritage of the ancestors in particular and the human race in general is transmitted. There is nearness of mother and baby in the pre-natal state, and it is a reciprocal, exchanging, total relationship. Then there is the mutuality of mother and baby after birth, prolonged in the human species because of its primary value in personality development. One of the best ways of counteracting some of the basic insecurity in youth today would be providing, in the first days and weeks of life, a great deal more of the skin-to-skin nearness of calm and secure mothering in loving, tender, physical ways.

Gradually the baby becomes able to transcend the physical distance of mother's periodic absence and still feel her presence, her nearness beyond physical touch. Insofar as can be determined, the first effort to think, the first formulation of a symbol with which to think, is when the child puts together the touch, the taste, the smell (and with modern mothers it is a lot of varied smells), the sounds and all of the senses that go into operation when mother is present; the integration of these into an "experience." Whether he sees it as an eidetic image on the screen of his mind or just "feels" it, mother is out there and she is still with him as a presence, a symbol. When the baby has learned to hallucinate mother successfully, begins to be able to accept nearness beyond physical touch, he is ready to permit her to go farther and farther away and still feel secure. He knows she will return. He accepts emotional nearness as a fact of human experience. This becomes the basis for what is later experienced as emotional-spiritual-social nearness of the closest adult relationships.

This most essential environmental element in stimulating the development of human potential, in keeping the self open for growth, is the kind of accepting closeness—feeling, interest, responsiveness—described most often as *love*. Love is one of life's basic energies seeking to express itself. At birth the baby is adapted simply to its nurtured role and its love energy focuses upon self. A most important part of self as then experienced is the mother; in fact, all experience is unitary at this stage of development. Within the child's need of response from the mother, and his own reaching out to her, lies the potential for love of family, friends, country, world, and infinity. The need to give love is quite as great as to receive, but as the child develops he can love others only in proportion to the wholesome opinion he has of himself. This, in turn, is quite dependent upon the manner in which the child is loved.

Whether expressed directly by simple touch, through abstract longings for achievement and beauty, through the multi-faceted desires which culminate in the union of a man and woman, or in the realm of ideas and symbols, love is life's most energizing force. It seeks to cohere all life forces, and in turn to make individuals cohesive through fellowship in the family of mankind.

But it is essential to remember that no matter how skillful one becomes at experiencing love on other than a physical basis, he never loses his need for nearness in the physical sense. In its absence he substitutes potions, lotions and preoccupation with appearance or health, or with the "other person" in the marriage triangle.

A great deal of the struggle *the adolescent* has to face is tied up with the need for nearness. However, he has found in growing up that nearness not only generates love, it can bring hurt. In this period when he is trying to assert himself, to prove himself, to move from childhood to adulthood, much of the struggle comes out of conflict in the need for nearness. In fact, the more the home offers in terms of nearness at adolescence, particularly if sexuality cannot be faced consciously, the greater may be the threat to the adolescent.

As noted earlier, adults do not adequately take into account the seriousness of the conflict provided youth by: (1) enough maturity for physical sex need to be emerging, (2) the overwhelming need for nearness to parents, and (3) the fact that sexual feelings tend to arise within that nearness. Adolescents can become terrified of finding sex needs arising in relation to siblings, or to father and mother. This may precipitate open rejection of parental care at this stage. Then it becomes necessary to find new sources of nearness outside the family, in the school, church, or neighborhood, which accounts in part for the great hold of the peer group upon the adolescent. It contains the answer to many of the sexual explorations of this period, some helpful and some harmful. In many of the most serious problems commonly treated psychotherapeutically, the point of attack could very well be this most basic human need, nearness.

For instance, many psychotherapists and counselors do not get very good results in dealing with homosexuality. Many others who believe that the condition is treatable obtain good results. One of the reasons for failure with people who have this kind of difficulty is that it is treated primarily as a sexual problem, which basically it is not. In the search after nearness, and in the presence of hurts that tend to make one afraid of healthy kinds of nearness, one has to find unnatural substitutes.

Perhaps one other illustration will clarify. Take the period of intensive dating and courtship leading to mate selection, especially for those adolescents and young people who have been hurt in the closeness of growing up, or by the absence of healthy nearness. Add to that the efforts of society, under the guise of protesting youth, to make them afraid of that which they need most. How quickly boys are taught not to show certain kinds of feelings! How early girls are warned against openness, nearness, closeness! Don't dare do this! Lest what? Lest you get hurt. This is carried over into dating practices: Don't show yourself, don't reveal yourself, don't let him know what you're really like—he might not like you. Don't show him what you really think—he might not like you to think that. Don't deal with what is conflicting, you would fight and disagree and maybe break up.

Dating youth try to find with each other the lost nearness of childhood which they had to renounce with siblings and parents. Moreover, now the need for nearness is stimulated and pushed ever more intensely by emerging sexuality. If each person in the couple is rebelling in his own way against parental control or familial value systems, they may not be able to discuss these vital issues because of fear of disagreement. This blocks communication between them. Still the need to share, to give, and the need to receive becomes greater and greater. They must have each other at all costs.

The compromise solution is to find a way to have nearness and yet avoid the kind of conflict and possible rejection that might come if they discussed these controversial issues. Often physical affection becomes the one way to have some of the essence of nearness and yet avoid hurts that would come from verbal sharing of ideas and feelings. Open conflict might bring separation and they can't bear loneliness. Eventually the need to share becomes greater and greater, resulting in increasing physical intimacy. Physical affection becomes the one way of having closeness without running the risk of verbally induced hurts similar to those experienced already in growing up.

Take such a couple into *marriage*. Now the need to share, the need to reveal the total self and be accepted, is greater than ever. But since the necessary skills of communication never have been developed, efforts to share more intensely may lead to hurt. He expresses himself; she doesn't understand, rejects, and he is hurt. Then each of the couple pulls away from ways of sharing that lead to conflict, which may lead to a total breakdown in the relationship. Frequently they fall back into the one way of communicating found already in their sex experience where some of the essence of nearness can occur. But at the end of one year or five years of marriage they may seek help with a sexual problem.

Examination of what happened to end such passionate relating of a couple often reveals that they did have a very good relationship sexually, but—in the absence of other kinds of nearness and other kinds of shared-ness—all of life's messages got chanelled into this one form of expression. Any line of communication, similar to a telephone system, can take just so many messages at a time before everything goes a-jumble. Typical in these marriages is the expression through sex of love, fear, shame, loathing, bitterness, and hostility; the relief of all sorts of physical and emotional tensions; the need to share at any and every level—intellectual, social, emotional. They try to express all of this almost exclusively through the sex drive. Then one day this line of communications, like an overloaded telephone circuit, breaks down. Their sex life is a mess, either non-existent or conflicted, and they come for help. By this time they usually have a great deal of pent-up bitterness, and are making accusations that "he must not love me anymore, must have a girl friend." "She must never have loved me, or we're incompatible." Then they say, "What have we left? There is nothing!"

Many other values in the human sphere, whether systematized or individual, seem efforts to find as much as possible of this most necessary ingredient of reciprocal nearness. When this need is frustrated by blocked communication an almost unbearable loneliness, often ill-defined and vague, sets in and resentment and recriminations ensue. Any imaginable kind of symptom may result, which is described as the real issue when a couple comes for help.

This discussion has been an effort to reduce growth to its simplest components, but human personality does not remain simple for long. Through the simultaneous processes of differentiation and reintegration the total person grows, each step becoming complicated by incalculable multiples. Through example, instruction, experiences both traumatic and pleasurable, the individual comes to perceive things in particular ways and to develop "sets" which determine his behavior. This gives *value* to certain experiences in that they facilitate satisfaction, growth, and self-realization, or they bring pain, illness, isolation, or other forms of discomfort, or simply do not lead to gratification. Such value systems may be imposed from without by parental figures, or they may evolve through experience. Hopefully the last will apply increasingly as the child grows. Such a value system likely will have much in common with the values derived through the experiences of others, although in other ways there will be tremendous diversity. Among the most universal values of man are: growth is more desirous than non-growth, flexibility than rigidity, change than non-change, love than non-love, communication than withdrawal, fellowship than isolation, health than sickness. There are, of course, variations in emphasis upon these values from culture to culture and from person to person.

Man's tendencies to mal-develop are out-growths of healthy tendencies. The human energy system tends to operate with the minimum energy for efficiency for what it needs to accomplish. Often this means that the easiest way is chosen, especially if serious hurt has been encountered, which may prove to be an expensive shortcut. New ideas are implanted, ideas which would open the self to growth; but the traumatized energy system wants to remain stabilized, does not wish to be disturbed or exposed to possible pain. Therefore, the new idea is fenced off, hemmed into a corner, and as a result the possible growth is prevented. Anxiety comes, and there is a shake-up and an effort at reorganization of the self in order to remove the source of anxiety. But once the process of integration is at work, there is a tendency to closure, to put things back together again, in the quickest possible way. This need for equilibrium may short-circuit the chance to grow. Yes, the self wants to rid itself of a troublesome part, but it does not want to risk being destroyed.

Even hostile aggression grows out of a healthy drive. It is simply the "push" of growth, which becomes defensive when threatened and takes on a destructive quality when seriously hurt.

The greatest pain of man is the opposite of love, which is not hate but rather *isolation*. To feel cut off from those whom one cherishes, to be separated from fellowship with what one considers ultimate in his hierarchy of values, this is the sickness unto death; the sickness out of which most troublesome symptoms grow. Only in deprivation of love does one become stingy, rigid, fearful, defensive, and destructive. In love's absence, growth is delayed, and in its contortions and misapplication growth is warped;

yet there is growth. Innate potential does not give up easily. Even when it has been dormant for years, the stimulus of genuine love from another, once it penetrates the shell, may activate the potential and renew the process of growing, loving, and becoming. In this sense, falling in love is an effort to "treat" oneself, to break isolation, to grow again.

All growth, psycho-socio-physical growth, comes from within, but an environment characterized by loving acceptance helps. Progressively then, an individual is the product of what he is born with, including tendencies to growth and self-realization, what happens to him in the environmental milieu, and what he has done and does with these.

Belief in the dignity and worth of every individual is essential if the counselor is to be of assistance to the clients individually and together in freeing themselves for growth and change; for competency, autonomy, empathy, and creative marital interaction.[4] The counselor helps to ventilate, explore, support, clarify; he joins in the search for objectivity, new perspective, new potential, new insight; and his greatest function is to be a source of understanding love. How to apply this love in pre-marital counseling requires the best a counselor has to offer as a scientist and an artist.

II.   A Family Frame of Reference

One does not understand an individual except in the context of his parental family, and further light is found in projecting him into his anticipated family. He is a part of his family and they are a part of him, and here his strength and weakness reveal themselves. Pre-marital counseling calls for a consideration of two individuals who have a unique relationship with each other, and with others within their parental families. Therefore, the pre-marital counselor must have a family frame of reference, as well as an individual orientation. Of necessity the counselor must focus upon maladjustment in individuals and within marriages and families, but he should be just as well versed in what comprises individual and family health. What are the healthy factors to be found in this particular prospective family? The "family frame of reference" is developed at some length in Chapter 2, The Nature of Marriage.

C.   GOALS IN PRE-MARITAL COUNSELING

Culture not only makes people too sick for successful marriage, it provides opportunity for healing and growth. The tradition of engagement

[4] Foote, Nelson and Leonard S. Cottrell, Jr., *Identity and Interpersonal Competence, A New Direction in Family Research.* Chicago: University of Chicago Press, 1955.

provides an opportunity for correcting or learning to utilize many of those factors which have already been discussed as making up both the strengths and inadequacies of two personalities involved.

I. The Purpose of an Engagement

In putting together the experiences of hundreds of youths, along with the findings of many family life educators, engagement is seen as providing an opportunity for:[5]

1) The total process of learning to undertand and relate to each other in all circumstances. "I" and "you" become "we."
2) Undoing unwholesome attitudes developed through earlier conditioning and dating experiences, and exploring the male-female likeness and differences in general and as applicable to each couple.
3) Understanding and evaluating each of the parents, the parents' relationship to each other, the relationship of each to his parents, and the future relationship of the new family to the old family.
4) Determining the kind of marriage and family life desired by the couple, and the beginning of thinking, feeling, and reacting in this context.
5) The continuation of individual growth and acceptance of responsibility, in an atmosphere of love and appreciation, with the "push" of sexuality as one of the driving forces.
6) Working out attitudes and plans for work and family financing.
7) Exploring attitudes toward children, and coming to a beginning plan of how they should be reared.
8) The exploration of personal development and of family life in the larger context of social and spiritual reality.
9) Solution of problems in the feeling and expression of affection, including specific preparation for sex life.
10) Planning the general and specific details of the wedding.
11) The development of long-range family goals, life purposes and values.

II. Pre-marital Counseling Goals

The goals of pre-marital counseling are closely related to the total process of engagement outlined above. The first task of the counselor is to help engaged couples examine their *total readiness* for marriage. Although

5 Waller, Willard, *The Family, A Dynamic Interpretation*. Revised by Reuben Hill, New York: Dryden Press, 1951; also Blood, Robert O. *Anticipating Your Marriage*. Glencoe, Illinois: The Free Press, 1955.

they may have assumed such readiness, it is by no means assured. Their choices are to get married just as they are in spite of the dangers, to break up a relationship that can only be unhealthy or soon end, or to set about in earnest getting ready for marriage with the counselor's aid.

Three areas of investigation claim the counselor's attention if he is to understand each person and to visualize them as a married pair: (1) Personality formation and feelings; (2) Role perception and attitudes of each about self and about the others; and (3) Past failure-success in close personal relations. In this process each may come to a better undertanding of self, of the prospective mate, and of the relationship they are growing. All such knowledge begins with the knowledge of self.

1. Things to be done

There are many areas which are related to personality development and to marriage relationship about which the young person needs to know as much as possible. Much of this knowledge has been attained in the process of growing up but it needs to be corrected and supplemented by rigorous study of the marriage and family literature available. But facts are only the beginning point of learning. The failure or the success of a marriage seems to be more dependent upon attitudes, feelings and habituated behavioral patterns than upon the knowledge of facts. Various specialists have estimated that 75 to 90 per cent of the factors involved in the meaningfulness of marriage are due to these less conscious, learned processes of relating and responding in close personal relationships.[6]

One of the foremost tasks of any young person who is contemplating marriage is the discovery of his basic selfhood and the *continued growth* of himself as a person; this is the first goal in pre-marital counseling. The kind of equalitarian marriage desired by increasing numbers of young people demands the highest possible level of growth of those who undertake it. Although marriage itself can be a maturing process for an individual, he must have attained a reasonable degree of adult growth and responsibility if he is to carry his end of the multi-faceted responsibilities of modern marriage. It is through the wholeness of healthy self-identity that one can experience the oneness of heterosexual relationship, and thus further stimulate his growth as an individual of worth.

Perhaps *skill in communication,* discussed further in Chapter 3, is as important as any other one factor in developing a healthy marriage. In spite of the almost overwhelming mass communication to which the citizenry is

[6] Waller, Willard, *Op. cit.*

subjected, there is ample evidence that in more intimate relationships this is a nation of noncommunicators. Early in development children are taught by example, if not by word of mouth, to conceal their real feelings about many things. All too often this is taken over to the dating stage by youth, basing their experience upon the "line" of a deceptive front. Dating and courtship catch young people at a period when egos are easily threatened. They are in the process of moving away from parents and yet have not proved themselves fully as adults. If they have been conditioned against exposing their inmost feelings lest they be hurt, then deception will play a major role in dating. Although not often put into words within the dating experience, one of the mottoes that seems to underlie much of this period of development is: "All is fair in love and war, especially deceit."

When two people enter into an engagement, or formally or informally assent to begin thinking about marriage, attitudes and techniques based upon deception as protection for the ego will be detrimental. A truce must be signed and time allowed for redefining roles and restructuring relationships to the end that they begin to understand each other and much of their own complicated make-up as individuals, and begin to evolve techniques for honest and forthright relating.

Without specific and deliberate intent to do otherwise, courtship and engagement may serve only as a continuation of subterfuge and camouflage of the basic personalities under a smoke screen of passionate love, and as an opportunity for more intensive and exclusive rights to individual satisfaction. Social pressures are such that many status-conscious youth, although concluding separately or together that they might best break up, go into marriage because of familial and community expectations once the engagement has been announced. In a relationship which has meaning in spite of the conflict, there is a tendency to camouflage injured feelings and differences of opinion in order to maintain the delusion of complete agreement. To make this possible, often one of the couple develops a policy of giving in. This sets a pattern of smothering one personality, along with giving the other undue leeway in self-expression and a resultant false feeling of self-adequacy. This tends to turn into a missionary endeavor on the part of the more aggressive one to overhaul the personality of the yielding one.

A question asked by every honest couple many times in the earlier development of their relationship, but with a great deal more seriousness at the time of the engagement, is: *How do we know it is really love*, the kind that will last? There is no final answer to this question. One cannot know love in the future sense. The most meaningful married love cannot be experienced during the engagement except in its very incipient or embryonic state. It is something that begins and then continues to grow, or does not grow. There are many couples, who, using any objective testing method known, are "in love," but who by all means should not get married. Their love is capable of growing only to a certain point, real as it may be up to that time, but then the marriage would disintegrate. Love must continue to grow or it dies, after being buried under frustration, resentment, and possible hatred. For these and many other reasons, being in love is not the best manner of determining whether or not a particular couple will make a permanently meaningful relationship.

Some people handle this by entering into marriage with the full intent of divorcing if it fails to offer as much as they expect. This expectation can be carried out because divorce is relatively easy. On the other hand, entering into a marriage without any sense of permanency to the commitment means that the relationship has three strikes against it before it has a chance to get on solid footing.

There is an approach that has a high rate of success in determining the potential for growth of love in a relationship, but it is an expensive one in terms of personal effort. It is the approach of total readiness outlined in this book; a process as dependent upon "homework" by the engaged couple as upon the counseling process.

Learning to communicate with honesty, sincerity, and intensity is one of the greatest means whereby the unmarried can prepare for a meaningful life in marriage. Attention will be given later to some of the many areas that call for this kind of careful communication.

Continued growth, and the development of communication skills between the particular couple have been discussed. This leads to a third goal within the total process of preparation for marriage; that of developing problem-solving skills. The effort to face up to and try to resolve, or to accept as unsolvable, the many areas of difference that exist or might exist between a particular couple, as well as maximizing potential for growth, is dependent upon effective communication skills. Much of the process of preparation for marriage is opening up the crucial areas of life and projecting the young people into the future, enabling them to visualize the kinds of problems and challenges awaiting them. They can develop skills now in handling the conflicts that will become the basis of the additional know-how necessary for handling problems in these same areas later in marriage.

2. Some Things Must Be Undone, Too

By the time people reach the age of marriage it is amazing how much of their daily living consists of fairly fixed patterns and habits, most of which are quite healthy. Indeed, without the economy of habits there would not be enough energy to get through the day, what with all the decisions to be made about tying shoes, chewing food, combing hair, and perhaps even about kissing mother or wife goodbye on the way out to school or to work.

On the other hand, there are many areas of habituated expression which can get in the way of intimate man-woman living in marriage. Part of the responsibility of a young couple who are preparing for marriage is to undo this unhealthy conditioning and replace it with newly learned forms of behavior that are less destructive, and more promising of satisfaction within marriage. For instance, the man may have been conditioned from boyhood against feelings of tenderness, gentleness and sweetness, and into a brusk, matter-of-fact aloofness that will leave a wife feeling unappreciated and unsatisfied. All too many men, and not a few women, become ill at ease and even embarrassed at the mention of these qualities which seem so necessary to fulfillment as a lover and as a parent. Parental and social expectations may have succeeded all too well in convincing the woman from girlhood that she does not have sexual feelings, or if so she does not express them, or that it is the husband's responsibility to see that she is satisfied or a fault of his technique if she is not. The process of preparing for marriage provides an opportunity for masks to be removed, for barriers to be melted, for each to become spontaneous in those feelings which are fundamental to a growing marital relationship. Moreover, it is necessary for the couple to learn how to express hostile or hurtful feelings with each other without feeling any unusual threat to the relationship. Without learning how to handle the worst kinds of feelings it is inevitable that these will accumulate and that efforts to control them will block out the more pleasant kinds of feelings and attitudes. By learning to handle all kinds of feelings with each other, old patterns of responding can be ferreted out, understood, and laid aside as they are replaced by new patterns of responding and communicating.

In summary, the counselor's goals with the engaged couple are: (1) to test the growth and growth potential of each personality, (2) to develop skills in and to stimulate spontaneous communication, and (3) to expose areas of stress, and develop problem-solving skills. Either by individual or group contact he helps them face up to existing problems and additional ones that can be anticipated. He can help them create an environment in which to clarify hindrances to growth and relating, to stimulate and capitalize upon feelings of adequacy, and to develop skills in relating and problem-solving which facilitate growth, both of the individuals and of the relationship. In this kind of relationship their love can continue growing. A new family circle established by such efforts then becomes the nursery of a new generation of more competent marital partners. If the engaged couple learn that this intense process threatens unduly their love for each other, if they cease to relate well and their love fails to grow, the counselor can assist them in terminating their engagement with learning and health rather than hurt.

Why can't all of this be accomplished by the couple alone, by studying all the facts of family living? Knowledge of facts is only one small part of readiness for marriage; attitudes, feelings and learned patterns of responding are of much greater significance.

Along with the continued growth of each as a personality, and the development of communication and problem-solving skills, a couple must begin to gain the know-how of relating meaningfully in marriage. It has been indicated that relating within the affectional and sexual areas is not enough, and, indeed, that this can camouflage the necessity for preparation within the many other areas of life that are just as vital to marriage. So much of the past has been closed off and has become unconscious that it is very difficult indeed for young people to open up the many areas of life to the free kind of communication that is called for here. The more hurt there has been in particular areas of development, the more reticence to remember.

The primary purpose served by "content" or factual material—whether in a textbook, within journal articles, films, or lectures—is to serve as a stimulus toward remembering, toward discussing with the counselor and the prospective mate. New learning in relating can occur around the reactions that follow.

Since the "facts" of marriage vary from culture to culture, from social class to social class, religion to religion, country to city, and person to person, and since feelings and attitudes carry much greater weight in a marriage than does knowledge, the challenge is to help the couple open up the vital areas of life for intensive communication, continued discussion, and a search for problem-solving skills as differences of opinion come about between them. The areas of life discussed in Chapters 9-11, along with the methods and techniques of this text, will serve the counselor as he assists in this challenging task.

Chapter 2

THE NATURE OF MARRIAGE

Courtship, engagement, marriage and family relations have inspired many volumes, with much of the basic content made readily available through popular publications.[1] In spite of this, it is not unusual for couples, even those who have studied "The Family" as a basic course in high school or college, to find this material strangely foreign to their own plans for marriage.

There can be many blocks to a fundamental overhauling of basic attitudes toward family living. These range from the ingrained teachings of parents and church, to deep emotional hurt, to the rugged independence of healthy youth. The combination of counseling and instruction which is possible in specific preparation for marriage seems to provide the ideal time, setting and method by which such knowledge can come alive for the individuals separately and together in terms of their approaching marriage. Together the engaged couple comprise a unique relationship, with potential all its own, somewhat independent of what other marriages may be, but they must work together to develop this relationship. Such intelligent youth may put off seeking outside help, sometimes to their detriment, because of the determination to work out their own problems. Yet, when they do come for assistance, they realize that counseling is an endeavor in which they and the counselor share, that they do not surrender their autonomy. They get maximum results in minimum time because they are strong enough to make intelligent use of the counselor. Pre-marital counseling gives them first hand knowledge of the hard work on their own which is essential in meeting lifelong needs, as well as a picture of how to make wise use of a professional.

This and the following chapters will serve to make the world of "family" data manageable in terms of a particular couple.

[1] Blood, Robert O., *Anticipating Your Marriage*. Glencoe, Illinois: The Free Press, 1955; Christensen, Harold T., Editor. *Handbook of Marriage and the Family*. Rand, McNally, 1964; Duvall, Evelyn M., *Family Development*. Philadelphia: J. B. Lippincott, 1957; LeMasters, E. E., *Modern Courtship and Marriage*. New York: Macmillan Co., 1957; Waller, Willard, *The Family*. Revised by Reuben Hill. New York: Dryden Press, 1951; and Winch, Robert F., *Mate Selection, A Study of Complementary Needs*. New York: Harper & Bros., 1958.

A. MARITAL EXPECTATIONS

Perhaps the most fruitful beginning place in preparation for marriage is a careful examination of what the couple expects in contrast to what can be realistically expected from this particular marriage. Romance, passion, fear of disagreement, and the "law of least action" can work against such an effort, but it can be accomplished with a counselor's assistance.

I. What is Expected of Marriage?

Relationships or institutions have their *raison d'etre* in individual needs. The need to be, to become, to fulfill one's potential, comes to expression in the form of wishes or desires for new experience, security, response, and recognition, all of which are dependent upon other people. The basic need for nearness as a continuing source of emotional sustenance has been discussed in Chapter 1. All of these needs have taken on added socio-psychological value and complication in today's culture, which emphasizes the dignity and worth of every personality, and which has become primarily pleasure-oriented.

More recently determined values centering around economic, status-conferring, reproductive, socializing, affection-response, and security-giving functions of marriage are challenging the historical principles of family life; namely, monogamy, permanence, fidelity, and love. On the other hand, marriage with its multi-dimensional aspects continues to provide the framework in which most adults seek to fulfill their principle drives and needs. The emphasis today is increasingly upon mutuality of satisfaction without which the relationship is threatened. To appeal to the modern couple marriage must promise: mutual satisfaction of sexual urges; mutual expressions of affection and love in addition to the sexual; sharing in responsibilities of procreation and care of children; sharing of interest in friends, recreation, worship, and creative work; mutual sense of security, belongingness, and status; and, stimulating self-development and self-expression. One or more of these at a time have been functions of marriage since the beginning of family life. Perhaps the difference today is that most people expect a rather high degree of satisfaction simultaneously in all these areas. Never in the history of mankind have so many expected so much from marriage and family living. Often these demands are coupled with a low frustration tolerance, narcissism and inadequate skills in relating. Intense reactions often follow disappointment in any of these expectations, setting into operation forces that also tend to block relating in other areas.

The potential of marriage is being advertised adequately in school, college, and church, and via the press, radio, and television. The lag is in the "know-how" which is not so easily taught or acquired. Each couple must understand that meaningful marriages do not come magically through choice of the right mate; they are grown by constant effort. It is well to expect one's own needs to be met in marriage, but it is equally important that each anticipate meeting the needs of the other. The person who is most capable of fulfilling his potential as an individual will be aware of and feel the urge to meet the needs of a mate. The degree to which expectations can be realized depends upon the ability, experience, and willingness to experiment in interpersonal relations by each of the couple. Perhaps more so than in other relationships, what comes from marriage is determined by what is brought to it, and continually invested in it, by two personalities, each with relatively fixed and yet changing sets of needs, values, and interests.

B.   MALE AND FEMALE ROLES

In no other relationship do the two-sided needs of humanity—i.e., the need for individuality and the need for nearness through relationship—find such opportunities for fulfillment and for threat as is present in modern marriage. Among the most dynamic factors entering into a marriage relationship are the role patterns brought by the man and by the woman, along with the ability and willingness to shift roles in emergencies. These factors are easily overlooked because they may be more or less unconsciously motivated and maintained. Often conscious perceptions are the obvious side of an ambivalence toward male and female functions. These can be exposed, reevaluated and integrated through a counseling experience.

Confusion of male-female roles has proved to be a most disturbing factor in marital relations, particularly as it has affected the psychosexual development of the child. Part of the increase in neurotic sex behavior today can be attributed to this confusion of roles. In adult sexual life firmly embedded dominance and submissive needs become entangled with the more superficial role concepts of the two people and endless conflict can result.

Once men were men and women were women and both were glad of it, or so the popular songs would have it. It seemed enough for the dictionary to define *male* as the sex "which begets young" and *masculine* as denoting that which is "opposite to female, especially vigor, strength and independence." *Female* described that sex which "conceives and brings forth young," and *feminine* delineated those qualities which are "opposite to male; i.e., those deeper, more tender, more gracious qualities." [2] Today the picture is not so clear. Separately and collectively, the many social forces making for the revolution and evolution in the family scene during the last half century have torn down the distinctions in male and female functions. In the emancipation of women the only way many knew to become equal was to become "masculine." Usurpation of the male role became the goal of the day, not true self-determination. Thus history has witnessed several generations of lost women who have in turn helped produce generations of inadequate males. Many adult women of today prepared for a career as their primary drive, but at the same time tried to keep in touch with men— just in case. Some of these have continued to find themselves torn between a career on the one hand and marriage and family on the other. These "divided" women have been described over and again in books and journals, and written upon the pages of experience in every community.

Slowly women are coming out of this morass into an awareness of self-hood that permits the flexibility to find one's way through the varied and cyclic courses of life. A new generation of women is emerging, a generation who, out of re-discovery of self, can at one and the same time prepare for a career which will bring personal fulfillment and the ability to make a living for themselves, and make special preparation for marriage and parenthood. These women work out a career outside the home and a career within the home, simultaneously or alternately, as circumstances dictate.

To be sure, many women have not attained this state of self-discovery and self-acceptance, and only as inward emancipation from each one's own feelings of inadequacy is attained will it be possible for her to gain full self-respect and serenity. Many women are developing this new strength, the real strength of womanhood, and as a result finding themselves an ever-increasing force for creativity within the culture in general and within their homes in particular.

To the same degree that a question mark has been put around the traditional distinct functions of woman, the roles and functions of man have been challenged and confused.[3] Counseling offices and many other services

[2] Rutledge, Aaron L., "Male and Female Roles in Marriage Counseling" in *Pastoral Psychology*, October 1962; Farber, Seymour M. and Roger H. L. Wilson, Editors, *The Potential of Woman*. New York : McGraw Hill Book Co., 1963.

[3] Strecker, Edward, *Their Mother's Sons*. Philadelphia, J. B. Lippincott, 1946; Strecker, Edward and Lathbury, Vincent T., *Their Mother's Daughters*. J. B. Lippincott, Philadelphia, 1956.

of detection and treatment of family difficulties attest to the terrific struggle going on in much of modern womankind and mankind. It is especially confusing as they seek to integrate into the marriage relationship continually changing role patterns expected by the mate and by the culture. Today men, perhaps more slowly than women, are beginning to rediscover themselves and become more adequate mates and fathers of children.

But the sources of confusion have not been put to rest. This culture will never return to clearly defined roles for men and women. To the contrary, there will be less and less distinction between what is described as distinctly male activity and female activity. But, as people become healthier specimens of human nature, the absence of rigid distinctions in function will make less and less difference to their sense of value as individuals, and greater flexibility will lead to more creative self-fulfillment through marriage. Meanwhile, pre-marital counseling becomes a necessity, not a luxury, for those who would get off to a clarified beginning in growing a meaningful marriage. The success of the couple depends upon what each brings to the relationship, the roles perceived and lived by each, including a willingness to shift roles when necessary, how they learn to give and receive affection, their determination to make the marriage work without thought of quitting, and a growing ability to diagnose and solve problems. The man must fill roles of lover, husband, companion, father, and bread-winner; the woman, those of lover, wife, companion, nurse, mother, budget manager, and often a partner in making a living.

Fixed role patterns in one mate and the expectations of the other often conflict in marriage. Workable techniques in problem-solving learned through pre-marital counseling can change harmful habits, relieve emotional stress, clarify issues, and develop insight which will result in personal and social growth. Failure to develop effective problem-solving techniques can leave a marriage in perpetual turmoil. With professional help young men and women can develop the potential to understand themselves and each other, at least to the extent of meeting adequately each other's needs and expectations. Many not only learn to adapt to expectations in a particular situation but are flexible enough to shift roles if necessary because of crises or because of personality change in the mate.

C.   CRITERIA OF A HEALTHY MARRIAGE

Just as all too little is known about what composes health in an individual, the counselor is confronted with the absence of any systematized picture of what comprises marital health. Yet some workable frame of reference becomes increasingly important as he seeks to help each couple discover the potential for health within their marriage and to move toward its realization.

I. The Nature of the Marital Relationship

Jung [4] has expressed a theory of marriage in a fascinating manner, in keeping with his view of dichotomous human needs, with one side repressed or undifferentiated and the other conscious and active. As a part of his concept of masculinity-feminity, he gave to the male "soul-image," hidden deep within the unconscious layers of the male personality, the name of "anima," the embodiment of the female principle of man. This term describes all the traits in men often considered feminine: tenderness, gentleness, creativity, interest in the finer things of life; along with pettiness, spite, indecisiveness and rage. He named the masculine counterpart in women the "animus," attributing to it such traits as decisiveness, assertiveness and other similar "masculine" characteristics in their rudimentary form. Men who have undifferentiated or unrecognized anima will be fearful of expressing tenderness and affection, while the woman with an undifferentiated animus tends toward the clinging vine type who is unable to express opinions or make decisions. In some cases men become so identified with the anima as to become only effeminate caricatures of men. The same thing may happen to an animus identified woman who becomes overly masculine and opinionated.

So-called love at first sight, according to Jung, often is based upon the sudden discovery of the unknown, unfulfilled side of self (anima or animus) in the other person. This constitutes the promise of fullness, wholeness, fulfillment. The unknown aspects of one's own personality are projected on the mate in the love relationship. To an extent, this may be one of the purposes of marriage in the first place. Yet, the fact that so much of the attraction is based upon unknown and often despised elements of self creates a relationship pregnant with ambivalence and potential conflict. Jung's concepts, while giving undue support to stereotypes of what is naturally male and female, and expressing only one of the endless prospects for complementarity of both healthy and crippled needs, are at least suggestive of the potential for counseling use.

This is the nature of the human species; the need for such complementarity is a central hunger in the search for satisfaction in marriage

[4] Jung, C. G., *Two Essays on Analytical Psychology*. Pantheon Press, 1953; Clark, Robert, *Six Talks on Jung's Psychology*. Pittsburgh: Boxwood Press. 1953.

or even in briefer relationships. This complementarity remains normal so long as each member of the relationship can relate spontaneously in this reciprocity of individuality that makes for a wholeness of marriage; a lesser but reasonably healthy complementarity can be had by those whose crippled needs can be accepted and allowed for in the totality of the marriage.

Any functioning whole represents more than the sum of its constituent parts. The principles that govern the behavior of an individual cannot be applied directly to relationship behavior because the psychological processes involved at the group level comprise a different dimension, a different biosocial organization.

Just as with the human organism or any energy field, the marital relationship has unique properties of its own over and above the total personalities which merged in the marriage. The two personalities enter into a new level of organization, much as would two merging electrical fields, and thereby create new qualities unique to the new whole, the marriage relationship. This does not mean that the old elements, the two personalities, need be grossly altered. The unique properties of the marital relationship preserve dynamic relations to the individual personalities of husband and wife. Just as an individual cannot be understood except in the context of his psychosocial field, a family or a marriage relationship can be understood only if all members of the family unit are taken into account. When a man and woman marry, they formulate a relationship which in a functional sense becomes a new "personality."[5]

II.   Research Criteria

Scientifically validated data on what constitutes a meaningful marriage is scarce and tends to be oriented to the more conforming elements of middle class American culture. According to Waller,[6] available research indicates that a marriage is successful in proportion to fulfillment of the following criteria: the love sentiment is fixed on the mate; smoothly functioning accomodations minimize conflict, stabilize the relationship, and yet leave it open to constant change and revision; common activities and experience have given rise to a fusion of purposes, duality of participation, common memories, and other forms of solidarity; the prevailing dominant roles of spouses are compatible and complementary, and the role of

[5] Ackerman, Nathan W., *"The Diagnosis of Neurotic Marital Interaction,"* Reprinted from *Social Casework,* April, 1954. Family Service Association of America; also, Rutledge, Aaron L. "The Future of Marriage Counseling," *Merrill-Palmer Quarterly*, Vol. I, Summer 1955, pp. 141-147.

[6] Waller, *op. cit.*

each is satisfactory to the other as well as to himself; the marriage gives both partners a sense of security and belongingness; furnishes a wholesome background for rearing children; meets the ego demands of both parties adequately; economic problems are solved, or have a reasonably good chance of being solved when certain contingencies are met; and, large areas of freedom for self-development and self-expression are provided for in all fields which do not threaten the relationship itself. This sounds entirely too utopian to apply *in toto* to the average couple.

Waller and Hill [7] have outlined five distinct limitations emerging from an analysis of these summarized findings: (1) The criteria used bias the studies in favor of conventionality and conservatism; (2) The factors most highly associated with success in marriage in these studies are unconfirmed for the most part by more than two or three studies and are questioned by others; (3) If valid, the factors probably are valid only for the early years of marriage; (4) The studies were limited in application to the white, urban, middle class from which they were drawn; (5) About 75 percent of the factors that really count for marital success are left unaccounted for. They broke down this vital percentage of overlooked dynamic factors as: the role patterns brought to the relationship; the ability and willingness to shift roles in emergencies; the success-failure history of past intimate relationships of each; the capacity to give and accept intimate love; the presence of expectations of success, determination to succeed, or some expression of unwillingness to resort to separation or divorce; and some measure of problem-diagnosing and problem-solving abilities of the pair.

Foote and Cottrell [8] have set forth six values believed to be common to most American culture, which serve both as goals and as measurements of interpersonal competence within the family relationship. They are: (1) Health, or maximum use of the organism; (2) Intelligence as applied in daily living; (3) Autonomy, or self-governing abilities; (4) Empathy, or healthy relating to others; (5) Use of judgment, or decision-making ability, and (6) Creativity, or the ability to develop and utilize flexibility and adaptability in life situations. These criteria, if present in each of the spouses, theoretically would result in a healthy marriage relationship. In turn, a meaningful marriage relationship would stimulate the development of these valued individual traits.

[7] *Ibid.* pp. 360-361.
[8] Foote, Nelson K. and Leonard S. Cottrell. *Identity and Interpersonal Competence: A New Direction In Family Research.* Chicago: The University of Chicago Press, 1956.

A healthy marital relationship, according to Ackerman,[9] is characterized by a clear awareness of shared, relatively realistic, stable and flexible
goals which are positive rather than defensive in emphasis. In the chief
areas of shared experience—emotional, social, economic, and parental—
there is a modicum of compatibility. Conflict is chiefly related to reality
factors and under control. Mutual understanding and equality results in an
empathetic acceptance of differences and of residual immature needs, which
makes of difference a stimulus to growth rather than a source of conflict.
Shared pleasure, responsibility and authority leads to a reasonable
fulfillment of goals for the relationship and for the further development of
the partner as well as the self. There is a relatively high positive complementarity as husband and wife and as father and mother. Trends toward isolation, disintegration, and regression are minimal. This sounds as utopian as
Waller's summation, doesn't it? Still these criteria can serve as guidelines
in eliciting the potential for meaningful relationship of a particular engaged
couple.

D. MARITAL DIFFERENCES AND CONFLICT

The multi-faceted social milieu and the hodge-podge population of
today produces a never-ending variety of individuals and families. To the
degree to which husband and wife can have the courage and the security,
the self-acceptance, which enable them to be true to themselves as
individuals and through their marriage, to that degree will there be healthy
family life.[10]   Each individual seeks within his or her field of eligibles
for that person who gives greatest promise of providing him or her with
maximum need gratification. Winch [11] saw love for another as response to
the composite promise of meeting those personality needs which one cannot
meet for himself. Such a concept of love coincides with the concept of
nearness outlined in Chapter 1, provided one fact is kept in mind, namely,
that one of the needs one cannot meet for oneself to the fullest extent is
to have a person beyond himself to love.

The basic biology of life is a complementarity of male and female.
Such pairing of opposites to gain greater fulfillment permeates the entire
physical, social, emotional, and intellectual life of mankind. The earlier
marriage research indicated that "like seeks like" as a mate. Similarities
in appearance, race, religion, education, social class, although slowly

[9] Ackerman, op. cit.
[10] Rutledge, Aaron L. "Evidences of Strength in the Modern Family." Journal of
Home Economics, Vol. 48, No. 5. 1956, pp. 323-326.
[11] Winch, op. cit., pp. 88-90.

breaking down, have tended to be the rule. It becomes increasingly evident, however, through a deeper study of motivation and of the marriage relationship, that at the emotional level it may be the differentness of response patterns of the other person, promising to meet unfulfilled personality needs, which leads to marriage. There is unlimited potential for continued personality growth as two people fulfill and complement each other in marriage. This is the reciprocity of healthy nearness, two distinct individuals simultaneously making the life of self, and of the loved one, more complete through spontaneous giving, receiving, and relating.

I.   The Function of Marital Conflict

It is open conflict or apathy from unresolved stress that leads many couples to the matrimonial junk heap. Waller [12] compared marital conflicts to personality conflicts in that they both originate at one of three levels: those growing out of erotic needs; those concerned with ego involvement or false pride; and those resulting from cultural definitions and confusion of roles.

1.   Sources of Conflict

Sex Factors in Marital Conflict. Before marriage the couple often are bound together by tension of unfulfilled acts and the anticipation of satisfaction of strong sex drives. This can give a tremendous push to the feeling of closeness and need for each other. These needs tend to be more cyclic in nature after marriage, leaving periods when the need for each other is not so pressing, making it easier for conflict to arise. In the growing marital relationship a satisfactory sex life can stimulate a feeling of interdependence and mutual sharing. The frustration of unsatisfactory sex relations can spread bitterness and disturbance, but even then the detrimental results seem to be in proportion to the lack of unity and of communication in the basic relationship. At the same time, allowance must be made for the occasional marriage of two fairly grown-up people who love each other and find most of life satisfying; yet the sexual inadequacy of one or both ultimately destroys the marriage. Sexual love in marriage is closely interwoven with feelings of respect for the mate and the marriage, love of children, group loyalties, and self-esteem, all of which are woven into the fiber of married life. Therefore it is not difficult to see that trouble in any area of life may reflect itself in sexual maladjustment.

---

[12] Waller and Hill, *op. cit.,* pp. 272-294. An excellent discussion of conflict to which the author is indebted.

Just the reverse also is true, in that serious lack of sexual adjustment can lead to maladjustment in any other area of life.

The Clash of Ego Involvements. False pride or the neurotic self seeks a separate or divisive gratification. It is based upon desire for status, competitive strivings and self-protective tendencies, and is found in abundance in immature married people. They can be seen in alternating cycles inflating and deflating the ego of each other, leading to hurt, resentment and either overt or covert conflict. Often sexual problems are due to a mingling of these unhealthy ego motives with sexual needs, resulting in frigidity, impotence, sterility and varied other problems. Care should be taken to detect such symptomatic responses during pre-marital counseling.

Cultural Definitions of Marital Expectations. The wide difference between unduly high expectations in marriage and the attainable has been discussed above. Many conflicting expectations are ethnically or religiously or, in the broader sense, culturally determined. When fused with deeper personality conflicts, these cultural differences become particularly potent.

2. Types of Conflict

Marital conflict of whatever origin may be primarily covert or overt. Folsom[13] has discussed three categories of overt conflict: (1) Acute conflict, common to early marriage and the new problems of later marriage, with intense expressions of hostility, is usually transitory but it wrecks the relationship if it persists unresolved. (2) Progressive conflict has directional trends. Every quarrel tends to destroy the sentimental aspects of the couple, leaving them more ready for renewed battle. These conflicts move from crisis to crisis, spiral-like, until arrested at some point or until the relationship is severed. (3) Habituated conflict applies to those issues in which the couple have not and will not agree. The entire marriage relationship may be centered in a pattern of habitual stress, with conflict between the couple serving as life's most interesting diversion, although it may be destructive of their emotional health. These tend to be cyclic or recurrent, and each of the overt manifestations is associated with covert conflict.

3. Results of Conflict

Responses to conflict are varied, and may be external, internal, or both. Various forms of withdrawal and withholding are common. She is hurt and withdraws to avoid further hurt or to hurt him. He is hurt or deprived

[13] Folsom, J. K., *The Family and Democratic Society.* John Wiley and Sons. 1943 p. 447.

and withholds because she doesn't give. These may take the form of refusal to talk and to show affection, sulking and pouting, frigidity, or impotence, to name only a few manifestations of broken down communication.

One of the most immediate overt responses to conflict is quarreling. Quarreling is destructive if it is directed at the whole person or at the weakest parts thereof, striking at ego defenses, or if directed at the marriage relationship as a whole. On the other hand, it can be a useful technique of adjustment, particularly in the early marriage relationship. Productive quarrels tend to be characterized by:[14] being limited to a distinct issue or issues, so as not to involve the entire relationship; free expression of ideas and of emotions by both persons, followed immediately or later by calm expression of the conflict by both as to stated problems, underlying issues, reactivated hurts and fears, conditioned emotional responses and personality needs; leading to insightful decisions which contribute to adjustment.

The process of change in marriage will be continual, whether positive or negative. Marital growth can best be assured through real understanding rather than trusting the false rapport of "everything is all right just because we're in love." The transitions from single to married living necessitate many changes in the value systems of each of the couple, as self-centeredness becomes marriage and family centeredness. Their mutual needs, backgrounds, and interests will determine further areas of change, as will their conscious efforts at the solution of disagreements.

Marriage conflicts may end in complete reconciliation and subsequent good relations. Or the result may be less satisfactory in the form of accommodation or compromise in a less pleasant, yet effective truce. Overt conflict, rather than always threatening to destroy a marriage, may be merely the sparks from the anvil of life where a healthy relationship is being beaten out. As such it is evidence that both personalities are alive, that neither is surrendering or being smothered out. The two are becoming one in relationship, but each personality is being preserved. Overt conflict can be evidence that hurt feelings and resentment are being expressed and faced rather than being repressed or denied and turned into poison. Conflict can be an evidence of growth, and it may become the means of strengthening the relationship by sloughing off unhealthy habits, relieving tension, clarifying issues, and developing insight. But "when streams of communication within a marriage become dammed off, the backwaters of accumulated hurt feelings,

[14] Binkley, Robert C. and Binkley, Frances, *What's Right With Marriage.* Appleton. 1929, Chapter 17.

misunderstanding, and resultant bitterness contaminate the spontaneous springs of love and relatedness." [15]

Marriage demands the best in maturity but this does not mean that couples necessarily are mature to begin with. Marriage can be the greatest single stimulus to continued growth and maturation of young people who are determined to make their relationship work. If the conflict in such a marriage is too prolonged or intense it can become a way by which the marriage calls attention to the unknown threats deep inside one or both individuals. It may result in withdrawal or attack, or it can push the couple toward further examination of self and the marriage, including the use of a counselor.

One of the primary functions of pre-marital counseling is to ferret out the probable areas of stress in the prospective marriage, maneuver the engaged couple into conflict, and assist them in developing diagnosing and problem solving skills, along with an appreciation of each other's individuality.

E.   THE ROLE OF NEUROSIS IN MARRIAGE

How does a neurotic marriage differ from the healthy complementarity discussed earlier? Just as neurotic [16] behavior represents malformation, malfunction, maldirection, or reaction formation of normal forces, so it is that neurotic complementarity is the distortion of a healthy push toward true reciprocity of relationship. The way in which motivation to marriage can become distorted is simplified if viewed as "layers": (1) at the surface level, most couples continue to be attracted on the basis of similarities — i.e., color, education, religion, and social class. (2) At a deeper level, as in the discussion of complementarity, couples are attracted in terms of oppositional traits; i.e., their personality traits and behavioral patterns seem to "fulfill" each other, making for a wholeness otherwise unattainable. (3) The third level is seen in the similarity of underlying need, the emotional sustenance so necessary to continued maintenance and growth of selfhood.

So far, so good. But how does this process become neurotic? If mate selection is contaminated by the necessity of conscious and unconscious rebellion against the parental families, the partner becomes an unwitting

---

[15] Rutledge, Aaron L., "The Future of Marriage Counseling," *Merrill-Palmer Quarterly*, Vol. I., Summer 1955, pp. 141-147.

[16] For a discussion of neurosis see Freud, Sigmund, *A General Introduction to Psychoanalysis*. New York: Liveright Publishing Corp., 1920. Chapters 16-28.

pawn in the hostility. An immature adult who has to *use* the fact of marriage to prove his adulthood is likely to demand a certain type of wifely behavior to maintain his delusion of adequacy. The exploitation inherent in such a situation ultimately generates hostility and attacks by her, that he will experience as "castrating," thus setting into operation a cyclical set of dynamics similar to what he experienced in his parental home. The normative need of male and female to complement each other—based upon undeveloped but non-traumatized areas of the self—become thoroughly contaminated if one or both of the partners are neurotic, potentially psychotic, or otherwise grossly crippled emotionally. If the unconscious is a reservoir of repressed hurts and distorted, insatiable hungers the concept of neurotic complementarity can be a mild description indeed of a relationship hell. The mate is perceived as savior, healer, restorer, and perpetual succorer for psychic wounds that cannot be healed and residual appetites that cannot be satiated, guaranteeing that he will fail. Even if he succeeds in some of the functions, that very fact may threaten to bring into consciousness the unperceived and rejected crippled side of the other, and still guarantee that the mates will be objects of gross ambivalence. Thus it is that the second "layer " of motivation for selection of a particular mate often is the opposite behavior patterns—i.e., dominant-passive, introvert-extrovert—which represent over-reactive personality defenses. However, underneath, at the third layer, they are attracted by the basic similarity of crippledness and unsatisfied hungers from a traumatized past.

In some instances such neurotic conflict destroys the marriage; whereas, in others it gives the relationship "meaning" for each crippled spouse. At the mate selection state, complementary neurosis may be the determining factor. The counselor must be able to identify the neurotic patterns of engaged couple interaction and see them in the context of total interaction, if the possible effect upon the relationship is to be evaluated. The effects upon the future marriage may be relatively localized, diffuse, or both. Neurotic disturbance of a marital relationship usually is the creation of both partners.

One person, feeling inadequate and incomplete, unable to live a whole life, finds another who can complement or complete the syndrome of personality need. A woman, with strong repressed needs to rebel against what she perceives as the strictures of femaleness may choose a man who becomes alcoholic, has affairs, is sexually perverted or otherwise inadequate. She may protest this male freedom or failure and yet wear the robe of female martyrdom with agonizing pride. The fact that she is living out vicariously the repressed side of her crippled self often becomes evident when, through counseling, he begins to make rapid changes toward health. She protests that counseling is making him worse, or she has an affair, begins to drink excessively, uses drugs, or becomes mentally ill, as the previously hidden side of her personality asserts itself. Of course, this whole picture may be seen with the wife as the actor-outer and the husband the martyred member of the conspiracy in neurotic living, in which one is the hell-raiser, and the other the protector of home, ideals, mores, religious ideals or law, but who in reality is just as maladjusted.

As seen earlier, immature adults often tend to "parentify each other," each pushing the relationship toward the needed form of parent-child relationship or it may assume the dynamics of sibling rivalry. This places upon the marital relationship an impossible load as it is forced to assume compensatory and curative functions. If those compensating needs give way to decompensation, the marriage progressively disintegrates. But if the neurotic individual marries someone who makes it possible for him to strengthen himself against neurotic regression, and gives support to his healthier tendencies, he may become not only an adequate mate but a fairly effective parent. The adult can change and grow in marriage if the proper emotional environment is created. In fact, for many adults, the responsibilities and privileges of marriage are the greatest incentive to continued personality growth. On the other hand, two personalities who remain neurotic can build a marriage relationship which is meaningful for them and fairly healthy by any externally applied criteria of measurement. The opposite is true also; that two healthy individuals may together produce a marriage relationship which is neurotic or unhealthy.

The ultimate effects of the neurosis of the individual partners on marital health are determined by the dynamic part that neurotic conflict plays in the complex process of integration of the personalities of the partners into the reciprocal roles of husband and wife.[17]

[17] Eisenstein, Victor W., Editor, *Neurotic Interaction in Marriage*, New York, Basic Books, Inc., 1956, Chapters 4-6; Grotjahn, Martin, *Psychoanalysis and the Family Neurosis*. New York: W. W. Norton and Co., 1961; Ackerman, Nathan W., *The Psychodynamics of the Family*. New York: Basic Books, Inc., 1958; Ehrenwald, Jan., *Neurosis in the Family and Patterns of Psychosocial Defense*. New York: Harper and Row, Hoehen Medical Division, 1963; and Chance, Erika, *Families in Treatment*. New York: Basic Books, Inc., 1959.

F. SOME MARRIAGE TYPES

For thousands of youth the stereotype of the patriarchal family is taught at one level, the highly distorted democratic ideal at another, and what is practiced may be hardly recognizable from the viewpoint of either. The conflict between these positions within the individual and between the couple can come to fruition in marital stress or apathy which leads either to the marriage counselor's office or to the divorce courts.

Families in general today suffer from a lack of clear-cut values, goals and norms. The marital and family norms originating in rural social conditions of a century ago have been found inadequate and in many cases discarded. One of the reasons for rejecting or breaking away from elderly parents and in general turning away from the "extended" family today is to keep them from bringing along the past, or reactivating it from deeply imbedded recesses in the unconscious of the new generation. Having freed itself in a measure from the restraints of the past, the nuclear family is cut loose without anchorage until new values and norms are established, or until the old ones have been modified to fit into new and complicated social situations. There is conflict about the rejected past, between the old and the new values, and because of the discrepancies between both of these and behavior. Basic values must be discovered or brought up to date if modern marriages are to survive. Sex needs, acceptance needs, companionship needs, and economic needs all enter into the motivation for marriage. These must be given attention as new value and goal concepts are formed. The modern family has the threefold task of discovering individual and group values, organizing these into a meaningful hierarchy, and then integrating this new picture with the culture of which it is a part. In the absence of adequate counseling the inbuilt expectations of marriage may be much more determinative than taught ideals. These internalized needs tend to mirror the characteristics of the immediate families of origin, but they are also related to larger social issues and currents in the culture; i.e., minority biases, economic conditions, political and religious philosophies. These are incorporated into the developing personality, which in turn gives the old forces a new twist, and are modified further when two individuals with such a mixed heritage unite in marriage. Caricatures of a few "family types" will serve to illustrate the endless variations of dynamics and behavioral patterns to be found among engaged and married couples,[18]

[18] Rutledge, Aaron L., "The Essence of Family." *Merrill-Pelmer News*, Vol. IV, No. 5, October 1961; Berelson, Bernard and Gary A. Steiner, *Human Behavior, An Inventory of Scientific Findings*. New York: Harcourt, Brace and World, 1964.

reflecting elements of culture, family patterns, personality dynamics, and even the modern practice of psychotherapy.

I. Marriages That Reflect Elements of Culture

This culture is fond of such terms as good family, happy family, successful family, peaceful family, Christian family, or democratic family which are used in family life literature as if they actually delineated a particular entity. Couples often come for help believing that their marriage can be made over into some preconceived ideal type, frequently the democratic marriage.

Increasingly, *democracy* in the home, with many variations to be sure, is becoming the model for young couples.[19] With apology to the Constitution, a portion of the marriage ceremony might be re-written as follows:

> We, two democratic individuals, desiring to make our abode together, in order to form a more perfect union, establish justice, insure domestic tranquility, provide for the common defense, promote the general welfare, and secure the blessings of liberty to ourselves and our posterity, do hereby unite ourselves in the bonds of matrimony.

Democracy in the family means freedom of thought and expression, the greatest development of individual potential, and the opportunity to share alike in both privileges and responsibilities. A democratic family is of the people, for the people, and by the people. It is a cooperative effort to meet the needs for love, understanding, achievement, and recognition to the greatest advantage of the husband and the wife, and in such a manner as to create a wholesome atmosphere in which children can learn the art of interpersonal relationships. Democracy demands a life-long emphasis upon creating through mutual effort an atmosphere of understanding friendship, problem-diagnosing and problem-solving partnership, along with wholehearted devotion to each other and to goals arrived at through consideration of mutual and individual needs.

Equality seems basic in the democratic concept of marriage and family life; equality of rights, privileges, and responsibilities. But along with equality must go the acceptance of major responsibilities in terms of individual talents, innately determined functions of men and women, training, and available time. Marriage is a giving, receiving, sharing fellowship. Yet each couple has the right to determine how democratic

[19] Beasley, Christine, *Democracy in the Home.* New York: Association Press. 1954.

their home will be. Noble as it sounds, the emergence of democracy in the family has not been an unmixed blessing. In many cases one or both of the couple will be incapable of democratic functioning, since equalitarian family life demands the highest level of individual maturity. Some of these marriages, replete with every conceivable hurt, seek help when their version of democratic living evolves from laissez faire to anarchy. The pathway of any democratic effort is strewn either with the wreckage of conflict or with monuments of successful interaction; perhaps a mixture of both. People are continuing to experiment with democracy in the home just as it is being subjected to trial and error in many countries of the world. A few are discovering the joys of shared living, and are guaranteeing its workability by mutually delegating areas of major responsibility according to individual capabilities, availability to tasks and other criteria.

The Master-Serf Marriage. The tenant farmer system is rapidly passing from the American scene and yet a residue of its components still expresses itself in family life. The owner-tenant farmer type of family is characterized by: "I own the land, house, tools, crops; yes, and really the people too. They work for me; I give them what they need, as I define what they need. If they cooperate, keep quiet, and give me no trouble, we get alone fine." The husband, wife, or both may be the "owner," with others filling the place of serfs. This "stay in your place" marriage represents the same dynamics seen in some communities as: "A good nigger knows and stays in his place"; "Puerto Ricans are wonderful people in Puerto Rico." Family balance depends upon following preconceived roles for each family member; someone does the perceiving and others are second class citizenry to be kept in line, or who choose to stay in line.

When such a marriage deteriorates it may rapidly turn into a warring camp. The relationship is based on the philosophy that members of one sex are the superior creatures, should demand their rights, punish when these are challenged or neglected, and perhaps administers additional punishment just to keep the mate in line. The semi-sadistic, semi-culture-based kind of emotional, verbal, and physical cudgelings expressed when this type of marriage gets out of balance know no limits.

II. Marriages That Repeat Family Patterns

Some young couples start their life together almost as a replica of some aspect of their own family of origin. The natural tendency to establish families somewhat similar to the family of origin can upon occasion produce some grotesque distortions of human potential. In psychodynamic terms these frequently can be described as "transference marriages."

The Parentified Marriage. The central task of growing up is to find one's identity as a human being. This can force the child into trying on various stereotypes of male and female in order to gain from the parents the emotional sustenance so necessary to preserving himself as an entity, however segmentalized or crippled it may leave him.[20]

In the absence of a warm relationship between two adults which would manifest itself in every facet of life, including the sexual, the child may become aware of only the *parental* aspects of being adult. Later this can lead to a "parentified" type of marriage in which the roles are those of a pseudo child-parent relationship. One of the couple, needing to be an adult through "parenting" another, chooses (or is chosen by) a mate who needs to preserve the only "role" he knows, that of a child. These dynamics become endlessly complicated in that one who fits into either of these patterns is likely to have unconscious needs to play the opposite role. This means that even in a neurotic way the mates cannot be adequate for each other. These marriages make possible a socially acceptable survival, but such child's play is a poor substitute for the relatively unencumbered and spontaneous interaction of two "whole" adults. A few common situations illustrate the phenomena.

The "Mother-Son" marriage is a common expression of the parentified relationship. This is the woman who as a girl saw or experienced only the mothering aspects of femininity. Mother's affectional and sex life, her relating as a total adult, were absent, hidden, or danger-fraught. As a result the girl was conditioned to express her adulthood only through being a mother, desiring both to emulate and to displace her own mother. Marriage becomes a chance for her to get a family for whom she can be a mother. She chooses a man who has to be a boy or needs primarily to be mothered; and there are many such candidates, products of unhappy marriages of crippled men and women. The male child of an unhappy woman is particularly vulnerable, catching the hatred she has for self and for husband because of her unhappy lot. There may be enough drive toward healthy relations and enough desire to get away from the slavery to his own mother to push such a youth toward marriage. Yet he has to marry a mother figure, not an adequate, total female.

[20] For the type of parenting that produces inadequate marriage mates, see Strecker, *op. cit.,* and Strecker and Lathbury, *op. cit.*

Many such marriages seem to work quite well for months or even years, depending upon the degree to which the two sets of needs complement each other. A shift in need patterns brings acute conflict. Typically, this woman seeks help because her once fine husband has become a terrible husband. He is drinking, refusing to come home at night, gambling or running around. In an oversimplified way, this is what has happened. The marriage was "good" because she served well as the mother he needed, at the same time finding her chief satisfaction in that process. But she has become either such a poor mother that he must rebel or such a good mother that he has grown. When little boys grow, the next step is adolescence and adolescent rebellion. Now he is sowing wild oats. Good mother to her little-boy husband, she cannot tolerate being a mother-wife to an adolescent-husband. She tightens the reins and he kicks over the traces all the more.

This dilemma, perhaps forcing into consciousness for the first time some of her unrealized potential as a woman, leads to further stress in the marriage. In other marriages, through the process of daily living, the emotionally stunted wife grows into a more complete woman and then finds herself endlessly frustrated because the husband cannot shift roles and become an adequate adult male lover and companion.

The Sibling Rivalry Marriage. Along with learned stereotypes of what is male and female, together with the fact of conflicting and overlapping stereotypes, an individual may react as if men and women were different kinds of creatures, either to be avoided or used as pawns in life's struggle. This can amount to the worst aspects of extreme sibling rivalry in a marriage, with sides chosen along sexual lines. These stereotyped expectations, full of inconsistencies, can become the major tools whereby two immature adults put on costumes and enter into the contest of marriage to see who can get the most out of it, with little ability to live spontaneously or to share. When children are born to such a spurious union they become further sibling competitors in the juvenile tug of war for "my way, my rights, my pleasure, my, my . . . mine."

A wife is highly offended that her husband has a girl friend. She misses the contest-oriented life which they once enjoyed. Early in marriage she changed jobs repeatedly to keep a salary larger than his. He traded cars to keep a flashier model than hers. She excelled at polo, but he continued to fall off the horse. Then it was swimming. She outdistanced him and became the rescuer when he almost drowned. He couldn't hit a barn with a scatter gun; whereas she scared him to death clipping cigarettes from his lips at ten paces with a pistol. It does not make sense to her that he has surrendered in despair and spends hours just holding a woman's hands listening to music.

The Self-Sacrificing Family. The self-sacrificing family is characterized by: "I regret I have but one life to give, but one circulatory system of blood to pour on the altar of sacrifice, for my precious husband (wife, or children)." Such an attitude often enslaves the cared-for mate or child into having to serve the "perfect one" with unswerving devotion until death, or into being compelled to rebel and feel horribly guilty, with many emotional, mental, psychosomatic, and marital symptoms resulting.

III.   Marriages Reflecting Personality Traits

It should be no surprise that marriage reflects the two sets of personality traits brought to it by husband and wife. They produce a relationship that is more than the sum total of themselves, but the basic integrity of the self remains intact. Hopefully, each person is flexible enough to continue to grow and to develop new abilities to relate. The more immature and crippled the personality, the greater the tendency to act out in the marriage both earlier unresolved family dilemmas, as discussed earlier, and individual rigidities of personality structure.

There is the *sado-masochistic relationship* in which one mate gets major pleasure from hurting, and the other from being hurt. Onlookers frequently are amazed at the ability of one of a dating couple to make the other miserable, and no less astonished at the propensity for "taking it" that is manifested. This seemingly promising matching of needs often falls apart when one of the couple outgrows the former need, or when through a shift of personality dynamics the ambivalent need—e.g., the need to be hurt can be protection against the need to destroy—becomes dominant. Are these two seriously crippled individuals whose reciprocal needs will remain similarly patternized, or can disturbing shifts in personality be anticipated, either for reasons of health or deeper pathology in one of the couple?

A marriage familiar in counseling centers is composed of the *passive-dependent husband* and the *dominant-aggressive* woman. Although common to many elements of the population, this syndrome is likely to be openly complained about by Jewish clientele, adherence to the traditional ideal of male superiority and dominance notwithstanding. (It is likewise a typical syndrome in counseling centers serving other populations, but is less likely to be stated as one of the problems.) This pattern is so typical that it seems to demonstrate the truth of the saying, "Show me a patriarchy in name and I will show you a matriarchy in fact."

Such a pattern of interaction may be well camouflaged because consciously the couple both believe that they want the same type of marriage, whether one of equality and mutuality, or one in which the husband is "head of the house." They can deceive all the questionnaires and interviewers, along with themselves, by responding according to the marriage ideal superficially desired and accepted.

When a pre-marital counselor meets a couple like this, are these personality patterns relatively fixed for the duration of the marriage? Or, is one healthy enough to grow and shift, upsetting the balance? Is one crippled enough to have to assert both sides of ambivalent needs, whether simultaneously or in succession? Such shifts often occur just after the wedding, following a pregnancy, or any circumstantial shift. Can the counselor predict the fact and circumstances of such breakdowns in complementarity, and either discourage the marriage or prepare them for such crises?

To this syndrome might be added all manner of *adequacy-inadequacy pairings* for complementarity purposes that can become reversed or otherwise unbalanced, causing acute marital conflict.

The *rebel marriage* is commonly seen among the very young or the seriously disturbed. The marriage itself may be a rebellion, or the type of marriage may carry the hostile charge. Typical among the latter are some mixed faith and mixed nationality relationships. Counselors, priding themselves on openmindedness on such matters, often wish they could see more inter-racial couples who have basically sound personalities and a preponderance of healthy motivation for getting married. The opposite is all too often true, as the individuals act out their uncertainty of personal identity and their rebellion against unpleasantness in the previous way of life. Although there may also be a sound core of healthy attraction to each other in many of these inter-racial or otherwise mixed relationships, the counselor will need to assist them in either working through or understanding and accepting responsibilities for the rebellion, or the intra-psychic and community induced burdens will bog down and defeat the marriage. The added societal load these marriages have to carry could break many healthy relationships, not to mention those made up of basically crippled individuals.

The *manic-depressive syndrome* is about as common in marriage as in individual personalities. A basically depressed man, covering this symptomatology by means of introversion or devotion to career, is often attracted to a vivacious woman whose activities and style of life should tip the counselor off to a basically "manic" type of personality. These people frequently seem to be "just right" for each other until a shift of personality traits or needs occurs. With her depressed kinds of needs now being lived out vicariously through the husband, she is free to be even more outgoing. The husband, who cannot keep pace and whose needs cannot really be met by anyone, becomes threatened—whether or not she gets emotionally involved with other men—when her bubbling nature is not wholly devoted to him. All of this can happen in reverse when such a husband swings to a manic-like phase of activity with real or imagined sexual acting out. The wife whose repressed conflicts were being "satisfied" through his depression vicariously may now be tripped into a depression herself. All such symptomatology may not be pronounced enough to make the needs for psychiatric treatment evident, and yet be the major attraction for an engaged couple or represent the basic pathology of a marriage.

There are engaged couples in which one is seemingly healthy and the other always on the verge of a *schizophrenic reaction* (or other type of psychosis). This is likely to be hidden by the fact that the "sick" one has not as yet had a breakdown, or is now "well" under the ministrations of the seemingly healthy partner. (The "parentified" marriages discussed earlier may cover such deeper pathology.) The "well" one *must* marry an ill or potentially schizophrenic mate in order to vicariously live out, and thus defend against the schizoid elements (or other serious conflicts) in his own personality. Psychotherapists all too often treat the seemingly "sickest" mate without ever realizing that the triggering device for the psychotic break or other serious episode was what occurred in the apparently healthy mate; namely, the loosening up of ego-controls. This threatens to bring the repressed conflict into consciousness, but the risk is too great. Rather than permit this to happen, more stress is placed on the weak mate than can be borne, and the illness is precipitated. The seemingly healthy, but inwardly conflicted, mate can become wrapped up either in helping or condemning the "sick" one. Thus the repressed conflict is partially activated, displaced to the obviously problem-ridden mate, lived through vicariously, the guilt paid for through the inconvenience and discomfort, re-repressed, and control re-established —all without the person becoming aware of what is really happening, and all too often without therapist ever knowing that he has treated the wrong patient.

Consequently, counselors should be alerted by any case where a seemingly very strong and healthy person is determined to marry one who appears to be of borderline to seriously disturbed mental health.

In marriage, just as in every other aspect of life, there are the *lonely ones* who somehow discover each other in their self-imposed cells of isolation.

How nice, one is tempted to exclaim! Yet, the expectation that one individual can remedy the loneliness of another, when he can't even communicate with his own self, often becomes the source of major marital conflict and further withdrawal.

Closely allied are the *insatiable couples*, individuals who underneath are hungry sponges that can only sap strength until one or both are destroyed. Some of the narcissistic personality disorders would be found in these marriages. Major depressions sometimes follow the sequence of: (1) Activation of repressed needs through the stimulus and promise of courtship and marriage; (2) followed by the failure to be fulfilled; (3) with reactivating of a reservoir of hatred that may be turned toward the mate, but often ricochets back against self in a depression.

The *addictive syndrome*, not at all uncommon among engaged couples, has some similarities to the "insatiable" type, except that the symptoms tend to be limited to certain areas of life. Diagnosis of such relationships can be difficult even after years of marriage because of the intricate ways in which the underlying need—whether overwhelming dependency, hostility or guilt, etc.—is camouflaged. Just as an individual may drive himself to become superstrong to compensate for or hide a felt weakness, men and women unconsciously serve this function for each other. This may take the form of permitting the partner to live out any denied aspect of one's own self, and finding perverted vicarious meaning therein for the addictive need. Marriage itself may be the dependency addiction. Such a pathological relationship can be hidden by the normative need for relationship, especially in the infatuation characteristic of many engaged couples. When it becomes impossible for these addictive marriages to meet the unconscious distorted needs of one or both individuals, an open addiction may result, whether to alcohol, drugs, gambling, or distorted sexuality.

And there is the *asexual relationship* which can be so neatly hidden by what might be healthy ideals of "saving sex for marriage." This can be the sexually cold and inhibited woman and the passive, "seldom interested in sex," male. Or, some sexually crippled individuals consciously or unconsciously use one another as "covers" for either overt or covert homosexuality. By marriage they hope to prove to themselves or to others the heterosexuality which they cannot in fact bring off. Contrary to much popular and professional thought, a grossly inhibited woman, in her search for a male who will cure her frigidity, can appear to be so sexually adequate and promising that she traps the inadequate male, who is equally disappointed when she does not transform him into a sexual giant. Such unconscious needs may be catapulted into awareness or result in an endless variety of symptoms instantaneously by a wedding into which one now feels he was trapped; or, become evident only when other accumulated frustrations, or personality shifts due to either growth or conflict, become the triggering device.

Many highly idealistic, yet basically healthy youth are victimized by another individual whose inhibitions root in personality crippling or psychopathology. She thinks he has "saved himself just for me," but in fact he may have been too inhibited or ill to express himself sexually. This can come as a gross shock to the one who has consciously controlled sexual expression in spite of acutely felt need, and now feels liberated by marriage and wants fulfillment. Very often the same ideals that made for pre-marital chastity may dictate "now that you have made your bed, you must sleep in it," accounting for many stalemated and bitter marriages.

Counselors can sometimes spot the *compulsive-sloppy* dichotomy in an engaged couple, in which the *obsessive-compulsive* characteristics of one dictates a mate that is careless enough to want or warrant criticism about appearance, housekeeping, or personal habits. This very carelessness may be guarding against the same kind of unconscious compulsive needs, and thus result in a double dose of hatred for the perfectionistic mate. This resentment is matched only by that which operates in the one whose ritualistic needs—which camouflage a threat of personality dissolution and loss of controls that must be categorically denied—are challenged.

Even in something as common-place as the anticipated *working-wife/ working-husband* combination, a skilled counselor may find sources of future trouble. Is this plan for the future marriage a spontaneous expression of masculinity for him and of femininity for her, or is it a means of *proving* something to one or the other? If the latter, no marriage can be expected to refute deeply unconscious doubt about one's identity, worth, and rights as a member of one's own gender.

Chapter 3

COMMUNICATION, IN MARRIAGE AND IN COUNSELING

The nature of family interaction, as with all interpersonal processes, is dependent to a great extent upon the quality and quantity of communication. In turn, efforts to remedy relationship problems, or to invest positively in a forthcoming marriage, lean primarily upon this basic process of human interaction.

A. DYNAMICS OF COMMUNICATION

Recent clinical literature has underlined the role of *relationship* in making possible understanding, acceptance, clarification and change through counseling or psychotherapy. Basic to relationship is the process of communication, with its verbal and non-verbal components. Elements of communication—listening, symbolism, empathy—have been studied, but only recently has much attention been given to the total process of communication. One major contribution is *Communication* by Reusch and Bateson,[1] which is utilized freely in this discussion.

I. Definition and Apparatus

Communication is much more than the conscious, verbal transmission of messages. It includes all those processes by which people influence each other, whether verbal, gesticulatory, or the conscious and unconscious utilization of any or all organs of touch, taste, smell, sight, hearing, and balance. All impressions received from the self, from others, and from the total environment, and the retention of these as impressions for future reference, are integral parts of an individual's communication.

The Gestalt psychologists [2] have demonstrated that the communication apparatus must be viewed as a functional entity which does not fit into any of the theories of anatomical localization. Healthy communication is a

---

[1] Reusch, Jurgen and Bateson, Gregory. *Communications,* New York: W. W. Norton and Company, 1951.

[2] Koffka, Kurt. *The Principles of Gestalt Psychology.* New York: Harcourt, Brace and Co. 1935; Reusch and Bateson, *op. cit.,* pp. 16ff.

function of a total human being in relationship to self and others. This "apparatus" consists of the sense organs as receivers, the effector organs as senders, the communication center as the place of origin and destination of all messages, and the remaining parts of the organism which shelter and maintain the communication machinery. The number of incoming, outgoing and within-the-system signals is limited by the capacity of the intrapersonal network, the selectivity of receivers, and the skill of the effector organs. This is a highly complex and amazingly effective communication system; however, overloading jams the network and interferes with messages either by distorting or by blocking them from reaching their destination. This disruption causes anxiety and creates an anxiety-tension state which causes further blocking and "scrambling" of messages.

II. Growth Through Communication

The life and health of an individual requires that he be able to communicate in a competent manner within his psycho-social field where he is exposed consistently and repetitively to bombardments of stimuli. From birth, even before, the development of the child is dependent upon much more than nutritional sustenance. The physical and emotional stimulation of loving adults is necessary for basic development as an organism. (See "need for nearness" in Chapter 1.) Although transmitted at first largely through physical touch and comfort, the needs of the child increasingly demand added stimulation, which makes use of all possible means of communication. Communication facilitates specialization of function through differentiation and reintegration, and leads to maturation. Maturity as evidenced by communication and cooperation with others replaces more complete dependence upon physical and emotional assistance from elders. As indicated earlier, Saul [3] saw the progression to maturity in overlapping phases as the child moves from dependence to independence of the parents, from a state of primarily receiving to a give-get balance, from direct expression of hostility to understanding and utilizing constructively the energy from anxiety; and as the person learns to handle the battery of inadequacy feelings common to growing up, learns to distinguish reality, becomes flexible and adaptable, and accepts the responsibilities of genital sexuality. A system of interaction is established in which cause and effect cannot be isolated; stimulus and response are welded into a unit. Such a unit of communication

[3] Saul, Leon J., *Emotional Maturity*. Phil. J. B. Lippincott Co., 1947. pp. 1-22.

becomes a "value," or a preferred channel of communication and related-ness.[4]

III. Communication Tools and the Family

In early childhood the primary tools of communication are non-verbal. Henceforth, much of the most significant communication remains at a sub-verbal level. The child is born with an interactive system with which he begins to learn to interpret gestures as incipient acts, or short-cut acts. Acts, in turn, become a conversation of gestures. But as the child grows and his needs call for an increasing number of other people, who themselves are increasingly complicated, he must make the transition from meaning as defined by acts and gestures alone to acts as defined by verbal symbols. Verbal communication universalizes experience by reducing it to concepts, and thus the child is exposed to the wisdom of the family and of the culture. Communication with others demands that the sender must make use of his imagination to know how the message appears to the receiver. This he does by using his thought processes and the ability to "hear" himself speak. As these skills develop, minute adjustments in relating to others are made possible.

The family is crucial in the development of skills in all phases of communication. Long before a child has formed the first monosyllabic extension of himself, he has formulated the basic matrix of communication skills which are chiefly non-verbal. This has happened in the total context of "in-tune-ness" in the family. If, from conception, the child has been prized as a person of worth, if despite the dependent state of infancy he has been treated as an entity worthy of reciprocal closeness, if as a child self-identity and personal worth have never been undermined, if parents and parent substitutes have been facile in both the giving and receiving aspects of non-verbal sharing—then the child will have the required components for building an adequate communication system for the future. He will have the need and the strength to communicate his own message of self-hood to meaningful others, and will be an apt pupil as the family teaches and provides opportunities for acquiring the tools and skills of verbalization and linguistic symbols.[5] A child reared in an environment where both verbal and nonverbal communication is easy and spontaneous, and where some sym-

[4] Rutledge, Aaron L., *Marital Therapy: Psychotherapy with Marital Problems.* Manuscript in preparation, Chapter 7. Reusch and Bateson, *op. cit.,* pp. 8ff.
[5] Waller, Willard and revised by Hill, Reuben, *The Family.* New York; the Dryden Press, 1938, pp. 35-41. Rutledge, *op. cit.,* "Symbolism" in Chapter 15.

metry or uniformity prevails, probably will be emotionally healthy and able to relate meaningfully to others.

IV. Communication and Disturbance

The child who does not have an environment which provides ample opportunity for stimulus and response in communication, or where inconsistency is too great, is likely to become ill or otherwise a misfit. Too few "messages" to the communication system results in starvation. The non-stimulated child, often thought to be mentally deficient, may grow up with the inability to receive messages of genuine interest from others, or he misinterprets and distorts the intentions of others because of his own misperceptions. Moreover, not having received, he cannot give and thus is further isolated from reciprocal human fellowship. Excessive stimulation in certain areas, to the neglect of others, may result in spasmodic or unequal development of the child's ability to relate.

Mental hygiene can be viewed as the attempt to prevent the development of disturbances of communication which are indirectly responsible for behavior disorders. Reusch [6] has contended that all phenomena placed under the traditional headings of psychopathology are disturbances of communication which are defined partially by culture. The sick individual never developed a satisfactory means of communication, and therefore was unable to assimilate the divergent trends within the home or between home and surrounding influences. This resulted in a marginal status as compared to the bulk of people within his psycho-social field of experience. Stimulus of a kind continues to barrage him, but his readiness for action cannot be consummated. When fight and flight, as well as all means of communication, are blocked, the continuous alarm becomes a permanent anxiety state. The resulting disturbances many be organic or functional. Through prolonged tension from emotional conflicts, the internal communication may be blocked by failure to acquire skills, or by functional interference with the skills of transmission and reception one does possess. Interpersonal conflicts, such as in a marriage, relate to communication in a network composed of one or more additional persons. At the semantic level, the difficulty may lie in the failure to transmit the desired meaning, or perhaps in the distortion of the meaning that was portrayed.

Although Sullivan was more inclined to consider a breakdown in communication the result of personality disturbance, rather than it being the disturbance itself, he described with clarity verbal communications as

[6] Reusch and Bateson, *op. cit.,* pp. 37, 50-93.

evidenced in the therapeutic interview, viewing them as autistic disturb-ances.[7] Autistic refers to the predecessors of communicative behavior when the child has learned a word, toys with it and assigns his own private meaning to it, but has not as yet seen the meaning which will enable him to communicate with others. Something is absent, lacking. The patient may experience a loss of thought, become blank, or, in extreme cases, block completely. There may be peculiar misunderstandings or mistaken inter-pretations of the therapist's (or other's) questions or suggestions. The person may hear what is not said, the extreme form being hallucination. Stereotyped verbal expressions may occur which are non-communicative in nature, but seem to have some inner meaning to the patient. Sometimes he acts as though there were certain secret understandings between him and the therapist or other person; he may be coy and evasive as though the two were in secret agreement to ignore certain facts. When someone attempts this with a marriage partner he is not understood and often is misunderstood.

Sullivan[8] listed three types of disturbance in the gesticular aspect of communication which are vital to the understanding of what is occurring, and these may apply in treatment, in marriage counseling, or in a marriage. (1) Stereotyped gestures seem incongruous with the subject and occasion, as if cut off from the person; yet they have some unknown meaning. (2) Mannerisms are regularized peculiar bodily movements which are divorced from what is going on externally. (3) Tics or spasms of groups of muscles may seem quite separate from what is occurring except to register a tension level, but they also may occur in relation to specific stress.

People tend to be taught from early childhood that it is dangerous to think about certain topics, not to mention communicating freely about them. Both with the engaged couple and in a counseling relationship the counselor must be alert to how much interference is due to a life-long taught pattern, or symptomatic of deep-seated personality disturbance, or related to current marital conflict, and how much is due to a combination of these, plus the stress of the interview situation.

V. Communication and Cure

There is a hopeful note in the approach to the study of counseling through communication and this is especially true in pre-marital counseling.

[7] Sullivan, Harry Stack, *The Psychiatric Interview*. New York: W. W. Norton Co., 1954, pp. 189-193.
[8] Sullivan, *Ibid,* pp. 193-195.

Fundamentally, all people, regardless of limitations, can be helped to improve their skills in communication, although both the speed and degree of improvement fluctuates, depending upon a variety of internal and external factors. When communication of the individual with himself and with others has improved—which involves change in the content and process of perception—self-correction, and correct interpretation of stimuli from others provide the foundation for real change in the conduct of relating.

Communication permits the explanation of intrapersonal, interpersonal, and cultural aspects of events within the marriage and in the total social situation of which the client(s) and the counselor are integral parts. Within this conceptual frame of reference the counselor may have to focus upon certain aspects of communication, but at the same time it is imperative that he have a thorough knowledge of the total relations between individual, mate, families, and culture if he is to be of maximum help.

For all psychotherapists and counselors, communication is *the* method of influencing the client. The counselor aims at understanding disturbances of communication with a view to correction of the defective processes. This may involve both the undoing of already established patterns and learning and gaining experience with the basic elements of human communication. The fact that the overloaded, emotionally laden, lines of communication must be cleared through ventilation and catharsis before this learning and relearning can occur is of crucial importance in pre-marital counseling.

VI. Communication and Marriage

Just as mental illness is diagnosed at the point of breakdown of understandable communication with others, much marital pathology can be similarly described. Lack of communication here can be the illness, the symptom of a more basic illness, or the isolating effect of this illness. But once the processes of communication begin to weaken, symptoms grow and become further causes of conflict and of illness. The very symptoms themselves isolate the person, cutting him off from the healing forces that emanate from the mate or the larger group, and stifle the healing forces within himself. Restored communication brings a chance to be healed, although healing to a certain extent must also precede adequate communication.

So it is with marriage. At the root of most marital difficulties are two personalities; but, there was potential for growth of some kind of relationship, else a marriage likely would not have occurred or would not have endured for long. The need for, the goal of, and the process by which pre-marital counseling is accomplished are all rooted in both the interference with and the necessity of communication. Interference in the couple's sharing may center in a stunted or crippled personality of one or both mates, who either have never learned the basic elements of communication or who have cut themselves off from others because of traumatic experiences. The interference may lie in the nature of their particular relationship itself, where interaction brings about a dynamic relationship which is a product quite different from the individual capabilities and liabilities of the two people.[9]

Contrary to many clinical opinions, healthy individuals can have the kind of difficulties in communication—due to differing perception systems, or to semantics, or to failure in clarification and evaluation—that will lead to an unhealthy marriage.

In fact, the process of mate selection in this culture is conducive to poor communication in marriage. Children are taught from childhood not to communicate certain impulses, feelings, and interests. This is intensified in dating where each camouflages his real self and transforms the partner with a halo of projected needs. All too often there is mutual resistance to honest exploration, based upon fear of being found out and rejected. As marriage approaches for a couple, there may be a dual effort to discover and conceal. The need to know and possess pushes them into a closer relationship, but this closeness threatens to expose the "hidden" factors and they become anxious and withdraw.

Following marriage, as the intensity of love increases, restraints tend to be released, manners are forgotten, truth emerges, frankness overrides tact, and hostility may be expressed. As the total interaction intensifies it may become so upsetting that the couple cannot tolerate it. To stabilize interaction and maintain the relationship, they again begin to place limits upon self-expression. Gradually areas of life and kinds of feelings are added to that collection of reactions which must be avoided to preserve the relationship. Thus communication within a marriage becomes blocked and hurt feelings, misunderstanding, and resulting bitterness magnify and accumulate until little except anger and rejection are being shared, either directly or through withdrawal. Psychologically expressed, inhibition and defenses are mobilized, along with vigilance against the narcissistic injury that would accompany self-confrontation; much of this is unconsciously motivated, of course. As conflicted couples come to the marriage counselor,

[9] Rutledge, *op. cit.*, Chapters 1 and 2.

it is literally astounding how confused their communication can be. It is the rule rather than the exception that the picture each of them portrays of self, of mate, of specific incidents and conditions, and of the marital interaction in general are so different that it doesn't sound at all like the same situation. What is communicated verbally is misunderstood or distorted; what isn't said is just as confusingly interpreted. Acts and gestures, as well as generalized "feelings about" what is being communicated, whether creative or destructive, tend to be received as a grotesque facsimile of healthy marital communication.[10]

When the counselor enters this emerging picture with an engaged couple, disturbance, or at least anxiety, may be intensified because he endeavors to break down the dams to communication, threatening to release the pent-up dangers to self, to loved one, and to the desired marriage. Just as with individual psychotherapy, the progress of pre-marital counseling will be determined by the client's experience of communicating with other persons whose values and communication system are different. Often the threat of hurt is so great that an appreciable amount of time is required to establish in the counseling relationship an environment of safety in which some elements of the engaged couple's problems can be faced and shared. In some cases an even longer period may be necessary before the couple dare begin communicating freely with each other, lest they intensify the hurt. Painful though it is, pre-marital counseling can be excellent relationship insurance for the future marriage.

The *role of the pre-marital counselor* is crucial. The complications of couple conflict are such that distortion of perception by one or both prospective mates, perhaps also by the counselor, can affect the plan of help. The professional must be attentive to the content of the individuals' communication; and yet, if he is taken in by what one mate says about his situation or about his partner, either an idealized, distorted, or stereotyped picture will be formed. If he takes a superficial look only, he tends to over-generalize the situation and ignore the actual behavior of the man or the woman in-laws, and third parties. At worst, he will gain a distorted picture of the emerging relationship, which will make his influence a destructive one. On the other hand, he may be led to treat each individual as an isolated entity, not related to the mate. The counseling would tend

[10] Rutledge, Aaron L. "The Future of Marriage Counselling," *Merrill-Palmer Quarterly*, Vol. I, 1955, pp. 141-147; Slavson, S. R. *A Textbook in Analytic Group Psychotherapy*. New York: International Universities Press. 1964. Chapter IX.

to focus upon internal structure and dynamics to the neglect of the structure and dynamics of the relationship which is moving toward marriage.

If the counselor concentrates on being a "neutral observer" of man-woman interaction, he may fit them into character types and cultural patterns and be blinded to unique individuality and personal idiosyncrasies. To be more than an automaton, to understand individual trends and patterns and the interaction of individuals as well, the counselor must be a participant-observer. However, to become too involved in the immediate experience with either or both clients, and with their specific relationships to each other, is to overlook the more static factors of mores, social structure, and other social determinants of motivation and behavior.

In a word, a holistic approach—giving equal care to understanding the social milieu, the individuals, and the unique relationship created by them— is essential to effective pre-marital counseling. Such an approach is at the same time diagnostic or evaluative, therapeutic, and educational. The counselor's role as a participant-observer enables him to: determine to what extent each is aware of the rules, roles, and labels of married living; to observe the degree of reality with which each is in tune with the communication occurring in counseling and with the fiance(e); to evaluate the ability of each to handle the stimuli received, and whether each is stimulated or understimulated; to detect semantic problems in linguistic and symbolic aspects of communication, and the knowledge or level of learning in vital areas; and to gauge the effect of each client's communication, or lack of it, upon the mate.[11]

With both prospective partners involved in counseling, it becomes possible to check out individually and comparatively the effectiveness of both the sending and the receiving capabilities of the two persons, whether verbal or non-verbal, since engaged behavior is an open manuscript for the counselor to read. One may become even more disturbed about the approaching marriage if his sending apparatus is improved, while the mate's receiving or perception remains distorted. The counseling relationship gives each spouse a chance to share anxiety with a non-anxious and non-defensive person, and brings about enough relief and reassurance to make possible the toleration of the impact counseling makes upon the engaged relationship. Gradually each learns to utilize knowledge of self, of his situation, and of his part in it to correct himself and to be corrected. Successful communication in counseling can become the model for the

[11] Reusch and Bateson, op. cit., pp. 85-86; See also Rutledge, Marital Therapy, "Diagnosis of Marital Interaction," Chapters 11 and 12.

couple learning to communicate together now and later in the marriage relationship. The establishing of free and spontaneous communication either demonstrates that a relationship is unworkable or begins to pave the way for, give stimulus to, and demonstrate the advisability of a marriage for them. In time the couple must take over the functions rendered in counseling if they are to make a wholesome transition to self-sufficiency. The non-verbal aspects of communication, often repressed in growing up or blocked out through hurtful experiences, hopefully become freed through the process of "working through"—the process of making available to the ego the unknown or unconscious for evaluation and guidance—in counseling and in relating to each other. Empathic relating can be enhanced by verbalization of true feelings, once the process of intrapersonal communication has become effective. In turn, verbal sharing which is spontaneous and non-compulsive can sharpen empathic abilities.

At the preventive level, the chief function of the engagement process, and concurrent preparation for marriage through education and counseling, is to provide opportunity to learn how to communicate freely in every vital area of married pair living.

B. COUNSELING AND INSTRUCTION

The two primary means of communication through which adult personality is influenced are the multiple media of education or instruction, and of counseling or psychotherapy. Professional opinions on these two approaches to pre-marital counseling can be broken down into those authorities who: (1) advocate exclusively either education or psychotherapy as the choice method; (2) say education is for mass efforts, but dealing with the individual calls for psychotherapy; (3) insist that the didactic approach is contrary to therapeutic principles, fails to bring results, and may be destructive; and (4) contend that psychotherapy is a highly specialized form of education, a process of unlearning, relearning and learning.

I. Varying Viewpoints

There are a few psychotherapists who feel that long-term psychotherapy or psychoanalysis is the *only* way to change patterns of reacting, relieve serious symptoms, or bring about renewed growth in a stunted personality or improvement in relating skills. At the other pole of possibilities are a few educators who feel that instruction is the answer to all individual and marital adjustment or maladjustment; that the answer lies in gaining the maximum knowledge in terms of facts, statistics, and techniques.

In the extreme psychotherapy view, the contention is that all maladjustment is due to deep-seated, crippling inhibition, not to lack of information and skills. The emphasis from the exclusively psychotherapeutic view is that the successfully analyzed person would have no relationship problems, sexual or otherwise. To reverse it, if he had such problems, a successful therapy experience would automatically remove them and leave the person able to live in a spontaneous and healthy manner in all relationships.

To carry the educational emphasis to an equal absurdity, a few family life and mental health advocators tend to divorce certain areas of life— i.e., the religious, economic, sexual—from the context of the rest of life, especially from the total love relationship, and believe these can be modified through the didactic imparting of information and techniques. Prescribed reading may become a major tool in this approach. Amassed research, statistical norms, and various cults of intercourse, whether social or sexual, are peddled as the answer to all marital dilemmas.

It is all too easy for the family educator to peddle a supermarket philosophy of "pick what you want and pay for it," with the smooth-working techniques of the industrial world being taught as the model for happiness. Barter, "you meet my needs and I'll meet yours," is the mode of exchange in the search for mutual sex satisfaction or team work in marriage. To superimpose upon these unhealthy concepts of marital value the best of information is to have it distorted into something as superficial as "how to win friends and influence people" in the secular field or the distortion of "the power of positive thinking" in religion. Everything, including the mate and God, becomes a means of getting what one wants, which often pushes two lonely and starving people further into emotional poverty and isolation.

In actuality, there is no clear-cut distinction between educative and therapeutic approaches. This is made clear when one examines the extent to which some psychotherapists depend upon direct instruction, prescription of reading material, exhortations to certain behaviors and against others, admonition, and even threat; some of these operating in the name of a religiously based value system and some on the basis of their own brand of science.

Counseling and psychotherapy, on the one hand, and education, on the other hand, are two effective ways of attaining the same goals; two processes by which people learn and grow. Fundamental to the success of either approach, or combination thereof, is the application of certain basic principles of personality growth and change (See Chapter 1). To learn, to change, to grow, calls for some basic motivation that will push the person forward, enabling him to pay the price of temporary confusion in order to attain a new level of meaningfulness. A second basic requirement is that the life energies of the individual be free to be utilized in this process of growth and change.

II. How Ideas Are Used

A goal mutually held by both the average counselor and educator is that most individuals can unlearn harmful ways of reacting and behaving and learn to live in a healthy and creative manner. The underlying principles of learning apply equally well in education and in counseling when the person is free, within himself and among others, to learn. Stimulus to change comes from exposure to new ideas, whether they originate within himself, from a therapeutic suggestion, a book, or a classroom, or pulpit statement, or from a mate, or prospective mate. It now becomes fruitful to ask in what way new ideas are used by a particular person. Roughly the population might be divided among those who use new ideas to hamper growth, to further growth, and various combinations of these extremes.

There is a widespread tendency to hear what one wants to hear and utilize it to strengthen prejudices, stereotypes, fixed beliefs, feelings and ways of responding. The variety of ways in which new ideas can be used against self, associates, mates, children and counselor is astounding. To some, new ideas become additional pickets on a fence of unhealthy self-maintenance, bricks in a thicker wall of defenses against change and growth. Many of these people will need treatment on a long-term basis. Detection of disturbed patterns of behavior, along with strong defenses against learning, may indicate postponement of marriage until change has occurred through psychotherapy. Some will lack the motivation for treatment of any kind.

Other people, including many of those seeking preparation for marriage, habitually use new ideas, whether gleaned from literature or professional people, as a challenge to further growth. These may be able, or soon find it possible, to make creative use of direct suggestions or instruction.

Perhaps the largest percentage of marital clients, although basically able to utilize new ideas constructively, temporarily are incapacitated by bitterness, tension, and bogged down processes of thinking and responding. Once new ideas were an influence for further growth of the mates and of the relationship, but because of so much hurt anything new now is used defensively. This may be true in certain areas of life for any pre-marital client. Passion needs to be tamed enough to use its energy in preparation for marriage.

If instruction is used as a substitute for counseling, or if information is superimposed upon confused thinking or a disturbed relationship, the cure may be more destructive than the disease, as the couple now assume themselves to be adequately prepared for marriage.

The end result of this can be clearly seen when a married couple, seriously conflicted and anxious over failure to adapt sexually, set out to remedy their situation. They read books and attend sex lectures, but successful experiences evade them. The marriage counselor may check on their knowledge and find that they can recite all the facts of anatomy and sexual techniques, but "it doesn't work." They have heard from the ears up, but it has not permeated the rest of the person. To give more information or diagnostic opinions at this stage is merely to add weapons for them to use against each other. Instruction alone fails in cases of serious marital malady, but the skillful use of information within a therapeutic relationship becomes a vital tool for helping people. As bitterness and tension are reduced through counseling, outdated feelings and beliefs are moved out and there is space for more realistic ideas. Instruction, as an integral part of counseling, is effective to the degree to which the person can take new ideas, weigh them in terms of previous knowledge and experience, predict results, choose, try out, learn from, and then adopt or reject. Old ways of feeling and acting may reassert themselves, after having been temporarily resolved in counseling, simply because there is nothing new to take their place. Draining off tension and clarifying outmoded ideas and beliefs, eliciting and suggesting something "new" to take the place of the old, support as choices are made, guiding discussion until assimilation occurs, and giving encouragement as it is implemented is the essence of counseling and psychotherapy. Moreover, it is in accord with the best principles of education and learning.

When one of a married couple has understood himself, when the need to love begins to emerge in its fullness, suggestions, or instruction in previously unknown ways of expressing affection, or preparation of the mate to receive the love and to respond, can speed the development of a relationship. Reading and discussing a sound book may be of great help at this stage. Gradually they relax and learn and relax some more until spontaneous affection begins to emerge as a natural outgrowth of love. Many people have been too crippled to reach their original potential, but most couples are capable of moving toward the ideal expressed by Fromm:

"Love, experienced thus, is a constant challenge; it is not a resting place, but a moving, growing, working together; even whether there is harmony or conflict, joy or sadness, is secondary to the fundamental fact that two people experience themselves from the essence of their existence, that they are one with each other by being one with themselves, rather than by fleeing from themselves." [12]

To help the engaged couple to begin to approximate this growth and self-expression will demand a variety of education and counseling tools. Early in the contact the counselor should be able to determine whether this person on his own, or a couple together, is capable of using ideas as stimulus for growth. If there is serious conflict, it may be rooted in deep-seated personality disturbance. The first step then may be intensive psychotherapy for one or both of the individuals. In other cases the evaluative process may determine that the couple are ready for direct instruction, or that even the least amount of instruction or suggestion is a risk until some major relief and clarification have occurred through the early or prolonged stages of preparation for marriage. When tension is relieved through catharsis, stereotyped thinking corrected, and emotional blocking removed, the capacity of each person to use ideas creatively is enhanced. Then there is an opportunity for the counselor to become an instructor— the "parent" no father or mother could be—as they learn and relearn basic skills of learning and problem solving.

It becomes obvious then that preparation for marriage is a joint process of counseling and instruction; enough counseling to bring understanding and relaxation, and enough instruction, whether by suggestion or by eliciting from the individual's storehouse of knowledge, to replace that which has been uprooted and rejected.

Bret asked many questions about the desired frequency of sexual intercourse. After several hours of counseling he became comfortable enough to relive much of his earlier experiences, and to recall the sex attitudes in his home. He had been warned by parents and coach that sex expression would weaken him, destroying his ability to be a good ball player. Now he feared that frequent intercourse in the anticipated manner would make him weak and ineffectual as a man. After reliving in great detail these early threats, and his reactions to

[12] Fromm, Erich. *The Art of Loving.* New York: Harper and Row Publishers, Inc. 1956. p. 103; by permission.

them, after emptying himself of false beliefs, he was ready for instruction in the naturalness and healthiness of sexual intercourse in his approaching marriage.

Without first experiencing the catharsis of talking it out, and the corrective experiences of therapy, he would not have been able to utilize the truth. In fact, he had heard and read the facts before, but they were merely superimposed upon unhealthy basic convictions.

C. THE MERITS OF BRIEF COUNSELING

How long must the process of guided therapeutic communication last before an individual or couple becomes self-sufficient? Once short-term therapy tended to be discredited in favor of very long or psychoanalytic treatment. But the literature of the last ten years shows an increasing emphasis upon psychotherapy on a short-term, one to twenty-five or thirty interviews, once or twice a week basis, with close collaboration between counselor and client, including the joint setting of goals to be attained.[13] These briefer approaches can be given various names, including goal-directed therapy, sector analysis, brief psychotherapy, and counseling. Short-term counseling may be as directive or as non-directive as the particular practitioner cares to make it. There are many problems in the practice of brief counseling and not every client can profit by it or even tolerate it. Likewise, not all therapists can do successful short-term counseling, which may require more skill than a longer term relationship, in that there is less time for adequate diagnosis and less opportunity to correct therapeutic errors.

Growth comes slowly for many people and more time is required for real change to get under way. Deeper resistances and conflicts may not be discovered, since there is not enough time for satisfactory transference relations to develop between therapist and client, or for the needed working through of disturbing emotions. Some clients become so disturbed by more direct and intensive short-term efforts that they cannot tolerate the experience. Brief psychotherapy or counseling can produce seemingly miraculous cures by removing physical or other symptoms through catharsis and suggestion, but all too often the basic conflict is left untouched to sprout another symptom. It takes a sharp clinician to determine early the

[13] Ellis, Albert. "New Approaches to Psychotherapy Techniques," *Journal of Clinical Psychology,* Monograph Supplement No. 11, July 1955; an excellent summary review of journal literature.

counseling approach which has the best chance of succeeding, but pre-marital counseling in general is essentially short-term.

On the credit side of the ledger, short-term counseling can be a helpful method as preparation for other treatment, as a substitute for longer psychotherapy which is unobtainable, or as the preferred approach to certain cases. It may be acceptable to many clients who could not or would not seek longer term help. Attacking the client's current, disturbing problems may stabilize him short of a psychotic break. By concentrating more on personal relations than upon underlying urges and impulses, although it is urgent that the counselor understand these, the client is helped to evaluate his reality situation and to modify it or his attitude toward it. Brief goal-directed counseling may, through one facet of the personality, bring about changes in the total personality structure. This can be particularly effective with clients who have a strong ego structure with which to work, such as may be found among many engaged pairs. Brief counseling may avoid over-dependency and the danger of some clients continuing to regress through long-term help. That more people can be served is another distinct advantage of short-term counseling.[14]

In certain cases short-term, non-depth-oriented counseling with a trusted minister or professor gets similar results to longer term psychotherapy with the stranger who is the professional therapist. It would be easy to say that in such cases the problem was more superficial, rooted less in the unconscious, or that the changes were less deep and permanent. No doubt this is true in some instances, but many clients do make both comprehensive and intensive change under such brief contacts. Among the many factors accounting for this are readiness to face up to reality—whether it be a specific problem or getting ready for marriage in general—with a professional person who is known, whose roles are fairly clear, making for a mutually understanding relationship. Perhaps the central reason for

[14] Laidlaw, R. N., "The Psychiatrist as Marriage Counselor," *American Journal of Psychiatry*, 1950, Vol. 106, pp. 732-736; Rosenblum, B., "The Single Interview Case," *Jewish Social Service Quarterly* 1952, Vol. 28, pp. 257-265; Saul, L. J., "On the Value of One or Two Interviews," *Psychoanalytic Quarterly*, 1951, Vol. 20, pp. 613-615; Alexander, F., "Current Views on Psychotherapy," *Psychiatry*, 1953, Vol. 16, pp. 113-122; Chaskel, Ruth, "Short-Term Counseling — A Major Family Agency Service," *Social Work Journal*, 1953, Vol. 34, pp. 20-23; Moore, Eleanor A., "Casework Skill in Marriage Counseling," *Social Casework*, Vol. 34, 253-258; Pumpian-Mindlin, E., "Considerations in the Selection of Patients for Short-Term Therapy," *American Journal of Psychotherapy*, 1953, Col. 7, pp. 641-653; Meader, A., *Ways to Psychic Health*. Translated by Theodore Lit, New York: Charles Scribner's Sons, 1953; Thorne, F. C., "Directive Psychotherapy: Theory, Practice and Social Implications," *Journal of Clinical Psychology*, 1953, Vol. 9, pp. 267-280.

progress is the manner in which the trusted minister or professor role lends itself to the client's needs for identification much earlier in the process.

This can be illustrated with the minister. He is an authority figure; but when he is of the personality makeup to attract people to him for personal help, this likely will be construed as a benevolent authority. There is enough client expectation of the punishing or judgmental attitude to pull to the surface major hostile and rebellious identifications and feelings associated with earlier traumatic experiences, but an accepting attitude by the minister (again depending upon whether or not he is capable of this role) ameliorates these attitudes and in turn elicits healthier identifications. This may speed the working through of partial transference of various conflicts without the necessity of developing a full-blown tranference neurosis.

Whether or not such insight is verbalized, and verbalization does not necessarily make experiential insight more effective, the minister by title and by role symbolizes—as needed by the client—father, brother, mother, God, and successful man. There is something about the clarity of these roles, particularly for one reared in the church, which invites many who are troubled to deal quickly with what is bothering them. Even when the client does not have the courage or time to verbalize all conflicts, his feelings of inadequacy, hostility, frustration, confusion, guilt and isolation—in the presence of one who can give him opportunities for identifying with and working out feelings about so many of his family relations—come flooding to consciousness. This enables him to clarify the influence of others upon himself and to face up to responsibility. The facing up to self may intensify the feeling of isolation but the need to be "at one" with self, with the family, with man, with the cosmos—if met by a forgiving, accepting representative of a God of Love—may bring about the kind of release from tension and personality reorganization at the deepest levels which would take much more time and effort in another setting.

The long-term and continuing relationship of pastor and parishioner may provide ready-made transference situations for immediate use, so that a few minutes' conference occasionally, reinforced by group experiences in the church, can bring the kind of gradual change and growth comparable in both degree and quality to that attained in others by long-term intensive psychotherapy. Conversely, such an experience with a sick or markedly immature leader of whatever profession may result in further disturbances or blocking of growth. There are other notable cases in which the client, depending somewhat upon his concept of God and of a minister, coupled with the particular minister's condemnatory attitude, is threatened seriously in working with a pastor or priest. This may apply to any minister for a particular client, who may seek help from a neighboring church where he does not have to face the minister every week. Many cannot accept help from a religious source or from any other person who is involved in their daily life, particularly in an authoritarian role.

Similar to the minister, the role of teacher or professor may lend itself to both positive and negative transference dynamics. In cases of intra-family difficulty, the professor-counselor may more easily become a "family member" in the counseling process. This invites the speedy working through and clarification of role confusions, *if* the counselor's skills and warmth are adequate. There is equal potential for damage to the client if the counselor is inexperienced or under compulsion to direct the life of the client. An interpretative statement which seems to be mild indeed may completely overwhelm the client because of the extra value the opinion of the authority figure has taken on in the transference situation.

Short-term deeper counseling, even though there is some risk of unleashing destructive forces from unconscious depths, can release for creative living energy previously bound in containing conflicts and defending self. Subterranean resources for health, growth, and healthy human relationships may be released which cut short the necessary helping process.

Pre-marital counseling can be effective on a short term basis, even with fairly serious relationship problems, when each of the couple is stable enough to tolerate direct confrontations about his own personality or behavior problems. The emotional freeing of catharsis then enables a frontal approach to developing and utilizing the skills necessary to healthy interaction. Getting ready for marriage has a way of activating many of the struggles common to growing up and becoming adult. This fluidity, plus a desire to build a good marriage, can bring the engaged couple to pre-marital counseling with a high level of motivation to change and grow. This makes pre-marital counseling a rewarding experience for both client and counselor.

Chapter 4

THE METHOD AND THE COUNSELOR

Whether the counselor adopts a uniform approach to all preparation for marriage or plans for each situation on its own merit, there are certain basic considerations. What information is required? Desirable? What is the role of the counselor? Should the group approach be used, or one couple at a time, or should each person be seen individually?

A. NECESSARY INFORMATION

Both at the level of choosing a method and in the process of actually working with a couple, reliable information is vital. As the counselor collects this information, it may take on a segmented nature, but he must be constantly alert to seeing the facts in relation to the total person(s) involved. This necessitates as much information as can be reasonably obtained, both of a general and specific nature, about each person and his family background. The tools to be used will vary with the counselor and the situation, but the following outline discussion points to a few of the many possibilities.

I. Information Schedules and Inventories

Rather complete data on a client can be assembled as counseling proceeds, but necessity dictates some minimal information early in the contact, and the client may be asked to report early for the first appointment in order to provide this. The counselor may design his own blanks or use one of those in print. An example is the *Individual and Marriage Counseling Inventory,*[1] which provides initial uniform data on clients in the quickest possible way. Part A provides space for "personal data," which depicts the educational, marital, occupational, financial, religious, cultural, and health status, as well as listing the major problems with which the client wishes help. Part B is devoted to parental or "family data." Part C is a

[1] Rutledge, Aaron L., "Individual and Marriage Counseling Inventory," Merrill-Palmer Institute, Detroit, Michigan; available along with instructions for a brief record system.

guide for the individual to use in discussing the personal relationships in his family, but this should be used only with discretion. The average client who is seeking preparation for marriage can handle Part C of this Inventory well enough, but the disturbed client may find it upsetting. For this reason the folder should be stapled inside-out for general office use so that clients coming for help with serious emotional problems will not be called upon to fill out this part without special consideration. The final one half page of the folder is designed for those who can maintain only a simple record system, and provides space for the counselor to record dates of interviews, presenting problems, further problems revealed in counseling, and the outcome.

The Sex Knowledge Inventory[2] is used by some counselors to portray the client's sex knowledge and attitudes. It is an objective test which can be taken within forty-five minutes. The client chooses one of five possible answers to each question, and indicates those he wishes to discuss. This is not a "self-help" test but an aid to the counselor in demonstrating to an individual or couple where knowledge and attitudes are inadequate. Perhaps its greatest worth is in activating the many facts of sex in order to facilitate free discussion.

II. Marriage Prediction Tests

Terman developed a Prediction Scale of Marital Happiness, and Burgess and Cottrell formulated another similar tool. [3] These instruments have been modified through the years, and have been tried in varying combinations. In most cases they are based on reports made by married couples from narrow social class populations about factors before marriage as compared with adjustment in marriage.

The Value of Prediction Tests. Prediction tests are still in the experimental stage. Although the correlations of the majority of predictive factors with success in marriage are not so high in recent studies as they were in the earlier one, Burgess [4] has outlined their value:

1. Couples testify to a therapeutic and educational benefit in that it makes them realize factors to be considered in a successful marriage.

[2] McHugh, Gelolo, *The Sex Knowledge Inventory* Form X, Family Life Publications, Durham, North Carolina.

[3] Terman, L. M., *Psychological Factors in Marital Happiness*, New York: McGraw-Hill, 1938; Burgess, E. W. and Leonard S. Cottrell, *Predicting Success or Failure in Marriage*, New York: Prentice-Hall, 1939.

[4] Burgess, E. W., "The Value and Limitations of Marriage Prediction Tests," *Marriage and Family Living*, Vol. 12, 1950, pp. 54-55; See also: Locke, Harvey J., *Predicting Adjustment in Marriage*, New York: Henry Holt and Co., 1951.

2. Time is saved for the marriage counselor and the client by eliminating certain points that need not be covered in an interview.
3. Problems that might be overlooked if there were only one or two interviews may be located with these schedules.
4. Interference of the personal and social equation of counselor, his theoretical frame of reference, seemingly is reduced below that found in short interviews.
5. The prediction possible by the schedules puts the interviewer on guard against intuitively based prognosis.
6. They are a screening device which picks out persons or couples who need one or more interviews and sets aside those with high scores as not needing counseling.

The Disadvantages of Prediction Tests in general can be outlined briefly:[5]
1. They are constructed and standardized on a mass basis rather than being applicable to any one individual.
2. They fail to reveal a configuration of dynamic factors which are most significant in a marriage relationship, such as previous success and failure in person-to-person relationships, ability to give and receive affection, flexibility and adaptability in roles as changes are dictated by circumstances, and problem-solving skills.
3. They may lead to a directive or didactic counseling relationship rather than one which puts the emphasis upon the client facing up to his own problems and working out solutions; they invite the client to say "tell me."
4. What the tests tell is based upon inadequate knowledge about marital success which under the best circumstances would be difficult to measure.
5. Adams has shown that the prediction instruments do not take into account contingency, i.e., the prospect for the future in terms of in-laws, finances, job, social adjustment, sexual needs, children and health of the people.
6. They are weak in portraying the basic attitudes of the individuals, a factor which assumes major importance in a marriage relationship. This is closely akin to the constellation of dynamic factors indicated above, but is sufficiently important to underline it.

In brief, the methodology and findings, and even the differential relevance of criteria, vary from population to population, not to mention

[5] Burgess, *op. cit.*; Adams, Clifford R., "Evaluating Marriage Prediction Tests," *Marriage and Family Living*, Vol. 12, 1950, pp. 55-58. See especially discussion by Albert Ellis in this reference.

the multiplicity of additional factors that makes any one engaged couple unique. It is this unique couple, not mass screening, which interests the pre-marital counselor. The currently popular prediction tests, especially when carelessly applied, can be time-consuming, superfluous, and downright misleading to the engaged couple and to the pre-marital counselor. The best hope for helpful instruments for pre-marital prediction lies in finding ways to project and analyze the current and prospective interpersonal interaction of a particular couple. In the absence of such valid tools, the interview, coupled with validated personality tests when indicated, continues to be the primary method of eliciting the requisite understanding of individual and couple.

III. Pencil and Paper Personality Tests

Several brief pencil and paper personality tests have been used widely in pre-marital counseling. They have the advantage of simplicity, but most of them are far too incomplete and inconclusive to have much weight placed upon them as clinical tools except for gross screening. Whether it is the individual's motive to protect himself from the opinion of others, or against self-knowledge, or to boost his opinion about himself, many give an overfavorable picture of themselves. Conversely, the person who needs to suffer or to castigate himself will present an unfavorable picture. Many sophisticated high school and college youths are capable of "fixing" the answers deliberately, in terms of what they think they ought to be from reading text books in family life and human development.

Many of these weaknesses apply also to the interview as a tool. However, interviews bring all of the skills of the counselor to be used in observation, in ferreting out reality from unreality, and in clarifying feelings of the client over an extended period.

The *Minnesota Multiphasic Personality Inventory* [6] is a true-false pencil test of 550 items on the long and 350 items on the short form. It is sufficiently comprehensive to get a more objective picture of a personality than is possible on the lesser inventories. Also, it may be administered individually with cards. Scoring on the MMPI is in terms of ten regular validity and clinical categories—validity score, lie score, hypochondriasis, depression, hysteria, psychopathic deviate, masculinity-femininity, para-

---

[6] Hathaway, Starke R., and Paul E. Meehl, *An Atlas for the Clinical Use of the MMPI*, Minneapolis University of Minnesota Press, 1951; also Swan, R., The Application of A Couple Analysis to the MMPI in Marriage Counseling. Ph.D. Thesis, University of Minnesota, 1953.

noia, psychasthenia, schizophrenia, and hypomania—and several more recent experimental ones. None of these categories alone is meaningful apart from the whole test. Scoring is simple, but interpretation calls for advanced professional training. Some disturbing interpretations are frequently made around masculinity-femininity scales of this test. An MMPI on each of an engaged couple gives an interesting and often helpful comparison of the two personalities in terms of similarities and complementary traits. Even the MMPI can be "fixed" by some individuals, but the fixing is easily detected.

IV. Projective Tests

The most valuable tools in the clinical psychologist's kit are the projective techniques, particularly the *Rorschach Test* and the *Thematic Apperception Test*. They portray much more than projection; in fact, any patterned mechanism of reacting can be demonstrated.

The Rorschach Test [7] is in the form of ten ink blots reproduced on cards. The client responds in terms of what he sees in the blots. The dimensions of personality which are measured can be grouped under intellectual activity, psychological operation, and fantasy living. This is the basic psychological tool in measuring or evaluating personality structure, whether pathological or healthy. A Rorschach analysis may be used for diagnosis prior to or in the process of pre-marital counseling, and can be valuable in comparing personalities and reaction patterns of a couple. There is need for intensive research into the use of the Rorschach in pre-marital counseling since only scattered efforts have been made in using this tool to predict marital interaction, to discover how a couple have got out of balance in a marriage, to guide the marriage counseling process, or to guide engaged couples in facing up to the probable areas of conflict to be encountered. The potential is great in the hands of a skilled psychologist, but this is no tool for a novice.

The Thematic Apperception Test (*TAT*), standardized by Murray,[8] is made up of pictures which provide stimuli for the client's stories. Nine classes of determinants may be at work as the test is administered. The

[7] Rorschach, H., *Psychodiagnosis*, translated by P. Lemkau and B. Kronenberg, New York Grune and Stratton, 1942; Beck, Samuel J. *Rorschach's Test*, New York, Grune and Stratton, Vols. I & II, 1949; Anderson, Harold and Gladys Anderson, editors, *An Introduction to Projective Techniques and Other Devices for Understanding the Dynamics of Human Behavior*, New York: Prentice-Hall, 1951, pp. 101-148.

[8] Murray, Henry A., *Thematic Apperception Test*, Cambridge: Harvard University Press, 1943.

concept of "thematic" derives from the themes of client involvement, and "apperception" denotes the perception of the pictures in terms of one's own needs. As a diagnostic tool the TAT ranks close to the Rorschach in usage, although complete recording, scoring and evaluation are complicated and time-consuming. It produces a wealth of material related to the client's own problems and mode of response to key issues, and paired tests are helpful in predicting the marital conflicts of a couple.[9] Clinicians may select a smaller group of the cards to administer for specific purposes.

The *Four Picture Test,*[10] developed by a pupil of Rorschach, lends itself to simpler use as a therapeutic tool. The client makes a story by combining and arranging, according to his own choice, four vaguely drawn pictures which portray states of existence—personality alone, with one person, with many others, and socially alone. FPT is limited as an individual diagnostic tool, but it can help reveal the multi-faceted dynamics of love relationships, jealousy, social ambitions and crises, fears, wanderlust, mistrust, longing, narcissism, neurotic fatigue, suicidal and homicidal tendencies. As with the TAT, the recording and diagnostic evaluation of the data is time-consuming, but the pictures can be used short of a complete test to stimulate a client who has difficulty in communicating.

Psychodrama and Sociodrama are forms of planned experience in which the counselor encourages the client to achieve maximum autonomy in self-projection. He may utilize such projection techniques as role-reversal, double-ego, substitute-role, mirroring, improvisation, dream presentation, monologue, dialogue, soliloquy, wordless psychodrama, and hypnodrama according to his training and the circumstances. These techniques have been evolved in the quest for a combination reality test and therapeutic method with individuals but can be adapted easily to a couple.[11]

V. Intelligence Tests

Seldom is the pre-marital counselor called upon to administer an intelligence test for IQ purposes as such, but these tools may be used to "pair" the ways of responding of an engaged couple. If the counselor is not skilled in testing, he will refer to a psychologist for such an evaluation; therefore, only a few of the most common instruments will be mentioned. The simple "pencil and paper" tests which can be administered in a group

9 Anderson and Anderson, *op. cit.* pp. 181-278.
10 *Ibid.*, pp. 149-180.
11 Moreno, Jacob L., *Who Shall Survive?* Rev. Ed., New York: Beacon House, 1953; Anderson and Anderson, *op. cit.,* pp. 662-675.

or to an individual will not be discussed since they are of little value when any degree of definity is required.

The Stanford-Binet Scale of Intelligence, Revised Form, is administered individually and is an effective tool.[12] Another valuable test to determine mental age is the *Wechsler Adult Intelligence Scale.*[13] The eleven separate groups compiling the scales are divided into six verbal and five non-verbal, covering areas such as information, comprehension, digit span, similarities, picture arrangement, picture completion, block design, arithmetic, digit symbols, object assembly and vocabulary. These two comprehensive tests have the advantages of being administered by a trained clinician, can be given in abbreviated form if indicated, and have significance for diagnosis of both personality strengths and weaknesses far beyond the determination of mental age.

Harrower has worked out a very helpful summary blank for test findings which records the "paired" strengths and liabilities of each mate, utilizing data from Rorschach, TAT, Bellevue-Wechsler, Szondi and drawings.[14]

VI. Tests and the Disadvantaged Population

Except for the grossest screening of the mentally ill and the mentally deficient, modern tests—whether self-administered personality surveys, intelligence instruments, or projective techniques—are risky indeed with that large element of the population that might be described as disadvantaged, underprivileged, or lower socio-economic. Most such tests are so culture-bound (usually to middle and upper class norms) that the results are misleading and oftimes completely erroneous.

Take the intelligence instruments as an example. Any test of native capacity for intellectual functioning must assume roughly equivalent backgrounds of the individuals used in test standardization and the subject now being tested. Such is not the case when applying the Stanford-Binet or Wechsler Adult Intelligence Scale to a disadvantaged Negro or white population. Negro children from underprivileged backgrounds test notoriously lower on intelligence tests than middle class white children, as do environmentally deprived white children from mountain and other isolated rural areas. Both the Negro and the white lower educational groups have in

[12] Anderson and Anderson, *Ibid.* pp. 581-605.
[13] Wechsler, David, *The Measurement of Adult Intelligence*, Baltimore: The Williams and Wilkins Co., 1944; Anderson and Anderson, *op. cit.,* pp. 544-580.

common many of the "I.Q. limiting" factors in their early histories; namely, poor prenatal and neo-natal nutrition and medical care, inadequately educated parents, teachers and clergy as stimuli to development, the limitations of available schools, the tendency to disrupted families with many children, and many resultant self-defeating personality characteristics.[15]

There is little published research on the use of projective personality tests—i.e., Rorschach or Thematic Apperception Test—with either lower socio-educational Negroes or Whites, but tentative findings of the author would indicate that one almost has to rewrite the norms for these tests, lest all of this population be labeled abnormal or of borderline potential and health.[16] In a depth study of nineteen hard-core, never-successfully-employed Negro men, all showed such gross anxiety on the Rorschach as to be labeled "in need of treatment." Tendencies toward flight through withdrawal, evasiveness, failure, and passivity were serious enough to be labeled pathological—except that, given the life-long environmental settings of these men, these traits probably represent the most effective means of survival. Furthermore, it was clearly demonstrated that there is no culture-free test for this population. The *fact of a test*, whether intelligence, personality or academic content, is in itself a cultural contaminant, predetermining gross anxiety and poor performance. This does not automatically mean that tests are not to be used, but caution is the order of the day with the culturally disadvantaged population.

By whatever means it is gained, there is no substitute for a basic factual picture of each of the engaged couple, including the history of past successes and difficulties in intimate relationships. How a man got along with mother, sister, father, brother, or previous girl friends can illuminate the current engaged relationship, and aid in projecting what he is going to be like in the marriage once the glow of passion begins to subside and the daily realities of living come to the fore. The woman's history of past relationships is equally crucial, of course. If either has been married before, or had a relationship with someone that approximated a marriage, this will provide further revelation of how this personality is going to react within the new family setting.

[15] For summation of research on "Negro American Intelligence," see Pettigrew, Thomas F., *A Profile of the Negro American*. Princeton, New Jersey: D. Van Nostrand Co., Inc., 1964, pp. 100-135.

[16] Rutledge, Aaron L. and Gertrude Z. Gass, *Nineteen Negro Men, An Experiment in Manpower Retraining*. Jossey Bass Publishers, Inc., 1966.

B. THE COUNSELOR

Among those chosen by engaged couples for help in preparing for marriage will be ministers, medical doctors (especially general practitioners, gynecologists and obstetricians), psychologists, psychiatrists, professional marriage counselors, and a variety of other counselors, including family service personnel, other social case workers, college professors and family life teachers in high schools. It is to be hoped that the counselor will demonstrate healthy attitudes toward love, marriage, sex, children, and the many areas of human interaction. Basic in this attitude would be the utmost respect for individuality and the encouragement of young couples to work out their own destiny in the light of history, and of their inborn and developed potential.

I. The Counselor's Resources

If the counselor is to aid young people in preparation for marriage, he must measure up at two crucial points: as a storehouse of the latest knowledge and information in the total field of human development and relationships; and as the kind of person who by his very being creates a suitable environment in which understanding and change can occur. The latter may be the most important, but more will be said about that later.

If the counselor is to be a source of information and aid in the evaluation of attitudes and beliefs, he must be familiar with the basic and latest thinking in many broad areas of knowledge which are outlined in Chapters 9-12. At least he must know where to put his hand on such data at a moment's notice. This does not mean that his role is to purvey facts and figures or that pre-marital counseling should be primarily didactic sessions. It does mean that an intelligent understanding of a great body of human experience will color this attitude as he relates to youth who are preparing for marriage. It influences greatly the suggestions he makes for seeking further help from other professional persons, books, and articles, as well as the way time is utilized with a particular couple or group of couples.

It is important that the counselor of engaged couples have access to and know how to utilize whatever resource persons can serve him or the couple—law, finance, insurance, religion, genetics, medicine, psychology, psychiatry. However, the parading of experts before a group of young people is not adequate preparation for marriage. In fact, it may be dangerous because of its tendency to segmentalize life, reinforcing such tendencies already rooted in the personality and reinforced by high school and college educational pressures.

II.   The Role of the Counselor

In both individual and group endeavors there should be *one counselor* or leader who is responsible for: the total process of getting ready for marriage, including the use of other resource persons; the integration of the entire process in terms of the American family scene and what each couple wants from marriage; and the personality and group dynamics emerging. The overall goal of pre-marital counseling, then, is to see that all phases of married living receive ample attention and that the combined sessions add up to a meaningful whole.

One-sided or partial attention to any area of life can cause difficulty. Preoccupation with a family history can arouse or reinforce fears of inheritance, or of "slipping back" to an earlier renounced way of living. Indiscriminate reviewing of parental family relationships, without time and support for handling conflicts, can reactivate hostilities with resultant guilt, leaving the person in a state of increased anxiety. On the other hand, an out-of-context focusing upon fine backgrounds, similarities and other purported assets can create a false sense of security. The ill-advised use of personality or psychological test results can create or reinforce fears of illness and maladjustment, and intensify impressions of superiority or inferiority. Prediction tests can create a false assurance that all is well, and the couple, left without doubt that they should be able to adjust, may make little practical effort to establish a working basis for handling problems. Blind dependence upon prayer and scriptural reassurances, or pronouncements of *the* way to family success, can camouflage deep-seated fears and create a false sense of security. Unwise dependence upon the outer expressions of religion—church attendance, urging a religious home or a democratic approach to life, etc.—important as these can be, can gloss over emotional problems which need special attention prior to marriage. The same can be true of a glib pledge to establish a democratic home. The outgrowth of unwise medical handling can be a variety of "organ neuroses," frigidity and other anxiety-laden difficulties.

Pre-marital counseling is not an authoritative ordering or forbidding, nor the repressive type of suggestion which denies problems and gives false reassurance. As such it will be rejected by the mature youth, but it will hurt the immature in that his unhealthy dependency needs are reinforced. Intellectualized interpretation merely succeeds in building a fence around problems, without resulting in personality reorganization or the learning of more effective patterns of adjustment. Exhortation and the extrication of promises and pledges at emotional peaks are of the same order.

Lest this book tend to point toward only one kind of leadership, a word of qualification is in order. Each counselor must develop his own approaches, and in the meantime will be most effective when he is using methods with which he is comfortable. This may mean that he is primarily didactic, authoritative, permissive, or any combination of these traits. Hopefully, as he gains maturity and experience, he will become increasingly flexible and capable of responding in terms of the needs of the particular individual, couple, or group. Only then can the maximum capacity of individuals for understanding themselves and for creatively relating to each other be realized through counseling.

Each couple has the right to work out a marriage relationship to meet their own expectations and needs, hopefully modified in terms of reality; not one which necessarily will fit into that desired by the counselor, or that which is expected in any social class, ethnic, or religious group. For instance, a completely democratic, equalitarian marriage may be the religious ideal or the middle class ideal of today, but it demands a level of personality development which can be attained only after considerable growth. Such growth is not likely to occur in an authoritarian counseling atmosphere.

As in all face-to-face relationships, what the counselor *is* speaks louder than what he says. This is never truer than in preparing youth for marriage. The process will be vitally affected by his view of his own role, or of the meaning and purpose of marriage, and his own emotional and educational biases. A healthy personality has the utmost respect for individuality and the ability to encourage young couples to work out their own destiny. Such an individual has a minimum of need to impose upon or treat in an authoritarian manner those who ask his guidance.

The counselor is important in terms of what he represents, as well as what he is. To some he is a representative of the law, God, science, education, society, or class structure. Although many of these traits may be represented, perhaps, for the young person who is approaching marriage, the counselor takes the place psychologically of the parental figures, who are not felt to be adequate for this stage of life. This has advantages and disadvantages. The counselor may by his reactions, or by not being alert to the use being made of him, reinforce the authoritarian, castigating forces operative in the young person from childhood. The entire process of preparation for marriage thus can be turned into a hostile struggle or into a passive reinforcement of repression and submission.

The skillful counselor becomes the parent the youth *needs,* not necessarily that which he has had or even wanted. He is the parent and the not-parent; the ideal parent who understands, clarifies, encourages, grants freedom, and who expects the young person to take on the traits of adulthood and its responsibilities in the emotional and sexual realm, as well as economically and socially.

III. Self-Help for the Counselor

This means that, through an ever-increasing self-understanding, the counselor must be a growing person. The extent to which he will be a help or a hindrance will be determined by the degree to which his energies are unencumbered and free-flowing. He must learn from the principles which he applies to others how to be free, and keep himself free, for relating helpfully to people in counseling. They have come for help; not to help him. This does not mean that he does not receive help. One reason for entering any profession is that it helps one live himself, but at least the counselor should be able to keep his needs out of the engaged couple's way, and at least fifty-one percent of the help involved in the process should be going to the clients.

The counselor may learn how to help himself through any combination of life experiences, all the way from just growing up to personal psycho-therapy. Some people learn to face up to self in prayer or in self-analysis, whereas for others these become the perfect camouflage of the real self. A professional colleague with whom one can talk out confused feelings about particular cases or problems can be invaluable to any counselor. Writing out one's thoughts and feelings, or talking them out to a tape recorder can often help.

If the counselor fails to remain alert to himself as he deliberately keeps in mind the interest of the people with whom he works, he will repress many urges, longings, and thoughts of his own. This is particularly likely to happen if the inclinations are contrary to his idealized image of himself as a counselor. With such unexpressed, even unthought, urges trying to reach consciousness, and his conscience saying "no," untold energy is tied up in keeping these hidden from the self. Thus the counselor may be unalert or preoccupied with unconscious fantasy rather than being free to interact with the individuals with whom he counsels.

How does he free himself? By facing up to his impulses, ideas and interests, and putting them into conscious form where he can deal with them. This can be done by finding time, after the client has gone and cannot be affected, to let the imagination run in free association and fantasy. Perhaps the most important requisite to working in pre-marital counseling is that the counselor have adequate sources of love, affection, and emotional security outside the helping aspects of his work, such as mate, friends, and other interests.

C. FEES

Pastors and family life educators often think of pre-marital counseling as an extension of the educational assistance to which parishioners and students are entitled. It may be beneficial for young people to receive this service without cost, as an extension of the interest adults have in them. "Getting something for nothing" does not apply fully since the couple do invest their time and effort.

Those who are in a position to charge fees find that this can be a beneficial tool in itself, establishing the principle of paying for what one needs, including professional help. Money is a helpful aid in involving one in counseling by increasing the investment in and responsibility for the process. In general, particularly in this culture, people value an experience even more if they invest money as well as time.

Fees for private counseling may be prohibitive for many young couples, but counseling agencies usually can adjust charges to the income. In this way the benefits of fee charging can be had without unduly burdening the engaged couple.

D. THE METHOD

What are the relative merits of special individual and group counseling in preparation for marriage in contrast to that provided in on-going groups established for more general purposes? Such group efforts may be made in discussions of dating, courtship and marriage provided by "Y's," churches, clubs and other groups set up for the education of youth. In the school setting one may make use of established courses in family life, personal living, sex education, emotional development or guidance to contribute toward the preparation of the class members for marriage.

I. Family Courses

Many high school and college courses on "Marriage and Family Living" are taught from the sociological point of view. These make use of statistics and the results of research to approach the subject of family life as a social institution. Some courses are "home management" oriented, and others are psychologically oriented, stressing emotional development. A growing number of courses with titles such as "Personal Adjustment" and "Family Living" emphasize the ways in which individuals grow and attempt to meet their needs within various types of family structure. These employ in teaching a blending of home planning, sociology, psychology, and other behavioral sciences.

"Marriage and Family Living" is an emotion-laden subject for youth. Having their thinking focused upon self in an analytical frame of reference can be upsetting to students, but so can a statistical approach to family living. Emphasis upon such facts as the high percentage of divorces, or upon the sick and unhappy people who come from broken homes, can precipitate major anxiety in class members who see themselves in the statistics. Discussion of such subjects as quarreling, too few common interests, insufficient demonstration of affection in a home, frigidity, and fears regarding childbirth can be threatening to class members who are reminded of their own family situation. As students begin to be aware of the extent to which such environmental factors may have influenced their development, as old conflicts are reactivated, considerable anxiety may be generated. New ideas, even though positive, can be especially disturbing in the context of courses on marriage and family living. Every "family" idea has significance in the personal development of the student, and therefore has the potential of temporarily disrupting his equilibrium. He may be made anxious by some recognition of his personality problems and develop anticipatory anxiety as he foresees the stresses and possible failures involved in his own future married living.

In a family course Jack and Jill filled out a marriage prediction schedule which indicated that they were "not compatible." The passion they felt argued that this was not sufficient proof, and, not feeling free to discuss the problem with even the course instructor, they were married. The secret fear that their marriage would not work was repressed. Conflicts not resolved as they arose were "forgotten" but they added to the hidden reservoir of fear that the marriage would not work. It lasted only two years. Personal counseling of the two young people concurrent with the course of study probably could have led them to a meaningful adjustment or to a realistic picture of the unwise relationship, thus preventing the marriage.

Teachers may decry any responsibility for personal feeling or implications of subject matter for an individual student. One said, "My job is to teach. Subject matter, not counseling, is my responsibility. I deliberately plan material so as not to call attention to oneself. If a student contacts me after class with a problem, I tell him he is taking the wrong approach, that we were not talking about personal problems. I just don't talk to him about it."

With troublesome feelings being activated, students may be forced in self defense to block off the disturbing emotions and think of the daily course material only as data unrelated to themselves. Being threatened and left to rely on their own resources, they begin building defenses against looking at the self. Information is relegated to a compartment of the mind to avoid disturbing the equilibrium of the whole self. Though this allays immediate anxiety, the repressed conflict makes the person even more anxious in the long run. Benefit from such a method of education is minimal. The student learns to parrot facts and statistics but his behavior is not modified, unless in the direction of rebellion on the one hand or rigidity on the other.

This is not to say that students should not be challenged to look at themselves and their families; just the opposite is intended. One must be led to question the way things *are* before he can be challenged to gain further understanding or attain a higher level of development; but emotional disturbance without aid in resolving it is not helpful. Time must be allowed in the schedule for individual counseling.

To avoid segmentalization of subject matter, and to meet other needs of students, courses might be built around establishing and maintaining *man-woman relationships* and family life. Another way of effecting such a holistic emphasis would be to build a course around *attitudes* toward marriage and family living. Such an approach would examine any area of life from the many possible points of view, but always at the level of feelings and attitudes of students in the context of the whole of life. Segments of behavior of an individual or of a couple would be examined but consideration of their implications for the family, the community, the nation and the world also would be an integral part of the process. Through such a procedure students are freed from the limits imposed by logic-tight compartments to become creative in individual and family living.

Risks inherent in functional education are easily over-looked. For instance, students may be encouraged to change continually toward more effective realization of *socially determined* objectives. This is *status quo* oriented rather than stimulation toward evolution of more effective ways of living. This is adjustment, but it may or may not represent growth and realization of potential of youth.

Need for Ventilation and Assimilation. Another danger, particularly when efforts in a family life course are limited to the class period, is that newly acquired information and attitudes simply are superimposed upon basic, static, systematized ways of responding in interpersonal situations. Light may be thrown on problem areas and at the same time point to a more challenging way of life, thus stimulating choices which are best under the circumstances. Misery continues, however, when insufficient "working through" leaves the activated inner conflict to haunt the person with guilt and anxiety.

This was seen in bold relief in youngsters reared in textile mill villages in the South. As modern ideas intruded into these in-grown communities and family situations, a desire for self-advancement was created. In college these youths were possessed by driving ambition to rise above their families —financially, educationally, socially; in fact, to find a new life and a new family. They tended to feel guilt over rebellion or feel lost and alone, belonging neither to the old nor to the new way of life. Many left college to return home. Others drove on to success in the university and in jobs and established families based upon more democratic ideals. Some became ill or chronically unhappy because attitudes centering about the old way of life never had been dealt with consciously, and the inner struggle between two ways of life, old and new loyalties, continued to fester and hurt. Similar dynamics can be seen with other rural populations recently moved to the city, or in the upwardly mobile Negro population. The teacher-counselor has the opportunity to assist such youth in working through their stresses, guilt, fear and anxieties, liberating them for growth into new dimensions of family living geared to their own potential and needs.

Before new facts can express themselves in attitudes and behavior as components of the personality, they must have been understood in relation to one's self and assimilated into the self. "Talking out" problem areas and uprooting outmoded stumps of ideas is the best way to prepare for the planting of new ideas, allowing for later spontaneous action. Former distorted views and feelings must be recalled to the level of awareness, understood and consciously discarded before new ideas can be integrated. Ventilation of feelings followed by discussion can facilitate the assimilation of new ideas so that they become an integral part of the individual.

This requires a block of staff time for students to confer confidentially with their teacher-counselor. Administrators should recognize this individual attention as a part of the teaching load of family life education, not simply an over and beyond the call of duty task. To fulfill adequately this need, the persons assigned to teach personal development and family life should have basic training in guidance and personal counseling, as well as possessing a wholesome appreciation of the personalities developing under their leadership.

Unless the teacher is a skilled counselor, his role in unusual situations is one of detecting anxiety and tension and referring the student for assistance. On the other hand, many teachers can become understanding listeners and at least help to clarify issues and feelings by leading the student to look at his problem in the perspective of the rest of life. Instead of feeling "my life is a problem" the student may come to feel: "Here is my life and there is a problem in it." The next step is looking at alternative ways of handling the problem, or, if the situation cannot be changed, cultivating acceptance and less disturbing feelings about it.

II. Pre-marital Counseling

Historically there have been three major opportunities to do specific pre-marital counseling with the about-to-be-married couple: one or both sets of parents, the physician, and the clergyman. In this culture it has been difficult indeed for parents to render any specific assistance in relationship problems. The young people are in the very process of marriage declaring their separateness, their independence and self-sufficiency. This is accompanied by wholesome inclinations not to take relatives in on the secrets of the new relationship. In most states blood tests for venereal infection are prerequisites to a marriage license, and in thirty-seven of these there are requirements for a medical examination. These requirements have made it possible for most couples to have some medical contact prior to marriage, although little has been done in most cases beyond signing a certificate. In the great majority of cases, requested contraceptive advice was given, specific questions answered, and the whole matter treated quite perfunctorily. Suddenly physicians are awakening to both the need and opportunity for specific preparation for marriage—along with an awareness that they have not been prepared for this role through medical training. (See Chapter 8)

For that large element of the population reared in close proximity to religious teachings, there has been a tradition of weddings being performed by the clergy. For generations little or no attention was given to the couple except to rehearse the wedding ceremony and "talk to" them about the place religion should play in the new family. With the proliferation of opportunities for training in pastoral counseling, this picture is changing. An ever increasing number of clergy from all the major faiths want to do something more specific about preventing marital unhappiness and insuring family success.

The minister in particular has an opportunity to utilize the many individual and group contacts to educate both in the need for and the content of preparation for marriage long before the wedding date is set, but this takes time.[17] Planned Parenthood Agencies have rendered a valuable but limited service of prescribing and instructing in the method of contraception requested by the woman. Usually this request was made very late in the plans for marriage and she was not expecting anything else to be done for her. She obtained the contraceptive advice in this manner, went to a physician or a clinic for blood tests, and then to a justice of the peace or clergyman for the wedding ceremony.

Almost no one thought of the total needs of the woman, not to mention the needs of the man. This situation prevails today. The 1964 annual meeting of the American Association of Marriage Counselors, devoted to pre-marital counseling, made it crystal clear that, other than a few university based counselors, very little formal pre-marital counseling is being done except with the seriously disturbed.

In the case of both clergy and physician, along with those marriage counselors who are interested in engaged couples, the cry is frequently heard, "How do you get them interested? How can you get them to come earlier than a couple of days prior to the marriage when it is too late? It has become increasingly clear that the professional must find some frame of reference and practical plan to do realistic pre-marital counseling, along with long-range education of the public about the importance of such services. For current about-to-be-married couples a "gimmick" is needed whereby they can be enlisted in preparation for marriage.

III.   A Suggested Plan

The experience of the author is that once adequate pre-marital counseling is made available on university campuses, couples are highly desirous of taking advantage of it. However, in almost all other circles this is not the case. Ministers report difficulty in getting couples to consult them even a week before the ceremony, physicians don't see them until the last few hours, and other counselors don't see them at all unless they have some gross personality problems that demand psychotherapy. In view of the vast breakdown in marital interaction, coupled with advances in counseling and

[17] Morris, J. K., *Premarital Counseling, A Manual for Ministers.* Englewood Cliffs, N. J. 1960.

psychotherapy, some experimentation is highly in order. Since some professionals have demonstrated excellent results, not only in preventing divorces, but in enriching the lives of couples through pre-marital education and counseling, the burden to make pre-marital counseling available and to educate the public to accept it seems imperative, indeed.

In the historic long and world wide search for more effective and more acceptable means of birth control, "the pill" has promised to become the most effective method ever devised. It is being much more widely accepted than could ever have been expected, even by its developers.[18] Research has demonstrated conclusively that even the lower socio-educational levels of the population find this an acceptable method of birth control and are inclined to follow instructions quite correctly and faithfully. One of the extra blessings of "the pill" lies in the unusual opportunity it offers for pre-marital counseling. Throughout the nation magazines—everything from dignified journals to "digests" to "True Love" magazines—have told the story of the pill. This includes the fact that to be protected a woman must have been taking the pill during the cycle prior to intercourse. Thus, girls of every socio-educational level are being taught that they should report to physicians or clinics and begin taking the pill following the menstrual period which precedes the wedding. A test for cancer should be made prior to prescribing the pill, which necessitates a physical examination. This brings the woman to the physician, or to a center for contraceptive advice, a month prior to the wedding, rather than a few hours before, as has been the case in the past. The pill can become the needed "gimmick" or point of contact with prospective couples. If the clergy and the family life teacher will take advantage of this "month of forethought" in preparing for marriage and sex life, work out connections with Planned Parenthood Agencies or other clinics or practitioners for such service at a reasonable cost, and see that professional counselors are provided to work through problems and integrate the total experience for each of the couple, the opportunity of the age is at hand.

To illustrate what could be done, a suggested plan of preparation for marriage in the context of a planned parenthood agency (other clinics or groups of practitioners could do likewise) is outlined herewith:

A "package" of services could be planned and announced to the public through the press, religious organizations, physicians and others. If enough

[18] For an excellent analysis of the discovery, research, uses of, and answers to many questions regarding oral contraceptives, see *A Prescription For Family Planning, The Story of Enovid*. Distributed gratis by G. D. Searle Company, 1841 Broadway, New York City.

resources were available, radio and television announcements would certainly be in order. The clergy, family life teachers and youth leaders could join in telling the facts about the "month of forethought" in preparing for sex life and marriage, and in advocating use of services provided both the man and woman, whether or not "the pill" is the contraceptive method of choice. This would be a deliberate attempt to take advantage of giving the various pieces of medical examination, serology, and contraceptive prescription as occasions when counseling sessions could be held for those who wished them. The counseling could be made more acceptable if it were offered as an integral part of the package of preparation. Such counseling should be done by skilled professionals only so that people are not put into the hands of incompetents. The counselors could be on the staff of the Planned Parenthood Agency, or on loan from any other likely source.

The goals in this package, particularly in view of the minimum counseling sessions, would be limited and simple: (1) to correct mis-impressions in the sexual area or any other area; (2) to give basic information as it was indicated and to help them talk through and integrate the new knowledge; (3) to help make their total expectations of marriage realistic, alerting them to any areas of stress that can be expected in their particular relationship; and, (4) to provide such a meaningful experience with professional people who care that it will be natural for them to return if they have major difficulty in the future.

Step 1: It is required that the engaged couple come together to the clinic, *both of them* to receive a basic physical check-up. (See Chapter 8, The Physician's Role in Preparation for Marriage.) This will take care of the requirement for a medical exam in states where it is necessary, but it can be sold as desirable and expected regardless of the law. It will also clarify whether or not the woman shall be placed on "the pill" or choose another desirable method of contraception. Either prior to the physical, or immediately following completion thereof, the first counseling session can be held. This may be with individual couples, seen separately or together, in which individual histories, and the chronology of their relationship, can be obtained. This will provide a general impression of the emotional health of the individuals, along with some of the potential of this man and woman in building a marriage. In all probability, it will be more feasible and practicable to see them as individuals and solitary couples on this first occasion rather than as groups of couples. There may well be a direct effort to sell them on the value of counseling, by using both revealed problems and unrealized potential, as a way of getting ready for marriage.

Step 2: One week later the couple return to the clinic to have blood tests made, and for the first counseling session. These sessions may be with individual couples, or groups of three or four couples could be set up, for this series of services. (See Chapters 5 and 6.) Admittedly, so long as it is within the required time allowed by the state law before marriage, blood samples could be taken on the first contact. However, this is a deliberate delay of serology work to make it easier for the couple to accept the next individual or group counseling session. The counselor's knowledge of the individuals and couples gained in the first contact may lead quite quickly to discussions of some of the most relevant areas on which a couple can begin to build a more realistic relationship.

Step 3: A week prior to the wedding ceremony the couple will return for the reports on serology, which are necessary to get a license. This visit may also include a brief medical discussion with the couple, interpreting any findings that would be relevant to their living together as man and wife. Most of them will be anticipating the counseling session planned for this occasion, which will focus upon any items that are causing anxiety, or go further in pointing out areas in which they need to work in the future.

Step 4: This session will be scheduled for a few weeks after the marriage. The "bait" that will make it urgent for them to return is the importance of having the contraceptive plan in which they have been instructed checked out and re-prescribed. The counselor will be on hand to talk over with them their marital relationship to date. This can be accomplished couple by couple, or it could well be done with three or four couples together, especially if it were the same couples that had met together before. This can be in the nature of a check-up, alerting them to potentially harmful areas of conflict, helping discover ways of working together in developing problem-solving skills and assisting them in relating more creatively.

Step 5: Four contacts will be minimal indeed in effecting any basic change in the kind of marriage the individuals might attain. If enough professional counseling is available, an ongoing group counseling experience of ten to many sessions can be instigated at any time enough couples are willing. Perhaps a group can be sold on the idea of beginning group counseling with two sessions a week immediately after the initial contact at a month prior to marriage. In a longer range educational campaign couples, particularly those referred by the clergy or family life teachers, can be led to begin more intensive group counseling a few weeks prior to the medical examination. Other couples—either those who, in the absence of major conflicts, are motivated to work at developing a meaningful relationship or those in whom enough conflict is uncovered to indicate serious difficulty unless they did have specific help—can be sold on the idea of beginning an on-going group counseling experience either immediately after returning from the honeymoon, or at the time when they return for the contraceptive check-up.

As time goes on, such a program can have individuals at all stages of this procedure, either following the minimum package of four sessions or adding to this on-going group counseling prior to marriage, after marriage, or a combination thereof.

Financing such a package can be expensive, and yet charging an adequate amount for those who can afford it is more than justified by the services rendered. The package deal—a physical examination for both the man and the woman, gynecological services for the woman, contraceptive prescriptions, and serology for both covers the kinds of medical services which otherwise would have to be paid for piecemeal, adding up to a good many dollars. Of course, an adequate fee for the counseling sessions—$15-$25 per session for individual counseling, and $10-$15 per person for group counseling, being something of the going rate—can make the package prohibitive. This means that it is often necessary to find some method of underwriting most of the cost of the counseling sessions. Likewise, some underwriting of the costs for the medical and contraceptive aspects would be indicated for many lower income couples.

This kind of package can be experimented with in a variety of settings and in a variety of ways to the end that adequate preparation for marriage can become available to the average couple in the average community. Because of the renewed emphasis on population control, along with the necessity of such programs as aid to dependent children and welfare, it is probable that the next decade will see either governmental or community agencies regularly providing contraceptive advice. Such service probably will be limited to the bare essentials, rather than providing the larger package which has been indicated in this recommendation. This could mean that gradually the pioneering role of the Planned Parenthood Agency might be replaced by governmental agencies. This proposed plan of total preparation for marriage would give a larger goal to Planned Parenthood and again provide an opportunity, in cooperation with other professionals, to pioneer in a total service to total youth in total marriages. Physicians, professional marriage counselors and the clergy could help a great deal in making such an integrated service possible by joining hands with Planned Parenthood Agencies in such endeavors.

E. PROBLEM-SOLVING ORIENTATION

An earlier chapter has stressed the value of utilizing the engagement period for specific preparation for marriage. The chapter on communication highlighted the necessary emphasis upon developing understanding and relationship skills. Closely related to this is the necessity of growing problem-solving skills which will enable the couple to make creative use of conflict as discussed in Chapter 2. The glamorized and romanticized feelings of love need to be tempered by the realities of human problems to be encountered in marriage in general, as well as those to be expected in their particular relationship.

Landis,[19] in a pilot study, discovered something of the difficulty involved in adjusting in certain areas of married life. Classified according to the longest time required to adjust, regardless of age at marriage, years married, or years of education, the areas were: sexual adjustment, spending the family income, social activities and recreation, in-law relationships, religion in the home, and associating with mutual friends. A survey of 557 physicians in North Carolina indicated marital problems among their patients in the following order of frequency: For men, the problems of most concern were sexual adjustment, money, and dissatisfaction with the amount of affection shown by the wife. For women, sexual adjustment, fear of pregnancy, and dissatisfaction with the amount of affection.[20] These sequences may or may not hold true for a cross section of American couples but clinical experience demonstrates that these do represent common marital problems in most segments of society.

Put to the counselor in many forms, marital conflict frequently is focused upon such concepts as: "personality," by which is meant any combination of incompatibility, such as failure to respect one's rights, authoritarianism or cruelty, irritability, moodiness; sexual conflict, centered around lack of mutual satisfaction or the love triangle; lack of empathy or "we" feeling in the home, with the children, and in regard to religion, along with lack of purpose in living; money and buying; non-support and desertion; relatives; and a complex of symptoms frequently labeled as drinking, drug addiction, gambling, and "raising hell." The frequency of these complaints to the marriage counselor is the joint function of the socio-cultural milieu from which the clients come, the precipitating crisis or triggering incident, and

[19] Landis, Judson T., "Length of Time Required to Achieve Adjustment in Marriage." *American Sociological Review*, Vol. XI, No. 6. 1946, pp. 666-699.

[20] Herndon, C. Nash and Ethel M. Nash, "Remarriage and Marriage Counseling," *The Journal of the American Medical Association*. May 5, 1962. Vol. 180, pp. 395-401.

the particular role of the counselor. Whether he is known primarily as a family case worker, a priest, a psychologist, a psychiatrist, or a marriage counselor, well may shape the presenting problem when help is sought, although it tends to have much less to do with the basic or covert problems which emerge if counseling proceeds far enough.

The case of Mr. and Mrs. Z. illustrates well the fact that any one complaint may cover many other basic and symptomatic problems at any particular stage of marriage.[21]

Mrs. Z., 38 years, married to a junior executive in a local company, came by appointment to discuss "marriage problems." She was very tense, not because of fear of communicating with the counselor, but due to pent-up anxiety and acute headaches. In spite of the tension, she could have passed for several years her junior because of the way she dressed and a well preserved figure. She talked in rapid-fire manner, beginning with a rather lengthy exposition of her husband's virtues.

She described the husband as hard-working, patient, kind, drank little, didn't chase after women, attended church regularly, was well thought of in the community, made every effort to get whatever she wanted for the house or for herself. After 40 minutes this testimonial ended abruptly with a statement which came out in a mixture of rage and squirming desire. "He's too damned good. That's it, good for nothing! What I need is a real man!" It wouldn't have been so hard to take this had they had children, although she hadn't really tried to get pregnant and didn't want to now. She felt if their sex life had been adequate they would have conceived.

She talked a great deal about the hopeless state to which their marriage of nine years had deteriorated. They married when both were 29, a few months after he was inducted into the Armed Forces. The weekends then were pleasant indeed, leading to a great deal of sexual expression. When he returned from the Service, sex did not seem to be so important to him, and the frequency of sexual intercourse declined. When he attempted intercourse he often was unable to finish or climaxed much too soon. Long periods of abstinence followed. When she was particularly passionate in the evenings he would beg her to turn over and go to sleep, saying that if he could respond at all he would come to her later. Rarely did he wake her and only occasionally was he able to respond adequately. She was irritated by being awakened and having him attempt intercourse immediately. This was especially annoying since it didn't satisfy her. Sometimes he disturbed

[21] Reported in detail in: Rutledge, Aaron L., "Experimental Techniques With Marital Problems," *Merrill-Palmer Quarterly*, 4, 2, 1948, pp. 88-99.

her sleep by stimulating her. At times he was asleep when he did this. He was unkempt in appearance and refused to bathe regularly. She told of increasing advances by a local professional person who seemed to be aware of her unmet sex needs and wished to cash in on them. For a long time she had shunned every thought of infidelity but lately had considered such an affair; she had had a blow-up with her husband over her unmet needs and told him about her extra-marital dreaming. She was thinking seriously of entering into such a relationship or getting a divorce.

Throughout this conference and several subsequent ones the client manifested a weird picture of burning anger, intensive sexual desire, and just plain misery. In spite of marked efforts at control she frequently broke down and cried. Once she said: "You don't know what it is to be a woman, know you're a woman, want love, want sex and yet your husband be impotent."

At the end of the first interview she had listed the following problems: tension in the marriage, aches and pains, inadequate mate, sterility, wartime marriage growing apart, premature ejaculation, orgasm inadequacy, general sexual incompatibility, lack of cleanliness, the "other person," thoughts of divorce, and impotence. In the two and a half years of hard work with this couple, the following additional problems were discussed: mother-in-law, mate ignores spouse, inability to conceptualize the problem, first marriage hangover, disagreement about conception, step-child, differing temperaments, clash over income and spending, friends and religious differences, refusal to talk, and endless quarreling.

Had the couple sought help any time during the earlier years of marriage, they might have named any of these symptoms as *the* problem. Certainly at many times in the history of the marriage any of these complaints could have appeared to be the real problem. Any of the problems might have been the central conflict, only a symptom of the conflict, for in time effect becomes cause in a vicious cycle of marital stress.

The marriage counselor must spend most of his time in trying to resolve such complicated marital problems. In pre-marital counseling there is an opportunity to invest directly in both individual health and meaningful relationships. The high level of motivation frequently found in the engaged couple (See "Readiness for Change" in Chapter 1) should be capitalized upon by the teacher, clergyman, physician or counselor. The diagnostic understanding of individual dynamics should enable the pre-marital counselor to project a relatively sound picture of the kinds of conflict inherent in this anticipated union. The counseling process provides an opportunity to maneuver the couple into most of the kinds of serious conflict which they will encounter later in life together. In this way they can develop the necessary beginning understanding, communication patterns, and problem grappling skills necessary to marital success. On the other hand, they may learn that the arguments really arise from basically crippled personalities who should not get married until essential change is effected through individual psychotherapy.

As the "new" and the "old" are critically evaluated, there follows alternate periods of incubation and discussion, the emerging of new ideas, plans and techniques, and constant communication with each other. The new is utilized until it, having replaced the older, becomes "first nature." Through individual and group efforts, each of the couple can come a long way before the wedding in self-understanding, understanding acceptance of the mate, and in developing skills in communication and problem solving. Often pre-marital counseling can bring them farther along in building a meaningful relationship before marriage than most couples have achieved after a year or two of married living.

Chapter 5

GROUP PREPARATION FOR MARRIAGE

"Groupings," essential to survival of all living creatures, are of even greater significance to the psychosocial prosperity of man. Inherent in his very nature, psychosocial cravings are stimulated in the family and life-long patterns are developed for gaining satisfaction in these areas of life. In turn, most individuals aspire to marriage as the socially acceptable way of re-establishing a continuing opportunity for meaningful grouping.

A. THE GROUP PROCESS

Group psychotherapy takes its major leads from the basic nature of human groups, including their organization and methods of relating.

I. Natural Groups

The major groupings that influence the development and function of man, disparate to some degree and yet often coextensive, are clearly set forth in Slavson's chart, along with the major contribution of each grouping to personality development. His *Textbook in Psychoanalytic Group Psychotherapy*,[1] one of the outstanding contributions in this field, is utilized freely in this discussion.

MAJOR CONTRIBUTIONS OF SUCCESSIVE GROUPS TO
PERSONALITY DEVELOPMENT

Order	Group	Major Contribution
1	family	acceptance, unconditioned love
2	nursery or play	social experimentation (socialization)
3	school	creative-dynamic expression
4	same-sex	identification (socialized), sexual reassurance
5	heterosexual	heterosexual adjustment
6	occupational	social adequacy, economic security
7	adult voluntary	social acceptance (socialization)
8	family	mating, parenthood, self-perpetuation

[1] Slavson, S. R., *A Textbook In Analytic Group Psychotherapy*. New York: International Universities Press. 1964, p. 14; permission of the publisher.

Any group milieu, to provide the greatest assistance in development, must provide acceptance and respect, where performance can fluctuate from minimal to maximum capacity without fear of failure because of real or imaginary inferiorities. The entire educative process—the totality of nurture, development of motor and intellectual skills, self-expression, and interactional patterns—of which schooling is only a small part, occurs in this context. To whatever extent, in the course of personality development, these opportunities were lacking, inadequate, or distorted, re-education and psychotherapy become necessary.

II.   Scientific Groupism

Slavson [2] believes that "groupism" represents the latest evolutionary attainment, a task at which man is yet in kindergarten; a fact that is amply demonstrated in today's marital difficulties. Although the "science of groupism" has a long way to go, it is being tested in every area of modern life, from nursery school to post-graduate training, from outpatient treatment to the management of institutionalized patients and prisoners, from community relations to international affairs.

III.   Group Psychotherapy

Group psychotherapy as a discipline can receive only introductory attention here, but much of the methodology of pre-marital counseling is dependent upon knowledge and skill in some "school" of group treatment or group dynamics. In addition to the broad and specific knowledge pertinent to every phase of married living, and individual counseling skills, the pre-marital counselor must possess group leadership skills. Some of these principles have been learned through the combination of training and experience which have made him an effective educator, pastor, or clinician. Hopefully he has had, or will obtain, supervised training in group work techniques.

Phillips' [3] introductory text on social group work emphasizes the individual growth of group members and the development of the group as a whole for social usefulness; goals easily applicable to preparation for marriage. A condensed definition of group work skill applies to the pre-marital counselor. It is the ability to work in the process of interaction with a group of people toward a clearly defined goal. The leader must possess a

[2] *Ibid.*, p. 21; following Ward's stages of evolutionary development, chemism, bathmism, zoism, and psychism.

[3] Phillips, Helen U., *Essentials of Social Group Work Skill*. New York: Association Press, 1957.

sense of "process," of interaction, and the capacity to direct it, respond to it, and contain himself to the end of achieving a balance of interactional forces within the group. For more advanced emphasis, the works of Slavson, Moreno, and Bonner [4] provide helpful background for pre-marital counseling.

B. PRE-MARITAL GROUP THERAPY

Group psychotherapy has been widely advocated as a way of saving time and thus reaching more people, with the inference that individual sessions would be preferred if there were just enough time. Actually, experience has demonstrated that frequently more time is utilized per person for those seen in a group setting. If each is seen privately for screening and preparation for the group, if he blocks emotionally or is upset by the group, or wants to discuss something alone with the therapist before sharing it in the group, or develops a need for more intensive personal therapy, the time factor becomes greater and greater.

Group psychotherapy in general is beginning to hold its own with the individual method; indeed it can be the preferred method, especially in preparation for marriage. There is learning and healing potential within a group beyond that found in individual psychotherapy or counseling. A great variety of meaningful ways by which couples can relate, react, and respond can be elicited in the group so that the counselor does not have to assume a didactic role in most areas. Changes in thinking and feeling come about with group support that might be resisted if suggested directly by the counselor. Sometimes confused feelings or transference reactions can be examined with greater ease within a group than in the presence of just the fiance and the counselor, or of the counselor alone. Old hurts can be healed, the isolation of guilt can be broken, and fellowship restored with oneself and with others within an understanding group. The group can permit the individual to lose himself briefly if he must, but also can focus upon him or upon the couple's interaction if it is needed. Feelings of shyness, inadequacy, rebellion, or fear can be faced together, and be resolved or accepted, as each works out the riddle of being himself in a social milieu in an approaching marriage relationship.

[4] Slavson, S. R., *op. cit.*:—, *The Field of Group Psychotherapy*. New York: International Universities Press, 1956; Moreno, Jacob L., *Psychodramatic Treatment of Marriage Problems*. New York: Peacon House, 1945; and Bonner, Hubert, *Group Dynamics*. New York: The Ronald Press, 1959.

I. Group Dynamics

Here are some of the dynamics common to groups, all of which have relevance for pre-marital counseling, depending upon the make-up, goals, leadership, and procedures in operation (paraphrased from Slavson): [5]

(1) *Interaction* may be spontaneous or directed, laissez faire or guided, without structure or with ground rules. Neutralization and compromise are common management techniques, whether induced by client or counselor, for the control of interaction.

(2) *Interstimulation*, an outgrowth of interaction, occurs through attitudes, conduct, acts, emotions and ideas—largely in the realm of action and thoughts. It may be constructive or destructive, whether guided or unguided.

(3) *Mutual induction*, confined to the area of emotion and feeling, is the process whereby one person becomes "charged" by the presence of another. This describes particularly well the state that exists between an engaged couple in or outside a group, as well as the equally interesting and useful occurrences between other group members.

(4) *Identification*, whether positive or negative, occurs on the basis of emotional prototypes, i.e., similarities in personality, background or experience, making possible vicarious catharsis and "spectator therapy."

(5) *Intensification* of feeling, with possible-acting out, following the reduction of ego and superego controls in the group is sometimes benevolent-constructive and on other occasions hostile-destructive.

(6) *Assimilation*, aiding in the processes of socialization and group cohesion, can be contra-indicated in pre-marital counseling, in that it might discourage the unique development of each individual and of each separate couple.

(7) *Integration* is operative in groups, as well as being a central dynamic in individual personality. The pre-marital counselor tries to prevent individual (or couple) absorption into the group Gestalt. Each individual, while able to utilize interaction, should become increasingly capable of detaching himself from the total group and then re-establishing himself in other groups, including the sub-group of his own engaged relationship.

(8) *Group cohesion*, around common objectives and interests, can easily subordinate the interests and needs of both individual and couple participants. It is a function of the counselor to see that this does not occur.

(9) *Polarity* tends to produce rigidity and fixity, whether the center around which it organizes is the counselor, other group members, or the

[5] Slavson, *Ibid*, pp. 45-51; permission of the publisher.

group-as-a-whole. Unless multiple polarities are encouraged, as individuals and as couples change, corrective and re-educational experiences are hindered.

(10) *Nodal and antinodal behavior* describes respectively the acting out periods and the inactive or silent periods common to all groups. The intensity and alternation of these portray the relative stability of ego controls and personality integration of individuals; and, in a somewhat unique way, the stage of development of the "marital personality" or the couples present.

II. The Nature and Intensity of Pre-marital Counseling

The previous chapter made clear the great variety of individual and group efforts at preparation for marriage, but the focus here is upon the more intensive experience. Group experiences may be viewed in terms of "depth," but even here there is difference of opinion. Some therapists view any treatment as relative and conditioned by specific circumstances of specific clients. Others would apply the depth concept only when an all-out effort is made to reorganize the patient's psychic economy, so that the id, ego, and superego function harmoniously and effectively in all life situations. Pre-marital counseling may consist of any combination of, or intensity of what Slavson has tried to distinguish as separate processes, namely, group counseling, group guidance, and group psychotherapy.[6] Likewise, pre-marital counseling may utilize any focus or combination of foci, or centeredness, whether total group, situations, sub-groups (couple), intrapersonal dynamics, techniques (i.e., problem-solving), ideas, theory or philosophy of marriage, etc.

III. Anxiety in Pre-marital Counseling

One of the needs which push an engaged couple toward marriage is the promise of relief from the state of tension common to this period of life. Normal affectional, sexual and status needs are in a state of suspended anticipation characterized by a state of anxiety. If this is complicated by gross neurotic anxiety in either partner, or by intense conflict between the couple, whether overt or defended against, the level of anxiety can become well nigh unbearable. As a result many engagements are ended either by a precipitate wedding or termination. As an effort to manage such normal and neurotic anxiety, couples tend to move toward premature closure

[6] *Ibid,* Chapter IV,

against external forces, whether benevolent or restrictive, and to cling to their own assumed state of enforced calm.

A certain level of anxiety is necessary for the beginning of any therapeutic endeavor; indeed, much of the effectiveness of psychotherapy, including group pre-marital counseling, is dependent upon the creative stimulation and utilization of anxiety. There is an optimal level of anxiety for the progress of each individual and couple. This need for therapeutic anxiety, and the tendency toward couple closure, makes necessary some key that will unlock the relationship to corrective and re-educative experiences for which the engagement should be used; a function in which group counseling is uniquely effective.

As Slavson[7] has clearly delineated, groups initially evoke anxiety in all people. This diminishes somewhat with acquaintance and length of membership in the group, but, with rare exception, the average person never feels as comfortable in a group as he does with one individual; notwithstanding the opposite tendency to experience the group as a support and allayer of gross anxiety. Any group provokes rivalry for attention, recognition, acceptance, power, and status. Attitudes and responses toward groups tend to be replicas of family experience, and the derivative hostilities and aggressions (along with constructive emotions) that accompany such adjustments are implicit in all group relations. The individual, in accordance with ego strength, expects attacks, rejection, rivalry, and aggression somewhat according to the previous experiences in the family of origin. These expectations, and the resultant hostility and guilt, result in further anticipation of misuse.

Will these new individuals, this group as a whole, delimit and constrict his freedom of action, be critical of his unguarded conduct, opinions, and personality as a whole? Both conscious misgivings and unconscious and repressed feeling tones already associated with groups are aroused. The dread of discovery for what one really fears he is, and about which he feels guilty, causes some to take on a facade of social amenity, while others attack or withdraw into self-isolation as a means of self-protection. When an engaged couple pool and exchange their anxieties and defenses, the need to resist the discovery and confrontation being engendered by the group can become intense indeed.

In the prototypical responses lies much of the value of the group approach to preparation for marriage. These are actual people, dealing with actual situations, in the context of preparation for real marriages, being upset by

[7] *Ibid,* pp. 31-33,

the same incidents and feelings that they will carry into their anticipated family. Here is a field of reality, providing both stimulus and utilization of anxiety in developing understanding of self, of mate, and of means of coping which will serve them well in the future.

IV. Effectiveness of Pre-marital Group Therapy

To varying degrees, each individual will manifest such personality malformations as impaired libido development, blockage of autonomous strivings, faulty indentification models, neurotic conflicts with guilt and fear, defective self-image, ambivalence, and a variety of organic and constitutional factors. This means that in pre-marital counseling, in addition to the educative and re-educative element, whether in content or relationship skills, several psychotherapeutic functions are operating; namely, libido redistribution through cathexis displacement, ego strengthening, superego correction, and self-image improvement. As Slavson summarizes,[8] thus "accommodative, selective, and inhibitive capacities are enhanced through the freeing of the psychic forces that have been bound up or drained by pathognomonic intra-psychic processes." The group setting is most effective as a corrective of the ego, because of its reality property, the inevitable multiple identifications and transferences, the catalytic influence of the patients on each other, its service as a field for testing one's ego functioning, its opportunities for improving the self-image, and it's mirroring of reactions and behavior, as well as other effects of a similar nature inherent in a group.

Pre-marital counseling takes advantage of the natural heterosexual grouping of two people, moves it from relative isolation into a group of couples, which is a prototype of the larger community, where educative. re-educative and corrective means of developing relationship competence can be brought to their assistance.

C. AN ILLUSTRATIVE GROUP PROJECT

In order to be more specific, *one way* of setting up and operating a group of couples in preparation for marriage is demonstrated herewith. It might be wise to peruse the content material of Chapters 9-12 before proceeding, as well as Chapter 7 which outlines the necessary considerations in building a new family.

[8] *Ibid*, pp. 34-35,

I. Setting Up The Group

Criteria must be established for selecting any particular group of couples who will work together, whether it be availability, similarity or dissimilarity of such factors as age, education, religion, previous marital status, and emotional health. The engaged couples available at the moment, and the kind of group the marriage counselor prefers to work with probably will be the primary determinants.[9] Exceptions will be discussed in the next chapter.

Let the hypothetical group consist of three to five, say four, engaged couples who are planning to be married in four months to a year. Agree to meet in a two hour session once a week for sixteen weeks, and get a commitment from each couple to spend at least two hours together in private discussion for each hour spent on material in the group. Suggest that each person keep a diary of reactions, questions, and interests following each session which he may share with the marriage counselor.

Prior to bringing the group together, the leader will have obtained certain basic information on each of the individuals and their families. *The Individual and Marriage Counseling Inventory*,[10] discussed earlier, serves this purpose. It should be filled out in duplicate so that each may keep a copy of his own Inventory to aid in discussions with the fiance(e). It should be made clear that the information is confidential until each chooses to discuss it with the fiance, and that discussions of threatening material may be postponed until the individual feels comfortable enough to share. Part A, "Personal Data," and Part B, "Family Data," should be filled out in advance of the first session. Part C, which incidently should not be used with seriously disturbed clients except with adequate safeguards, calls for essay material on "The Personal Relations in My Family." It may be written in advance, or preferably after the sessions are under way. This, along with interviews and any psychological tests, becomes the initial core of knowledge about each couple.

II. Movement of the Group

Now that the four couples are assembled for the first session, sitting in a circle with the leader, recognition is given to the mutual purpose which brings them together. It should be understood that they will become an

---

[9] *Ibid*, Chapters VI and VII.

[10] Rutledge, Aaron L., *"Individual and Marriage Counseling Inventory."* Detroit: Merrill-Palmer Institute, 1956.

intimate group in which much will be shared that has heretofore been known only to themselves. This calls for certain commitments, depending upon a plan worked out by the group. For instance, if they come from various parts of the city and from different churches and schools, the group imposed limits may be much less than if they all come from one school, church, or neighborhood. In the last case, they may wish to commit themselves to limiting discussions of the content and dynamics of the sessions to the room in which they meet, and to the private talks between the individual couples. Without such commitments remarks can be made to roommates, classmates, or friends that will be regretted later. The group will want to agree that traumatic experiences and other personal data shared within the group will be treated as highly confidential, not to be repeated to anyone.

The marriage counselor will point out that each person may find that he wants to share some feelings with him before discussing them in the group. This is designed to avoid springing upon the fiance feelings or incidents which are too traumatic to be accepted at the time. Sometimes feelings may be aroused which, if expressed at the moment, would be destructive, but the knowledge that the counselor has time to see each person will mean that it can be worked through and brought to the group in a less striking form. By announcing that each member of the group will be seen individually, those who come for appointments at first do not feel singled out or worse off than others. It also makes it easier for the counselor to suggest a private conference with a member when indicated, whether because of non-participation, hostility, undue anxiety, or other reasons.

A helpful way to break the ice with such a group is to let them introduce themselves, giving a thumb-nail sketch of their growing up, and certain things about their experiences as couples, such as the length of their acquaintance, interest in being in the group, and marriage plans. This can be done rather rapidly and yet it gets everyone talking. Immediately the counselor has a chance to spot the many kinds of personality dynamics in the group, as he connects voices with previously collected data, and projects his picture of how couples will react. In the first session the counselor will spot most of the difficulties to be encountered in the group, from the eager beaver to the withdrawn mouse. A variation, which provides further insight into how a couple relate, is the simple suggestion that each couple tell about themselves. This lets them choose who talks first, who discusses what, and how.

Now that everyone is acquainted and certain ground rules have been laid, time has come to chart the future of the group. Three courses of action are possible: (1) the counselor may decide how the group experience is to be conducted, either in detail or in broad outline; (2) the group may decide to discuss whatever is on their minds at each session; or (3) they may decide to spend the remainder of the first session planning the following meetings.

For this hypothetical group, the leader does not wish to structure the process to any great degree, but rather to stimulate them to move in the way that promises to be most meaningful for them. Yet, if no plan is formulated, the concerns of the most outspoken may crowd out the quieter ones and also omit equally vital but more painful issues for everyone. Can this first session be used to name the main areas of interest in preparation for marriage, with sufficient breadth to prevent interference with spontaneity but with enough specificity to avoid wandering and omitting? After some discussion of the three alternatives, the group well may come to essentially the position discussed below. Or, if stated as a conviction of the counselor that it is the way to proceed, it is likely that the group will accept it with the understanding that they can change the plans as they proceed.

As they discuss what enters into preparing for marriage, the counselor jots ideas or topics on a chalkboard. Sometimes the list will be quite limited until the suggestion is made that *all* the areas of concern in married living are vital in preparing for marriage, and that these relations must be anticipated and entered into now through discussions. Then the list on the board begins to grow.

When the field seems adequately covered, it is suggested that the many ideas which are similar might be grouped into several broad areas. This lends itself to assigning a topic or descriptive phrase to each group of issues. Now the question of priority of topics arises, as well as the amount of time to be spent on each. This leads to expressions of special interest areas and begins underlining the importance of the interaction of couples, and of the group, in the total experience of getting ready for marriage.

Suppose the hypothetical group works out the following priority of subjects, allotting two periods of two hours each to each topic, except that the first is to receive only one session. This is a practical decision based upon having spent one of the sixteen sessions in getting started and upon the suggestion that the engagement-love-sex theme will permeate all remaining sessions.

Their outline follows:

1. Engagement, Love, and Sex
2. The Parental Home
3. Our New Family Begins
4. Work and Finances
5. Children
6. A Family Faith
7. Special Preparation, Such as Pre-marital Medical Examination
8. The Wedding and Honeymoon

One member of the group suggests that this makes it easy to read material on the subjects in advance. Others agree, but the leader points out that it is even more important to talk out feelings and beliefs with the fiance, the group, and the counselor.

Engagement, Love, and Sex

The *second session* begins with a further look at why this effort at preparation for marriage. Quickly they come to the omnipresent question among young engaged persons—how do we know it is really love? After bantering this about they turn to the counselor. He is aware both that his response may cause too much focus upon himself so early in the group and that they need to know what kind of leader he is. He suggests that the honest couple may well ask this vital quesion, voiced many times in their earlier development but with a great deal more seriousness now. Then he comments somewhat as follows:

"Meaningful married love cannot become known during the engagement, except in its very beginning, embryonic state. Rather, it is something that begins and then grows, or doesn't grow. There are many couples, who, by any objective test, are 'in love,' but who by all means should not marry. Their love is capable of growing only to a certain point, and then the marriage would disintegrate. Love must continue to grow or it dies. Love must be active, or it is hidden by frustration and hatred. As your leader, I am assuming that you are in love, really in love, else you wouldn't be here. However, being in love is not the best manner of determining whether or not this will make a good permanent relationship."

The reactions are a mixture of shock and embarrassed laughter. He waits for them to recuperate and refocus on how one does determine this vital question. Someone suggests that one purpose of engagement is a trial period, but others counter that it really isn't a trial since "once you're publicly engaged everything pushes you on into marriage."

This leads to a detailed discussion of the purposes of engagement. With some suggestions and summation from the leader they agree that: The all-important purpose of an engagement period is to determine whether, in each of the major areas and relationships of life, there is enough in common and enough creative potential to make possible a lasting and meaningful relationship. Discovering this potential still is not enough since many marriages do not survive the testing period. Therefore, the engagement should be spent in discovering both liabilities and assets and in formulating techniques and accumulating experience in the solving of problems. in order to produce an environment in which love can grow, flower, and find fulfillment.

At this point the group begins to notice the similarity between the purposes of engagement and the topics set up during the previous session for exploration in preparation for marriage which has been left on the chalk board. Engagement is seen as a process, both in the sessions and when the couple are alone, whereby they will learn to interact verbally in many ways, just as they might be expected to do later in marriage. There seems to be an unspoken assent that if this creates an environment in which their love continues to grow, then marriage is the natural culmination. If, on the other hand, they create the kind of environment which tends to smother or destroy love, it will be best that it be discovered before entering into a legal contract to live together forever.

The *third session* finds the group rather quiet, as if the seriousness of engagement and marital preparation has sobered them. The counselor, by way of rephrasing the previous discussion, points out:

"Short of special efforts, engagement may serve only as a continuation of subterfuge and camouflage of the basic personalities under a smoke-screen of passionate love, and as an opportunity for more intensive and exclusive rights to each other. To maintain the delusion of complete agreement, there is a tendency to hide injured feelings and differences of opinion. One of the couple tends to develop a policy of 'giving in,' and thus sets a pattern of smothering one personality, giving the other undue leeway in self expression and a false feeling of self-adequacy. This easily turns into a missionary endeavor to change the yielding one.

In this intimate and exclusive relationship conflict should be expected, including an occasional quarrel. The answer lies in the art of communication which should be so freely established that all differences can be faced and experience gained in solving problems in such a way as to maintain and strengthen the relationship. These differences and conflicts should be explored most thoroughly. At the same time, individuality must be encouraged to grow and develop.

Stated in broad terms, each major area of life should be explored intensively with a view to self-understanding, mutual understanding, discovery of assets and liabilities of each other and of the relationship, and to the gradual development of a functioning plan of life. Unless such a working relationship is well under way before marriage, love is not likely to have a conducive environment in which to grow, and, although potentially a good union, the marriage may become a fatality in the first months of necessary adjustment."

One girl, joined immediately by other members of the group, calls attention to the problems of engagement, including the expression of love and affection. Feelings are expressed about how far an engaged couple should go, the "jitters" resulting from pent-up feelings, the tendency for sex to become all important to the exclusion of other interests, etc. This discussion occupies the group for the first hour of the third session.

The Parental Homes

Some of the group want to talk about the new family to be created by their marriage, but immediately others point out that the family they were "patterned" by is that of their parental homes. The remaining half of the *third session* is spent in discussing more or less superficial facts about each set of parents, the siblings, and style of life. Some hedging is evident. Toward the end of the period the counselor suggests that each write out an account of the personal relations in his family, using Part C of the *Inventory* as a guide, and that a carbon copy be kept for personal discussion with the fiance when each feels free to do so. The suggested outline is as follows:

1. My father as an individual, including personality changes
2. My relationship to him through the years
3. My mother as an individual, including personality changes
4. My relationship to her through the years
5. My parents' relationships to each other:
    1) Which was dominant? By choice or by necessity?
    2) Which was submissive? By choice or by necessity?
    3) Describe what you know about their relationship:

      a) As two personalities
      b) As a financial team, or otherwise
      c) As members of their community
      d) In handling problems
      e) In dealing with children
      f) Their affectional life, including sex relations

6. Discuss your brothers and sisters:
    1) Their reaction to parents
    2) Their reaction to each other
    3) Your relationship to them individually and collectively

7. Evaluate both constructive and destructive influences upon your-self and upon the remainder of the family from both the short range and long term points of view.

The *fourth session* finds the group discussing the material which had been activated by the written assignment. Each is surprised, some a bit shocked, but in the end each seems delighted to have a better understanding of his own and the fiance's parental home. The session ends with questions about the possible effect of all this upon the new family they want to establish.

Beginning A New Family

During the *fifth* and *sixth* sessions they discuss such questions as parental possessiveness, whether the new family should live with either of the parents, in-laws, maturity, responsibility, expectations of marriage, current and future possible conflicts, roles of husband and wife, and many other vital areas.

By this time, aided by the diary material turned in at each session, the counselor knows each person and couple quite well. The group also has an amazing grasp of the stresses in each couple. This environment encourages couples to enter into conflicts which, with most people, are held off until after marriage. A few individual conferences have removed emotional blocks in one or two people, and taken the push out of the hostility in another group member. They are relating well, both in terms of negative and positive feelings. Reports are that the couples are spending increasing amounts of dating time discussing vital interests.

Work and Finances

The *seventh* and *eighth sessions* are given over to work and finances. The early discussions bring out marked differences in feelings about income, handling money, debts, installment buying, the wife's working, and buying or renting. Insurance, savings, and housekeeping are kicked around. Then follows a meaningful discussion of the kinds of jobs for which the men are preparing, with emphasis upon the relevance of the job to the kind of family life each couple have begun to see they want. Discussion continues around the woman's dual career, in the home and on the job.

Children

The *ninth and tenth sessions* are devoted to children—how many, when, how they are to be reared, readiness for parenthood, discipline, education, and sex guidance. Sharp differences of opinion between couples arise, areas which previously they have not dared discuss. The sources of many feelings are made evident as the individuals try to reactivate their own childhood feelings. All agree that they have opened an area that will need intensive attention now and also after children are born. Several ask for individual conferences at this point.

A Family Faith

Sessions *eleven* and *twelve* find the group exploring the religious similarities and differences among the couples. A couple of the same faith are surprised to discover that they have more basic differences in religious beliefs than one of the mixed faith couples. The discussion moves into the meaning of their rejection of certain beliefs during high school and college. Several of the group report further discussions with their minister or priest. They are seeing that it was the more childish or immature aspects of religion which they had doubted, and conclude that each must grow a value system of his own, and that the couple must work together in this.

Emotional and Physical Readiness

The *thirteenth and fourteenth* sessions are devoted to emotional and physical readiness for marriage. Two of the couples who are marrying immediately after this group experience ends already have had pre-marital physical examinations, and have discussed it briefly with the counselor. They enrich the discussion the first day on this topic. The other couples have their physicals between these two sessions.

One girl goes home to the family physician rather than use the doctor recommended locally. He frightens her by getting concerned about a slightly tipped uterus. He mentions possible surgery, which subsequent examination by a specialist proves she does not need. Others have questions about what the doctor meant by certain terms, or suggestions. During these sessions the group members are warm and supportive, healing many wounds and aiding each other in replacing fear with fact and faith. They feel they are "like a real family," "like we have known each other for years." Two of the men express fear of childbirth for their wives and this leads to relaxed discussions of the whole process.

The Wedding and the Honeymoon

Fifteenth and sixteenth sessions. The discussion of childbirth is continued by one couple who has discovered some basic hesitancy at becoming parents. Then attention turns to honeymoon fears and expectations, mixed feelings about the wedding, and other plans of each couple.

Just as the final minutes of most sessions were used for integration, the final hour of the last period is reserved for pulling things together, relating discussions in one area to all other areas, and talking over the use of professional help if and when it is indicated in the marriage. They recognize that the segments of behavior of the individual and couple which have been examined must be considered in terms of their implications for the family, the community, the nation, and the world. Through constantly relating each part to the whole of life and to the whole of their relationship, these youth are freed from the limits imposed by logic-tight compartments and stereotyped thinking to become creative in individual and family living.

III.   Illustrative Feelings

Throughout this process fact is important primarily because of its relation to feeling and attitude. A diary or journal provides an opportunity for the individual to capture fleeting questions, feelings, and marginal thoughts, as well as thinking through on paper some puzzling incident or memory. This can be invaluable in guiding the counselor, as well as furthering the sharing process with each couple.

The following are excerpts from such group discussions and the diaries of participants:

Jim says:

"All I can recall about early childhood is drudgery and boredom. I had a hard time in school until about the fourth grade . . . changed schools and the new kids were wonderful to me, helping me to catch up. First time I felt wanted. . . .

"In high school and college I turned to the "Y" for companionship. Was wrapped up in projects; enjoyed the contact with leaders and the fellows. They became my family."

On the surface these facts seem to balance each other; family fails, and others form a family for the youth. But behind this quick statement is a life of hurt from deprivation of love. Has it been healed or just repressed? He will need to ventilate a great deal of this as the group proceeds.

Garcia tells the group from time to time:

"I am the son of a minister who was always busy. Seems I never had a moment with him alone, and not many with the whole family together. My brother was several years older and my sister still older; and we had little in common. . . ."

"Mother had to use illness to get daddy's attention and she tried it on me for awhile. I began to accuse her of this and go on out to play. I took over two younger boys down the street—became the leader in most we did from about seven to sixteen, including sex experiments. . . ."

"Felt insecure in school; some said preacher's kids are the meanest; others that they should be an example. One way or the other, it was constantly thrown in my face. I was compared to my brother and sister by teachers who had taught them. When I did O.K. it still wasn't as good as my sister. If I got out of line, I was being just like my brother. . . ."

"The minister's family was set apart, although respected. I was always reprimanded by mouth or paddle when I threatened this stereotype. . . ."

"Although confident elsewhere, I didn't date until my third year in college. Then it was an average of once a week; some mighty perplexing problems came then. . . ."

"The more I think of marriage the more ideal I feel mother was as a wife and mother. I am lucky indeed to have my dad; other young people stress this to me. Both of them seem unusually well adjusted. . . ."

Has he worked through resentment and seen the parents in truer perspective? Or, has he begun to feel guilty, and is he now trying to atone?

Simon opened the discussion of parental families with this:

"My parents divorced a year after I was born. Mother got custody, turned me over to her parents for adoption and left the country. I asked many questions about my real parents. All answers were colored in favor of my real mother, or just turned aside on account of my age.

"My grandparents were good to me in their way, but very early I didn't believe them, either about the satanic nature of my father or angelic nature of mother. Along in adolescence I tried various ways of tracing the record of my family in the courts. All at once I just didn't want to go on and I quit; guess I feared if what they said was true I might discover some hereditary taint. . . ."

"(Upon returning from the Service) I renewed the search, and about a year ago found my dad. I found there were *really* two sides to the story. He had been forbidden to see me throughout childhood on threat of death by my grandfather. Peace warrants had been taken out to restrain him from trying to see me. Grandfather actually fired a gun at my dad's feet one day. After I ran away from home at 14 my real dad had often searched for me.

"Now I find that mother was a spoiled brat. Dad says not to blame her since she was emotionally sick, and her parents believed every tale she told about dad, who admitted he made some mistakes. I've felt quite comfortable since seeing dad . . . everything sort of fits into place."

On the second day of discussing parental families, Jonz said, almost as a memorized speech:

"I was born in the mountains of Tennessee. During the depression years we never had enough to eat. Mother and Dad fought repeatedly. When I was 4 Mother was sent to the state hospital and immediately after that Daddy went to the pen for bootlegging. I lived in a boarding house for a year or so; was taken out by a fine family. I loved them very much, but I became so unruly and they were puritanical; so they had to take me back to the agency. I was turned over to a state orphanage . . ."

In his diary that night he wrote:

"I couldn't tell it in the group, but the manager of the orphanage beat me until I soiled my self. I was deathly afraid of him, and sometimes would soil myself when I saw him coming my way."

"At nine I was removed to a Christian orphanage . . . it was beautiful and the house mothers were wonderful. I was happy there until 13½ when my oldest brother took me out to his place. He was a drunkard. The contrast was so great I could hardly stand it. At 16 I got into the armed forces."

Jonz has many strengths or he wouldn't be here in one piece trying to get ready for marriage. But can he learn not to expect Suzy to fulfill all the unmet needs of childhood? They will need to give much attention to expectations, and to the development of problem-solving skills.

Henry sketched his background like this:

"I am the son of a farmer-factory worker. I was so much younger than my siblings that I was almost an only child. We didn't have much but Mama saw I got more than the older children say they got. Daddy wasn't doing so well at work so mother contracted some work at a small factory with a relative of ours, into whose house we moved. He drank a lot, and would spend all the profits and then we didn't get paid. I challenged him on this. He ordered me away so I joined the Navy at 16. I reenlisted when that stretch was up. Now I am trying to finish teacher training on the G. I. Bill."

Later in discussing children, he recalled:

"A teacher stands out in my memory. If we made a poor grade she let all the other boys in the class use their belts on us. They beat me pretty badly because I made it so hard for them to catch and hold me."

The Diary of a Girl

Almost without exception the several hundred young people who have experienced group preparation for marriage with the author have worked intensely and involved their total selves. Typical of this is the college girl who kept a diary during the process and later gave permission for it to be used "for the cause." The following extracts illustrate her personal involvement:

First Week. "My family has influenced me so very much that it is difficult to look at the whole picture objectively. Somewhere along the way they gave me the opportunity to grasp Christian ideals for life. I guess I am amazingly calm compared to their reactions . . . Mother was always the submissive type, even in her parents' home. Everything had to be just perfect for Daddy no matter what any of the rest of the family wanted. Mother has rebelled against her role and plays martyr, seeking sympathy, or using other "womanly wiles" such as tears. She has a tendency to have emotional outbursts, crying and screaming. I have tried many times to take her into my confidence, to ask her advice, to get her to help me to learn cooking, to establish grounds on which we might be friends, but usually she tries to belittle me. She has betrayed my confidence and seems to really prefer her martyr role, and does not wish to relinquish her childhood control over me . . . "

"Daddy especially was a member of the 'children should be seen and not heard' group. He seemed to expect perfection from us, and it was obvious that he was proud of us only when we appeared nearly perfect . . . Mother was rather unpredictable because sometimes she would be extremely harsh and other times she would just let things slide. She must have believed that a routine spanking every day would keep us on our best behavior, although it looks as if she would have seen it did not . . . "

"My parents are not very affectionate toward each other around anyone. I remember during my late childhood often wondering if they really loved each other. They never mentioned sex relations in any way before me; however, from one conversation with mother a number of years ago about having children, I believe that she is the kind of woman who just endured sex relations for daddy's sake."

". . . I want my home to be full of love which easily is visible. However, I have developed traits of selfishness and laziness which will never be helpful in establishing the type of home I would want. Once in a while I catch myself imitating the martyr, self-pity attitudes of mother. I also find myself fearful to undertake a project unless fairly sure of success . . . My family has influenced me through the years in never thinking constructively about marriage . . . I have had life too easy as far as material things are concerned; yet I lack a real sense of inner security. My relationship to my parents left an unfulfilled need for affection which I did not recognize for a long time, but which has caused me to expect a little too much from my friendships. Continous belittlement gave lack of self-confidence and a pessimistic outlook on the future, but my ability to recognize this has helped me to keep this from getting the best of me."

Second Week. "I have been concerned about unconscious, piled-up feelings and their possible influence on my marriage. In the group it is thought-provoking to see how each feels about things, especially the boys regarding sexual intercourse . . . I am impressed by the need to learn to express affection in many other ways than sex.

Third Week. I am impressed by the intense preparation for marriage that seems to be needed; the need to learn to communicate; comforting to know that many couples have the same problems we have. I feel a tremendous need to know more about sex.

Fourth Week. I begin to feel more confident that I can accept the responsibility of marriage. I have been impressed by an article on "Pre-Marital Sex Relations" and wonder if when a couple goes that far they do not become pre-occupied with sex and fail to get to know the real personality of each other. Have begun to see something of the total process of readiness for marriage which is the real purpose of engagement.

Fifth Week. Following our discussion in class Fred and I have been drawn closer together as we discuss children and their rearing. This led me to discuss my feelings about childbirth a little with him; I concluded I needed to be around children more, especially babies and would try to get a job this summer working with babies.

Sixth Week. In thinking about finances I realize that I have to form better habits of spending and saving; perhaps this is the biggest problem I will have. Have had too much and spent foolishly in college. As we think of living off one teacher's salary we must avoid credit and installment buying.

Seventh Week. One of the best sessions yet this week. A surprising experience to really have our feelings about children come out, especially the men. (Note: Most of those present did not want their wives to have babies because it would hurt them; they would feel guilty if the wife should die.) Fred was absent but we plan to talk this over in detail; have much to talk over with him about childbirth and children.

Eighth Week. I wish we could have a socio-drama in class in which practical, every-day situations which confront couples could be worked out.

Ninth Week. Have been reading *One Little Boy*; plenty to think about. Have usually thought of childbirth and child rearing in selfishly fearful way; am beginning to get a new perspective. Will be glad when we study about children in detail . . . would like to talk privately with the counselor about that . . . fear that the discussions of finances are not practical enough; interesting feelings about roles and expectations in marriage.

Tenth Week. We talked about the wedding ceremony and a lot of things involved. To me it should be expressive of the personalities and meaningful to them. I have always felt that it should provide a happy atmosphere in which the couple dedicate themselves to each other and to God and by which the new family receives public recognition and approval.

Eleventh Week. Sexual intercourse is the highest expression of love between two persons who seek to have a complete feeling of spiritual, physical, and psychological union, and who seek to give to each other the greatest creative outlet possible.

Twelfth Week. Communication—a problem of ours. Fred and I have made progress already in understanding our needs and feelings . . . Very interested in our discussions of sex; be glad if the leader would discuss thoroughly the wedding night; I would like to learn these things. It is comfortable to know we two are getting the same preparation for marriage.

Thirteenth Week. Especially appreciate the thorough discussion of contraceptives. We just cannot plan for children for the first two years of our marriage since he will be in school. . . . Details of pre-marital examinations started today. It is helpful to have details of the examination but I have never had any fears or worries about this, so it is no problem for me.

The anxiety-laden points stand out in her diary as the group process proceeded. Especially was she tense in early discussions of the parental family, at times appearing to be lost in fantasy. In daily activities, as well as in the group, she was an interesting mixture of a mature young lady and one evidencing many residual needs from childhood. She showed anxiety in the expression of affection; quite tense after petting and not knowing what to do about it. She was anxious lest she not find ways to make possible a happy and meaningful home.

The expression of feelings around childbirth during the fifth and seventh weeks were especially significant. Again, she was too tense to talk in the group discussion, but was able to discuss the matter somewhat with her fiance. She continued to work hard at the unconscious level, as well as at the conscious level, with her fears about childbirth.

By the ninth week she began quizzing the counselor's secretary about her reason for marriage and what kind of preparation she thought was necessary. Then she made an appointment with the counselor, asking for help in working out some of her problems. She began by discussing feelings about childbirth, a subject which terrorized her. She felt there was not only fear of pain but something akin to rejection of children. Since she had never been around younger children, she reiterated the plan to work with them during the summer months in order to learn about them.

In the twelfth week there was fascination and concern with sexual development and experiences. By the following week she had begun to relax somewhat about this and could join in the discussions of contraceptives. This relieved some of her fears of unwanted pregnancy. Her insistence in the thirteenth week that she never had any fears or worries about a premarital physical examination amounted to whistling in the dark. In the next individual counseling session she blocked, but through guided association was able to reactivate fears about medical care, and relived a traumatic experience with a gynecological examination at the age of ten when the mother had "told the doctor what I did." She recalled jumping from the examination table, screaming at the doctor and running from the office. That doctor wrote a letter demanding that she apologize to him because "a child doesn't treat a doctor that way." Working through these feelings in counseling accomplished a great deal for her, and facilitated further discussion of feelings with her fiance.

The diary ceased at this point since her needs were being met through counseling and continued group discussions, not to mention her relationship with the young man. She was seen regularly for another three months of individual counseling as she worked at self-understanding and continued to grow personally and in the relationship with her fiance and future husband.

Traumatic Incidents

Between group sessions Tom brought to the counselor a letter he had received from another man. It had shaken him; he was afraid to tell Lily, and yet wanted to. "I know I'm not a homo, but why was this fellow attracted to me?" Here are excerpts from the letter:

"My reason for writing this letter to you is that I want to tell you something that I had planned to tell you the other night but couldn't because those boys came in. . . . Since meeting you and talking to you, I have thought about you very much, and I have fallen in love with you. You may have already noticed it or at least you should have by the way I act when I am with you. Actually I had not planned to stop when I saw you. You attracted me and I couldn't resist. And thanks to fate, a conversation was started between us, one which I shall never forget. You not only attract me intellectually but physically as well, and I believe we have much in common or at least we have the same ambition. . . .

"Of all the boys I have ever known I have yet to find one to compare to you. I am convinced that if I were to search the world over I would be unable to find one boy I could love the way I love you, nor would I find one to be your equal in intelligence, ambition, understanding, etc. I only wonder why I hadn't met you before. You may think I am crazy for writing and you may not even like me at all, but one thing that you can always remember is that my admiration, adoration, and my love for you shall never cease, not with the end of time. . . . This is from my heart, trying in a feeble way to explain to you exactly how I feel about you. . . . I had rather sit and look at you than do anything else. Can we have a date so we can talk this over? Love."

This approach by an overt homosexual had upset Tom. After protesting too loudly, he confessed to the counselor that he might be a homo after all. Then he told of some older boys making him suck them off while holding a knife to his throat. He was about nine and, along with terror, could remember a thrilling sort of excitement. He had repressed this thoroughly, until now, but it was definitely tied to certain questions about his adequacy as a male. A few individual counseling sessions brought relief from these fears. There were no indications that he had strong homosexual tendencies. He became quite uninhibited in his affection and sexual attraction to Lily. (Subsequently, they adjusted well in marriage.)

Gloria lived in a girl's dormitory and was a campus "beauty." She painted over and over again a picture of her "ideal family." She was "prudish" in the group discussions of sex and affection. "Christian young people just don't pet until they are married." Yet she was deeply attracted to her fiance and her sex needs were emerging. She was depressed and withdrawn during two group sessions. The counselor invited her to talk it out in his office and she poured out a broken-hearted story. She had come in from a date all jittery with desire; yet feeling guilty about it. She had gone down the hall to sit on her "prayer mate's" bed to talk to her and to ask her advice. In the process of describing her feelings the two girls began to caress each other, culminating in Lesbian sex relations.

Gloria was overwhelmed with guilt and fear. Soon it became evident that the incident was the result of a combination of unduly inhibited heterosexual interests and circumstances. There was little doubt about the genuineness of heterosexual drives and interests. With some suggestions by the counselor of temporary "limits" as she felt her way, she decided she and the young man should learn to give and receive affection. This proved to be much more exciting and satisfying than the homosexual experience.

Smitty had made the group somewhat self-conscious when they described mixed feelings about their parents. His was the perfect family; dad was his model in life and he wanted his wife to be a carbon copy of mother. He championed rugged individualism, each going his own way, in marriage.

His conflicts did not work themselves out so quickly as those discussed above. He and Syl were to be married a few weeks after the group experience ended. During the preparation for marriage sessions he went for a physical examination. Rather than use one of the physicians suggested by the counselor, he consulted one recommended by "the boys." During the exam the doctor made sexual advances and Smitty went along with the homosexual experience. In the office of the counselor he was remorseful, genuinely concerned about hurting his prospective wife, but sure that his homosexual appetite was dominant, now that it had been reactivated.

Now he could recall wrestling with men at lunch hour on the job, trying to ignore the fact that he was sexually excited, except when it was called to his attention by an orgasm. His father was a professional man who had little time for the family. The mother "lived out" with the boy much of her unfulfilled emotional needs. As a small boy and as a young teenager he would sneak off while she attended circle meetings at the church and meet with a gang for sexual experimentation. This practice became less frequent when he became interested in high school theater.

He decided that the girl friend should be told that he had sexual problems and he wanted time to be sure they were resolved before marriage. She had suspected this and their engagement was broken. She was hurt, but grateful that it had happened now rather than later. She offered to date him any time and encouraged him in plans for intensive psychotherapy. He decided upon treatment because he felt immature, hated himself for being a homo, didn't know what he wanted to do in life, and was unable to love and marry a woman. (A casual contact with him five years later revealed that, after a year and a half of therapy and another year of "playing the female field," he had married another woman and they were getting along well.)

Another traumatic experience illustrates the unexpected. Griff and Maybelle had announced their marriage date after four months of courtship against her parents' wishes. They were to be married just after the preparation for marriage group ended. They were absent at the sixth session. Toward the end of the period the secretary brought in a telephone message from Griff. A childhood heart ailment had reactivated and Maybelle was dead. The effect upon the group was indescribable. They went to the funeral and to the graveside. When everyone else had departed, the counselor sat at the grave and finally convinced Griff that really she was dead, which he had refused to believe.

Griff missed the next session and the group wondered—afraid he would not return and afraid he might. The counselor wondered quietly what would happen to the group spirit if he returned, but this anxiety was ill-advised. There is healing in the group for whatever happens within the group context. Griff came for the next session. He worked through his feelings about her family; such statements as: "Why do you hang around here and grieve? You weren't married to her you know!"

After a very deprived childhood and later "finding himself" in combat overseas, Griff had returned home and dared to love for the first time. Maybelle's love had transformed him. After an overprotected, smothered childhood in which the mother had used the illness to bind and cripple the girl emotionally, she had thrown off restraint, loved and grown. Griff knew this and was grateful and pleased that she knew love before she died. He felt the group would understand and he knew that Maybelle would have wanted him to love again. Therefore, he continued in the group preparing for marriage. (It came five years later.)

D. MODIFICATION OF THIS GROUP PLAN

There is no end to modifications of the method presented here. Perhaps more than the four couples suggested can be handled by some counselors. Both of the engaged couple may participate or only one. In the absence of one, he can be kept in tune with what is happening through correspondence, and arranging for a visit to enable him to get to know the group or the counselor in person. Couples can be selected who are planning marriage in the near or distant future, or a mixture of both. Similarity, dissimilarity or a mixture of such characteristics as age, religion, education, and socio-economic background can be set up as criteria. Divorced or widowed people may be admitted or excluded, as may girls who are pregnant, according to the local setting.

Some groups invite a healthy married couple to join them as resource people at each meeting, although this may contribute to a "you tell us" attitude. The group may meet in a church, a "Y," clinic, school, or the counselor's office. The method advocated here also can be adapted easily to groups who are not engaged but want to discuss dating, courtship, and family life interests.

Most important of all, the approach can be adapted readily to seeing only one couple, regardless of the circumstances. Some counselors prefer the individual couple approach, and all must use it at times. All the way from initial contact, through the collecting and evaluation of information, the few or many conferences, on to the wedding itself—the process can be alike in its steps whether with one or a half dozen couples.

If the counselor has only a few conferences with a couple, it is obvious that all the areas suggested in this approach cannot be covered in detail. They must be telescoped into an awareness of areas that should have immediate attention, pointing out other areas which they must keep on working through after marriage. In short term preparation of one or a few hours the counselor often finds that he must structure the sessions somewhat, becoming the instructor rather than the counselor. Even then suggestive questions get better results, and precaution is in order lest help be superimposed upon basic problems. If there are serious problems in the relationship, smoothed over and hidden, the counselor may have to choose between not letting these be opened up, or confronting the couple with the advisability of postponing the marriage. For instance, opening deep-seated sexual conflicts just before the wedding can guarantee sexual failures. Sometimes the best that can be done for a couple who are determined to marry without delay, who cannot or will not enter into adequate pre-marital counseling, is to give them the kind of understanding that will cause them to return for help when trouble comes later.

Chapter 6

THE ONE COUPLE APPROACH

Preferential treatment has been given the group approach to pre-marital counseling. Group counseling is the method of choice for most engaged couples, but at the same time the procedure outlined is directly applicable to working with only one couple. Training in individual counseling or psychotherapy is assumed to be a part of the background of anyone aspiring to pre-marital counseling. Nevertheless, certain socio-personal conditions and pressures call for special attention and may necessitate somewhat unorthodox methods of handling pre-marital cases.

A variety of factors may call for seeing one couple at a time. They may seek help so late in the marriage plans that it is impossible to place them in a group. If they seek out a counselor who does not have access to an on-going group it is likely that they expect to be seen either individually or as one couple. Each well may have specific personality conflicts which he wishes to examine in confidence. Conflict between them may be so acute that it must be tackled directly, or their need to share in this area so great that every possible effort, including some which cause added anxiety, must be utilized to stimulate intensive communication. The needs and experiences of one or both of a couple may be so unusual or bizarre as to make it unwise, both from their point of view and for the welfare of the others, to handle them in a larger group. They might fit into certain groups but not the particular one available at the time.

A. SPECIAL SITUATIONS

There are special situations which make it preferable to counsel one couple alone, rather than with a group of couples, with either the couple, the counselor, or the local setting dictating the choice.

I. Forced Marriages

The concept of forced marriage brings to mind the "shotgun weddings" of comedy sketches and of real life. The counselor will work with cases in which the parents are forcing the marriage, but he should keep alert to other factors which can be just as oppressive. One of the couple may be using blackmail in any of many ways, or the superego of one or both can do the coercing. A compulsory marriage, for whatever reason, is a poor beginning for a new family.

Many youth are taught firmly that complete sex life must await full-blown love; "save yourself for the one you really love." This often back-fires, with youth using this rationale: "Since I am so deeply in love, it is all right to have intercourse." This, when followed by an onslaught of the superego, may lead to another conclusion: "Now that I have 'gone all the way,' I *must* get married." Many cultures have allowed sexual privileges to the engaged, without guilt. Witness the ancient Hebrew system of betrothal, and the religiously sanctioned practices of some Scandinavian countries to-day. The sequence—supposed love, justifying sexual intercourse—is quite common in America, but it is often accompanied by major guilt reactions, with marriage viewed as the one way to "make it right." This leads to a multitude of unwise marriages. The counselor must try to clarify added reasons for or against a marriage which is being forced by one or both of the couple. Sometimes the man, more often the woman, is using their sex experiences as a pressure toward marriage. Guilt and shame are poor bases for a lifetime relationship.

Current studies indicate that some forty to fifty percent of women and a higher percentage of men have sexual intercourse prior to marriage. Of the Protestant women who participate in pre-marital coitus, some ten to twelve percent get pregnant before the vows are said; this goes up to forty percent in groups where contraception is forbidden. A number of those who get pregnant will have previously agreed on marriage, feel that their love makes it wise to wed, and believe that for the child's sake, and their own reputation, all they need do is speed up plans. When this is the actual situation the counselor's role is essentially the same as preparing any couple for marriage, with the added reponsibility of helping both accept full responsibility to prevent the harboring of resentment toward the child or each other. Other-wise, this may become a factor in subsequent marital conflict, even though at present they are not unduly threatened by the pregnancy.

To others, pregnancy is a bitterly resented accident, or perhaps the woman deliberately got pregnant to force marriage, or the man suspects this to be the case. One or both of the couple are under pressure of the mores, a shot-gun, the law, or the superego to "make things right" and "give the child a name." Two wrongs never make a right. Pregnancy alone is the poorest possible reason for getting married. Such coerced marriages seldom provide a healthy home for the child and often break up after bitterness, infidelity, and when perhaps added children have been born into the unhealthy dilemma. Indications are that in from a third to a half of teenage marriages the girl is already pregnant, and the divorce rate of this group is phenomenal.

Unless the couple can find a sound total basis for a marriage, one that would have been wise without being precipitated by pregnancy, they should be supported in remaining single. This usually involves helping them take a responsible, although belatedly so, attitude toward the unborn child. What is really best for the baby? Being an unwanted child in a forced marriage? There are major exceptions in certain social strata where the unwed mother and the child are readily accepted into the community, but as a rule it is almost impossible for a single woman to provide a healthy home for her child. Hundreds of married couples are waiting to adopt such babies. The counselor can protect baby and mother from exploitation on the baby black market by guiding her to a Family Service Agency, Florence Crittenden Home, or to other public adoption agencies. The task has just begun if he is to help the woman and the man profit from the experience through counseling.[1]

Abortion, either before the marriage or instead of it, is the solution to pre-marital pregnancy sought by an increasing number of youth and adults. Kinsey found that 88 to 95 percent of pre-marital pregnancies ended in abortion in spite of its illegality and religious condemnation. Among all the single white females in his sample who had experienced coitus, 20 percent had undergone abortions.[2] It is not too uncommon for a counselor to find one or both of a couple burdened with guilt about one or more abortions, seeking another pregnancy as if thereby to gain atonement. This sought-after pregnancy, whether consciously or unconsciously motivated, may occur prior to marriage, or the inner push toward a wedding ceremony may be viewed as prerequisite to conception this time.

Many counselors would be quite comfortable to have an obviously pregnant woman and her intended husband as an integral part of a pre-marital counseling group. In some settings, neither the individual nor the remainder of the group would be hindered. In other situations, however, there would be enough tension associated with the pregnancy to indicate seeing them in a one couple approach. Extreme reactions of guilt and shame usually should be dealt with in individual sessions, and then with the couple together if

[1] Vincent, Clark. *Unmarried Mothers*. Glencoe, Illinois: The Free Press. 1961.
[2] Calderone, Mary S. *Abortion In the United States*. New York: Hoeber and Harper. 1958.

indicated, and later in the group if other facets of their counseling are occurring in a group setting.

II. The Divorced and Widowed

There are many settings in which a known-to-be-divorced individual would be unduly embarrassed by being a member of a pre-marital counseling group, although technically there is nothing to contra-indicate the practice.

Increasingly religious bodies are freeing their ministers to do what seems best to them, having considered all the circumstances, when one or both of a couple who have been married and divorced want to get married. Some leaders continue to hold tenaciously to a legalistic interpretation of the Scriptures. To them the murderer and rapist can be forgiven and begin over, but not the one who makes a mistake in marriage. They well might reconsider a few factors common to religious beliefs: Not every marriage is the result of "what God hath joined together"; "God is gracious to forgive whatever kind of sin", and, "forgiven sin is not held against one."

With the inadequate mate selection process of this culture, and the scanty preparation for married pair living which is the rule, a considerable percentage of marriages will continue to fail. Most of these people remarry. Current research reveals that many of them do attain a meaningful relationship after one or more attempts at marriage. The second home may be far healthier for the children than living in the original warring camp. Obviously many people do tend to repeat in the second marriage the same mistakes as in the first. But this need not be true if churches, clinics, and professional people helped, rather than condemning, by providing education and counseling. Many factors can be made to work in favor of the second or later marriage succeeding. The average couple at first marriage is 19 to 20 years of age, whereas the average second marriage is in the early 30's. Many of them are highly motivated to avoid repeating the hurt of the first marriage and to build a healthy home. They may not need more preparation, but they certainly can use as much help with their marriage as anyone else. The advantages and disadvantages of divorce, the welfare of children, and the possible assets of subsequent marriages are outlined in Chapter 9.

In that most divorced people would profit from the same pre-marital counseling as any other about-to-be-married couple, there is little to contra-indicate group counseling. Insofar as a major share of the needed counseling must focus around emotional hurts, fears, bitterness, or individual psychopathology, a combination of individual psychotherapy and one-couple-counseling might be preferable.

One might use the same principles in determining whether to counsel the *widowed* in a group setting or individually when they are planning remarriage, except that this does not raise as many value judgment questions in the minds of either clients or counselors.

III. Complex Sex Problems

The group counseling report in Chapter 5 demonstrates conclusively that sexual concerns can be an integral part of group pre-marital counseling. And yet, certain complex sexual problems can unduly divert the concerns of the group from the primary task of learning to relate healthily in the sexual area. Overt homosexuals create such a high level of anxiety for most non-homosexuals that it can be unmanageable. Any type of problem may be brought to awareness in a group setting, but remedial efforts in such areas as homosexuality, fetishes, impotence, and extreme frigidity usually respond best to a combination of individual therapy and one-couple-counseling quite similar to marriage counseling. Some of these problems could be handled in group psychotherapy if it were set up to treat the emotional problems, but the intensity of focus necessary to get results can take too much of the time usually allotted to handle total man-woman interaction in pre-marital counseling. An amazing number of sexually handicapped individuals misguidedly seek marriage as a cure to their pathology. Most such marriages should be postponed until adequate treatment has been provided.

IV. Addictions

Drug addicts, alcoholics and other "addictive" personalities pose problems sufficiently intense, if not different, to call for separate therapeutic efforts. Some counselors would slough off this concern in the conviction that such people should not marry in the first place, at least not until psychological treatment had proved successful. It is not so simple, however. Couples, both of whom know themselves to be addicts or chronic alcoholics, come for help, fully expecting the counselor to assist them to a happy marriage. More often, he discovers in the first exploratory interview that one of them is addicted and then it becomes clear that one or both expect him to be the miracle man, bringing about a reformation. It may be discovered that two people are addicted to each other, counting on the relationship to meet enough of their crippled dependency needs to keep away the necessity of bottle or needle. Some of these people seem to have quite meaningful (in the supportive sense) liaisons for a while, including sex life. When the relationship begins to lose its fascination, and yet is necessary to self maintenance, one or the other will begin to press for marriage. The other gets frightened of the responsibility, and in this crisis they seek professional help.

Much was said in Chapter 2 about the complementarity of marriage relations, including the neurotic or crippled personality factors. Although there is always risk in generalizations, this was never more glaringly illustrated than in alcoholic marriages. They prove to be such a "lock and key" relationship that the counselor learns to focus immediately on both the healthy and unhealthy facets of their particular complementarity. Over and again, when an alcoholic mate is treated to the point of giving up drinking, the previously "dry" mate becomes an addict, an alcoholic, or emotionally ill. These two personalities sought each other, driven by subliminal awareness that they were kindred souls, each feeling he could have his own insatiable needs met by this particular person. This may be camouflaged by, "I and only I can help him," but really means, "He and only he can help me." A common occurrence is the woman whose forbidden urges are deeply repressed and the man who "drinks and raises hell." He was that way when she married him or was the type of personality that could be "driven" to drink or sexual acting out as the need might be. Consciously the woman is hurt, martyred, and seeks to reform him. All the while his condition is strengthening the repressive forces within her. At the same time, unconsciously she can enjoy the behavior of the man, which brings vicarious expression to her own similar hidden needs.

This complementarity can be turned into an asset in many alcoholic or addictive marriages, especially so if the pre-marital counselor can assist them in working through these relationships prior to marriage. If some resolution, at least understanding and balance, cannot be gained he would do well to advise against the marriage, especially in view of what might be the fate of children born to such a union.[3]

One of the keys to effective work with such couples is the counselor's ability to understand the implications of complementarity as it works in a healthy marriage and to enable the couple to utilize this as building material for the best relationship of which they are capable.

[3] Burton, Genevieve, "Group Counseling with Alcoholics and Their Wives," *Marriage and Family Living*. 24, 1, 1962. pp. 56-61.

V. The Grossly Neurotic and Personality Disorders

Slavson [4] has cautioned that patients who lack a minimal capacity for object relations, ego and superego sufficiency, and those with serious sexual disturbances are unsuitable for group psychotherapy until these difficulties have been remedied through individual psychotherapy. Specifically, he rules out of the group treatment category individuals with anxiety neuroses, neurotic character, compulsive-obsessional, cyclothymic personalities, perverts, hypochondriacs, and true hysterics. Likewise he eliminates those with such "characterological" disorders as: inadequate primary relations, inadequate ego development, inadequate superego development, intense sexual disturbances, psychopaths, regressive infantile characters, and extreme narcissism.

Applied at face value, this would eliminate from pre-marital group counseling a great block of engaged individuals. Practically, his caution serves as guidelines to expected difficulties, types of groupings, seriousness of symptoms that can be utilized or tolerated, and the depth and goal of such premarital counseling. This field—group therapy in general and pre-marital group therapy—is too new to become dogmatic about what *can* be done.

Some caution is well taken, particularly in that basic guidelines and limits may have to be set if clients with certain symptom syndromes are admitted to pre-marital group counseling. The hypochondriacal patient who endlessly preens his symptoms before the group mirror can defeat pre-marital counseling for himself and others. The more extreme obsessive-compulsive individual tends to monopolize group time endlessly, taking off on countless detours, usually with little benefit to himself or to others. The grossly phobic may stimulate the needs of others to conceal or withdraw. On the other hand, these neurotic exhibitions can be used at times by a skilled counselor to pull forth into awareness similar characteristics of the healthier group members so that they can be utilized in the counseling process.

The concept of neurotic complementarity was used earlier in describing the psychological needs of the addictive personality. Obviously, neurotic traits are quite common to mankind, which makes it difficult to determine which neurotic needs can be worked through effectively in a group setting and which must have more intensive individual care. Perhaps the best guideline is the question of whether the time and energy necessary to handle

---

[4] Slavson, S. R., *A Textbook of Psychoanalytic Group Psychotherapy*. New York: International Universities Press. 1964. pp. 190-192.

this aspect of a case will detract that person or other group members from the total task of readiness for marriage.

At the mate selection stage, complementary neurosis may be the determining factor. It is the counselor's task to diagnose what is happening, including the neurotic patterns of couple interaction. These must be seen in relation to the healthier complementarity of the couple and, in turn, both types of interaction must be viewed in the context of the total man-woman relationship. Awareness of the "family types" discussed in Chapter 2 will aid in guiding some problem-ridden couples toward a meaningful marriage, albeit a struggling one, or in giving up the relationship as unworkable.

VI. The Mentally Ill

Psychotic individuals respond differentially to group psychotherapy when fundamental treatment is the goal. Schizophrenic patients can be handled in groups if the goals and techniques are reality based and controlled. Careful attention must be given to ego strengths if schizoid personalities are to be placed in pre-marital group counseling. Paranoiacs and gross depressives are risky candidates for any group treatment.

Should the mentally ill be permitted to marry? The fact is that thousands do get married in a prepsychotic state, or while a psychosis is in remission. Many are ambulatory schizophrenics, depressives, or fit into other diagnostic categories. A concerned relative or an examining physician often will refer these, hoping the counselor can talk them out of getting married, or perchance use pre-marital counseling to get them to the professional help called for by the illness. In most cases, either or both of these tasks will take priority over pre-marital counseling. In a few cases, however, marriage, if carefully planned for and given support, spells the difference between self-maintenance in the community and permanent institutionalization. This calls for careful collaboration of medical and psychological specialists in such areas as contraception, tranquilizers and other supportive treatment.

Initial guidance of such couples can best be done individually and conjointly with the engaged partner, although the follow-up supportive care may be ideally accomplished in a group of clients with similar needs.

VII. Panic Reactions

Doubts about an approaching wedding are common if not universal. Complete absence of such feelings probably means that they have been repressed, rather than that they never existed, or were faced and resolved. Confronting the doubts, examining them in the light of present reality, is an integral part of any pre-marital counseling. Usually these conflicts are managed and understood and the marriage plans proceed. At other times anxiety is heightened to an intolerable level both in and out of counseling. Two frequent reactions are (1) breaking the engagement, and (2) fleeing into an earlier marriage with the hope of ending the painful anxiety.

Common Anxiety. If the stress is mild and it seems inevitable that the couple will proceed with the ceremony, the counselor may be justified in "a patch job" of reassurance. Opening certain repressed areas for detailed examination just prior to the wedding might guarantee failure early in the marriage. It may be wiser in such cases to concentrate on building the kind of counselor-client relationship which will make it easy for them to return for help when problems come to the fore later. Here is the way not to do it:

> A young Jewish couple recently graduated from college were to be married in four days. His widowed father thought they should live at his home. The girl would do it, but obviously it was not her choice. Wanting to do things right, they decided to consult a counselor. A friend referred them to a "psychiatrist." He said their deep-seated problems must be brought into the open for handling. Since there wasn't much time he would use sodium pentothal. Through most of the morning he probed into the man, and then spent the afternoon with the girl under sedation. Then he saw them for a few minutes to report: "Young man, I've discovered a father complex in you, very deep-seated. And your fiance here is marrying you because of unconscious desires to be a mother to you. . . . Oh yes, you can get married but you both must return to me at once for therapy or your marriage won't have a chance." They would need to pay him now for services rendered, $500.00. Just to help them plan definitely to return for therapy they were to pay him another $500.00 as a down payment on future therapy.

> The next day the rabbi noticed how distraught they were as they said the honeymoon trip to Florida had to be cancelled, because they had paid all their savings to the doctor. The rabbi learned that although the medical doctor was practicing as a psychiatrist, he was not a member of the A.P.A., nor had he done any training in psychiatry. When threatened, the doctor returned the $500.00 advanced on future treatment. The rabbi took the couple to a professional marriage counselor who could help undo the damage.

If there is time, or if the problems appear to be bizarre, the counselor can suggest that these difficult problems should be handled before marriage, whether they root in personality disturbances or in their relationship to each other. Often prolonged individual psychotherapy is necessary for one or both, and this can be coordinated much as is done in marriage counseling, if they continue to plan on a future marriage.

Panic Reactions. The counselor won't handle many cases of pre-marital counseling before he is confronted with a full blown panic, which dictates individual treatment. An approaching marriage may appear so ominous that the personality controls which have worked for years threaten to break down. Some of these cases can be handled in the context of pre-marital counseling if wedding plans are postponed, but others require intensive long-range treatment. This case will illustrate both the problem and the techniques of diagnosis and therapy.

The young man came to a minister, whom he had heard speak once, three weeks before his wedding day. He was so worried that he couldn't get out to look for an apartment, eat, or sleep. Now he was overwhelmed with a feeling that something dreadful was about to happen. Afer learning that the man had been interested in two other girls but suddenly lost interest, the pastor pressed as to what was really bothering him. He blurted out, "I get sexually satisfied only from women's clothing." The panic did not subside, so the pastor brought him to a counseling center.

The notes on the exploratory interview follow: He is a 26-year-old single male, five feet six, 135 pounds; was receiving Catholic instruction and was to be married one month from the first interview, having been engaged to the girl some six months; high school education, served in the army four years, ending four months ago; works as a clerk typist. He is one of four siblings; a 29 year old male, married, insurance adjuster, no children, 27 year old female, married, housewife, three children; 22 year old half-brother, factory worker, married. He lives presently with his mother and step-father, the third husband of his mother. He works part of two shifts which makes twelve to fourteen hours per day.

Upon taking a seat he said his problem was fondling and wearing female apparel, getting his sexual satisfaction therefrom. He reported that he had known this girl to whom he is engaged for years but they had become serious fairly recently; perhaps he had pressured her into plans for marriage. He had thought that he could control his problem and go ahead with marriage, but upon finding the date approaching, announcements going out and a shower being given for the girl, he began to panic. He described it as one part of him pushing toward marriage and another part afraid. He feared being caught in a compromising situation with female apparel, thus embarrassing and hurting his wife, his mother, his younger married brother whom he likes, and letting down his own father who "recommended" him to the girl's family. His father, who divorced the mother when this patient was one, is now married to an older sister of the girl to whom the patient is engaged. Also he is afraid of the girl's family who are "very close knit and her dad might get a shotgun to me."

He described the girl as having led a sheltered life, a very good kid who knows little about sex; some concern that he might be exploiting her in pushing her toward marriage and also when he tries to fantasy having sex experiences with her, when she is such an innocent kid. He said that in their marriage, "I would be her strength. . . . a father, a brother, an uncle . . . and a husband." He likes most her gentleness, something he has always wanted.

For some time he has dated her twice a week, this limit due to his work schedule. During many of these dates he experienced an erection throughout the date, felt great pain, but would just walk it off after leaving her, did not want to masturbate when excited by her. Once he realized that marriage was definitely approaching he lost all ability to get sexually excited. He said: 'It's not paralysis . . . not paralysis, but just no erection.' At this time the realization that he had a sexual problem of many years duration hit full force. He had heard this minister speak some time in the past and now recalls saying to himself, 'Some day I'll have to talk about this problem and he will be the man.' He thought he would be understanding and says he found this to be true.

In looking further at relationships to women he described at least two other experiences where he dated girls for a period of time but never let it get close to marriage; he thought about it but evidently they did not know about his interest in marriage. He described his mother as very strong and dominant but not really affectionate now, just an "easiness" between them. He says in the teen years there was very definitely a lot of affection; too much so, he thought. He illustrated this: when he was about eighteen she would insist upon kissing him goodbye every time he left the house and this bothered him a great deal; he didn't think it was right and broke it off.

His real father left home and they were divorced when he was about one year of age. Later the patient visited him and his new wife but was told that he was his godfather; he learned differently when about 20. Mother married again when patient was about 2 to a Spaniard who was an alcoholic. He felt that his mother's third husband, whom she married about ten years ago, had a basically good attitude toward him as a boy, but he remembers being kicked by him. He described his childhood role in the family as being "in the middle, wanting but not receiving love." He described this third father as moody all week although he keeps on working, but loosening up on the weekends when he is drinking. The attitude between them now is just one of accepting the fact that each other is there.

In exploring relationships to other people through the years, he had few close friends earlier and two or three during his stay in the Service, but this did not sound convincing. When asked what kind of people they were he described jovial outgoing persons. One gets the feeling that rather than this being friendship, the patient warmed himself in the outgoing, seemingly happy attitude of these other people. He mentions several times his liking his youngest brother; essentially no mention of other siblings.

He volunteered little about his early life; seems repressed or blocked here, so was not pressed. Several things seem to center around the age of fourteen. About this time he remembers putting on women's undergarments and taking them off but "that is all the significance it had." Later he began to get stimulated and to masturbate on these occasions. He named a traumatic experience when he was about fourteen (later corrected to somewhere between ten and fourteen). He thinks that mother had some sort of genital surgery. He can't understand why but she and the step-father insisted that the patient observe the mother's genitals in this condition. He remembers being shocked and sickened by this. A great deal could have been elicited at this point but this was saved for therapy.

The patient recalled beginning masturbation somewhere around the fourteenth year but it did not seem to be important until about eighteen, or at least he could not remember it. He thought perhaps it was because high school was interesting and he was busy. Upon graduating he worked a year and then entered the Army for a four year stretch. Masturbation, while making use of women's clothing, intensified about the eighteenth year. He doesn't keep women's clothing around, lest he be detected. At home mother's underthings usually were available, or he would see them in windows of stores and get excited, occasionally purchasing some. Occasionally he masturbated without the aid of these garments, but only rarely and even then he felt very guilty. In spite of feeling shame and guilt, the experience of masturbating with women's undergarments would re-occur within a few days. In describing the fantasy during masturbation he indicated that he puts on the garments, parades around, particularly in the bathroom where he can't be seen, taking dance steps like a woman. He says that there are no men or women in the daydreams, just himself. He told how he would smoke a cigarette like a woman, the limp wrist, etc.

He described periods of great stress over this problem while in the army, although he has struggled with it consciously since eighteen, perhaps earlier. He was a clerk in personnel work and described how many papers on homosexuals came through the office; some being sent to mental hospitals, some discharged and some court-martialed. Somehow he managed to hold himself together. He considered himself "a step higher than the homosexual" but knew full well that his sexual concern would be treated as perversion if it were detected. Often he was afraid to go to sleep lest he talk and give away his secret. Insofar as he knows no one ever suspected and no one has ever been told by himself until he consulted the minister this week. When asked to describe a typical incident in which he might get sexual satisfaction from clothes he indicated: He might be in a bar drinking with some fellows. The girls who were dancing would not attract him if they were large or poorly shaped. If one were well-proportioned he might get sexually excited watching her. If he were drinking the ideas would come out more freely, ideas which during the day he would push out of his thoughts. In watching the woman he would get sexually excited, then let down and feel "a calm satisfaction." Temporarily it looked as though he were being sexually excited by a girl, but in checking this out it was not the girl but the visualization of her underwear with himself in the place of the girl. It was he with the beautiful shape dancing on the floor. This was checked out in relation to several incidents, and in every case confirmed.

He volunteered rather proudly that he had intercourse with women some thirty-five or forty times since he was eighteen. Soon after going into the Service he was in one of the islands, was drinking some and was propositioned by a girl. He went along with her to a room where he described himself as clumsy and not knowing what to do; the girl had to show him. He continued to have sexual intercourse, always with prostitutes or some similar person, as often as he had an opportunity while in the Service. He describes the sexual experiences with prostitutes as very enjoyable, much better than masturbation with the aid of women's underwear. He said that he never had any particular regret about the experiences; he was seemingly glad of the fact that he did have normal sexual desires.

When asked about dreams he said that most of them were "solid" dreams that had nothing to do with sex, but quickly volunteered a sexual dream which is repetitive. There are two people but they are not very clear. He sees himself in the situation trying on female garments. The two people there have no sex relations and he is not sure whether they are men or women. The dream ends with his having a wet dream. When asked to tell of one of his "solid" dreams which had nothing to do with sex he told of a recent one. He was in an arena where there was some sort of sporting activity. There were many girls, Mexican or Spanish dancers. He went up to one, talked to her and put his arm around her and they went for a trolley ride together.

Plans for the future. During high school he wanted to go to college but this didn't happen. He likes to write short stories but has never mailed one. He did have some dreams about being a journalist of some sort but believes that if he were to get married now he would go on working as a clerk-typist where he is.

Alcohol. He carefully avoided drinking until he got in the Service, then drank, mostly beer, almost every night. Only four or five times was he drunk and then he always knew what was going on; was afraid to get too drunk lest he talk and give away his secret. Yet drinking seemed to let the sexual ideas come into consciousness more freely than otherwise. Says he is not drinking now.

After repeated checkouts it still seemed that the most difficult period of this man's life began about three weeks ago. He panicked after finding himself moving rapidly toward marriage, but having lost all ability to respond sexually to his girl friend. He thought of running away but then realized he had been struggling with this for ten years and had to face up. It was not pressed but there was little evidence of concern about suicide at that time. Nor was there indication of hallucinatory experiences. He did indicate that he had not eaten a wholesome meal in two weeks, sleeps fitfully, waking up almost as soon as he drops off to sleep. Obviously he has lost weight and is under a great load of tension.

His own statements were used to pin down the fact that he should postpone the marriage while seeking help. When asked if he knew that postponing the marriage would mean that he lost the girl, would he proceed with therapy anyway, he replied, "Definitely. I've struggled with this long enough and cannot handle it. I've got to have help." It was suggested that he need not tell her the nature of the problem unless he wished. To his concern about what the family should be told, it was suggested that the fact of his deciding with the therapist that he had problems was sufficient. It was agreed that he would postpone the marriage, and not leave here struggling with a decision about it. When asked to give his ideas of what it would take to help him, he explained, "There is no trap door through which this can be dropped." He thinks a lot of things could be explained to him, why and what they mean, but mostly he guesses it would have to be talking it out. He asked how long, and this was turned back to him. He hesitated and then guessed "at *least* a year." This was re-enforced, and it was suggested that he not even think about a marriage date at the present time.

As the interview was closing he said that there was something he must tell before he left. About three months ago he stopped at a filling station late at night. A guy came running out of a theatre with other men in chase. There was a lot of confusion and he learned that the man had been 'doing something to a little girl.' His first reaction was one of sympathy with the man and then the idea hit him full force: "What if I should do that?" Since then each time he sees a little girl the fear hits him. Later he modified this to say that if he spent four or five hours with his little niece, the idea might occur to him only once and he would quickly shove it aside. He said it is not a desire to do anything to a little girl, but a fear that he might. This idea hits him sometimes when he is driving along in a car. He was assured that there would also be help with this kind of problem.

A thorough diagnostic study and therapeutic plan was followed by three years of individual psychotherapy, the last six months of which included pre-marital counseling as he related to another woman whom he subsequently married.

B. OTHER NEEDS FOR PSYCHOTHERAPY

It is commonly agreed that every known personality problem walks in under the guise of "we need marriage counseling." These people may feel that marriage counseling carries less onus, or maybe they can admit only the symptom, not the cause of the discomfort which may reside in their own personality. To some extent this is true of pre-marital counseling requests also. It is well to educate the public to the significance of pre-marital counseling as a positive investment in the life of a couple together, but the counselor must at the same time be alert to the underlying personality problems which "seek" solution via marriage and preparation for marriage. A careful diagnosis at this time often leads to the recommendation of individual psychotherapy both to resolve problems and to reactivate personal growth. Some engagements end when one or both begin treatment, but others continue. Just as marital interaction can be utilized to ferret out and highlight behavior and personality dynamics, the engaged relationship may provide both the motivation and the anxiety that makes treatment necessary enough to overcome resistance. Later, when the value of psychotherapy has become clear, the person may continue whether or not the engagement survives. Many former clients have reported that their individual psychotherapy proved to be at the same time pre-marital counseling for marriage at a later date, even if to another individual than the one with whom help was sought initially.

Chapter 7

BEGINNING A NEW FAMILY

The pre-marital counselor must be oriented to the basic knowledge in the many areas discussed in Chapters 9-12—psychology and psychotherapy, human development, religion, socio-cultural influences, family relations, genetics, family law, medicine, sexology and economics. Keeping informed in so many areas is a constant and life-long process of study. Even so, one cannot be expert in everything. The counselor should cultivate a working relationship with resource people who are competent in each of the professional areas in which his own abilities are limited by training or by personality factors. Perhaps an organization of this content around an anticipated new family unit will make it more accessible for both counselor and couple. The following topics seem most pertinent to the average couple: the wedding and honeymoon; love, sex and children; making a home; attitudes toward elders; family break-up and remarriage. Because of its interest and significance to the engaged couple a separate chapter is devoted to the pre-marital medical examination.

A. THE WEDDING AND THE HONEYMOON

I. The Wedding

The counselor may not feel that detailed plans for the wedding are important enough to discuss in counseling sessions unless a specific problem arises. However, enough tension producing problems center around the wedding plans, particularly as the date approaches, to make this area almost a miniature moving picture of the future marital relationship. It is all there —individual personality dynamics, the relationship between the two persons, the impingement of external factors like finances and job, the expectations of relatives and friends, and the individually and jointly held attitudes toward each of these components. By working out the many kinds of feelings clustering around the wedding plans and the ceremony, almost every facet of life will be brought into focus. Therein lies an opportunity to assist them in understanding and reorganizing, where indicated, individual perspectives. Some, not all by any means, of the "I" and "mine" must become "we" and "ours."

Parents and friends can be so persistent that the young couple may need a good deal of support in making this their own wedding, based primarily on their own wishes. Knowing the tendency of some parents to splurge, exhibit, and exploit the wedding, adding to the strain and tension for the couple, the counselor may suggest a few guiding principles to help in sorting out what is most significant when a formal wedding is planned. They may want to use these principles with parents, the officiating clergyman, and caterers to guarantee a more relaxed and enjoyable wedding. They are:

Neither the parental family nor the new family should be left destitute by the cost. If the wedding is to be a religious rite, then an atmosphere of joyful worship should be created and maintained. If it is to be a legal procedure only, this question may not arise. Elaborate trappings and numbers of attendants should not be permitted to detract from the bride and groom, nor from the vows. Decorations should be simple and dignified rather than abundant and detracting. Receptions and parties before and after the wedding should be kept to a minimum which will not tire the couple nor cause undue tenseness. The couple should participate verbally in vows which have been made meaningful to them. They have a right to refuse to resist the wear and tear of family and friends who want to run the show.

Some counselors have used the marriage vows as the basis of meaningful discussions in pre-marital counseling. The traditional aspects of the vows may seem to collide with some of the modern concepts of marriage which the couple wish to incorporate into their relationship. It isn't healthy to take vows with reservation, as when one feels that he has to edit or omit parts of them from his acceptance while committing himself otherwise. The pastoral counselor will have greater opportunity to utilize marriage vows for counseling, but it is available material for any counselor.

There is something unique about each couple which well might be incorporated into the wedding vows, although the guests would be unaware of its deeper significance. One couple, finding they disagreed about parts of the traditional vows, and agreeing that they didn't like other parts, worked intensely at this matter for a while. Then they asked their counselor to help them re-write the vows in terms of a democratic marriage, within a liberal Christian tradition, and in the light of their own process of preparing for a new self-determined family. Although this would be too much attention to details for many couples, it is illustrative of the wealth of meaningful content which can be included in a wedding ceremony. In addition to the obvious and the covert meaning for the couple, it served an educative function for relatives who might thereby grant uniqueness to this relationship. Here, then, is their wedding ceremony.

Minister to the Audience:—

Friends, you have been invited to share the joy of a couple who have chosen each other as husband and wife. According to the Christian principle that for this purpose a man and woman shall leave their parental families and begin on their own, they desire to establish a new family.

They love each other, but mature judgment tells them that love alone is not enough; that it must have an understanding environment in which to grow. Out of this exploration has come the realization of amazing similarities of personality traits, likes and dislikes, and an array of mutual interests.

Also, differences have been revealed, but they accept these as assets, giving spice and variety to their relationship. It fits well into their feeling that individuality should be maintained, as well as union established, in the marriage relationship. It is in accord with their belief that husband and wife are equal and share alike in all the responsibilities of married living.

Getting to know each other has involved coming to an understanding of family backgrounds and experiences, friends, social, and educational interests. Although of the same religious denomination, they have felt it wise to explore religious beliefs with a view toward continued growth and development of their faith.

Attitudes toward work and finances have been discussed, and plans made for the future that will promote security and at the same time be conducive to family living.

Knowing that it represents a vital part of husband-wife relationships, these two have studied the role of sex in human life, and have formulated an ethic as a guide for the future. They see sexual energy as a gift from God, a basic part of human nature, to be accepted gratefully and used for purposes in harmony with His will, in keeping with the best interests of mankind. They see sexual feeling as an important part of the total emotional development, a powerful stimulus toward the assumption of adult responsibilities of loving and of caring for a family. It affords an opportunity to learn how to have one's own needs for affection and love met and to meet those of the mate.

Sex expression within a happy marriage is a source of health for the entire person. The emotional overtones of adult love, the giving and receiving of love, flavor all of life.

This couple know that when they have reached a certain stage in their development and efficiency as partners, lovers, and homemakers, there will emerge a natural craving for the fulfillment of their love in children. They believe that the conception of a child at the height of love, and caring for it until it is born and afterward can be the ultimate in creativity on the human plane.

Minister to the Couple:—

You have come to the beginning of life's most difficult, and yet most thrilling adventure, the establishment of a permanent relationship to one person. It is a relationship in which the love of God can best express itself to each of you, and through you to others.

You will want it to be a stable, and yet ever-changing relationship, in which your love can spring forth, mature, flower, and bear its fruit. A good pattern for that love is given in I Corinthians 13: "Love is patient and kind, love is not jealous or boastful, is not arrogant or rude. Love does not insist on its own way, is not irritable or resentful, it does not rejoice at wrong but rejoices in the right. Love bears all things, believes all things, hopes all things, endures all things. Love never ends—Faith, Hope and Love abide, but the greatest of these is Love."

*   *   *   *   *

.............., in the spirit of such love as this, desiring to establish a home where you can learn to meet her needs for affection and love, and have your own needs met, and where children can grow in calm security, we understand that you have chosen .... to be your wife and the mother of your children.

He answers: That is true.

................., in the spirit of this love, desiring to establish a home where you can learn to meet his needs for affection and love, and have your own needs met, and where children can grow in peace and security, we understand that you have chosen .... to be your husband, and the father of your children.

She answers: That is true.

Minister (receiving ring from best man) says: You will now make your vows.

He (turning to her) says: ...., just as I am, and as I hope to become, I offer myself to you as a husband whose love will try to be tender, patient, thoughtful, and understanding, through all the experiences of our life.

(He pauses and receives ring from minister) As a token of my faith in your love for me, as a sign of our mutual hope of bringing to each other continued happiness, I give you this ring (places ring) and pledge you my love and devotion forever.

(Minister receives ring from matron-of-honor)

She (turning to him) says: ...., in keeping with that spiritual union which already we have experienced, I accept your ring, and, I accept you as my husband. . . . I present myself as your wife, promising a love that will be tender, patient, thoughtful, and understanding, through all the days of our life together.

(She pauses and receives ring from minister) I should like to give you a ring also, in the assurance that our love springs from, and shall be guided by, the Love Eternal. *(places ring as she speaks.)*

* * * * *

(The couple kneel before the altar, and the audience bows)

Minister says: Inasmuch as .... and ...., before God and these witnesses, have dedicated themselves to the establishing of a home, I declare that, will all the responsibilities and privileges attend-

ing, they are husband and wife, united in their love for each other, in their love for God, and in His love for them.

* * * * *

Minister prays: Our God, these are your people, and the home hereby established is their home under your guidance. Their first act as husband and wife is to kneel here in worship of the Eternal Love out of which their love for each other was conceived. We thank you for the assurance that you accept their love and their home, and that you will grant your continued blessings throughout their lives together. Make them and their home mediums whereby your love can reach others, even as it reaches them. Amen.

II. The Honeymoon

Honeymoon plans are made more exciting by sharing, and yet the counselor and the minister are about the only persons in whom the couple dare confide. They need suggestions for preventing tension and tiredness. By letting them tell him about it the counselor can help them relax and make wiser decisions. Over and above much of loving and sex, what do they hope to accomplish on the honeymoon? The love-making aspects will be more meaningful and less strenuous if seen as part of a quiet vacation period, set aside for the general purpose of broadening the base of understanding and interaction, of crystalizing plans for the immediate future, and to attain initial sexual adjustment.

If dream castles are too tall, the honeymoon all too often becomes a bad memory. Counseling may help them know that initial experiences of living in such close contact can cause friction and disappointments, but that when faced together this can further their developing relationship. They should know that fatigue and tension are the greatest barriers to successful sex experiences. It is just as important to know that failures or misunderstanding on the honeymoon need not have lasting traumatic influence.

Some couples would like to eliminate the honeymoon or make it very short. It is well to support them in this decision if their reasons are sound. Some people adjust best if they go about daily routines from the beginning of marriage. Of course, many others make creative use of a relaxed vacation at the beginning of their married life.

B. LOVE, SEX, AND CHILDREN

I. Love and Sex

Much has been said about the part played in modern family life by the concept of "romantic love," the Hollywood version of romance, as it has become the ideal of the average high school and college youth. There is little doubt about the destructive influence of the sort of "delicious insanity" which popularly is called love. There is reason for special concern when the inference is made that once this bloom of romance has faded there is nothing left in a marriage.

On the other hand, modern families are trying to make something positive and healthy out of the concept of love. One of the weaknesses of much earlier family life in America was represented in the philosophy that it was unladylike to be romantic or unmanly to be sweet and tender. Many adults of today find it difficult to relate warmly to their spouses, or to their children and friends, because they were trained to conceal honest emotions. Superficial as it may be, the modern concept of romantic love with its expressions of affection, at least on the physical level, has served to highlight the value of love in a family life. Of course many have confused love and passion, mistaking the whole for the part. On the other hand, there are young men and women who, through getting a little taste of love and affection, in both its giving and receiving, have continued to search for and find a more complete, mature, and creative love relationship. They create a new environment in which their children can grow, mature, feel secure and move into adulthood able to give and receive affection. This ability is the prime requirement for healthy family living. The degree to which many young people are attaining it, with a minimum of professional help at crucial periods, is one of the brightest spots in today's culture.

Love of this deeper variety is desirable as a basic, ever-present flavoring influence in the home.[1] At the same time marriage becomes an opportunity for the growth of love, since abiding love is not born fullgrown. It is a product of constant, thoughtful effort, and years of cooperative enjoyment and suffering. It is characterized by patience, restraint, and sacrificial devotion to mutual interests and values. Such love emanates spontaneously from one who has been well loved and feels lovable. "Love," says Buber, "is not the enjoyment of a wonderful emotion, nor even the ecstasy of a Tristan and Isolde, but the responsibility of an I for a Thou." But even the responsibility,

[1] See West, Jessamyn, *Love Is Not What You Think*. New York, Harcourt, Brace and Co., 1959,

if love is genuine, comes naturally, not as an unpleasant duty assumed. No matter how it is experienced as an extension of the self, love calls for courageous work if it is to grow and to permeate the practicalities of everyday living. In this connection, West [2] has written:

"Every man is a hero far from the bayonet; EVERY woman a heroine of love until she starts practicing the arduous craft—particularly with a man with whom she has fallen in love. . . Love is never the measure of the person loved, but of the person loving."

To be comfortably human is to be loving, and again, as West says:

"To be happy is to be given the opportunity to express that love. To be blessed is to have love returned. Love is not what you think. It does what mind cannot do, it goes where mind cannot follow. Its nature is transcendental and when we love we at once transcend ourselves and are most ourselves."

Sex becomes both a means of expression and a result of such love between a husband and wife. Hopefully, each is a unified whole capable of relating as loving sexual beings. But love and sex have been so completely separated through the years of growth and experiences for some youth, that major difficulty arises in efforts to express them together with one person. The average young man and woman either lack sufficient information in the sexual expression of love, or have wholesome attitudes jumbled with a hodge-podge of misinformation, fears, and inhibitions that impede spontaneous sexuality. Bringing about clarification and reintegration of attitudes and feelings in the areas of sex and love can be one of the major functions of pre-marital counseling.

One of the best books to be used with a couple, in that it both provides valuable information and sets a holistic frame of reference for sex and love, is Calderone's *Release From Sexual Tensions*.[3] But there is no substitute for detailed discussions of the intricacies of sex and love, both with each other and in the accepting environment of pre-marital counseling.

Increasingly modern youth are insisting upon the right to plan their families, which means that contraception becomes an important item at the time of marriage. Because of its importance a separate chapter has been devoted to sexual preparation for marriage.

[2] *Ibid.*, pp. 17, 38.
[3] Calderone, Mary S., *Release From Sexual Tensions*. New York: Random House, 1961.

II. Children

A couple are not ready for marriage until the process of working through their feelings about children is well under way, and until tentative plans are made as to when, how many, and how their children are to be reared. The procreation and rearing of children must be an integral part of family living; neither the one and only reason for, nor merely a by-product of, marriage.

When and How Many? The number of children a couple have will be affected by many factors, including: fertility, age at marriage, financial status, living conditions, education anticipated for children, expectations of their social and religious groups, health of the wife, degree of adjustment in marriage, and chance.

Readiness for parenthood varies from couple to couple, but usually one or two years can be used well for becoming adjusted to each other. By that time a mature couple who have found their married life growing in meaningfulness probably will begin to long for fulfillment in parenthood. Undue prolongation of the time of conception may tend to close the family to "outsiders," as life becomes so settled that the couple fear the disturbing influence of a baby. A couple may want to have all their children early in order to free the wife earlier for resumption, at least part time, of the career for which she prepared. In fact, for a variety of reasons, statistics indicate that the average first marriage bride today adds up like this:

Married at 19, when she has already been employed outside the home, to a man about 20. She has her three plus children by the time she is 25. When she is 30 the youngest child is in school part of the day and she returns to part time employment.

About one couple in ten find it impossible to conceive a child. This usually is an unknown quantity as marriage plans are being made. Individuals who, not wanting children, have been surgically sterilized, or who know themselves to be sterile for other reasons, may conceal the fact lest the mate be offended. Children by previous mates, married or unmarried, likewise may be a difficult but nonetheless vital subject for discussion. The counselor may have to take the initiative in uncovering some of these hard-to-discuss facts.

American culture has undergone quite a cyclic change in *attitudes toward children.* In the early days of factory exploitation of child labor children were a distinct financial asset, just as in the earlier farm economy. Child labor laws were passed because of mixed motives of protecting the labor market for adults and genuine desire to protect children, and as a result children became a financial liability. Another result was the overprotection of older youth, barring them from employment which could be a primary factor in their growing up to be responsible citizens, and therefore contributing to delinquency.

All of this change has made little difference in the birthrate of the laboring population, but several decades saw the decline of middle class birthrates, especially among the college educated group, made possible by more available contraceptive assistance. Recently the birthrate among the college educated has been swinging upward again. Being able to plan children when they are desired is one of the greatest steps in the self-realization of a family.

It is interesting to note other historical transitions in the attitudes of parents toward children. Many young people today are preparing as specifically for parenthood as they once worked for a college degree or a career. From the earlier attitudes—"children ought to be seen and not heard" to "eat in the kitchen and not bother adults," "little animals to be trained" rather than individuals in their own right—the pendulum swung to such an extreme that the little *homo sapien* was placed upon a throne and mother and dad bowed more than the proverbial three times in his direction. This focusing upon the child, making him the very center of family life, the hub around which everything revolved, inevitably produced great anxiety by intensifying the resentment parents felt about having their own lives molded and shaped completely around children.

Among the greatest evidences of health in modern families are the tendencies toward self-reliance and self-realization. This may be conceived of as self-realization of individuals within family units, or, when focusing upon the family unit itself, in terms of self-realization and self-fulfillment of the family. A growing number of these parents are showing their adequacy in the way they utilize the "experts" in child rearing and family guidance. One of the most disturbing factors in family life in the last decade or two was the impression left by popular media and some more dignified educational efforts that only the experts knew how to rear children. To be fair, it must be said that most of the real authorities in the field made no such claims, but their popular interpreters left the impression that parents were a "bunch of ignorami" who could only carry out the prescriptions of a doctor of child development. The end result was a generation of parents with intensive inadequacy feelings, contributing to an environment of uncertainty, insecurity, and anxiety in which the child grew and developed, an environment in which he "caught" anxiety much as he might catch the measles.

Under the aegis of this philosophy, many individuals related to the family came to feel as inadequate as did the parents. One can easily sketch the hierarchy of inadequacy feelings of those days. Parents felt inadequate in the face of teachers; teachers and ministers felt inadequate in the face of psychologists and educational specialists; psychologists and educators before psychiatrists; and psychiatrists in contrast to psychoanalysts; and an occasional psychoanalyst in relation to God. Several generations of children have been emotionally upset as parents tried earnestly to carry out what they thought to be the instructions of one and then another expert. Their children learned the hard way that this does not work; that there is no such thing as a textbook which will guide in the total development of a young personality.

This has left many parents afloat, but gradually some are getting their heads above the water. Taking authority off the pedestal makes for a healthier use of professional assistance. Both professionals and parents are beginning to realize that each child brings with him his own built-in calendar of development; that he is his own best textbook. This permits more intelligent use of assistance in discovering principles and in learning to "read" the particular child, with parents knowing full well that they must work out the application of such principles within their own family context. This rediscovery of resources within themselves as parents is one of the greatest developments of present day family life.

Recently there has been a revival of the belief that parents have rights too. This renewed emphasis on equal rights of every individual within the family situation is to be encouraged. Waller and Hill [4] have emphasized the reciprocity of benefits in the parent-child relationship, and this is becoming evident in many families. There is mutuality of benefit in meeting the basic needs for response, recognition, and belongingness; of opportunities to learn in the laboratory of daily living about human nature and social relationships as life is seen in the raw. Parent and child have the opportunity to gain new insight into life processes as they look at life through the eyes of the other generation. There is opportunity to gain insight into self in the intimacy of home with the frankness of other loved ones as a mirror. The reality and the symbols of authority become actualized in parent and child as one serves as a symbol and agent of authority and the other learns to relate to and utilize this authority, these symbols, and these persons. Parents and children develop tools of communication as

[4] Waller, Willard, *The Family, A Dynamic Interpretation*. Revised by Reuben Hill. New York: Dryden Press, 1951.

children pursue the great process of discovery and parents learn how to become both teachers and fellow learners. Parents tend to develop habits, to fall into ruts; but children, by constantly disturbing the status quo, are a stimulus to continued growth and development. Parents are learning to make home a relief from the shallowness, the brashness, the callousness, and the cruelty of everyday life in the community at large; a "cushioned retreat" for growing, striving children.

Some of the older generation are concerned about the noisy, rowdy families of today, and yet many of these families have learned to make a place where one can "feel the way he feels" and, within certain limits, "be what he is." Consciously or unconsciously these families have hit upon a great truth, one of the tenets of clinical practice, that only when one can express in some form his bad feelings can he be free to give full and spontaneous vent to his good feelings.

Even such self-actualizing families must keep one ear to the ground of social expectations, but they dare to experiment, to live, to be, to create. This is evidenced in the great variety of family life seen today. Those who expect one kind of family life to emerge from the present boiling pot of human emotions and family dynamics are in for disappointment, for tomorrow's family will have as its outstanding characteristics uniqueness and differentness. American family life will continue to produce a variety of individuals, a variety of personalities, which will in turn produce an endless variety of family life. One way of looking at this is to say "what a hodgepodge!" And yet, the multi-faceted social milieu of today and tomorrow calls for just this variety of family life and for the variety of individuals produced by these families. To the degree to which families have the courage and the security, the self-acceptance, which enables them to be true to themselves, to that degree will they grow a creative family life.

Some leaders decry the fact that the modern home is so loosely constructed, that there is a dangerous lack of family unity. This lack of close identity with parents is a disturbing factor in the make-up of many individuals. On the other hand, it cuts down on the previous tendency, particularly in middle-class America, to project lost ambitions upon the child. It waters down the influence upon the child of a disturbed family member. The simple expedient of having the child exposed to many persons to the same degree as with the father and the mother gives greater selectivity of objects of identification, both personal and occupational. As such, the loosely constructed family unit may be more conducive to self-determination and self-affirmation than the older, tightly knit family system. To be sure, many children cannot bridge the gap between the lack of identification within the family unit and the opportunities for it outside. But many do; particularly those who in their early years have experienced an intensive respect for their individuality and the kind of warm and accepting environment which is conducive to the development of inner security. Parents who have created a healthy environment for their children early in life tend to evidence a degree of comfort as these children in turn work out against them the kinds of feelings inherent in the growing-up process.

Without guidance, seldom will the engaged couple go to the trouble of working out thoroughly plans for *rearing their children* in advance of the wedding. The counselor can help each analyze the way he was reared, and see that this is discussed thoroughly with the fiance with a view toward agreement before a child is born. If one of the couple has been married before, it can be equally important to work through those experiences. Children by a former marriage call for extra efforts at accepting the past and planning for the future.

Too many couples get married and then become parents merely as a by-product of sex. Each begins reacting toward the child in the way in which he was reared, or, in the case of rebellion against parental examples, just the opposite. What happens to the child if these parental patterns are different? The most destructive force in the life of a child is lack of love; but second to it, and closely related in the mind of the child, is basic and continuous inconsistency.[5]

Development of Values. One of the most meaningful ways of helping a young couple review and compare the influences of their own families upon themselves, and at the same time anticipate their influences upon children yet to be born, is provided by this chart from Patty and Johnson. It focuses upon the evolution of values within the family setting at particular life periods.[6]

[5] Baruch, Dorothy, *New Ways in Discipline; You and Your Child Today.* New York: Whittlesey House, 1959; Bossard, James H. S., *Parent and Child.* Philadelphia: University of Pennsylvania Press, 1953; Brody, Sylvia, *Patterns of Mothering; Material Influence During Infancy.* New York: International Universities Press, 1956; Foote, Nelson N., and Cottrell, Leonard S., Jr., *Identity and Interpersonal Competence: A New Direction in Family Research.* Chicago: University of Chicago Press, 1955.

[6] Extract from *Personality and Adjustment* by William L. Patty and Louise Snyder Johnson, New York: McGraw-Hill Book Company, Inc., 1953. Pp. 163, 164, 165, quoted by permission of the publisher.

LIFE PERIODS AND VALUE STAGES

Life Period	Start of core values in affection-security
Early infancy (parturition to toddling)	Mouth-centered sensitiveness Interest-excitement versus frustration-rage Exteroceptor-enteroceptor balance
Late infancy (toddling to walking)	Affection-security more varied and active Auditory-visual-tactual sensations added to mouth sensitiveness Self-concept beginning to organize newly assimilated experiences around core values Playmates start second-level sociocultural values Awareness of boy-girl bodily differences; comparison with self as a standard Toilet training and self-feeding establish core values related to "cleanliness" and "full acceptance" Verbal symbols indistinguishable from objects
Early childhood (about age three to five, inclusive)	Affection-security now largely reassured through experimentally independent actions and temporary regressions to "nest situation" Self-concept begins to show contrast between "self" and "other" Awareness of bodily differences leads into start of male or female role values Exploratory abilities result in rapid increase in contacts with material and socio-cultural worlds Verbal symbols become moderately distinct from referents, but with limited dependability.
Late childhood (about age five to eight, inclusive)	Affection-security now largely assumed, but requires occasional verification Self-concept now orienting to sociocultural at "pal" level, experimenting with privacy Self-other distinction fairly clear Boy-girl differences now central values; some heterosexual explorations Verbal symbols becoming distinct from referent objects in imaginative sense also

Early adolescence (about age eight to thirteen, inclusive)	Affection-security now mostly "approval"
	Self-concept now in "gang" stage, with need to be different from earlier behavior standards and reactions to authority
	Self-other distinction sharp, sometimes painful and hidden by "fads"; your adult world versus our world versus baby things
	Boy-girl differences rapidly becoming man-woman differences, although awkwardly
	Verbal symbols now gain abstractness, making possible start of thought or worry about religion, fair practice standards, morals
	New emotional experiences puzzling if not prepared for by earlier knowledge
Late adolescence (about age fourteen to seventeen, inclusive)	Affection-security now a mixture of approval and adult love, with many habit regressions or infantilisms
	Self-concept now adding adult appearance and freedom values, with some evidence of self-responsibility
	Self-other distinction now almost complete, applied to parents also
	Boy-girl differences now man-woman relationships but with limited scope, experimental
	Verbal symbols adequate to most abstract thinking, overgeneralization of ideals and heroes
	Adult emotional experiences such as man-woman love, parental love, adult love of own parents beginning to take form
Youth (about age eighteen to twenty-two, inclusive)	Affection-security now centered in career plans or ambitions, with man-woman love meshing into plans
	Self-concept now includes vocation and social mannerisms, standards of comparative ability, secondary group affiliations, and some philosophy of life
	Man-woman relationships adult except for economic and parental aspects
	Verbal symbols now losing some of the tendency

to be over-generalized, but skill in dealing with abstractions still increasing through usage

Adult emotional experiences achieve more definite form, although still somewhat experimental

Early adulthood (about age twenty-three to twenty-seven, inclusive)

Affection-security now centers in husband-wife relationships, with home maintenance, career advancement, social acceptability as contributors

Self-concept integrates with affection-security processes

Man-woman relationships become adult as self-concept incorporates spouse and offspring into itself. Love as giving as well as receiving becomes the specific "love emotion"

Verbal facility increases chiefly through continued increase of alertness—with improved abstract thinking

Late adulthood (about age twenty-eight to climacteric)

Apparently little change in values listed above, except for some loss of alertness and compensation through greater background of experience. Security factors of career emphasize more than "toehold" factors

Climacteric (about age forty to sixty, but not well defined)

Somatic changes, appearance of organic weaknesses not noticed earlier; psychological problem of change of family pattern from parenthood to grandparenthood, loss of ambition due to limitations on future progress, acceptance of self as is rather than as expected to be in the future; facing of old age and stepping aside for youth to progress

C. THE FAMILY LIFE CYCLE

By the time an engaged couple have gone this far in discussing children, the relevance of a look at the total family life cycle will seem quite in order. This concept of family life is discussed in detail in Chapter 9.[7]

[7] Glick, Paul C. "The Life Cycle of the Family," *Marriage and Family Living.* XVII, 1, 1955; Duvall, Evelyn Mills, *Family Development*, Chicago: J. B. Lippincott, 1957. pp. 5-21; See also discussion in Chapter 2.

I. Rites of Passage

How do children become adults in this culture? More primitive cultures
have arranged for quite dramatic transitions from childhood to the new
state of adulthood. But modern culture has been all too prone to prolong
the no-man's land of adolescence well into the twenties or even thirties for
many youth. There is little clarity in how a boy becomes a man or a girl
a woman. In many cases the only way to get parents to concede adult status
is to get married. This is no small factor in many unwise marriages.

In examining their own relationships to parental figures the young couple
have an opportunity to facilitate their own passage to adult status, all the
while remaking the groundwork for their own later role as parents of maturing youth. Central to this concern will be a consideration of the responsibilities of maturity.

II. Relation to the Old Family

The socio-cultural and family life data outlined in Chapter 9 will provide
additional resources for the study of the family life cycle idea, but counseling must assist the couple in both specific and general understanding of
their own two parental families.

The two sets of parents exerted the initial and the most prolonged influence upon the development of these two personalities, and thus will play
the background music for this new duet in life. For each of the couple to
understand himself and the mate, it is necessary that each understand his
parents and his reactions to them. Also significant is an understanding of
other members of the parental families—siblings, grandparents, and others
—with emphasis upon relationships. Particularly crucial will be differences
in standards of living, dominance-submission patterns, systems of discipline,
and temperament between the two parental families, along with aspirations
of the couple. More important than any of the facts is how each feels about
these many elements in the make-up of the prospective mate's family and
about the mate's current aspirations. Counseling can only begin the process
if they have not discussed it previously, but at least they can be given an
impetus toward continuing these discussions on into marriage.

They must know that making changes in the parental family is not the
purpose, but, rather, increasing their own understanding and changing their
own feelings about the facts, along with seeing that the older families are
not given a chance to interfere unduly in this marriage. This calls for the
couple being mature enough, or rapidly becoming so, to live a self-sufficient
life. Perhaps they do not see that in this culture all the conveniences of liv-

ing with relatives may be more than out-weighed by the necessity of privacy in developing intimate interactions, by the tendency of well-meaning relatives to interfere, and by the need to learn to depend upon and develop their own judgment and resources as a new family. Often a little distance will facilitate emotional separation from parents, along with the necessary readjustment. A happy solution for many young couples is to live far enough away from relatives to avoid keeping everyone in on everyone's business, yet close enough to allow for visits and sharing the more positive experiences of life. In cases of greater emotional dependency, psychotherapy alone, not distance, will make it possible for youth to live an independent life.

Counseling can challenge the couple to continue their total development as individuals and as a married pair. They must learn to take off rose-colored glasses and see each other as real persons. They have come a long way from total dependence upon parents to a stage of independence of the parents and must live up to this responsibility. It may be that until now they have thought of life primarily as receiving; now they are learning to make giving equally important as the home is established. Too close dependence upon parents can hinder this vital process.

Although some parents may be opposed to the independence of their married youth in the beginning, most of them come to respect the self-sufficient, unencumbered adult son or daughter much more than the emotionally crippled child who remains dependent upon the parental home. Nonetheless, much parental selfishness and possessiveness is camouflaged by professed love and over-protectiveness toward young adults. It may become important in extreme cases for the counselor to intervene with possessive parents, helping father and mother see that "for this cause came they forth from the womb."

Sometimes the problem of the clinging parent is complicated by the need of youth to be dependent upon parents after marriage. A good approach here is to stress with the young person, perhaps also with the parents, the need of the parents to be on their own now, so that they may begin to rediscover each other after years of centering attention about their child. The parents should not have the burden of rearing another group of children, but rather should be free to develop other interests which will renew their zeal for life and make subsequent years happier for themselves. Assisting parents in their "empty nest" stage is an exercise in mature living now, as well as preparation for this critical facet of the couple's own family life cycle when it comes.

III.   Attitudes Toward Elders

Concurrent with the tendency to over-dependence in this culture, is a rebellious separation from the value systems of elders. Independence and self-adequacy does not necessitate the rejection of parents and elderly relatives. In fact, however, one of the characteristics of American family life has been the increasing rejection of elderly parents and grandparents. As life expectancy has risen, the displaced older person has become a natural as well as a family problem. Resistance to having elderly parents in the home is made up of many factors, including finances, housing, and desire for independence. However, what seems to be the most significant factor has hardly been mentioned in the literature.

Americans are characterized by status climbing and other forms of self and family advancement. An analogy with the adolescent may help to clarify the struggle. The adolescent must face himself, perhaps even rebel against his parents and their protective love, if he is to become a self-sufficient adult. If the youth is not yet the man he wants to be, close association with the parent activates the dependency needs that would hold him back. Therefore, he is more comfortable if left largely on his own. Similarly, generations of young Americans have aspired to a "higher" way of life than that experienced in their parental family. Part of this aspiration resulted from the striving for superiority and "success," sometimes neurotic in nature, taught in the culture. But an appreciable amount of it can be credited to inherent urges toward growth, health, and self-realization. Such growth—whether of an educational, social, financial, or value nature—is threatened by the tug of *status quo* and the guilt engendered in leaving the old way of life. Growth of a new way of life may be interpreted by the parents, and thus by the young person, as parental rejection. The old way is always there as a threat to the young adult. What if I don't make it? What if I slip back, take the easy way?

Having the old folk in the home can keep the past alive and become a major source of anxiety in the new way of life. It threatens to activate dependency needs, to make conscious the resentment, guilt, and shame associated with moving into a way of life different from that of the parents. The young couple still have not succeeded in all their aspirations and hope to see these gained by their children, as well as seeing the present gains maintained. Having the grandparents near the children with their different grammar, manners, and values may be a distinct threat to these goals.

Family life in America has been at the adolescent stage in relation to parents and grandparents. In the meantime, many children have had to grow up without older people in their environment, cut off from much of the cultural heritage the presence of elderly people would have brought. These children miss something quite significant in their own development of values for all of life, including preparation for later maturity.

As adolescents mature, their attitudes toward parents tend to mellow and they become more accepting of the old folk. This is true to some degree with "adolescent families." Gradually some realize there is a place for older persons and re-admit them to the family circle, although sometimes this is only at the utilitarian level of baby-sitter. In a few generations there will be more homogeneity within wide blocks of American family population. Newcomers to social class levels will tend to level off, establish new sets of values and become secure therein. As the culture becomes more stable and social climbing a less compulsive drive, the important role of elders in the development of children will be rediscovered. In an encouraging number of families this transition has already occurred. The pre-marital counselor has a unique opportunity to help each couple in this vital process.

D. MAKING A HOME

Soon after marriage, usually prior to it, the new family must choose a location, a building, plan the financing, and create an "atmosphere" for the new home. This covers a wide variety of subjects to be considered in preparation for marriage. (See Chapter 5 for a demonstration of the use of similar material with actual engaged couples.)

I. A Place to Live

The couple may be quite realistic in their plans for a home; where they will be living; in an apartment or a house. Rent costs may determine this. But many couples overlook the cost of utilities and added furniture necessary to renting a complete house. The popular cry is that buying is cheaper than renting, but hidden costs such as insurance, taxes, and upkeep upset this dream for many. Winnick and Shilling [8] will be of value at this point. It is easy to waste money in indiscriminate buying of furniture before the couple are settled somewhat permanently, and before they are sure of changing tastes.

The home must be cared for. Will they share the chores, or is this to be considered "woman's work?" Many men who agree with the wife that she

[8] Winnick, Louis and Shilling, Ned, *American Housing and Its Use.* New York: John Wiley and Sons, 1957.

work to supplement the income are adamant against sharing in all phases of housekeeping.

II. Work, Finances and the Family

A reliable mark of maturity and of satisfactory vocational adjustment is the degree to which one gets pleasure from the actual doing of his job, rather than from the reward only. The healthy person gains major pleasure in productivity and creativity. A reasonable income is vital but that it should be earned under conditions favorable to wholesome family life is even more important. Husband and wife need each other, and children need to have two parents active in their lives.

The counselor will need to help the couple explore expected income and the total financial situation. Some ventilation of the feelings of each about work and money is quite essential since money carries many symbolic meanings.

Will the wife work, and how long? After the children are born? Do the parents subsidize the marriage and will this cause them to assume the right to direct the new family, or cause the young couple to feel obligated?

How is the money to be handled? Who is to be treasurer or business manager? Will they share each financial responsibility? Will a separate or joint bank account be used? Have they given ample attention to budgeting? Equal sharing in all planning and spending calls for the greatest maturity, and by necessity this may not be their plan if one cannot handle money wisely.

Have they faced the tendency of young couples to insist upon beginning at the same level of living as that in their parental home? This can be done, but usually only by way of installment buying, the distinctly American curse upon young families. They will need to see the dangers inherent in charge accounts, loans, and mortgages. Cash and carry can be rough but it is conducive to living within one's income. They will need to discuss and work through savings, responsibility to worthy causes, and insurance plans. Because of its actual and symbolic significance Chapter 10 deals with finances and life work in relation to family values in great detail.[9]

[9] Feldman, Frances L., *The Family In A Money World*. New York: Family Service Association of America. 1957; Black, Hillel, *Buy Now, Pay Later*. New York: Wm. Morrow and Co., 1961; *Money Management Booklets,* Household Finance Corporation, Prudential Plaza, Chicago 1, Illinois.

III. Religion

Religion can be a difficult subject for serious discussion for counselors as well as for clients. This accounts for its all too frequent omission from pre-marital counseling as practiced by non-clerical counselors.

If the couple belong to different religious groups, it is wise to see clergymen of both faiths. Usually religious leaders make every effort to help clarify beliefs and practices, including inconsistencies between the two religions. But all too often the counselor hears: "We went to the priest and got the Catholic line; to the pastor and got the Baptist line; now we're more confused than ever." The counselor must help them become calm and relaxed enough to examine issues and make wise decisions. Religious differences can become a source of serious disturbance in a marriage, or they can be turned into an enriching element in family life. Even when the religious consultation has been adequate, the pre-marital counselor can help to integrate religious considerations into the total preparation for marriage. This includes careful examination of religious feelings, beliefs, questions and doubts. Among the most critical issues are the desirability of attending services, attitudes toward control of conception, rearing of children, and the interrelationship of religious and cultural backgrounds.

It is not the counselor's role to decide for them, but he can assist in examining all the factors, and then encourage them to work it over together until they feel sure of guiding principles. This may involve visiting each other's church, and even other churches. Sometimes it is easier and more satisfactory for both to change, choosing a third church, if they begin to feel at home there in the expression of their faith. Some sacrifice on the part of both usually is worthwhile in order to be united in their religious life, providing an integrated spiritual atmosphere for the home and the children. Many couples will decide to maintain their individual relationships to the church of their childhood, and put the emphasis upon learning to respect and appreciate their differences. If so, attitudes toward the religious guidance of their future children will need special attention. Whatever changes are indicated in religious affiliation and practice might well be actually put into operation prior to the wedding, or the course of action definitely agreed upon as a step immediately following marriage. Otherwise, the more resistive mate procrastinates and the "leaven" of life becomes a bone of contention.[10]

[10] Pike, James A., *If You Marry Outside Your Faith; Counsel on Mixed Marriages.* New York: Harper and Brothers, 1954; Bossard, James H. S. and Boll, Eleanor, *One Marriage, Two Faiths.* New York: Ronald Press, 1957; Lydon, R. J., *Catholic Teaching on Marriage and Divorce.* New York: Catholic Information Society.

Resolving interfaith problems is only one step in preparation for marriage and family living. Working out the beginnings of an effective personal faith, and relating these two faiths, is the heart of the process of spiritual readiness for family life. Only a faith and a value system wrought out through personal searching, trying, comparing, and experiencing can be an effective force in daily living.[11]

Getting to know and understand the parental family of each should have focused attention upon the particular religious emphases in both the healthy and disturbing features. Out of evaluating these should come some idea of changes which will facilitate spiritual growth for these two individuals and their new family. Introspection and talking it out by the couple are necessary in this process of arriving at a meaningful faith.

Religious ceremony or ritual in the family, centering around family devotions and the commemoration of special days, can become the means of instilling in children the concepts of religion held by the parents. These can be passed along either in a narrow, restricted fashion, or the process of growing values can be learned in a spontaneous, healthy manner. The religious atmosphere may be one of boredom, meaningless repetition, or domination by one member in an authoritarian way. This keeps hurtful, resentful, or other feelings of dissent from being expressed, thus making people ill and miserable. On the other hand, each of these functions can be participated in by the youngest to the oldest in a family, spontaneity can be encouraged and reality-facing can become basic in a healthy life flavored by a joyous faith.

The individual family unit becomes the means of passing on whatever is of value (and the destructive also) in a culture, a religion, a form of government, along with the process of valuing or growing values. It prepares the child for participation in (or withdrawal and isolation from) an ever-enlarging family, beginning with playmates, school mates, and extending to an array of friends and acquaintances. The role played in the greater human family will relate directly to one's role in his own family. Most religions place great emphasis upon families and, in turn, religion thrives best in the family and depends upon it for propagation to new generations. Either love and trust or hate and suspicion reach out from the family to the community, to the nation, and to the greater family of mankind.

Given the frustrations, irritations and hurts of modern life, religion may render a major service by helping an individual to accept his own imperfec-

[11] Rutledge, Aaron L. Perpetuation of Non-value. *Mental Hgyiene*. 43, 1, 1959. Pp. 64-70; Rutledge, Aaron. "Value and Psychotherapy" in *Marital Therapy*, Manuscript in preparation.

tions, which must come before he can really accept, forgive, or relate freely to another person. Religion can stimulate the self examination necessary to change and growth. The ideal of service based on a spontaneous love for people does much to guide and to integrate, to bring reverence for life, and to stimulate further growth of individuals. It challenges a family to make creative use of the tremendous potential of today's complicated life. It can guide in reconciling responsible living with all of the invitations to irresponsibility through high pressure advertising, installment buying and living beyond one's means, and the baiting of materialistic appetites to the detriment of other human values.

But what about the couple who are atheistic or humanistic in orientation rather than belonging to any organized religious group? A careful perusal of the principles found in the above discussion will apply equally as they work through the value systems treasured by their parents and by themselves as individuals. The counselor will find additional suggestions for guiding a couple in discussing religion in Chapter 10.[12]

E.   FAMILY BREAK-UP AND REMARRIAGE

With all of life's forces pressing toward marriage, family break-up may not be a very challenging topic for pre-marital discussion. To be honest, it can be threatening indeed. And still, it too is a part of the family life cycle.

Death is the greatest dissolver of marriages, and the one frequent cause of family break-up which is universal; yet, it is seldom discussed as such in pre-marital counseling. Little attention has been given in the literature to family break-up by death as a social problem, but it will be faced repeatedly by the counselor in terms of bereavement stress, loneliness, sexual maladjustment, problems with children, etc. One may not be ready to live freely until he is—individually and familially—prepared for death. Death comes sharply into focus for the counselor when the bereaved person comes to discuss remarriage.

The second major type of family break-up is that seen in *separation and divorce*. About one sixth to one fifth of the men and women who live an average life span are divorced at some time. This only partially portrays family break-up. Some authorities estimate that almost half of the couples who enter into a husband-wife relationship ultimately separate. Many

[12] Allport, Gordon W., *The Individual and His Religion; A Psychological Interpretation.* New York: Macmillan Co., 1950; Doniger, Simon (Editor), *Religion and Human Behavior.* New York: Association Press, 1954; Angyal, Andras, *Foundations for a Science of Personality.* New York: Commonwealth Fund, 1941; Bonthius, Robert H., *Christian Paths to Self-Acceptance.* New York: King's Crown Press, 1948.

others continue to live together in a state of open conflict or bored indifference.

The engaged couple will be particularly interested in working through feelings in this area if either of their parents were separated or divorced, although it can be a strenuous task. Other couples will need particular guidance here because one or both of them have been divorced. By reworking the previous marital experiences, whether their own or that of parents, including hangover feelings and problems around the divorce, the way is paved for positive preparation for a new marriage. The counselor must understand the factors causing divorce, and the effects upon the couple and their children. Remarriage has become a common phenomenon, and increasingly the divorced are seeking professional help before entering into another marriage. Each person must realize that he had a part in the earlier marital failure and that he has deep-seated reactions to the hurt involved which might affect a new marriage.

In spite of a high percentage of break-up of couples, Americans continue to become the most married people in the world. More couples are breaking up, but at the same time more people are being married than ever before in history. One way of looking at the broken home is that it finally comes apart at the seams when it no longer has meaning for the persons involved. Much of the literature focuses upon the unhealthy trends in personality which ensue in separation or divorce. These emphases are true to legal experience and daily work as a counselor would reinforce statistics along this line. But the marriage counselor needs to see in clear perspective the strengths in modern family living, for it is upon these that counseling must build.[13]

Overt conflict can be viewed symptomatically as evidence of deepseated maladjustment; but also it may be simply the sparks from the anvil of healthy experiences. The older way for respectable families was to stifle feelings, grin and bear it. Clinical experience underlines the destructiveness of personality for both adults and children inherent in such a method. The modern trend of bringing such conflicts to the surface where they can be dealt with is much more in keeping with the principles of mental health.

A large number of people seek separation or divorce for the simple reason that through the process of trial and error the marriage has not lived up to the high expectations with which they entered the relationship. The last few generations of people have been led by many efforts—including

[13] Rutledge, Aaron L., "Evidence of Strength in the Modern Family." *Journal of Home Economics.* 48, 5, 1956, pp. 323-326.

the press, radio and television, the theatre, and literature of all kinds, as well as the classroom and church—to expect more from marriage than has ever been expected in the history of man. Many of today's finest youth— including by any measurable standard, some of the most mature or maturing persons—find themselves so frustrated in a marriage which falls far below fulfilling the promises held up that they end the experience. The very health of some individuals leads them to break up an ill and seemingly hopeless relationship. This does not necessarily mean that goals, ideals and expectations should be lowered and preparation for marriage eliminated. It does mean that a much better job should be done of tailor-making the marital preparation for the particular youth or groups of youth. Young people must be helped not only to set goals in marriage, but in obtaining the know-how of attaining those goals.

The intensity of a mental illness portrays the negative, the symptoms, the liabilities of the personality, the hidden conflicts; yet at the same time it reveals something of the strength of the person as he grapples with conflicts and seeks integration on a higher level of effectiveness. In the same manner, marital conflict, even that ending in divorce, may be an indication of great strength of personality and thus of potential within the marriage. If gotten to in time, this strength could be capitalized upon in working at resolving the difficulties within the relationship, thus making possible a higher level of personal and marital integration, growth, and usefulness.

The engaged couple needs to work through not only feelings about any marriage break-ups in their own past, but to clarify beliefs about the possibility of a divorce when they have conflict. Pre-marital counseling introduces them to the availability and use of professional assistance that serves as a prototype for resolving future conflicts, usually without resorting to separation or divorce. Goode, Bernard, and Emerson will be helpful to the counselor in taking a balanced look at the carry-over effects of marital break-up.[14]

[14] Goode, William J., *After Divorce*. Illinois, Glencoe: The Free Press, 1956; Bernard, Jessie. *Remarriage, A Study of Marriage*. New York: Dryden Press, 1956; Emerson, James G. *Divorce, The Church, and Remarriage*. Philadelphia: Westminister Press, 1961.

Chapter 8

THE PHYSICIAN'S ROLE IN
PREPARATION FOR MARRIAGE

Those young people who are foresighted enough to enroll in a marriage or family course in high school or college, or those who enter into pre-marital counseling, learn to appreciate the value of a thorough pre-marital medical examination. Most people, to the contrary, view it as a legal nuisance to be fulfilled in the quickest and cheapest possible manner. An outstanding gynecologist recently testified that in all his practice only one couple had expected a complete physical in preparation for marriage. That couple did want more than a blood test, but even then the opportunity failed because he did not understand the request until they wrote back denouncing his ineffectiveness. This puts the spotlight on both sides of a critical issue; not enough couples ask for pre-marital physicals and not enough physicians use the opportunity to demonstrate the value of such service.

Most states require blood tests for the detection of venereal infections. Realizing that such tests are only partially successful, as well as believing that other health factors should be checked, thirty seven states have legal requirements for a pre-marital physical examination in addition to blood tests for both individuals. The degree to which all of these requirements are circumvented was illustrated in a recent report by Dr. Sylvester W. Trythall.[1] In a survey of 2,500 Michigan patients he found that only thirty-five per cent had received the required physical examination although ninety per cent favored the law and its observance. He also reported an active bootleg market in medical certificates provided either by the physician signing without performing the examination, an assistant forging the signature, or a commercial laboratory providing the blood tests and certificates.

It seems evident that propaganda based on the fear of venereal infection is singularly unimpressive to the marrying public. Enforcement of the law is dependent upon the physician and health departments. Much more effec-

[1] Trythall, Sylvester W., "The Pre-marital Law, History and Survey of Its Effectiveness in Michigan," Paper presented before American College of Osteopathic Obstetrics and Gynecology meeting in Detroit, Michigan, February 18, 1964.

tive would be an education campaign sponsored by physicians, clergy, counselors, teachers and the law directed toward the positive values of the pre-marital physical checkup.

Perhaps it is unrealistic to speak of the physician's *duty* in adequately preparing a couple for marriage when he is not trained in counseling and when the couple are asking only for a minimum examination in order to obtain a marriage license. Hence, it is best to think of the physician's pre-marital *opportunity*; a tremendous opportunity for preventive medicine, making optimum use of his legal opportunities to render complete medical services, and thereby contributing to the health of the couple and their forthcoming children. (See Chapter 4 for a plan of pre-marital counseling around the use of contraceptives.)

Medical schools in general have not prepared the doctor for this important task, especially in handling its emotional aspects; nor has graduate training in counseling adequately dealt with it. Even more significant is the failure to assist professional students to gain insight into their own emotional and sexual development and adjustment, which would make them comfortable and understanding with self and with others.

Lief [2] contends that because of a curious kind of prudery in the medical schools many physicians are surprisingly ignorant in a field where they are supposed to be wise. He quotes the English psychoanalyst, D. W. Winnecott:

> The doctor's long and arduous training does nothing to qualify him in psychology and does much to disqualify him. It keeps him so busy from 18 to 25 that he finds he is middle aged before he has the leisure in which to discover himself. It takes him years of medical practice and the struggle to find time to live his own life before he can catch up on his fellow creatures, many of whom have lived a lot by the time they are 25.

Lief found in his own research that medical students, in striving for mastery, "put intellectual matters above emotions, security above pleasure, service to others above self-service (at least at conscious levels), exactitude above fantasy." While conforming to the public image of a good doctor, he is "not usually able to develop a warm, intimate relationship with his wife" (nearly two thirds of medical students today are married). Most of these marriages do not break up but many are troubled and stormy. In studying the sexual attitudes of medical students, Lief found much ig-

[2] Lief, Harold I., "What Your Doctor Probably Doesn't Know About Sex." *Harper's*, December, 1964, Vol. 229, No. 1375, pp. 92-98; quoted by permission of publisher.

norance, obsessive-compulsive concern, guilty fears and moralistic attitudes that would grossly interfere with pre-marital or other psychological counseling. Several tendencies are common among such physicians with patients: (1) To probe mercilessly to satisfy his own curiosity, (2) to react with disgust, contempt, or sarcasm, or (3) to over-identify with the patient's problems as similar to his own. Thus, it becomes mandatory that the physician, as well as the psychological counselor, prepare himself through self-study, consultation with marriage counselors, painstaking experience, and follow-up of cases.

A. THE MEDICAL EXAMINATION IN GENERAL

To be sure, the medical exam usually focuses only upon the physical aspects of marriage, but the couple's sexual aspirations can be capitalized upon in selling a complete physical as an integral part of total preparation for the privileges and responsibilities for family living. Important as sexual and other physical information is in the approaching marriage relationship, facts that are new to the individual can be transmitted most effectively in the context of an accepting emotional environment, much like a counseling relationship. It is not easy for the physician, who is "supposed to know the answers and tell the patient," to shift gears and make listening his major tool. Yet, it is necessary because unhealthy attitudes must be uprooted before newer, healthier attitudes can take root and grow. Without catharsis first, facts pertaining to health or to sex life will be superimposed upon old and outmoded attitudes.

This means that the pre-marital physical requires a great deal more time and patience than most office calls. A minimal package would consist of: an interview geared to eliciting any points about which the patient is anxious, and to pick up leads for further check, followed by the indicated lab work; a subsequent appointment given to the actual physical examination, to be followed or accompanied by an explanation of functions and any difficulties. In addition to the time involved, the physician who plans to participate in preparation for marriage must be aware of certain other factors: the fee should not be prohibitive; an unusual combination of maturity, understanding of human emotions, including one's own feelings, and a special body of knowledge is unnecessary; and the physician could best be a family person, or at least possess healthy attitudes toward love, marriage, and sex. A doctor who is tense about any of these areas will generate or intensify uneasiness and anxiety in the patient.

The somewhat meticulous explanations at points in the following discussion are geared to the simple language and care necessary for the client to understand what both the counselor and the physician are talking about.[3]

I. Physical Factors

Both the man and the woman should have a medical checkup at least six weeks prior to marriage, including laboratory work necessary to reveal any organic difficulty or physical illness. In addition to the immediate benefits, the pre-marital examination can have the added effect of establishing a relationship which will be conducive to periodic returns for information, medical checkups, and assistance with problems. A meaningful experience with a physician prior to marriage is the surest guarantee that the woman will feel relaxed and confident with him or with another doctor when she becomes pregnant or when she has any illness or difficulty.

It is important not only that the man have a physical examination, but that he know the physician who examines and may treat his wife and family. For this reason, as well as for the interpretations to be made to them separately and together, *the same physician* might best be used by the man and woman in preparation for marriage. This does not pose a problem for the general practitioner or internist, but some gynecologists and obstetricians are unaccustomed to doing physical examinations or consultations with men. When undertaken as preparation for marriage, it has proved to be a rewarding practice indeed. The minimum to be expected is that, having completed the woman's physical, the physician have one conference with the man and then see them together. If they are moving from the vicinity, the physician can urge them to arrange for the family doctor or gynecologist chosen afterward to contact him for any significant findings.

Blood tests will be made to determine the possibility of syphilis. A careful history of any venereal infections is essential. Many cases were treated with penicillin until external symptoms disappeared, but the spirochete took refuge in the blood stream or the central nervous system. Any record of previous venereal infection therefore deserves meticulous follow-up.

The Rh factor will be explained in simple fashion if the couple have shown concern, particularly emphasizing that it is less important than some people now think, and explaining what could be done if the rare chance of difficulty should develop. Now that most such babies can be saved, many feel it is better for the physician to know and the couple not to know—at

3 *Ibid.*

least not be concerned about—when risk is involved. Others would insist
that the couple should be made aware of such factors, but hopefully it can
be done without setting off undue anxiety.

When serious illnesses are uncovered in the physical examination, the
physician has the responsibility of leading the couple to deal realistically
with the situation. It seems unfair to permit a couple to get married when
one has a limiting illness, without the other being adequately informed.
Leading them to face facts together is a major step in removing what could
become a disturbing source of conflict and anxiety in the marriage relationship.

II. Emotional Factors

The physician who is qualified to do so may go further than checking
organic factors, determining whether attitudes are healthy or neurotic. If a
professional counselor is involved in the referral, the two will coordinate
their efforts to this end.

One of the common unwholesome outgrowths of careless medical checkups is the formation of, or confirmation of, "organ neuroses" in the overly
anxious personality. A physician's preoccupation with such organs as
heart, lungs, or uterus without explanation, or with only brief statements,
may convince the client that something serious is wrong.

The physician should be alert to the emotional factors in physical illnesses which are discovered. Too quick reassurance, based upon superficial or even thorough medical examination, may have the effect of repress-
ing existing fears about one's health; thus, the causative psychic conflict has
time to become more complicated. If a patient is convinced that he has a
certain illness and the doctor does not find this to be true, the natural thing
is to assure the patient of the falsity of his conviction. Yet, what happens is
that the anxious patient feels the superficial examination revealed the illness, that the doctor therefore feels it unnecessary to go further, and is reassuring the patient falsely of good health to keep him from becoming more
concerned. An anxious patient may well be unable to accept a medical fact
when he *feels* the contrary. On the other hand, if the fears and complaints
are talked out until the emotional charge is dissipated, medical assurances
have tremendous value. Many people need an extra few minutes, and some
a few hours, with the physician or a counselor to help assimilate new ideas
of health which have been revealed by the examination, having felt for so
long that they were "sickly."

Many mental and emotional disturbances can be detected in the pre-marital medical examination. It is doubtful that a couple should be permitted to

get married without such disturbances being tactfully and skillfully brought into awareness where a solution becomes possible, or adaptation to them can be effected through skillful counseling. Again this calls for close collaboration with the referring counselor. If no counselor is involved, and if the physician does not feel adequate to deal with the emotional problem and to assume responsibility for it, a suitable psychotherapist should be found for them. Referral should not be a one-way street. It is equally as urgent that physicians learn to refer to counselors and psychotherapists.

In something of the same category would be such marked emotional immaturity or neurosis as to prevent the couple from being adequate parents. To be sure, marriage may provide the challenge to growth which will in time develop their potential as parents, but a physician may be wise to encourage a couple to postpone having children until a reasonable period of individual growth and development of their relationship has transpired.

III.   The Use of Medication

It is most essential that the physician and pre-marital counselor obtain a detailed history of the use of medication in the past and the present. Most of this can be elicited as history, but the exact nature of medication (including old prescriptions that the patient continues to have filled) is often unknown except to the prescribing physician.

Thyroid Therapy. Thyroid conditions and the treatment involved can be related to the health of a marriage in many ways. A slow functioning thyroid can lead to lethargy, semi-depression, lack of interest in sex, and a "don't care" attitude in general. There are a few cases in which this condition is brought about by prolonged use of medication, which was necessary in slowing down an over-active thyroid, but which has been continued too long. On the other hand, efforts to stimulate an underfunctioning thyroid through medication can backfire in a variety of ways. Take, for instance, a man who has fallen in love with and is marrying a woman with a low functioning thyroid, finding in this kind of female the style of life, general interest level, and personality characteristics which are necessary to his own adequate functioning as a male in the marriage. (This is illustrated in the earlier discussions of neurotic complementarity in marriage.) When a physician discovers an inadequately functioning thyroid and prescribes medication for the woman, major shifts can come about in her basic attitudes toward life, and in available energy. Here is a case in point:

Mr. T. had fallen in love with and married a woman with a low functioning thyroid, finding in this kind of female the speed of movement, general interest level, and personality characteristics which were necessary to his own adequate functioning as a male. In the pre-marital examination, the physician prescribed medication. Almost immediately major shifts came about in her basic attitudes toward life; she became vivacious, wanted to join a church, go dancing, and have friends in.

In many marriages this might have been a change welcomed by both mates, but this type of man, with his own psychological economy based upon having the former type of wife, felt that "this is not the woman I married." His sex interests were slowly paced and specific conditions had to be met for him to perform. She had little sexual desire previously, but now he thought she was "insatiable." She wanted regular sexual experiences and expected to be satisfied. As often happens to this type of male personality, he became even more incompetent under her pressures, and resentment toward her became acute. She, not aware that she had changed or was expecting him to change drastically, began to accuse him of being interested in someone else.

Only the physician's alertness in referring them to a marriage counselor when the wife came in for an "irritation" saved this marriage from breaking up.

Similar dynamics can operate when it is the husband who is receiving thyroid medication. In either case, it does not automatically follow that a high or low thyroid output slows down or speeds up sexual life, since many other factors may help account for such transitions. However, such a vital role does the thyroid play that it certainly should be taken into account, and resultant psychological factors and their relationship to the marriage should be kept in mind. All such transitions tend to take on added importance when there is a basic personality conflict or difficulty in communication between the couple.

Similar attention should be paid in cases where hormonal therapy is in process or is prescribed as a part of the pre-marital medical attention. Some hormonal treatment intensifies sex need and ability to respond in certain patients, and slows down desire or ability in other cases. Much of the results are unpredictable in view of complicating psychological problems and might well be postponed until the psychological treatment has been completed.

Barbiturates and Alcohol. Literally thousands of people in the United States are addicted to barbiturates, which are all too readily available. The degree to which these drugs alter personality can be amazing. More familiar, perhaps, is the slowed-downness or lack of ambition that can come from over dosage and accumulation of residual drugs. In some cases toxic psychosis results. Although it should be a well known fact that barbiturates and alcohol don't mix well, it is not infrequent to find such a combination at the basis of a disturbed marriage.

Mrs. M. had been a sophisticated modern housewife for several years until the husband died. She then became a successful business woman until married the second time, continuing to function in the "country club and cocktail set." Alcohol had been a daily part of her existence for all of her adult life and it didn't make sense at all to her that she should be considered a problem drinker by her husband of a few months.

She had become increasingly "nervous" and her physician had prescribed phenobarbital until she became readjusted to married life. They were referred to a marriage counselor by an attorney. On several consecutive nights she had provoked the husband, seeking a fight. Finally, when she had become quite violent, he had slapped her in self defense. She remembered the physical violence on his part, but had amnesia for her role in this. It soon became evident that she was continuing her practice of a glass of wine at lunch, a beer with the girls in the afternoon, and a couple of cocktails in the evening, interspersed with doses of phenobarbital. The results were nigh fatal for her and her husband.

Marijuana, heroin, etc., although not as frequently encountered in premarital counseling, can provide a major problem in some early marriages. Sex and drugs are often thought of as "going together," but the picture is not that which the public often suspects. Under the stimulation of or the sedation of certain drugs, sexual interest may be heightened; however, many of the drugs tend to reduce the ability to respond sexually, although there may be strong sexual components in the individual fantasy and collective talk which accompanies smoking "pot" or otherwise indulging in drugs.

Tranquilizers and Stimulants. The great American cure-all of tranquilizers and stimulants can be a real culprit with newlyweds. Although mild dosage of tranquilizers may take off the edge of pre-marital tensions, and may permit a fuller sexual involvement of tense and inexperienced people, over-dosage, or prolonged usage can grossly interfere with, or actually make it impossible for a man to respond sexually. The woman's interest in sex or her investment in and determination to gain satisfaction therefrom can be grossly slowed down, even making her psychologically frigid. Closely allied to the interference with sexual life is the degree to which tranquilizers can produce a lethargy which can be maddening to a mate who wants to be more active socially, recreationally, etc. The picture can become confused indeed when both tranquilizers and stimulants are used. Tranquilizers can take away the extra bit of anxiety necessary to involving an emotionally disturbed person in individual psychotherapy or pre-marital counseling, for that matter.

B. THE WOMAN

Since adequacy as a sexual partner is a central concern in requesting a complete pre-marital physical, the best approach to an understanding of what is significant may be through a brief description of the cyclical behavior of the female during sexual stimulation and satisfaction. Masters and Johnson have made more extensive and intensive studies of female sexual response than all other researchers combined and much of their findings will be paraphrased here. So crucial is their work that every article indicated in the footnotes should be carefully studied by the counselor and physician.

I. Cycle of Sexual Response

Whether sexual stimulus be due to psychological factors, or to physical contact by self or by another, or any combination thereof, there is a relatively well defined phenomenal sequence in the human female. This cycle of sexual response can be divided into four relatively discreet phrases: (1) excitement, (2) plateau, (3) orgasm, and (4) resolution. The Masters team has demonstrated that the major anatomic changes in the vagina develop primarily during the first two of these stages—excitement and plateau.[4]

Excitement Phase. A universal accompaniment of sexual stimulation is the engorgement and lubrication of mucosa tissue. Salivary glands produce excessively, the mucosa tissue of the nose increases until breathing through nasal passages may be difficult and excess moisture can cause nasal dripping. Vaginal lubrication starts within 5 to 15 seconds from the beginning of sexually stimulating activity.[5] Most sex manuals have attributed lubrica-

[4] Masters, W. H.: The Sexual Response Cycle of the Human Female. I. Gross Anatomic Considerations. *Western Journal of Surgery, Obstetrics and Gynecology.* 68:57-72, January-February 1960.

[5] Masters, W. H.: The Sexual Response Cycle of the Human Female. II. Vaginal Lubrication. *Annals of New York Academy of Science.* 83: 301-317, 1959. See forthcoming text by Masters, Williams H. and Virginia E. Johnson, *Human Sexual Response,* Little Brown and Co., April 1966.

tion to the glands of Bartholin, but Masters and Johnson have clearly demonstrated the sweating phenomenon in which the vagina and the walls of the vaginal barrel look like a "sweat beaded forehead," until the droplets coalesce into a well-lubricated surface, preparatory to coital activity. The Bartholin glands seem to provide emergency lubrication, secreting only after prolonged stimulation. This delayed but concentrated drop of fluid adds so much lubrication that many mistakenly feel the woman has an ejaculation.

Despite size, shape or degree of availability, the clitoral response of a woman typically follows a pattern, beginning somewhat slower than does vaginal lubrication. The response cycle is usually more rapid if the clitoris is directly stimulated than if sexual stimulation is more generalized, but the same phenomena occur nonetheless. As sexual tensions rise vasocongestion increases the diameter of the clitoral shaft, but rarely is the length increased. There is a microscopic tumescent reaction in the glans clitoris, tightening the integument (skin). In some women this tumescence is pronounced enough to give the appearance of a clitoral "erection."

The minor labia increase to approximately twice their relaxed thickness, which provides external elongation for the vaginal barrel. Heightened vasocongestion begins to bring a color change in the "sex skin" of the minor labia, including the clitoral hood. The labia majora, in a nulliparous woman (who has not had children) continue to flatten out against the pelvic rim until they seem non-existent. For the multiparous female (more than one child), they may increase in size from two to three times through engorgement depending somewhat upon the degree of varicosity. As the excitement phase intensifies they spread out laterally from the vaginal opening.[6] At the height of excitement the skin of the body, especially in the region of the diaphragm, thighs, and small of the back, takes on a thickening, reddening appearance somewhat like the measles.

During the excitement phase the inner two-thirds of the vagina begins a distention reaction which bring expansion "not only in the vaginal axis and the anterior-posterior plane, but also in the transverse diameter at the mid-cervical plane." The uterus partially elevates into the body (false pelvis), withdrawing the cervix from the vaginal outlet. The end result is to begin a bulbous type of expansion which increases the circumferential diameter of the inner two thirds of the vagina much like an inflated balloon.[7]

Plateau Phase. If effective stimulation continues, the female enters the plateau phase of sexual response. Now both the shaft and glans of the cli-

[6] See Footnote 4; Also Masters, W. H. and Virginia E. Johnson, The Physiology of the Vaginal Reproductive Function. *Western Journal of Surgery, Obstetrics and Gynecology.* 69: 105-120 March-April 1961.
[7] *Ibid.*

toris "withdraw from the normal prudendal overhang positioning and retract against the anterior border of symphysis." That portion of the glans normally projecting from the clitoral hood when unstimulated withdraws deeply beneath the foreskin until it is quite difficult to observe. The overall reduction in clitoral length is at least fifty per cent. This sequence occurs regardless of the nature of stimulation but may be speeded up if the clitoris is more directly manipulated. If stimulation is relaxed, as in prolonged maintenance of the plateau stages, the overhang position may be restored, but upon renewal of stimulus the retraction reoccurs.[8] With heightening excitement the "sex skin" of the labia changes to a scarlet red, a sure sign of impending orgasm if stimulation is continued. The distention reaction of the *inner* two thirds of the vagina, begun in the excitement phase, continues as the uterus withdraws. The result is a balloon-like cavity well beyond the size necessary for any male penis.[9]

The vasoconcentration of the *outer* third of the vagina increases until it reduces the distention of that portion of the vaginal barrel by fifty per cent from that of the "excitement phase," but its pliability avoids any problem with penile intromission. This engorgement process makes ready the "orgasmic platform" for total sexual responsiveness.

Orgasmic Phase. The characteristic physical reaction of orgasmic response is the onset of regularly recurring contractions in the broadbased platform which has been created by vasocongestive reaction in the outer third of the vagina during the plateau phase. The orgasmic platform contracts 5 to 10 times with a frequency of five-tenths to eight-tenths of a second, the individual's characteristic rate being sustained until the fifth or sixth contraction, after which the time sequence slows.

The involuntary contraction includes the entire perineal body. The labia minora, the outer third of the vaginal canal, the rectum, the uterus, and the lower abdominal muscles contract in the orgasmic phase. "The transverse perionei muscles, the bulbocavernous group, the external or rectal sphincter, and the lower portion of the rectus abdominis are the muscles of primary response." [10] The pulsating sensations may be felt by the woman as

[8] Masters, W. H. and Virginia E. Johnson. "The Sexual Response Cycle of The Human Female." III. The Clitoris: Anatomic and Clinical Considerations. *Western Journal of Surgery, Obstetrics and Gynecology.* 70: 248-257, September-October 1962.

[9] Masters, W. H. and Virginia E. Johnson. "The Physiology of The Vaginal Reproductive Function." *Western Journal of Surgery, Obstetrics and Gynecology.* 69: 105-120, March-April 1961.

[10] See footnote 4; Also, Masters, W. H., and Virginia E. Johnson. "The Artificial Vagina: Anatomic, Physiologic, Psychosexual Function." *Western Journal of Surgery, Obstetrics and Gynecology.* 69: 192-212. May-June 1961.

either highly localized or generalized to the entire body. The more effective the total sexual arousal and stimulation the more complete is the total body response to sexual release. Muscles in the neck, face, eyes and throughout the entire body and extremities may develop spastic contractions. Most women seem to respond more completely if coital movement continues throughout the orgasmic experience. It is interesting that no specific reaction of the clitoris to the orgasmic phase has been noted in thousands of observations by the Masters team.

Resolution Phase. An orgasmic experience reverses the field of sexual response. Within five to ten seconds clitoral retraction lets go and the organ then returns to the normative positioning at about the same rate an ejaculated penis becomes flaccid. However, venous engorgement of the clitoral shaft may last five to ten minutes after orgasm. Without orgasm, engorgement of the entire genital area may last for an hour or more. With orgasm she returns temporarily to the plateau phase level of sexual stimulation and may remain for an indefinite time before dropping into resolution phase release. At this point she may find it possible to return to orgasm several times with proper stimulation. When the "sex skin" discoloration of the minor labia disappears, flushed face, taut muscles, expanded rib cage, and breasts which have been enlarged by up to a third, all return to normal. The clitoris remains extremely tender during orgasm and immediately thereafter, often negating the desire for further stimulation for at least a few seconds.

II. The Gynecological Examination

The gynecological examination should check the entire genito-urinary system for any unusual condition that would pose a problem in the menstrual cycle, sexual intercourse, conception, or childbirth. Chief among the organs of interest are the external genitalia, including *hymen* and *clitoris,* the *vaginal canal, uterus, ovaries, Fallopian tubes*, and the *breasts*.[11] While searching for possible physical complications, the physician should keep in mind that many "female troubles" are due primarily to emotional factors. The genital system is of such tremendous emotional significance to the individual that any suggestion of physical difficulty here can set off a chain of anxiety and reenforce lifelong fears. Physical findings which would interfere significantly with the healthy functioning of the individual must be dealt with; however, it is doubtful that slight physical variations from the

[11] Kroger, William S., and S. Charles Freed, *Psychosomatic Gynecology*, Glencoe, Illinois: The Free Press, 1956, Chapter 7.

norm should be mentioned just prior to marriage. When a woman has anxiety about menstrual difficulties it is doubtful that she should be pacified with "when you are married it will be all right"; a bit of advice which often backfires and destroys confidence in the physician. Unnecessary anxiety could be avoided if women were tipped off that menstrual cycles may fluctuate because of the tremendous excitement or anxiety associated with marriage and early sex experiences. Evidence that she is equipped admirably for childbirth is reassuring, but exceptional care must be taken in explaining factors which indicate complications in delivery which are only remotely possible.

The reproductive and glandular systems should be explained since most people have only a hazy acquaintance with physiology, and especially with the interrelationship of emotions and hormones in directing and controlling physical responses.

The Hymen. The physician will not assume that his unmarried client has or has not had sexual intercourse, but tactful inquiry may set the emotional stage for frankness. It may be of tremendous importance to an anxious girl to know, and to have her potential husband know, that the presence or absence of the hymen does not give a woman's "moral history." Of primary concern to a woman with a pronounced hymen is the difficulty it may cause in initial intercourse, and, in fact, the problem it may pose in medical examination. Dilation of the hymen, and of possibly constricted vaginal walls, can be done by the physician, by the woman under instruction, or by the husband after marriage. Dilation by the woman herself under instructions over a period of a few weeks is adequate in most cases, if she is ready for it emotionally and incorporates the preparation into total plans for marriage. A dilation of three fingers or an equivalent test tube will mean that penetration by the penis can be gained without difficulty if she is sexually excited. If it is a difficult hymen the woman should be discouraged from waiting for it to be broken in coitus, since this invites painful initial sex experiences. It may be advisable for the physician to effect dilation or surgical clipping of a rigid hymen under a whiff of gas which avoids associating pain with vaginal penetration. On the other hand, the physician must be alert to the girl whose emotional needs dictate that she be "deflowered" by the man she marries, and to the male who feels acutely the need for such an experience. Some men will react negatively towards the wife if dilation has been accomplished by anyone else, even medically by a physician. Discussion with the man usually removes such anxieties.

Tension can interfere with the pre-marital physical examination itself. The woman's reaction here is often a good guide to the information and explanations she needs. This is a new experience; she doesn't know what to expect, and tightens up at the approach of the physician. A simple advance explanation of each step makes his approach more meaningful and effective. All too often the physician's proceeding with the examination in a professional, yet matter of fact way, ignores and intensifies her inner qualms.

The Clitoris. Explanation of the role of the clitoris in the sex response cycle well may be indicated, somewhat according to the discussion earlier in this chapter, but care should be taken to avoid the kind of misleading impressions often conveyed in articles and texts. The nature of explanations can best be determined by the woman's own history. If through masturbation, intensive petting, or coitus she has learned to respond with orgasm regularly, the physician may feel like congratulating her good fortune and leaving the topic, lest mechanical instruction interfere with her spontaneity. In such cases the physician may well turn his focus in two directions: Instruction of the male partner; and joint discussions with them, since happy sexual experience depends upon interpersonal factors, as well as intrapersonal awareness.

However, many women, through either lack of experience or because of emotional blocks to responsiveness, are not so well prepared. Even those who have learned to stimulate themselves well in masturbation seem to forget the similar functions of the organs of stimulus and response in sexual intercourse. At the opposite extreme, but equally problematic, is an almost fetishistic preoccupation with the clitoris and other parts of female anatomy and response. What about the size of the clitoris? Is it positioned properly for coital contact? Is it too embedded in the clitoral hood?

Rarely indeed is there cause for medical concern with a clitoris, although the organs vary considerably in size, shape and location. Because of the epidemic distribution of some misleading contentions about female sexuality, the average woman who comes for pre-marital counseling, along with the average male, will need some corrective attention from the physician. Three of the most commonly held misperceptions about female sexuality are in regard to: *size, location,* and *desirability of direct stimulation* of the clitoris.

Competent observer that he was, making him as modern as the latest research by the Masters' team, Dickinson [12] long ago held that there was

[12] Dickinson, R. L. and H. H. Pierson. "The Average Sex Life of American Women." *Journal of American Medical Association.* 85:1113-1117.

no relation between the size of a woman's clitoris and sexual satisfaction. The Masters-Johnson research demonstrates that there is likewise no relation between clitoral *positioning* and sexual response, in spite of contrary theories of many writers.[13] In an effort to help free the modern woman for fuller sexual pleasure, the sex manuals have repetitively stressed the role of the clitoris as the center of female sexual stimulation and pleasure.[14] They have called for a degree of direct and prolonged stimulation of the clitoris which is impossible in most coital positions, and, even if applied manually, actually works against maximum responsiveness. Frequently this brings the female complaint: "I wish he had never read that book. He tries to operate me like a machine."

It well may be that male ego needs had much to do with the formation of twentieth century theories of female sexuality, since most of the investigators and writers have been men. Begin with a belief that the male has superior sexual prowess, add a generation of female partners who are too inhibited to respond spontaneously, confound that with resultant guilt over inability to satisfy those partners, and this makes necessary some theory of why the woman is not sufficiently stimulated to have an orgasm. An all male frame of reference leads the search for the most masculine appearing part of female anatomy, and the clitoris is elected to fill the role. This led to the formulation of special techniques of stimulation based upon masculine theories of the phallic attributes of the female. Once the necessity of direct clitoral pressure was postulated as the cure for frigidity and the guarantee of sexual pleasure, urging the necessity of married couples developing specific techniques for direct clitoral stimulation, both in foreplay and in coitus, became the logical next step for writers to take. Actually, except with the female in the uppermost position, continuing penile-clitoral contact is impractical to maintain. This had led to many derogatory attitudes by both men and women toward the anatomic fitness of the female to experience the greatest satisfaction in coition.

What are the established facts about location of the clitoris, coital positions, and stimulation of the clitoris in the female? Just as with other areas

13 See Bauer, B. A. *Women and Love*. (Trans.: by E. S. Jerday and E. G. Paul) New York: Liveright Publishing Corporation. 1927; Kinsey, A. C. et al. *Sexual Behavior in The Human Female*. Philadelphia: W. W. Saunders Co. 1953; Van de Velde, T. H. *Ideal Marriage*. New York: Covici Freide, 1939.

14 Stone, H. M. and A. Stone. *A Marriage Manual*. New York: Simon and Schuster, 1953; Van de Velde, *op. cit.;* Sadler, W. S., and L. K. Sadler. *Living A Sane Sex Life*. Chicago: Wilcox and Follett Company. 1944; and, Kleegman, S. J. "Frigidity in Women." *Quarterly Review of Surgery, Obstetrics and Gynecology*. 16: 243-248. 1959.

of female sexuality, Masters and Johnson [15] were the first researchers to conduct primary investigations in this area. Their findings challenge many of the marriage manual contentions. Here are a few illustrations:

(1) "Direct clitoral stimulation is less effective in developing and/or maintaining sexual tension than is indirect stimulation." Of several hundred women in the sample, no two individuals were observed using exactly the same manipulative techniques. However, one trait in common did stand out. Rarely did a woman directly manipulate the glans clitoris. If she did, this type of activity was not maintained very long; the glans itself was seldom touched and then only lightly and initially. Rather, these women applied stimulation to the general mons area, to one side or the other of the clitoral shaft. The fact is that the *glans* clitoris is so hypersensitive that too much contact causes a recoil and diminution of sexual pleasure. If a woman goes through the cycle of sex response to the plateau phase, regardless of the part of the body that is directly stimulated, the sequence of response of the clitoris will be the same.

(2) Considerably heightened sensitivity does develop in the clitoral area at the peak of sexual response, but for some unexplained reason the organ itself does not go through involuntary contractions at the time of orgasm, as do many other parts of the body. The clitoris is prone to be extremely sensitive immediately after orgasm so that further stimulation of it, at least for a few seconds, may be unpleasant.

(3) The most effective sexual stimulation comes about through manipulation of the entire mons area, along with other erogenous zones of the body, accompanied by the heightened emotionality that accompanies sexual intercourse. It is neither necessary nor desirable to stay in direct contact with the clitoris during the final plateau and the orgasmic phases of sexual response. Efforts of the male to recontact the naturally retracted clitoris at this time, which leads to cessation of manipulation of the entire mons area, can lead to much frustration and let down for the woman. To be sure, the clitoris plays a significant role in the final phases of sexual response, but the most effective stimulation is the result of "traction on the minor labial hood formed subsequent to penile distention of the vaginal vestibule." Even in normal retraction of the clitoris, it continues to be stimulated through the gentle tugging at the clitoral hood and the massaging symphyses of the male and female.[16] Since this holistic, generalized stimulus is more effective

[15] Masters, W. H. and Virginia E. Johnson. See footnote 8.
[16] The Kinsey research indicated that the minor labia are almost as sensitive as the clitoris in producing sexual arousal. See Kinsey. *op. cit.*

than direct manipulation of the clitoris, particularly once sexual interest has reached the plateau phase, it would seem that men and women are quite admirably equipped for sexual intercourse.

The Vagina and The Vaginal Barrel. Misinformation about the size of the vagina and the vaginal canal, and the relation of this to penis size, produces anxiety in many young women; notably those who have been influenced by crude tales of injury. The doctor can reassure the woman that her vagina is "infinitely distendable" under the aegis of sexual excitement adapting admirably to any size penis, as has been amply demonstrated by the medical research team of Masters and Johnson [17] reported earlier in this chapter.

Most women do not understand the intricate process of lubrication and distention which was outlined earlier in this chapter. This process is crucial to their sex life at any time, but especially for several weeks after the birth of a baby when the sweating phenomena of lubrication ceases altogether. It is not too early to inform her and her husband pre-maritally of this difference in readiness for intercourse, lest after fasting sexually before and after child delivery either of the couple become worried about her seeming lack of sexual responsiveness. Artificial lubrication makes it possible for her to cohabit pleasantly in spite of the fact that the vaginal canal temporarily loses its mucosa nature and becomes paper dry.

When fitting a vaginal diaphragm the physician should keep in mind the balloon-like distention of the inner two thirds of the vaginal barrel which accompanies sexual stimulation. If the barrier is fitted to relaxed muscles, it will become quite loose when, under sexual excitement, the uterus lifts into the false pelvis, thus increasing the depth and circumferential diameter of the lower vaginal barrel by several centimeters. This dictates a tight fitting in a relaxed state if the diaphragm is to stay in place well during coital movements to keep the cervical sufficiently covered with the spermicidal solution.[18]

The woman may well be informed about the band of contracting vaginal muscles immediately inside the outer third of the vaginal canal, including the voluntary control she can exert in intensifying sexual stimulation for her and her partner, the vasocongestion this area undergoes in readiness for coitus, and their involuntary contraction during orgasm. After a baby is

[17] Masters and Johnson, see footnotes 4, 6, and 10.
[18] Johnson, Virginia E. and W. H. Masters. "Intravaginal Contraceptive Study:" Phase I. Anatomy. *Western Journal of Surgery, Obstetrics, and Gynecology.* 70: 202-207. 1962; "Intravaginal Contraceptive Study:" Phase II. Physiology. *Western Journal of Surgery, Obstetrics and Gynecology.* 71: 144-153, 1962.

born she can restore the tonus of these muscles by deliberately exercising them.

Increasingly physicians are making vaginal smears to determine the presence of *cancer*. Incorporating this test into the pre-marital physical can be wise indeed, but when this is mishandled a woman may decide, "He suspects I have cancer." Thus a chain of worry is confirmed or begun. Careful advance explanation of this routine would avoid most of these fears. Breast examination for possible growths fits into the same category. Explanation of the normative role of the breasts in sexual stimulation and response may be indicated as a way of helping alert the woman to the total involvement of the body in her sex life.

Husbands, as well as wives, particularly in this culture, can be extremely sensitive about *body odors*, yet being too meticulous can become a disturbing factor. The manufacturers of douches have exploited the "cult of cleanliness" emphasis. Far more important than the possible physical damage by unwise douching are its psychological implications. A few physicians continue to advise douching after every intercourse, thus playing into the hands of the feeling that there is something basically unclean about sex. Women who know it is not an effective contraceptive device may continue to douche because they feel they have been made unclean. Such feelings are detrimental to a meaningful sex life. Unless some particular body chemistry or irritation of the vagina dictates douching, the vaginal canal is capable of self-cleansing, even following menstruation, with only an external bath. The naturalness and wholesomeness of vaginal and ejaculatory secretions needs to be established in order that relaxed attitudes may permeate sexual experiences. The physician has an opportunity to contribute either to the happiness or anxiety of the patient and of the couple at this point.

The Uterus. Since so much of the gynecologist's work focuses upon the reproductive system, it is natural that the ovaries, Fallopian tubes, and uterus receive special attention in a pre-marital physical. It must be kept in mind, however, that over concern can cause much difficulty with an anxiety prone personality. "Organ neuroses" can be intensified and focused by unwise handling of this portion of the medical examination. For instance, slight misplacement of the uterus need not impair healthy functioning any more than a crooked nose or a bowed leg interferes with daily living. Tremendous care must be exercised in mentioning such an anomaly, lest the woman misunderstand. One physician found that a woman's uterus was tilted, said she might need surgery, and left her so upset that this interfered with early sexual adjustment. Under similar circumstances another said:

"I want to talk to you about your uterus; not to alarm you but to reassure you in case some doctor mentions surgery. You have a healthy uterus; it is just slightly tilted. You do not need surgery. When you get pregnant let me check within a couple of months to see that the womb straightens out properly. You will have no difficulty beyond that which we can correct at that time."

Most women don't seem to know that the uterus contracts rhythmically during orgasm. This lack of knowledge is notable among those for whom the sensation of sexual climax is more global than localized. An understanding of this may not be too significant early in marriage, but it can become crucial later, in at least two specific areas: (1) unnecessary interference in sexual intercourse by pregnancy, and, (2) undue concern by the wife or husband about the kind of orgasm she is having. The pre-marital exam provides an opportunity for the physician to do a valuable bit of preventive education.

During pregnancy the woman may become more aware of the uterus' role in sexual response and this can become a source of sexual problems. Whether due to the extra pressure of the fetus, or to greater freedom to respond sexually now that the risk of conception is not a problem, uterine contractions can be more obvious. These movements unconsciously, sometimes consciously, remind the woman of "labor" contractions. The result can be a reflex action withdrawal from further sexual involvement which prevents her from having an orgasm. The woman who has a neurotic need to avoid coitus often grabs at this supposed threat to the baby as an excuse for negating that part of married life which she prefers to omit. Even the emotionally healthy pregnant woman, who very much desires sexual intercourse, can be made afraid by the unknown nature and feared consequences of the uterine contractions which accompany orgasm. The physician can alert the about to be married woman to any fears that may develop in this area at a later date. In an advanced state of pregnancy orgasm can contract the uterus so forcefully that the baby pushes up the abdominal wall several inches. In spite of this intensity, even within a few days of the normal time for delivery, a healthy fetus in a healthy woman will not be injured or dislodged. In fact, a good case can be made for continued orgasmic experience of the mother as one of the ways the unborn baby gets the extra stimulus, through the closeness of muscular contractions, needed in his evolving as a human being.

The woman should also know that nature's way of restoring muscular tonus to the uterus, after the birth of a baby, is through frequent contractions, with or without total orgasmic experience. A major factor in the resistance some women have to nursing their babies is tied directly to this phenomena. The breasts are a natural erogenous zone, and their significance in psychological sexual stimulation has been heightened by a gross cultural emphasis. A combination of factors—the need of the overly stretched and weakened uterus to re-tone itself, and the sexual stimulus of nursing—causes frequent involuntary contractions of the uterus. Subliminally the woman associates these contractions with the sensations of sexual stimulation and orgasmic response, which indeed it may be. When this fact is not openly faced, she may unconsciously equate this with incestual feelings toward the infant, and hence reject nursing. Knowledge of the simple facts of nature could relieve her of much anxiety. She can be prepared now for accepting nursing as something good for her as well as for the baby. The baby can be quite helpful in restoring her physically and emotionally for early resumption of full sex life with her husband.

Orgasm Adequacy. Today thousands of women and men are victimized by an orgasm obsession; literally possessed by the struggle for a particular type of climax. They read the popular editions of psychoanalytic theory, sex manual instructions are practiced with a vengeance, the added anxiety generates just enough extra tension to make the "prize" more elusive, and then accusations of inadequacy are leveled at self or mate. In 1963 the author, under auspices of the American Association of Marriage Counselors, led a two-day conference devoted to clarifying the phenomena of female orgasm. The report of these proceedings provides an excellent outline for study for the professional person, including an exhaustive annotated bibliography. Since most theorizing about female orgasm in the past had been done by male specialists, a unique feature of this conference was detailed reporting of women on what they actually experienced in sexual climax, which clearly demonstrated the need for some female sponsored research in this area.[19]

Clitoral or Vaginal Orgasm? Deutsch and other psychoanalytic writers [20] have espoused the theory that "vaginal orgasm" characterizes the response of the emotionally healthy woman. Conversely, mere "clitoral orgasm" is

[19] Rutledge, A. L., and David R. Mace. "Female Orgasm Conference Proceedings. American Association of Marriage Counselors." 1963.

[20] Deutsch, Helene. *"The Psychology of Women,"* New York: Grune and Stratton. 1945, Vol. II, p. 80; Beauvoir, Simone de. *"The Second Sex."* (Trans. by H. M. Parshley) New York: Alfred A. Knopf. 1952; Freud S. *"New Introductory Lectures on Psychoanalysis."* (Trans. by W. J. H. Sprott) New York: W. W. Norton and Co., 1933; and, Hitschmann, E., and E. Bergler. *"Frigidity in Women, Its Characteristics and Treatment"* (Trans. by P. L. Weil) Washington and New York: Nervous and Mental Disease Pub. Co. 1936.

adjudged to be the product of immaturity or neurotic fixation. How did this theory come about anyway?

In all probability the major factor was the description of new sensations deep within the body described by women to the psychoanalyst or psychotherapist. Without knowing the physiology of sexual orgasm, they attributed to the depth of the vaginal canal the contractions which Masters' [21] investigations indicate are due to the spontaneous contractions which the uterus commonly undergoes in orgasm, whether it was triggered by masturbatory activity (self or mate administered) or depth penetration by the penis. The "facts" behind what has been described as vaginal orgasm probably consist of two or more elements: (1) the woman liberated from sexual inhibitions responds more intensely throughout her body; once freed, the intensity and quantity of responsiveness is dependent upon the degree of emotional and physical involvement; (2) the responsive woman may feel acutely certain localized sensations of which she had not become aware previously, which perhaps had been blocked out of consciousness. Now that she recognizes the contractions in her body, which she does not know to be uterine, she, and often the therapist, interprets this as contractions of the inner vaginal canal, which does not occur. The uterus does react convulsively, however.

One woman who had become confused and blocked in her married sex life went through a necessary process of psychotherapy. One day she found herself enjoying sex with the husband, and experienced what no doubt would be called vaginal orgasm. Then she remembered having the same experience frequently in college while masturbating. Like many girls, she had inadvertently discovered that masturbation to orgasm may relieve menstrual cramps. If, because of clotting or any other reason, the cervical os is blocked during menstruation, there is a back-up of menstrual flow which distends the highly sensitized uterus, thereby causing severe pressure pain. The forceful orgasmic contraction of the uterus often dislodges the clot, normal flow resumes, pressure subsides, and the discomfort diminishes.[22] This particular woman thought it was amusing that she would get herself so confused sexually that she would have to go through intensive psychotherapy to rediscover some of the physiological facts utilized freely in her early life. She said, "Why, my early method was much more pleasant than Midol and much less expensive than analysis."

Based upon observation of thousands of orgasmic experiences with several hundred women, often using color photography which would permit

[21] Masters and Johnson, see footnotes 4, 9, 10.
[22] *Ibid.*

repeated intensive analysis, Masters and Johnson[23] insist that from an *anatomic* viewpoint there is "absolutely no difference in the responses of the pelvic viscera to effective sexual stimulation," regardless of how the stimulation occurs. The cycle of response of the clitoris, vaginal barrel, uterus, contracting vaginal muscles, and of the uterus conformed in exact detail whether triggered by superficial stimulation or depth penetration by the penis, coupled with extremely high psychic involvement.

Kugel's[24] research challenges the Masters-Johnson findings at several points, particularly in that he continues to distinguish between vaginally induced orgasm and that which results from more superficial stimulation. However, he also disagrees with the psychoanalytic position by insisting that inability of the woman to respond vaginally is not due primarily to psychological impairment, and that orgasm adequacy is simply a matter of good physiological functioning of muscles and nerves. His treatment consists of the toning of muscles through exercises, with particular attention to the contracting muscles just within the vaginal orifice and to the pubo-coxegeous muscle which surrounds the vaginal barrel about midway its depth, reaching from the rectal area up into the anterior pubic area. A cylinder is used by the woman under instruction as she practices a biting exercise to activate or restore these muscles to adequate functioning. He gives little credence to emotional conditioning in the treatment of orgasm inadequacy, and quite obviously overlooks the psychological value of such an authority figure as the physician taking this amount of personal interest in the sexual aspects of a woman's body and experiences.

As further evidence in his case for vaginal orgasm, Kugel,[25] contrary to the claims of most specialists that the inner two thirds of the vaginal canal has few if any nerve endings, postulates a highly sensitive concentration of nerve cells at two points near the pubocoxegeous muscle. If the vaginal area is viewed as the face of a clock, he locates these stimulus areas at 4 and at 8 o'clock. Masters denies the presence of such a phenomena, and, although he does not devalue muscular tonus as an adjunct to adequate sexual functioning, insists that in orgasm the pubocoxegeous muscle goes through just the opposite of contraction; namely, a "letting go" phenomena.

A further significant step will be made in understanding woman's normative sex needs if the findings of these two medical research positions can be

23 Masters and Johnson, see footnote 8.
24 Kugel, Arthur I., from professional conferences.
25 *Ibid.*

reconciled. Perhaps the findings of Kugel and of Masters are not so disparate as they or their followers might believe.

Kugel insists on the need for a deeper, extra, or fuller stimulus in order for woman to experience the maximum orgastic satisfaction, and posits an extra primary zone of intravaginal sensitivity. Masters, while holding that basic anatomic response of any orgasm is the same in sequence and kind, regardless of the type or location of stimulation, agrees that the higher the sex tension level can be raised, by either physical or psychological means, the grosser the orgastic experience throughout the body. With or without an extra stimulus center deep within the vaginal barrel, which Masters denies, coital movement with depth penetration brings added stimulation in at least several ways: intensifies the massaging of the mons area through male-female symphysis; maximizes the tugging of the clitoral hood and labia minora, which Masters believes to be the optimal clitoral stimulation; and, there can be no doubt that the sexually mature woman gets an amazing amount of psychological stimulation through the experience of depth penetration by a virile male.

There would seem to be no essential disagreement between these two men about the use of the vaginal contracting muscles just within the canal. Masters has stressed the vasocongestion that occurs there as sexual excitement heightens, which would automatically bring about a firmer and more concentrated stimulation to both partners. He and Kugel agree that these muscles can be voluntarily controlled during coitus, except at the moment of orgasm, and this becomes a means of heightening the pleasure of the woman according to her wishes.

The disagreement seems to be primarily in regard to the pubocoxegeous muscle which Kugel goes all out in repairing or strengthening as a primary tool in successful coitus, emphasizing the voluntary contractibility at the wish of the woman. Masters stresses the importance of this muscle insofar as tonus and management of the entire pelvic viscera are concerned. The disagreement seems to come precisely at the point of using this specific group of muscles as a way of contracting against the penis and thus adding stimulation to the female. Masters claims a notable involuntary expansion of the vaginal barrel at this point, whenever sexual stimulus is heightened; whereas Kugel, as well as some of the analytic authorities, have talked about contraction in the lower vaginal barrel at the time of maximum stimulation and of orgasm. Masters insists that contraction never occurs in the lower two thirds of the vaginal walls, but has clearly demonstrated involuntary uterine contraction. The more responsive the female is, and the more aware she is of her responses, the more it actually appears that the findings of these two men may differ only in small technicalities. The involuntary contractions of the uterus and of the abdominal walls can produce the depth sensation, along with the grasping sensation provided by the involuntary contracting vaginal muscles just within the canal, which add up to a holistic experience for the sensitive and aware woman.

It could be that the functioning of these two sets of muscles characterize two seemingly contradictory needs of the woman if she is to have the most complete sexual fulfillment. On the one hand, she must have the maximum of psycho-physiological stimulation in order to maximize the sex tension level throughout the body. Many women can experience this phenomenon to the fullest and yet never enter the orgasm phase of sexual response. In some cases they level off quite comfortably and return slowly to the resolution phase, but in other cases they are left miserable by the intensive stimulation sans satisfaction. From a physiological point of view, these women cannot find the triggering mechanism that breaks the tension barrier or releases the tension charge, regardless of the adequacy of intravaginal stimulation (some can do so with mechanical stimulation). Psychologically, this may best be viewed as the inability to let go, trust, or commit oneself to the state of lack of control that is inherent in the involuntary reaction of orgastic response.

It is highly probable that the difference in orgastic response with a particular woman is qualitative and quantitative rather than being due to a distinction in the organs or locations in the body which are involved. Orgasm tends to involve the entire physical-psychological being, although the primary locus of sensation may be determined by such factors as degree of bodily awareness, conditioning, spontaneity, emotional investment, accumulative sexual tension, and ability to completely surrender to the intensity of the experience at the triggering of orgasm.

Orgasm Inadequacy. One of the most common complaints brought to the marriage counselor or the gynecologist by both men and women today, is the inability of the wife to experience complete sexual satisfaction including orgasm. Herein lies a knotted dilemma for the physician and pre-marital counselor. In contrast, if major orgasm inability is discovered through the history or pre-marital physical exam in the male, few specialists would hesitate to urge treatment, and they might take a stand that resolution of the problem should precede marriage. A complexity of factors with the woman makes it much more difficult, both for her and her physician or counselor. For one thing, she can participate in sexual intercourse without coming to orgasm, and even in the absence of pleasure. There have always been women who lived long and useful lives without experiencing orgasm. However, the modern climate of expectation is different. Knowledge of the native endowment of the woman with the capacity to be sexually fulfilled, plus an all out emphasis upon equality of rights and privileges, the philosophy of mutuality in marriage, all add up to a multidimensional problem for the unresponsive woman and her mate.

The failure to be able to respond, in the face of demands that she respond, is related to the dilemma of female virginity as an ideal still widely held. The ideal wife is still visualized as virginal until marriage and endlessly passionate after marriage. If her sex experiences have been nil or minimal, where is she to learn? How is she to break down the inhibitions that have been necessary to maintain chastity? If, on the other hand, she has had frustrating sex experiences, these may have left her all the more confused. Many pre-marital sexual contacts are under such non-ideal and fear laden circumstances that the girl fails to attain orgasm. How is she to know whether this was due to deeply ingrained inhibitions or to the fears of detection or pregnancy? And then there is that common phenomena that does not come to light until after marriage; namely, the woman who could have orgasm with ease pre-maritally with her husband to be or another partner, while the act was taboo, but, now that she is married, cannot respond. With many young women the best sexual history comes around masturbatory practices, but even there guilt may have prevented her letting go and completing the entire sequence of sexual response from excitement through orgasm and resolution. Increasingly even those young people who cherish the ideal of pre-marital chastity are doing some experimentation as a way of meeting sexual needs of the moment and also as an effort to begin learning how to be able to respond more completely post maritally. This occurs through intensive petting, often to orgasm, with or without direct mutual masturbation. Indeed, some physicians and counselors recommend that certain engaged couples experiment with this type of sexual stimulation in their love-making in order to begin bridging the gap between pre-marital inhibition based chastity and marital spontaneity. This is usually much more successful than secretive experimentation of either of the couple with other partners. To a marked degree, sexual adjustment is something that happens between two particular people, not to people in general.

Hastings [26] has suggested the following outline for medical use in taking a history of suspected frigidity:

I. Etiology
   A. Due to chemicals
   B. Due to organic disease
     1. Systemic
     2. Local (including dyspareunia and menopause)
   C. Due to psychological factors (including vaginismus)
II. Time in sexual pattern
   A. Arousal (specify time)
   B. Genital union (specify time)
III. Specificity
   A. Absolute (frigid under all circumstances)
   B. Selective (specify)
IV. Duration or expected duration
   A. Acute (and probably transient)
   B. Chronic (and probably permanent)

In cases of psychologically induced frigidity or orgasm inadequacy, and most cases fit into this category, it is important to know if the failure to respond is generalized to all conditions or selective and occasional. For instance, a woman may respond adequately: With a husband, but no one else; with a lover but not with a husband; with servants or men of lower social order, but not with a husband or other men of equal social rank; with masturbation or during sex dreams, but not with any man; with a homosexual partner, but not with any man. Sexual disability may vary all the way from the woman who gets major pleasure from sexual stimulation but cannot consummate the experience with the spontaneous contractions of orgasm, on the one hand, to complete vaginismus in some cases. Vaginismus itself may vary from the mere tightening of vaginal muscles due to some temporary threat of discomfort, like the unaccustomed gynecological examination, to such an extremely painful and complete muscular spasm that even the well lubricated tip of the physician's little finger cannot be inserted. Malleson [27] has pointed to the importance of realizing that true vaginal spasm cannot be voluntarily produced by the woman to evade coitus; "it may appear in spite of the utmost *conscious* willingness to accept the coital act." The most common medical treatment for vaginismus is

26 Hastings, Donald W. *"Impotence and Frigidity."* Boston: Little, Brown and Company. 1963. pp. 84-85; permission of the publisher.
27 Malleson, Joan, "Vaginismus: Its Management and Psychogenesis." *British Journal of Medicine.* 2: 213-216. 1942; Also, Hastings, *op. cit.* Chapter 6.

teaching the woman to dilate the vaginal orifice either with fingers or a lubricated cylinder. The results may make coitus physically painless, particularly if the spasm is the result of a conditioned reflex, but this does not necessarily cure the orgasm inadequacy in the face of deep psychological resistance to sexuality.

Hastings [28] uses the following outline in checking out a woman's orgasm adequacy:

1. Have you ever achieved orgasm? Under what circumstances?
2. Can you achieve orgasm by means of masturbation?
3. Under what circumstances do you experience sexual arousal?
4. Have you achieved orgasm with a sexual partner other than your husband? (Fiance? If applicable)
5. Do you notice sexual arousal in dreams or with fantasy during the day? Upon reading erotic literature? On seeing suggestive movies? Etc.
6. Does arousal and orgasm occur under any other circumstances?
7. What are your usual responses during arousal and genital union?

To be sure, these are private matters, but the woman expects help and this means the specialist needs certain information. Usually the calm assuredness that says by action, "I need to know this and am sure you will cooperate," elicits the woman's trusting cooperation.

Most physicians and counselors are going to settle for inadequate sexual experience and know-how on the part of the average young woman; with less assurance that she will be able to relate adequately. They rationalize that only in marriage will conditions be ideal enough to experiment and to break down enculturated inhibitions. Under this rationale, which admittedly is necessary in many situations, the specialist can fail the woman and the couple. Gross blocking of sexual responsiveness simply is not cured by a marriage ceremony, in spite of the skill and patience of an adequate male partner. When such conditions are suspected, the physician will collaborate carefully with the referring marriage counselor, or some well trained psychotherapist, in determining whether to recommend treatment prior to marriage or subsequent thereto.

The medical examination ends with the physician's assisting the woman in facing any difficulties that are significant to healthy adjustment, including what can be done about them. If all is well, a few minutes should be spent with further questions and in impressing her with the simplicity and naturalness of sex life, as well as the fact that it takes time to adjust initially, and

[28] Hastings, *op. cit.* Chapter 6; permission of the publisher.

that growth in sex relations can be a life-long series of pleasurable experience. Adequate emotional preparation for intercourse through love making should be stressed, with attention to variations of need from time to time. Prolonged love making is essential at times; at other times a more direct approach is preferable. Instruction in contraception—whatever the method—should be accompanied by the same care and alertness to emotional needs. She should be encouraged to call the physician before or after marriage should any questions arise.

C. THE MAN

As much care should be exercised in the physical check-up of the man as with the woman, with an eye on his total health picture. Since routine sterility tests are not practicable with the woman, most physicians do not attempt them for the man unless it seems of specific significance for either physical or psychological reasons. Prolonged venereal infection may have sterilized the man. A history of undescended testicles or of glandular infections may call for sperm analysis. Occasionally a man has had a vasectomy for the convenience of birth control, perhaps during a former marriage where no more children were desired. There can be little doubt that a prospective wife is entitled to this knowledge. The scrotum should be checked for hydrocele or undue varicocele; the testes for size, consistency, and presence of any unusual nodules. The foreskin should clear the glans penis. Usually a history of penile erection under stimulation or upon awaking in the morning is adequate proof that there is no physical inability to respond sexually. Lack of virility is largely due to psychological factors rather than to physical disability. The prostate and prostatic fluid are examined for pus or other malfunction. Occasionally a male is unable to ejaculate, although he can adequately maintain an erection, or there may be pain associated with orgasm, which calls for further check-out.

I. Ignorance and Fear

The man may be much more resistant to sexual instruction than the woman, since the mores dictate that he be the sexually informed one. The physician may have to approach this area with caution, or even use the necessity to learn about the intricacies of female sexual response as incentive to get the discussion going. Actually men can be notoriously ignorant about their own sexual nature. Those without experience in sexual intercourse, as well as those who have had traumatic experiences or formed poor sexual habits, have many questions about their "maleness." "Will I jump the gun?" "Might I be unable to satisfy her? Be impotent? Too small? Too large? Sterile?" If defensiveness is removed by an understanding physician or counselor, the man will ventilate these fears, preparing the way for facts and reassurance.

An almost fetishistic concern about the size of the penis, and the possible relation of this to adequacy as a sex partner, is common. Actually, almost any male can be reassured that what counts is how he uses the penis in the context of a total relationship, not its size. Often his unwarranted comparison of himself with other males is based upon occasions when he viewed them in a flaccid state, where there is much greater variation in the size of penes than when in erection. An occasional man appears to have a basis in fact for concern about the size of his sexual organ, since in the flaccid state only the loose folds of skin seem evident. Usually this is a non-pathological condition best described as involutional penis. It is the same phenomena noticeable in most males as a tendency for the penis to withdraw into the body cavity under conditions of extreme cold. With these cases this occurs normally in the flaccid state, with the cavernosa shaft of the penis reappearing in an adequate erection with sexual stimulation. Folklore to the contrary, the average erect penis is about six inches in length. When the reverse phenomena occurs and the man is anxious lest an unusually large penis interfere with normal coitus, he can be reminded of the data reported earlier on the unlimited distendability of the female vagina and vaginal barrel when the woman is adequately aroused by sexual stimulation.

If the man is concerned about too early ejaculation, suggestions may be made for detecting the aura-like feeling just prior to ejaculation and slowing down by ceasing coital activity momentarily, or by thinking of something else. Thus he can learn to prolong the pleasure of maximum excitation for himself and his partner. Gross cases of premature ejaculation will require a more thoroughgoing treatment, a combination of psychotherapy and physical reconditioning, usually with the particular partner that is going to be involved.[29]

It is imperative that the physician become skilled in distinguishing anxiety which is quite common to the culture out of which the man originates from those deeper fears which are rooted in psychological crippling. False reassurance can be deadly with a highly neurotic individual. Impotence or homosexual difficulties are not cured by marriage. The outline suggested above in cases of frigidity may be adapted for use in eliciting information

[29] Rutledge, Aaron L. *Marital Therapy*, "Treatment of Premature Ejaculation." To be published.

about suspected impotence, or in getting a history of sexual adequacy. Referral of serious cases to the marriage counselor who sent the patient or to some skilled psychotherapist for psychological treatment is imperative.

II. Sequence of Male Sex Response

Historically a great deal more has been known about male sexual response than that of the woman. Nonetheless, this has not prevented the individual man from being woefully ignorant about his sexual make up and function. Parker's Manual [30] provides excellent illustrations of male sex organs, including the erection phenomena. Although the entire discussion may seldom be used with one patient, explanation of the natural sequence of male sex response should prepare the physician or counselor for detecting possible areas of difficulty.

Kinsey and Associates [31] have provided valuable statistical data on the incidence of sex experiences according to age, culture, and other factors. Already this text has paid tribute to the Masters team for its primary research in female sexuality. As a side interest, they have also carefully documented the sexual response sequence of the human male. The author is particularly indebted to them for discussions of this data.[32]

For comparative purposes Masters has used the same four phases of sexual response: excitement, plateau, orgasm and resolution. Allowing for variations between subjects, and from time to time with the same subject, certain of their observations show needed light on the topic. What happens then, when the male is sexually stimulated?

The *excitement phase* as a separate entity is shortlived unless the stimulus is varied and this stage deliberately drawn out. The first anatomic response is beginning erection of the penis, whether the stimulus be physical or psychic, brought about by the flow of blood into the cavernosa of the penis.[33] Complete erection may be reached within three to five seconds with sufficient stimulus, even though the total amount of sexual tension present is minimal. The vascocongestion may ebb and flow with the change of stimulus, short of the successive stages of sexual response. In fact, in the average male penile erection can be interfered with by such extraneous

---

[30] Parker, V. H., *"The Illustrated Birth Control Manual,"* New York: Cadillac Publishing Company, 1957, Chapter 3.

[31] Kinsey, A. C. et al, *"Sexual Behavior in The Human Male."* Philadelphia: W. B. Saunders Company. 1948.

[32] Masters, W. H. and Virginia E. Johnson, "The Sexual Response of the Human Male." I. Gross Anatomic Considerations. *Western Journal of Surgery, Obstetrics and Gynecology.* 71: 85-95. March-April 1963.

[33] Parker, *op. cit.*

factors as noise, or change of lights, even though sexual stimulation continues all the while. This is an important phenomena to keep in mind in checking out reports of histories of erection loss.

The primary erogenous areas of the male in addition to the penis are the scrotum, and rectal area. In one third of Masters' subjects nipple erection occurred, usually developing late in the excitement phase and lasting through the sexual cycle, and for many minutes afterwards. Direct stimulation causes the external rectal sphincter to contract both voluntarily and involuntarily either in the excitement or plateau phases of the sex cycle.

The normally loose scrotum begins to constrict, and the shortening of the cords causes elevation of the testicles during the advanced stages of the excitement phase. If stimulation continues unabated this process is completed in the plateau phase as the sac is both tightly constricted and congested.

Continued stimulation rushes the male from excitement to the *plateau phase*; in fact, as Masters points out, it is almost impossible to distinguish between late excitement and early plateau. This phase is characterized by gross vascocongestion of the entire body, as well as the genitalia. Mucosa tissue of the mouth and nose become congested, and, if the sex flush (previously described in the female) is to occur, it will be when this phase is well established. Whether it occurs as well as the intensity thereof seems to depend upon many factors, but primarily upon the nature and intensity of psychological influences. The flush begins at the diaphragm and spreads over the chest, to the neck, face and forehead, and perhaps over the extremities, and its fullest expression looks like the measles. Hyperventilation may develop late in the plateau phase, dependent upon the degree of sexual tension. The penis may increase further in size, especially the glans, which also may show some variation in color, changing to the purple of venous stasis. If this phase of tumescence is maintained two or three drops of fluid often appears at the urethal opening, and this frequently contains spermatazoa prior to ejaculation. This phenomena has led to conceptions both in and out of wedlock when male and female genitalia were in contact, but the male did not ejaculate. The author knows of several cases of "virginal conception" which occurred in this manner.

Vasocongestion increases the size of the testes by an average of fifty per cent during the plateau phase; the longer and more intense the sexual tension, the greater the increase. Testicular elevation continues as sex tension mounts until the sac is tight against the perineum. If the testes do not at least partially elevate the male will not ejaculate. One of the unexplained phenomena is the tendency of the left testicle to hang lower than the right.[34] Masters found that in many males the right testicle will fix itself firmly against the perineum in the early plateau phase, while the left might continue to move up and down in the congested scrotal sac, finally tightening immediately before ejaculation.[35]

If direct coital activity continues unabated the male rushes through the plateau phase to early orgasm, often reducing the time from intromission to ejaculation to two or three minutes. Not only is this insufficient stimulus for the woman; it grossly reduces the length of this highly pleasurable phase for the man. Practice in detecting the moment when further activity would bring involuntary orgasm and prolongation of the plateau of enjoyment becomes a joint task of most couples.

Orgasmic Phase. With sex tension, hyperventilation, and vasocongestion at a peak of intensity, the orgasm occurs as a series of involuntary contractions beginning at an interval of about eight-tenths of a second. Three or four major contractions occur, then slow down in rapidity, with minor contractions of the urethra continuing irregularly up to several seconds. These contractions occur in the "constrictor urethrae, bulbo and ischiocavernosi and transverse peronei musculature." Rectal sphincter contractions also occur involuntarily, usually limited to two or three times, and at times the buttocks contract, and occasionally there is striated muscle spasm.

Masters [36] discusses ejaculation in terms of two stages. During the first stage the contractions begin with the accessory organs of reproduction— vas deferens, seminal vesicles, etc.—and develop the sensation of "ejaculatory inevitability," which may last two or three seconds. Seminal emission occurs through the prostatic urethra, and prostate content is delivered to the seminal fluid several times during ejaculation. The second stage of ejaculation occurs as the seminal fluid is emitted through the penile urethra. The pressure is sufficient to propel the fluid from one to two feet in the absence of any obstruction. Once under way, the ejaculatory process cannot be halted, regardless of the degree of interference with sexual activity or interest. On some occasions ejaculations seem to be purely reflex action, but usually the highest cortical levels are involved.[37]

Ejaculation instantly sets into operation the *resolution phase* of the male sex cycle, characterized by both specific and general detumescence. The sex

[34] *Ibid.,* Chapter 3.
[35] Masters and Johnson, *op. cit.*
[36] *Ibid.*
[37] Retief, P. J. M. "Physiology of Micturition and Ejaculation." *South African Medical Journal.* 24: 509-514. 1950.

flush, if it has appeared, disappears rapidly in essentially the same order in which it appeared, beginning from the diaphragm. Immediately the penis reduces to about one and one half the unstimulated size, with secondary detumescence taking longer. Continued presence of stimulus may prolong this final phase of size reduction. The urethral diameter and urethral bulb returns to normal size. Scrotal sac congestion reduces and the skin returns to normal, rapidly or slowly, somewhat characteristic of the individual, although some skin thickening may be observable for two hours. Generally the longer the plateau phase was maintained, the longer the vasocongestion of the penis and testicles continues after orgasm. Hyperventilation is resolved with the rapid release of muscular tension, followed by an all encompassing sense of psychic and physical relaxation. Sleep often follows within a matter of seconds after ejaculation.

The physical findings, as well as any questions raised by the man, should be carefully discussed. The physician should have the dual purpose of getting across facts and at the same time being alert for instances of undue anxiety that might portray emotional problems. Some physicians will end the contact with the man at this point, while others will proceed to share any significant discoveries about the prospective wife. A joint session with the man and woman, sharing any significant findings, advice, or direct instruction can be invaluable to many couples.

D. THE CONTROL OF CONCEPTION

Careful instruction in controlling conception is an integral part of the pre-marital physical for both man and woman, and is one of those services that can best be rendered in a joint conference. It is best that each understand the methods to be used, even if applied by the other person. This means that the physician must be up-to-date in valid information on varying contraceptive methods, and it is extremely unwise to trust the advertising material put out by manufacturers. Greenblat's A DOCTOR'S MARITAL GUIDE FOR PATIENTS, and Guttmacher's THE COMPLETE BOOK OF BIRTH CONTROL [38] are reliable resources for the physician and counselor, as well as for direct use with the clients. The Planned Parenthood Federation of America is a constant source of the latest research in contraceptive practice.

[38] Greenblat, Bernard, "A Doctor's Marital Guide for Patients," Chicago: The Budlong Press, 1959; Guttmacher, Alan F., "The Complete Book of Birth Control," New York: Ballentine Books, 1961; both in economical editions.

I. The Older Reliable Methods

The rubber condom plus a spermicidal is the safest and most satisfactory method to be used by the man. Most couples begin with this and continue until the wife is fitted with a vaginal diaphragm. The condom has certain disadvantages, however. The penis must be erect before it is applied, which necessitates interruption of foreplay. This proves difficult for some men since it causes a "let down," and the wife's build-up of desire also may be hindered. The solution is for the couple to incorporate the application of the condom into the foreplay. Another disadvantage of the condom is that withdrawal must accompany the losing of erection lest the sperm spill over at the base and, contacting the moisture of her body, swim into the vaginal canal. Some conceptions occur by the man getting sperm on the hands in removing the used condom and transmitting them through contact with the vagina. A condom of inferior quality may break at the time the semen is emitted. Most companies make two qualities and the best are only slightly more expensive. An inch of slack left at the tip of the penis will help avoid breaking, as will ample lubrication. Incidentally, most people do not realize that petroleum products will deteriorate rubber products such as condoms and diaphragms.

For most women who wish to plan their pregnancies, the rhythm method of birth control is very risky in early marriage because of the fluctuation of ovulation time due to emotional stresses and excitement. The best method of conception control for many couples is the well fitted vaginal diaphragm with spermicidal jelly or cream, with a record of about ninety-five percent effectiveness. Most of the failures are due to occasionally forgetting to use the diaphragm or failure to apply it properly. Some of the most common errors in diaphragm usage, leading to unplanned conception, include: lack of understanding by the woman of how to place and check for fit; buying, without a prescription, the wrong size; failure to use spermicidal solution behind the barrier to guarantee that the cervix is covered; removing the implement soon after coitus for unnecessary douching; having intercourse many hours after initial insertion without reapplication of a spermicidal; and just being too lazy to apply it.

The diaphragm has the added value of interfering with sexual pleasure the least of any of the self-applied instruments, since it can be applied well in advance and is not to be removed for eight hours after intercourse. This allows time for elimination of the sperm, and removal with the bath becomes the natural thing to do, making it possible for the couple to remain together following intercourse. When fitted properly—and adjusted to emotionally—the diaphragm is not felt by the wife, nor does it interfere with the husband's pleasure. It is rare that a woman cannot be fitted properly.

Whether or not the young woman is to be fitted with a vaginal diaphragm before the marriage is a controversial subject. If so, the dilation of the hymen will have to be completed and care taken that the diaphragm is fitted to relaxed rather than to tight vaginal muscles. In the latter case, a check every few days for the first few weeks of regular coitus is necessary to see that the diaphragm still fits. If the girl is a virgin, most physicians seem to prefer to fit the diaphragm several weeks to three months following the marriage, so that dilation is completed naturally and repeated intercourse has brought relaxation to vaginal muscles. The physician should remember, however, that human needs are too variable to apply a rule of thumb to every person. On the other hand, determining the needs of an individual takes a good deal of the physician's time and some will not make exceptions. If the woman is to be fitted after marriage an appointment should be made so as to encourage her return. A diaphragm should be over-fitted (tightly) to allow for the enlargement of the lower vaginal canal which occurs naturally in sexual stimulation. Even so, the diaphragm serves primarily as a retainer for the spermicidal preparation and the patient should be instructed accordingly.

Some men and women find it difficult to trust a diaphragm because "just looking at it, it doesn't make sense." Usually the following procedure produces relaxation in the use of this method: with a model of the vaginal canal the physician explains anatomically how and why the diaphragm works; then determines the proper size and applies it, carefully explaining each step; then demonstrates checking for proper placement; she is asked to re-insert it herself; the doctor checks to see that she did it correctly. All that is needed afterwards is practice, checking with him if she has any questions. SEX WITHOUT FEAR by Lewin and Gilmore [39] has helpful pictures of the insertion of the diaphragm. In order to facilitate comfort and ease in its use, it may be suggested that the woman insert the diaphragm routinely in preparation for the evening during early marriage. This also eliminates having to interrupt love-making in order to prepare for intercourse. The husband likewise should be informed in the use of the diaphragm to enable him to trust the method.

Spermicidals which are used without an artificial barrier such as condom

[39] Lewin, Samuel A. and John Gilmore, *"Sex Without Fear,"* New York: Lear Publishers, 1950.

or diaphragm are not as reliable as either the condom or diaphragm method of contraception.

Although not highly reliable for most couples, the rhythm method must be mentioned, since it is the only acceptable plan for many people. The chart frequently used for determining days for intercourse or for abstinence is as follows:

If Shortest Period Has Been	First Fertile (Unsafe) Day is
21 Days	3rd Day
22 "	4th "
23 "	5th "
24 "	6th "
25 "	7th "
26 "	8th "
27 "	9th "
28 "	10th "
29 "	11th "
30 "	12th "
31 "	13th "
32 "	14th "
33 "	15th "
34 "	16th "
35 "	17th "

If Longest Period Has Been	Last Fertile (Unsafe) Day is
21 Days	10th Day
22 "	11th "
23 "	12th "
24 "	13th "
25 "	14th "
26 "	15th "
27 "	16th "
28 "	17th "
29 "	18th "
30 "	19th "
31 "	20th "
32 "	21tb "
33 "	22th "
34 "	23rd "
35 "	24th "

No simple and successful means of determining ovulation is available, which means that extra days must be allowed for safety. It is also well established that the time of ovulation can be affected by illness or emotional stress. The steroids have been used effectively in regularizing the monthly cycle of many women.

II. The Newer Methods

Nothing short of the word "revolution" describes the transition of the past decade or two in the field of contraception. Research studies are almost out of date before they have been published and the search will continue for simpler, more effective and economical methods of population control. One method is effective with one ethnic, religious, or socio-economic group and completely unacceptable to another.

The Pill. No development of modern times, including the exploration of space, has received such attention and acclaim as the oral contraceptive. Widespread experimentation began in 1956, but it was 1960 before the Medical Committee of Planned Parenthood Federation of America endorsed Enovid, the first of "the pills." Several compounds have now been approved by the Federal Pure Food and Drug Administration, with Enovid, Norlutin, and Ortho-Novum heading the list.

The oral contraceptives are based on a steroid chemical similar to progesterone, which normally prevents ovulation in order to keep the woman from having fertilized eggs of different ages in the uterus. The pill duplicates this suppression of ovulation. One pill is taken each day, beginning with the fifth day of the menstrual cycle, counting the day the flow begins as the first day, and continuing for twenty days. If menstruation does not begin, as is true of about three per cent of patients, the woman simply begins a new cycle of pills one week after she took the last one.

No woman, contends Guttmacher,[40] who has faithfully taken the pills according to schedule has become pregnant in any of the large scale tests. However, if a pill is omitted even one day in the cycle of twenty days, there is a chance of pregnancy. If the woman misses a pill, or forgets to begin until the sixth day of menstruation, she should use some other contraceptive method for the remainder of that month. When pregnancy is desired, the pills are simply discontinued.

The side effects which developed in one out of five patients in the early use of the oral contraceptives included slight gastro-intestinal disturbance,

[40] Guttmacher, Alan F. *The Complete Book of Birth Control.* New York. Ballantine Books. 1961—Chapter 5.

mild nausea and a bloated feeling similar to the early months of pregnancy. These usually disappeared after one or two weeks, if the medication was continued. The symptoms may be lessened by antacids such as Soda-mints, Tums, Gelusil, and it may help if the pill is taken with the largest meal of the day or just prior to bed. The occasional slight gain in weight is due to an increase in appetite, or to retention of fluids and can be dealt with accordingly.

Although sexual desire probably is not actually affected by the oral contraceptives, because of the absence of fear of pregnancy some forty percent of women reported increased sexual desire. The woman on the pill usually experiences no menstrual pain, has less flow, the cycle is regular, and usually there is lessened premenstrual tension or discomfort. There is only one caution; a nursing mother should not use the pill, since it does suppress lactation.

Most of the early research on side effects of oral contraceptives was based on use of the larger (10 m.g.) dosage which has now been made obsolete. Rice-Wray [41] experimented with six low-dose oral compounds:

Norethindrone acetate	4 mg.	
Ethinylestradiol	0.05 mg.	Schering, Berlin, Germany
Norethindrone	2 mg.	
Mestranol	0.10 mg.	Syntex, S.A. and Hormona, S.A., Mexico
Ethynodiol diacetate	1 mg.	
Mestranol	0.1 mg.	G. D. Searle & Co., Chicago, Ill.
Lynestrenol	2.5 mg.	
Mestranol	0.075 mg.	Organon, Inc., West Orange, N.J.
Norethynodrel	2.5 mg.	
Mestranol	0.1 mg.	G. D. Searle & Co., Chicago, Ill.
Lutoral	2 mg.	
Mestranol	0.080 mg.	Syntex, S. A. Mexico and Ely Lilly & Co., Indianapolis, Ind.

He found that these minimal dosages were as effective as the original large-dose compounds (also listed above), along with appreciable lessening

[41] Rice-Wray, Edris, "Investigating the Orals" in *Advances in Planned Parenthood,* Edited by Aquiles J. Sobrero and Sarah Lewit, Schenkman Publishing Company, Inc.. 1965, pp. 21-27.

of unpleasant side effects, and a greatly reduced cost. Coupled with this is the fact that the side effects in these low-dose compounds are not essentially different from each other. There is every indication that post-treatment fertility is not impaired and that babies born to women who have been on oral contraception are normal. By carefully eliminating pre-existing cancer, and keeping check through yearly Papanicolaou smears, clinics have been able to do the kind of research which dispels fears that the orals might be cancerogenic. There is now a growing impression that the drugs might be anti-cancerogenic in effect. Guttmacher [42] summarizes the pill against criteria of an "ideal" contraceptive:

1. Safety: The pill is harmless, for at least five years of use. There is no indication of damage to thyroid, adrenal, or other glands; nor to liver, blood, kidney, or other parts of the body; nor any adverse effects on ability to have children; nor any causation or stimulation of cancer of the uterus, ovary or breast.

2. Reliability: The pill, if taken as prescribed, offers 100 percent protection against pregnancy.

3. Side Effects: The rating is excellent for four out of five and most of the remaining twenty percent can be controlled or disappears with use. The smaller doses now being developed promise to eliminate this problem for most women.

4. Price: Although still somewhat expensive, the cost is constantly being reduced.

5. Simplicity of Use: The pill falls short here, because of the necessity of carefully following the prescribed regimen.

6. Reversibility: Ovulation ordinarily occurs during the cycle following termination of the pill.

7. Time of Use: It may be taken at a time completely removed from the sexual act.

In all probability the pill eventually will be approved by the Roman Catholic Church as a natural method of family planning. Already it has widespread approval as a temporary treatment as a means of regularizing a woman's menstrual cycle.

Although the contraceptive method of choice for each couple is likely to be found only after much experimentation, for newlyweds the pill has many advantages. In addition to total protection, it permits complete spontaneity and avoids the difficulties of mechanical fittings in the case of the virginal bride. The bride-to-be should experiment with the pill for a month

[42] Guttmacher, *op. cit.;* permission of publisher.

or two to adjust to any temporary side effects prior to marriage. (See Chapter 4 for a plan of pre-marital counseling built around oral contraception.) Oral contraception also makes it possible for the bride to avoid menstruation during the honeymoon, one of the perpetual problems in marriage plans through the ages.

The Intra-Uterine Devices (IUD). It is interesting to note how many of the modern methods of contraception have been present at least as possibilities in the folklore throughout the ages. Early medical history in Europe found a variety of metal pessaries being inserted into the os of the uterus as a means of preventing the migration of spermatozoa. Many of these came into disrepute because of the irritation factor and the possible relationship to uterine cancer. Recently there has been an upsurge of experimentation in this area, with thousands of control cases in many of the major cities throughout the country and in South American countries. The new intra-uterine devices are made primarily of plastic composition but at least one new implement is made of stainless steel. These come in spirals, loops, bows and rings, with and without "tails."

The following are a list of the six major types of IUD:

IUD	FOUNDER
Spiral 5 (large)	Margulies
Spiral 12 Diagonal J (small)	"
Loop 1 (small)	Lippes
Loop 2 (large)	"
Bow 3	Birnberg
Steel Ring	Hall and Stone

Hall [43] found that most complaints about IUD occur during the first two months after insertion. Bleeding was by far the most frequent, accounting for close to one half of the total. Pain was reported by about one-fifth of the women. Others complained about being unable to palpate the IUD to tell if it was in position and a few thought there were excessive protrusions of the tails of the objects. In terms of expulsion, it was found that women who expelled a device once were apt to expel it again. The most common cause for removal was bleeding, and secondly, pain. Following along after this was pelvic inflammatory disease, psychological factors, pregnancy and suspicion of pregnancy, desire to conceive, gynecological surgery, husbands' reported discomfort, and moving away from the clinic. Hall believed that

[43] Hall, Robert E. "Use of Intra-Uterine Contraceptives in an Indigent Population" in *Advances in Planned Parenthood*, Cambridge, Massachusetts, Schenkman Publishing Company, Inc. pp. 115-122.

most of the pelvic infections had an origin that predated the insertion of IUD's, or that the devices were removed prematurely and unnecessarily before treatment. In this study forty-three percent of the coils were either expelled or removed, compared with eight percent of Loop #2, and four percent of the bows.

In a study under the auspices of the National Committee on Maternal Health, Tietze [44] reports on more than 8000 women who had remained under continued observation, with another 2000 who had discontinued use of the device or who had been lost to follow-up. The aggregate period of use for the cases, both active and closed, was more than 89,000 "woman-months." He utilized all six types of the IUD.

A total of 163 women experienced one or more unintended pregnancies in this study; 995 had one or more expulsions of the IUD; and 895 had one or more removals of the IUD for relevant reasons.

Of the 163 unintended pregnancies, a known 84 occurred with an IUD in position. Of the remaining 79, classified as "device undetermined," it was thought that most of them were pregnancies after unnoted expulsion, particularly for the Birnberg Bow and the stainless steel ring, both of which have no appendages for ready inspection.

Of these expulsions, about one fifth were not noted by the wearer as having occurred. This highlights one of the ways in which extra attention is necessary with the IUD, since only frequent pelvic examinations will guarantee discovery of an expulsion and reduce the chance of pregnancy. In 776 of the expulsion cases, the same or another type of IUD was reinserted. Two expulsions each were reported for 186 patients, 3 each for 57 patients, and 4 each for 16 patients, and 9 had five or more expulsions apiece.

Removal of the IUD occurred for a variety of reasons, including irregular bleeding and pain, these two accounting separately or together for one half of all first removals. In the more than 10,324 cases, 138 asked for removal because they were now ready to conceive a child. Sixty-five percent of those who wished to conceive did so within six months after removal and 87% within one year, which are essentially normal percentages. Removals due to pelvic inflammatory disease was reported in 105 cases, with a slightly higher incidence for the spirals than for loops, and much higher for either one of those than for the bow and the steel rings. These statistics are complicated by variations in socio-economic status, sexual habits, and other diagnostic idiosyncracies of investigators and of patients. In 50 cases of

[44] Tietze, Christopher, "Review of Clinical Data on Intra-Uterine Devices" in *Advances in Planned Parenthood*. Cambridge, Massachusetts, Schenkman Publishing Company, Inc. 1965. pp. 97-105.

pelvic inflammatory disease the device was removed, while in 48 cases the condition was treated with the IUD in place. The pelvic inflammation occurred in 7 cases following expulsion of the device or removal for other reasons. About one-third of the patients with PID were hospitalized, with four undergoing surgery. In more than half the cases diagnosed as PID, a history of inflammation prior to insertion of the IUD was obtained.

Among the requirements listed by Segal [45] for admission to IUD clinics are:

1. No age limit.
2. Postabortal or postpartum patients not earlier than 60 days if amenorrheic, or at the time of the second menstrual period.
3. Physical examinations and Pap smears to be taken by clinicians at referring clinics to rule out any of the following contraindications for use of IUD:
   (a) Acute or sub-acute pelvic inflamatory disease
   (b) Suspicion of pregnancy or carcinoma
   (c) Menstrual irregularity and,
   (d) Myomas of significant size.

In terms of procedures, the physician and an assistant set up sterile conditions, insert the IUD, and instruct the patient on how to palpate the appendage of the device. A recheck consists of inserting the speculum and visualizing the presence of the nylon filament (tail) in the case of the Lippes loop, or the beaded appendage in the case of the Margulies spiral. For the Hall ring and the Birnberg bow, a uterine sound is used to palpate the device into position. A complete pelvic and cervical visualization is made, and a repeat Pap smear is taken if indicated. A discussion of possible side effects and precautions is had with the client.

In some cases, Segal confirms, the use of a tenaculum is required for dilation of the internal os, which can be quite painful. In many instances involving the bow or loop a tenaculum is used to straighten out the cervical canal and as a counter-pressure to the direction of the inserter as the device was fed through the tube. In many cases the pressure of the hand on the abdomen is sufficient and a tenaculum is not used, while in certain cases neither a tenaculum nor dilation is required. The bow, loop and spiral seem to be the easiest to insert of the IUD's, and are therefore less disturbing to the patient during insertion. Segal thinks that the degree of patency of the internal os and the degree of flexion of the cervical canal assist in the selec-

[45] Segal, Sheldon J. "Fertility Control: Charter and Uncharted Horizons" in *Advances in Planned Parenthood,* Cambridge, Massachusetts, Schenkman Publishing Co., Inc., pp. 107-113.

tion of the most suitable IUD, along with the emotional state of the patient, and any significant tension, or lowered pain threshold.

Many specialists feel that for the woman who can retain an intra-uterine device, this affords one of the most acceptable forms of birth control.

In addition to the clinical, biochemical, and physiological works of the endocrinologists, other disciplines have begun to be interested in contraceptive methodology. The most notable is the immunologist who has evolved a new sub-classification of contraception termed *immuno-reproduction*.[46] Efforts to induce the reversible aspermatogenesis in the male by active immunization with sperm or testicular antigens is underway. Already it is possible to completely slough all cells in the spermatogenic line, including spermatogonia, by immunizing guinea pigs with testicular extracts. Such extensive damage can not be reversed but it has been recently observed that immunized animals which produce azospermic ejaculates for as long as six months can return to full fertility. Naturally much must be done before these observations can be applied to contraceptive technology with human beings, although it has already been demonstrated that the principle of immunologically induced sloughing of seminiferous epithelium applies to the human male.

Virtually all the anti-spermatogenic compounds tested so far appear to have toxic side effects which contraindicate their adoption for human use, but pharmacologists know already that the testis is susceptible to direct interference by chemical agents. Several drugs act directly on the germinal epithelium without impairing Leydig cell production of androgens.

Amazing success has been gained in certain animal experimentations and successful gonadotropin-suppression has been gained for periods up to sixty days with the injection of synthetic progestins. Recent findings suggest that steroid control of gonadotropin release is mediated via the hypothalamus, so that the present oral contraceptives might most accurately be described as hypothalamic-blocking agents. Nothing is known currently about directly affecting the pituitary to prevent gonadotropin release.

Experimentation with the production of antibodies to the luteinizing hormone molecule, with the expectation that such antibodies combine with and cause the inactivation of circulating gonadotropins, is proceeding. There is a good deal of indication that either active production or passive transfer of LH antibodies can prevent ovulation or spermatogenesis.

[46] Ibid., pp. 29-37; used freely in this discussion.

Antiestrogens have been studied in the hope that they could interfere with the normal zygote passage or endometrial priming. A series of non-steroidal compounds have evolved with the characteristics of being both mildly estrogenic and mildly antiestrogenic. Ethamoxytriphetol and clomiphene are examples which produce a remarkable antifertility activity in animals if administered during the tubal transport of zygotes and while the blastocyst is free and uterine lumen.

III. Greater Complexity

Since the first break through with the steroids, the popular cry has been that "simpler methods" of contraception were just on the horizon. It becomes increasingly clear that the newer methods, as pointed out by Sobrero,[47] require multiple contacts between client and clinic. Increasingly this means that one of the determining factors in the success of contraception, on the one hand, and the peace of mind accompanying it on the other, is repeated contact between the patient and the physician and other personnel. Therein lies both the strength and the weakness of modern methods of family planning. Given adequate service and insensitive human contacts, and the methods themselves will be suspect. On the other hand, excellent public relations, sensitive attention to the emotional and physical needs of the client, coupled with the latest in information from this rapidly developing field, points not only to more successful contraceptive practice but to better health in general.

Just as the attitude of some physicians in the past toward the vaginal diaphragm and the amount of time it took to fit it caused them to disparage the method and thus confuse the populace, the same can happen today around the requirements for the oral contraceptive regimen and the intrauterine devices, as well as for any newer discoveries yet on the horizon.

Every individual and couple prepared for marriage should be urged to get in touch with the physician immediately if an undesired pregnancy occurs, rather than just fretting about it. The physician can help in several ways: (1) ventilation of feelings of resentment can clear the air and make it possible for the couple to talk with each other, help avoid one going on blaming the other or fearing that he is blamed, and hopefully result in genuine acceptance of joint responsibility for adult sexual behavior, (2) the woman can be kept out of the hands of charlatan abortionists, (3) possibly an un-

[47] Sobrero, Aquiles J., "Planned Parenthood Clinics and Medical Research: General Aspects" in *Advances in Planned Parenthood*, Edited by Aquiles J. Sobrero and Sarah Lewit, Cambridge, Massachusetts, Schenkman Publishing Company, Inc., 1965. pp. 1-9.

born child can be kept from brain injury through use of ill-advised drugs, and a referral can be made if psychological assistance is indicated. In thousands of cases the woman tries to cause abortion by taking any of a variety of drugs which she can get without a prescription through the beautician, bar tender, druggist, or acquaintance. It is almost impossible for her to take anything strong enough to cause an abortion short of killing herself; however, she can take many preparations that may cause damage to the brain of the fetus in its early stages of growth. These practices help account for the epidemic incidence of brain injured children today.

E. INITIAL SEXUAL INTERCOURSE

Initial sexual intercourse can be an anxiety laden area for many inexperienced young people. The physician will do well to elicit these feelings, often covered by superficial denial of concern, with a view to clearing the atmosphere for helpful pointers. Shyness and false modesty can be overcome if, after ventilating fears and misconceptions, they are encouraged to think in terms of the naturalness and fun of sexual experience.

The couple may need to be reminded that all that which has been learned about the tender expression of affection by both verbal and physical means can be the prelude to or accompany sexual intercourse. The entire period of engaged courtship has been in preparation for this and subsequent experiences together, and each intercourse can be a culmination of their need to share with each other. Loving words, gentle stimulating caresses, the lips, the breasts, the genitals, the entire bodies and personality come into play as each expresses feeling for the other. Then comes the giving of each to the other in complete sex union. At times foreplay is not necessary and can get in the way of one or both of the couple, but for initial experience it can be most vital and may always be desirable for some.

Initial penetration may be somewhat difficult in spite of preparation both physically and emotionally. The traditional position seems best to begin with: the wife on her back, knees drawn up, legs comfortably apart and both hands free for caressing. The husband is over her, one arm under her neck, carrying the weight of the upper body on the elbow, with the other hand free for fondling. The bulk of his weight is carried on the knees so as to leave her body in contact with his, yet free to move in any direction she chooses as she responds in rhythmic movements.

Initial entry may be made difficult by the husband resting too low on the knees, or too far downward from her body. In this position the penis goes directly against the hymen, which may resist, and this in turn may cause the vaginal muscles to contract and offer further difficulty in penetration. If he moves forward or slightly higher over her, penetration is made slightly above the lower and more resistant part of the hymen. Contact with the upper part of the vulva is very satisfactory to him, and the resulting stimulation of the clitoral area is pleasant to her, tending toward relaxation of the vaginal muscles. Pressure is applied gradually at the vaginal opening but still pressing slightly upward. The tissues just above the opening are quite pliable, and gradually relaxation occurs. If the wife tenses up, the husband can let off and continue caressing the external genitalia.

When the wife realizes that the vaginal muscles are contracting and causing resistance, she can help by concentrating on her desire to receive him. If she continues to feel the pressure of the resistance she can "push out" the walls of the vaginal canal, almost as if she were trying to expel an object from the vagina, except that she knows she is merely expanding the opening so as to receive the desired penis. This counteracts the slight resistance coming from the unaccustomed penetration pressure.

Entrance can be facilitated also if the husband holds the glans penis at the vaginal opening, pressing slightly upward and then downward, but then remains still in this position as she responds with gently pushing and receptive movements. This puts her in control where she can let off if she feels too much pressure, or vary the position or angle of entrance by hip movements and by guiding the penis with her hands.

When initial penetration occurs the husband well might remain still for a few moments until the wife relaxes. Gentle pressure, leaning the penis down against the edge of the hymen, stretches it with ease in most cases. If the wife continues to feel tense, thoughts about wanting to receive the penis, along with the same reaching, receptive movements described above aid further penetration and movement. Should there be too much difficulty involving pain, penetration can be deferred until later, and the couple should know that this does not mean failure. Sexual stimulation can continue, either manually or with the penis against the labia minora and the external vaginal orifice. This can be quite exciting to both and a satisfactory climax and relaxation can follow for each, or they can relax together and wait until another occasion. It is difficult for the inexperienced male to prolong ejaculation long enough to gain intromission if the hymen is particularly difficult. If he loses control she should understand and accept satisfaction through his manual manipulation until another erection is gained, usually much later.

The wife should know at the beginning of each sexual encounter to begin building herself up toward a peak of desire and thrill, utilizing bodily movements and the pressure of vaginal (and anal) muscles, and massaging the entire mons and clitoral area against her partner. This speeds her toward optimal excitement, culminating in completed satisfaction. The inexperienced woman should know that if for a while her climaxes are not very pronounced, this need not prevent enjoyment of the highly pleasurable plateau phase, followed by a "letting go" and gradual resolution in relaxation. Whatever she has learned about attaining orgasm earlier will be of value if it is not too laden with guilt.

She should be aware of the husband's feelings and learn to hesitate at his suggestion to keep him from ejaculating too early for her. Her peak of interest can be maintained by their stopping movement in a position in which the penis continues to press toward the clitoris, while he relaxes. If she is near a climax, his stopping may interrupt her mood, and even keep her from orgasm, when continuing to ejaculation might bring her to the peak of pleasure and to a climax. It is not easy for the man to know when to delay and when to continue; this comes only from experience with her and help by her. After intercourse in the traditional position has become easy enough, it is helpful, especially to the wife, if occasionally she assumes the uppermost position. This puts her in control where, by experimenting with bodily and vaginal movements and pressures, she can learn most rapidly how to be thrilled and satisfied.

A brief session with the couple together is a wonderful way to complete the doctor's part of preparation for marriage. One of the primary concerns of the physician who prepares a young couple for marriage is building the kind of relationship that will bring them back for help with any problems early in their marital adjustment. All too frequently they prolong returning until poor sex habits have been formulated and lack of adjustment has become a major source of conflict.

F. RECONTACTING THE COUNSELOR

In some cases the physician will be the only counselor involved, ending the consultations with an open door policy for any indicated return, on the one hand, and encouraging the couple to talk over together feelings and attitudes about the examination, as well as all other areas of their relationship. In many other cases the physician will undertake only the physical examination portions of this procedure, leaving all exploratory interviewing, instruction and counseling to the pre-marital counselor.

In no other area of professional work can careful collaboration of specialists pay such dividends in health for the individuals, the couple and the new family. Whenever initially referred by a counselor, the physician should return the couple to his care, with either a telephone or written report. It is constructive practice to suggest that they talk over the physician's findings with the counselor, who can be alert for misconceptions on their part, for residual anxiety, and can provide opportunity for assimilation and socialization of new ideas into total readiness for marriage.[48]

When the medical examination has been completed and discussed, and pre-marital sexual counseling and instruction is completed, what more can the physician and the counselor do? If they have demonstrated a healthy interest, the couple will know they have a friend and probably will return if assistance is needed. Yet their very desire to succeed and the professional efforts to help them may cause hesitation to return in the face of difficulties that indicate failure. Why not make it easy for them to remain in contact? Permission can be given for them to call anytime. An appointment for an early check-up can be made and even a six month or a year follow-up may be in order in certain cases. When difficulty can be predicted, it may be wise for them to have an appointment immediately upon returning from the honeymoon or about a month after the wedding.

The need for and importance of early supportive help to a young couple will have to be weighed against the dangers of too great dependency upon the professional, although this danger is great only with the exceptional case. In every case they can be encouraged to be experimental and openly communicative with each other in all things sexual. Problem solving and adaptive skills must be developed here, as in all areas of man-woman relationships. Sexual needs and interests change as personality grows and the marriage evolves. This can lead to a life-long sexual and affectional adventure for two individuals who choose to work out their destiny together.

---

[48] Names of competent marriage counselors can be obtained through the American Association on Marriage Counselors, Inc., 27 Woodcliff Drive, Madison, New Jersey.

Part Two

PREREQUISITE KNOWLEDGE AND THE CONTENT OF PRE-MARITAL COUNSELING

Chapter 9

PREREQUISITE KNOWLEDGE AND
RESOURCES - I

There is a vast body of knowledge from many fields which on the surface seems to be only incidental, but which in reality is basic to the science and art of pre-marital counseling. Resident in the background of consciousness, this understanding and its attendant attitudes becomes the foundation of an effective counseling relationship. This knowledge ranges from the mundane, through the scientific, to the mystical; from the physical surroundings, through a phenomenal body of data at varying stages of verification, to the scientific and philosophical assumptions underlying the frame of reference from which the counselor functions.

These areas of background information include personality theory, the various methods of psychotherapy, and a wide range of general and specific information centering around human development, socio-cultural and religious factors, family life, medicine, genetics, law, economics, sexual phenomena, and psychopathology. These are the raw materials, along with the life-long experience of the counselor and of the client, which are utilized creatively as the counseling situation calls for attitudes and insight not previously available.

The counselor must make a meaningful synthesis of this body of knowledge which is in a constant state of growth through addition, reorganization, and reintegration. An intelligent understanding of a great body of human experience will color and give substance to his attitudes as he relates in the counseling situation, and as he refers to other professional people.

The marriage counselor should first of all be well rooted in one or more basic professional disciplines at the graduate level, plus internship training in counseling or psychotherapy, including marriage counseling. There is no substitute for this scientifically disciplined use of one's self and of one's knowledge.

Inadequate though it is, space limits this discussion to an outline of the salient areas and a selective bibliography. The counselor can begin to organize existent knowledge and keep abreast of developments within these areas throughout his practice by using this outline as a guide for continued study.

A. PSYCHOLOGY AND PERSONALITY THEORIES

Within each of the major foci of psychology—clinical, counseling, Gestalt, etc.—will be found a variety of theoretical formulations: i.e., psychoanalytic, client-centered, learning theory. The following discussion will serve as a broad outline of study for the professional person who desires an orientation, as well as those who wish to study in depth.

I. Schools of Psychoanalytic Thought

Marriage counseling has been influenced markedly by psychoanalytic theory, with its orthodox and neo-orthodox variations. This vast body of theoretical formulations, often spoken of as dynamic psychology, is vital to pre-marital counseling, regardless of the basic professional background of the counselor. However, the quantity and diversity of literature pose a problem. There is no substitute for acquaintance with some of the primary works of such authorities as Freud, Jung, Adler, Rank, Ferenczi, Horney, Fromm-Reichman, Sullivan, Menninger. Then a book like Munroe's *Schools of Psychoanalytic Thought* can provide a meaningful exposition, critique, and attempt at integration of a variety of approaches to personality.[1]

II. Gestalt Psychology

Because much less has been written from the viewpoint of Gestalt psychology, and since this has just begun to be applied in clinical work, greater attention is given this discipline here.

Throughout history the pendulum has swung between two patterns of thought, the atomistic and the organismic, in a more or less constant attempt to distinguish between the primary or basic and the derived or secondary in human experience. At one extreme all phases of human endeavor are dominated by a pattern of thinking based on atomistic assumptions, whether theoretical, scientific, or practical. The emphases in political and economic thought and action, in science, in forms or styles of art—in fact in every area of life—take on an atomistic nature. As the atomistic movement loses its vitality, the entire cultural pattern shifts, and the pendulum begins to swing to emphases based on opposite basic assumptions. This latter

---

[1] Munroe, Ruth L., *Schools of Psychoanalytic Thought, An Exposition, Critique and Attempt at Integration*, New York; Dryden Press, 1955; Freud, Sigmund, *A General Introduction to Psychoanalysis*, Translated by Joan Riviere, revised edition, Garden City, New York: Garden City Publishing Co., 1943; ———, *An Outline of Psychoanalysis*, New York: W. W. Norton and Co., 1949.

approach is perhaps best designated as "organismic" in contrast to the "atomistic" approach.[2]

Contemporary biological, sociological, and psychological theories alike are variations of these two sets of basic postulates, those of atomistic-mechanism and those of organismic theory.

Conditioned reflex theory in a variety of forms has followed the atomistic approach. It presupposes that the whole is only a summation of its parts, but evidence against the conditioned reflex as an explanatory principle is found in the extremely unstable character of these responses. Even in animals they are built up with difficulty and very shortly disappear if repetitions with the original adequate stimulus are not continued.

Work in the psychology of perception from 1912 on led to the development of Gestalt or configurational psychology. Wertheimer, Koffka, Kohler, et al were prominent in initiating and contributing to this movement in Germany. Up to that time perception had been defined in terms of the mental elements of sensation and image, which were said to combine according to the laws of attention and association. The German team found these conventional theories and assumptions with respect to perception, and with respect to mental processes in general, inadequate to account for the facts.

The theoretical postulates of Gestalt psychology have been described as "organismic laws" because any performance of the intact, total organism is emphasized as an *organic whole*. The organismic view makes a physical as opposed to a psychic conception of behavior unnecessary because action and energy are regarded as neutral terms implying neither matter nor mind. The organismic explanation of modes of behavior makes constant use of the concepts *goal* and *configuration*. The principle of configuration underlies the functioning of all energy systems and sub-systems.

These organismic laws can be summed up as follows: [3]

1). The whole is more than the sum of its parts (the law of field properties).
2). The parts derive their properties from the whole (the law of derived properties).
3). The whole conditions the activities of its parts (the law of determined action).

[2] Wheeler, R. W., "Gestalt Psychology," *Encyclopedia of Psychology.* pp. 239-244.

[3] Wheeler, R. W., *The Science of Psychology*, New York: Thomas Y. Crowell Co., 1929, pp. 236-349, 493; Wheeler, R. W., *Readings in Psychology*, New York: Thomas Y. Crowell Co., 1939; Koffka, Kurt, *Principles of Gestalt Psychology*, New York: Harcourt, Brace and Co., 1935.

4). Parts emerge from the whole through an individuation process (the law of individuation).

5). Wholes evolve as wholes (the law of genesis).

6). The law of least action.

7). An energy system resists the disturbing influences of outside forces.

8). The law of configuration.

Behavior develops in man by the expansion of a total pattern that is integrated as a whole from the beginning and by individuation of partial patterns (reflexes) within the unitary whole. These organismic principles have modified the work of such scientists as Sherrington and Pavlov, and the traditional view of reflexes, as a basis for physiological theory of behavior. Nowhere in the physiology of the organism is there anything taking place which corresponds strictly to reflex action or to the building up of a whole from its parts. Parts are of later development. The organism-as-a-whole comes first.[4]

The task of Gestalt psychology is "the study of behavior in its causal connection with the systematic attempt to observe and describe the world as it appears to the experiencing individual." This method is of inestimable value in the investigation and understanding of behavior as an event in the psychophysical field. To the latter end, Koffka outlined the following steps:

(1) The organization of the environmental field must be studied, and that means: (a) find out the forces which organize it into separate objects and events; (b) discover the forces which exist between these different objects and events; (c) learn how these forces produce the environmental field as it is known in the behavioral environment.

(2) Investigate how such forces can influence movements of the body.

(3) Study the ego as one of the main field parts.

(4) Show that the forces which connect the ego with the other field parts are of the same nature as those between different parts of the environmental field, and how they produce behavior in all its forms.

(5) Do not forget that the psychophysical field exists within a real organism which in its turn exists in a geographical environment. In this way the questions of true cognition and adequate or adapted behavior will also enter the programme.[5]

Some Kindred Views. Gestalt psychology as an effort at correction in the mechanistic American system—giving as it did ample place to philosophy, religion, mythology, anthropology—was not warmly received at first. Even

---

[4] Coghill, G. E., cited in R. W. Wheeler, *Readings in Psychology*, p. 549; Wheeler, R. W., *The Science of Psychology*, p. 495; Koffka, *op. cit.*, p. 310.

[5] Koffka, *op. cit.*, p. 67-68.

now it is mentioned with trepidation in some circles. Nevertheless, Gestalt psychology with its field theory has deeply permeated American psychological thought. When this was pointed out recently a colleague replied, "Oh, but of course we are all Gestaltists now." This represents a back door admission of "the total approach to man" rather than a front door welcoming of the Gestalt theoretical system.

Each investigator has a tendency to give the results of his work a characteristic or distinguishing name. Consequently, much of the development in America stemming from Gestalt theory has not borne the name "Gestalt," but its principles have permeated modern developments, and organismic methodology is fast becoming the standard for much scientific investigation. Modern physics with its new theory of relativity, the new quantum theory, and the theory of the atom, is basically organismic in its frame of reference. The newer developments in sociology, biology, neurology, and psychiatry have been stimulated by this perspective.[6]

There are a number of theories that have been developed more or less independently of Gestalt psychology, which are in agreement with this theory in their opposition to atomism and in their emphasis upon the study of man as a whole. To this group belong the theories of emergent evolution; the psychobiology of Adolf Meyer; the personalistic psychology of W. Stern; the biological theories of Haldene, Uexkull, and Coghill; the holistic theory of personality of Angyal; child psychiatry, especially as developed by Kanner; and some of the social psychology movements.[7]

Gestalt influence can be seen especially in the field of psychosomatic medicine. In the early days the movement was threatened by the dichotomy of psyche and soma, with authorities tending to argue that diseases were determined primarily by one or the other, or at least to describe a particular illness as either psychogenic or organic in origin. The emphasis upon the total person rescued psychosomatics from this dichotomy with the emerging understanding that an illness is never just one or the other, but always a reaction of the total person. This still may mean that each illness will be located some place on a graph from primarily psychogenic in origin to primarily organic in origin, but with both psyche and soma involved.

The influence of Gestalt principles can be seen in the psychiatric field, particularly in the "relationship therapy" of Sullivan and others. Also it is illustrated in some of the better hospitals and institutions which try to make use of the therapeutic import of community living.[8]

[6] Wheeler, "Gestalt Psychology," *Encyclopedia of Psychology*, p. 241.

[7] Andras Angyal, "Gestalt," *Encyclopedia of Child Guidance*, pp. 174-175.

[8] Jones, Maxwell, *The Therapeutic Community*, New York: Basic Books, Inc., 1953

The more recent and specific contribution of Gestalt psychology to psychotherapy, and thus to pre-marital counseling, is discussed by Perls *et al* in *Gestalt Therapy.*[9]

III. Social Psychology

Psychology and sociology have blended into a fairly new science which has great pertinence to pre-marital counseling. Social psychology developed as the science of psychology—a systematic, interpretive account of human behavior—was applied to current social issues. It is based upon the belief that a psychology which is theoretically sound will be valid in practical situations. The social psychologist works primarily within the *interpersonal* behavioral event. As a social *psychologist*, he works from within the individual, but as a *social* psychologist the field of operation is the social habitat of man. Perhaps one of the most significant results of Gestalt psychology as a whole upon American Psychology was the stimulation and permeation of the developing social psychology. As early as 1936 Brown [10] synthesized organismic psychology and Freudian psychoanalysis into a field-theoretical approach to social psychology. Kurt Lewin, after coming to America, began to apply field theory to the social situation.

Krech and Crutchfield [11] list a number of major developments which led to the growth of social psychology and which also throw light on the specific interests of the field: (1) An increased recognition of the fundamental role that perceptual processes play in man's beliefs, attitudes, thinking, and action; (2) the new field of research which has been opened up by the development of group dynamics; (3) the accumulation and development of new data on techniques of measurement and investigation in the field of psychology; and (4) the necessity of integrating clinical and sociological data from psychologists, sociologists and psychiatrists.

The work of these two authors was influenced by perceptual psychology and the field theory of Gestaltists like Köhler and Lewin. Along with other writers in the field of social psychology, they attempt to clarify the principles that govern the formation and operation of beliefs and attitudes, and the functioning of higher order processes, and to see how these generalizations

[9] Perls, Frederick S., Ralph F. Hefferline and Paul Goodman, *Gestalt Therapy,* New York: Julian Press, 1951.

[10] Brown, J. F., *Psychology of the Social Order*, New York: McGraw-Hill Book Co., 1936.

[11] Krech, David, and Richard S. Crutchfield, *Theory and Problems of Social Psychology*, New York: McGraw-Hill Book Co., 1948: See the recent revision of this work: Krech, David, and Richard S. Crutchfield and Egerton L. Ballachey, *Individual in Society*, New York: McGraw-Hill, 1962.

may be applied to concrete social problems in order to understand and aid in their solution.

A section of the Krech and Crutchfield book is devoted to the changing of beliefs and attitudes of men, which has tremendous implications for any theory of psychotherapy or counseling, including preparation for marriage.[12]

IV. Learning Theory

Early Developments. Learning theory refers to the processes and principles according to which the human personality or "mind" develops and functions. The first great American proponent of a scientific learning theory was William James with his emphasis upon repetition as the law of habit. Thorndyke developed the "law of effect." Watson rejected effect for recency and later, under the influence of Pavlov, posited the theory of conditioned response.

All these theories have been worked over and modified by modern scientists, but a great deal of credence continues to be placed in the "law of effect." Still others believe that effect is not valid as a unitary universal theory of learning.

There are many recent developments in the broad area of learning theory, but only the concepts of Mowrer and Rotter will be outlined here, with some added comments on client-centered therapy.

Learning theory centers around the principles of hedonism (pleasure directed problem-solving) and associationism (conditioning), according to Mowrer.[13] Some authorities postulate a third principle of learning— rationality—but Mowrer sees this as a complex derivative of the first two. Hedonism calls to mind the "pleasure principle" of Freud whereby the individual is propelled by pleasure and repelled by pain. The living organism experiences discomfort or "drives," and then remains active until some response terminates the drive-state or motivation. Thorndyke saw this as the "law of effect" in infrahumans as they attempted to find satisfaction, or to lessen primary drives. In human beings most problem solving is directed at secondary (psychogenic) drives, emotional problems, rather than primary (viscerogenic) drives which usually are quite easily satiated. Once the channel of problem solving is set up it is easier to follow the next time.

Learning by associationism, conditioning, or conditioned response, occurs on the basis of contiguity or double stimulation, and is restricted to

---

[12] Krech and Crutchfield, *op. cit.*; Krech, Crutchfield, and Ballachey, *op. cit.*; See also: Stoodley, B. H., editor, *Society and Self*, Glencoe: Free Press, 1962.

[13] Mowrer, Hobart O., *Learning Theory and Personality Dynamics*, New York: The Ronald Press Co., 1950.

responses of visceral and vascular tissues which mediate "emotions" and are produced by the autonomic nervous system. Fears, resentment, and other emotions are acquired in this way. This kind of learning strengthens old drives, or brings new drives into being.

Actions and objects take on meaning or value as they enhance adaptation, adjustment, and integration. The development of neurosis comes about through identification with and imitation of those within the child's environment. Mowrer [14] believes that neurosis consists of an ego-superego conflict rather than an ego-id conflict, as Freud described it. The neurotic, as a consequence of family pathology, has failed to make a full-fledged, whole-hearted identification with the same-sexed parent. Identification takes two different forms. Developmental identification represents an attempt of the baby to reproduce parts of the desired parent. It is based upon the personal mediation of parent directed toward the *stimulus* side or *needs* of the infant. Defensive identification is based upon an attempt to resolve intolerable conflict produced by controlling parents, which means that their personal mediation is directed toward the *response* side or *behavior* of the child.[15]

Those attitudes and convictions, fears and loyalties, which make up the superego are learned in the same manner, according to Mowrer. In the healthy person, adult authority has been both internalized as superego and integrated into the ego. In the neurotic, adult authority has been internalized but not assimilated. This leaves the superego as a kind of encapsulated foreign body which influences conscious life only in the form of neurotic anxiety, depression, and inadequacy feelings.[16]

One of Mowrer's [17] outstanding specific contributions to pre-marital counseling is his discussion of identification as the "link between learning theory and psychotherapy." He sees resistance and transference phenomena in psychotherapy as an identification dilemma. In therapy the unaccepted, unassimilated superego is "extrojected" upon the therapist as the client repeats and relives the unresolved problems of his childhood relationships. Therapy thus provides a kind of "second childhood and a second chance at the unfinished business of growing up."

Rotter's Social Learning Theory utilizes psychological constructs for prediction and stresses the idea that basic modes of behavior are learned in social situations. An expectancy-reinforcement principle is fundamental to

[14] *Ibid.*, p. 599.
[15] *Ibid.*, pp. 596 ff.
[16] *Ibid.*, pp. 583 ff; See pp. 617-170 for "a study in conscience-killing" based on an analysis of the life and work of Poe.
[17] *Ibid.*, pp. 573-616.

the theory, i.e., behavior is determined by the nature and importance of the goals and reinforcements, as well as by the expectation that these goals will occur. The expectancy is determined by previous experience.

This approach to social learning theory is undergirded by seven basic postulates:

1. The unit of investigation for personality study is the interaction of the individual and his meaningful environment.
2. Personality constructs are not dependent on constructs in any other field of science but should be consistent with them.
3. Behavior described by personality constructs takes place in space and time and may also be described by constructs in other fields.
4. Behaviors describable with personality constructs appear in organisms of particular stages or levels of complexity and development.
5. Personality has unity. The individual's experiences influence each other, which means that previous experience is vital to prediction.
6. Behavior is directional; that is, goal-directed.
7. The nature of individual behavior is determined not only by the nature or importance of goals or reinforcements but also by the anticipation or expectancy that these goals will occur.[18]

Client-Centered Learning Theory. Rogers, although usually not associated with the school of learning theory, developed some tentative hypotheses in terms of client-centered learning that are of primary interest to the pre-marital counselor: (1) We cannot teach a person directly; we can only facilitate his learning. (2) A person learns significantly only those things which he perceives as being involved in the maintenance of, or enhancement of the structure of self. (3) Learning, especially if significant, often is a threat.

"Experience which, if assimilated, would involve a change in the organization of self tends to be resisted through denial or distortion of symbolization.

The structure and organization of self appears to become more rigid under threat. Experience which is perceived as inconsistent with the self can only be assimilated if the current organization of self is relaxed and expanded to include it."

(4) The situation which most effectively promotes significant learning is one

[18] Rotter, J. B. *Social Learning Theory and Clinical Psychology*, New York: Prentice-Hall, 1954, pp. 85-102; permission of the publisher.

in which threat to the self of the learner is reduced to a minimum and differentiated perception of the field of experience is facilitated.[19]

V. Psychological Practice

Once the practice of psychology was given over primarily to administering and evaluating psychological tests. The results were likely to be used by other professional people in adjustment and therapeutic efforts, leaving the psychologist as a technician. This continues to be a chief function on the Masters level, but more and more of the psychologists who complete doctoral training aspire to the practice of counseling and psychotherapy, along with a variety of other functions. In the dedication to research, teaching content, developing skills, and inculcating attitudes, psychology comes to include such areas as: human physiology, theory of personality, developmental psychology, social relations, psychopathology, appraisal of personality, clinical medicine and clinical psychiatry, psychotherapy and remedial procedures, methodology and clinical research, professional relationships, community resources and organizations.[20]

The practice of psychotherapy as a part of the psychologist's role has been impeded by the controversy over medical and non-medical psychotherapy, but even more so by the lag in psychotherapeutic training. As individual psychologists become proficient psychotherapists they function well with individual problems, and have an excellent background from which to begin pre-marital and marital counseling internship.

The pre-marital counselor must give particular attention to life-adjustive processes which are integral parts of most psychology texts. These include such psychic mechanisms as repression, rationalization, projection, introjection, withdrawal, regression, displacement, evasion, concealment, symbolization, compensation, substitution, and sublimation, along with such special reactions as depression and persecution. Concepts of self, conscience (superego), perception, unconscious, guilt, compulsion, and the role of feelings in human behavior will be within the every-day practice of the counselor. Whatever the original background, every pre-marital counselor must be knowledgeable of these dynamics.[21]

[19] Rogers, Carl, *Client Centered Therapy*, Boston: Houghton-Mifflin Co., 1942, pp. 388-391; permission by the publisher.

[20] Raimy, Victor C., Editor, *Training in Clinical Psychology*, New York: Prentice-Hall, 1950, p. 253; Levy, Leon H., *Psychological Interpretation*, New York: Holt, Rinehart, and Winston, 1963.

[21] Pennington, L. A., and Irwin A. Berg, editors, *An Introduction to Clinical Psychology*, New York: Ronald Press, 1948; Mikesell, W. H., editor, *Modern Abnormal Psychology*, New York: Philosophical Library, 1950; Noyes, Arthur P., *Modern Clinical Psychiatry*, Philadelphia: W. B. Saunders Co., 1948.

B. METHODS OF PSYCHOTHERAPY

Harper [22] has organized the journal and textbook literature of recent years into thirty-six systems of psychotherapy, all of which have a direct bearing upon pre-marital counseling. He gives a thumb-nail sketch of the basic tenets and techniques of each of these approaches. This brief book serves well as an outline for further study. Earlier, Ellis [23] had organized the major literature into five categories which are much more manageable in terms of this outline. Admittedly, there is much overlapping of these somewhat arbitrary categories.

Insight-Interpretive Therapy is based upon the belief that if the client understands fully his behavior, including its origin and significance, he will be more effective in modifying or accepting the behavior without anxiety. The therapist must gain as complete insight as possible into the particular person in order to facilitate development of insight by the client. Some authors put the major responsibility for this process upon the client, others upon the counselor, and some equally upon the two. Interpretation becomes the tool whereby the client is "given insight into his problem," or, in the terminology of other practitioners, aided in the process of evolving insight.

There are varying levels of interpretation which may be given in symbolic, representational, or direct ways. This interpretation may involve an entire sequence, beginning with preparation for interpretation and including analysis of defenses and resistances. Some would analyze less important symptoms first, while others would analyze transference material first, finally getting to character structure and defenses. The orthodox psychoanalytic approach is outstanding in this area.[24]

In the *expressive-emotive therapy* group are found those who give the client complete freedom to express himself and find his own way. Many

[22] Harper, Robert, *Psychoanalysis and Psychotherapy: 36 Systems,* Englewood Cliffs: Prentice-Hall, 1959.

[23] Ellis, Albert, "New Approaches to Psychotherapy Techniques," *Journal of Clinical Psychology,* July 1955, Monographed Supplement 11; For more recent texts on psychotherapy see: Bychowski, Gustav and J. Louise Desperts, editors, *Specialized Techniques in Psychotherapy,* New York: Basic Books, 1952; Standal, Stanley W., and Raymond J. Corsini, editors, *Critical Incidents in Psychotherapy,* Englewood Cliffs, N. J.: Prentice-Hall Inc., 1959; Buhler, Charlotte, *Values in Psychotherapy,* Glencoe: The Free Press, 1962; Masserman, J. H., *Principles of Dynamic Psychiatry,* Philadelphia: W. B. Saunders, 1961; Brammer, Lawrence M., and Everett L. Shostrom, *Therapeutic Psychology, Fundamentals of Counseling and Psychotherapy,* Englewood Cliffs: Prentice-Hall, Inc., 1960.

[24] Freud, *op. cit.*; Fromm-Reichmann, Frieda, *Principles of Psychotherapy,* Chicago: University of Chicago Press, 1950; Benedek, Therese, *Insight and Personality,* New York: Ronald Press, 1946.

techniques are used to facilitate this, such as reflecting what has been said, encouraging further free expression, general questions to keep the person moving on but taking care not to implant suggestions, and verbalizing feelings being evidenced. The belief is that if an accepting environment is provided in which the person can think, act, and feel the way he needs to— re-living, re-fearing, re-tasting, re-feeling experiences which are significant to him—gradually he will be enabled to become what potentially he is.

Actually, expressive-emotive responses are a part of most therapeutic approaches. The method deserves separate treatment bcause of the major emphasis sometimes placed here to the exclusion of other approaches.[25]

Relationship Therapy. All psychotherapy involves a relationship, but in recent years there has been an intensive emphasis upon the interpersonal relationship that comes to exist between the professional person and the client. This relationship becomes the primary object of study, with the belief that a personality can never be isolated from the complex interpersonal relations in which he lives and has his being. This view contends that emotional disturbances are in the area—at least manifest themselves there —of social or inter-personal relations.

By controlling and limiting the therapeutic relationship, much more so than experiences with the family or associates, it becomes safe for the client gradually to prepare himself for adjusting to more uncontrolled and unlimited relationships with others. In learning how to relate effectively to the counselor and communicate with him, the client learns social skills. Rigid moral standards and the superego are modified more in keeping with the attitudes of acceptance and understanding experienced with the counselor.

Because the counselor's reactions differ from those of the client's parents and of other authority figures, the client learns to evaluate himself realistically and to react more in terms of reality than in terms of past patterns of behavior. As counselor and client understand together, feel together, and within the relationship act together, the creative potential of both come to the aid of the client. By using the counselor as a person against whom to act out fears, suspicions, loves, and hatreds at a safe distance from condemning and misunderstanding society, the client becomes able to realize the true potentiality of his selfhood. This approach is related to Goldstein's concept of the "self-actualizing" person and Jung's state of "individuation."

There is a great deal of similarity between the relationship therapy of men like Sullivan and the use of transference and counter-transference

---

[25] Rogers, *op. cit.*; Ellis, *op. cit.*; Alexander, Franz and Helen Ross, editors, *Dynamic Psychiatry,* Chicago: University of Chicago Press, 1952.

phenomena in classical psychoanalysis. In fact, both could well be placed, at least in some of its aspects, under insight-interpretive therapy. Some of the modern psychoanalysts like Alexander, French, and Knight place primary emphasis upon utilizing the interpretation of current data within the life experience, and within the therapeutic relationship, rather than the genetic approach of Freud.[26]

The thesis of *activity-directive therapy* is that the counselor to whom the person comes for help is the specialist who knows how to proceed. Various tools are used, including case history, focusing, probing, directing client activity, confronting, conditioning, and the setting of goals and of values. Having determined what seems to be the central conflict or major issue, the counselor is free to keep the interviews focusing at these points. Another way of describing this is to keep the interview material focused upon "reality situations" rather than letting it wander into the past or into fantasy. (In applying this to pre-marital counseling the focus would be upon the reality of family conflicts and couple conflicts rather than making any effort to explore developmentally the basic personalities.)

Tentative goals may be set at first, with more thorough-going ones later, jointly by the therapist and the client. The individuality of the client must be considered in setting these goals, and the therapist has to be alert to the possibility of foisting upon the client his own goals, values, and way of life. Again this calls for understanding the client's background, general personality structure, assets, liabilities, needs, and degree of self-realization. The concepts of will power and free choice may be utilized to help an individual accept responsibility for himself. This can be carried out in a mild suggestive way, but some therapists would not hesitate to command or coerce the client to take certain actions in extreme cases.

The most recent development in this field is "rational-emotive psychotherapy." [27]

Recent literature has given a marked emphasis to the values of *supportive therapy*, an approach which was somewhat taboo in early psychotherapeutic literature. The "supporters" were accused of filling the role of a parent, armed with "authority and patronizing love," using persuasion, suggestion, hypnosis, confession and absolution, all aimed at encouragement and moral

[26] Sullivan, Harry Stack, *Clinical Studies in Psychiatry,* (Helen S. Perry, Mary L. Gawel and Martha Gibbon, editors) New York: W. W. Norton and Co., 1956; —————, *The Psychiatric Interview,* (Helen S. Perry and Mary L. Gawel, editors) New York: W. W. Norton and Co., 1954.

[27] Thorne, F. C., "Directive Psychotherapy; Theory, Practice, and Social Implications," *Journal of Clinical Psychology,* 1953, 9, pp. 267-280; Ellis, Albert and Robert Harper, *A Guide to Rational Living,* Englewood Cliffs, N. J., 1961; Harper, *op. cit.*

coercion of the patient into "normal" ways of thinking and acting. They were criticized for dealing ineffectively with the deeper sources of guilt and anxiety and for failing to stimulate personal growth.

However, support may include experimenting with ways of handling hostility or guilt; substituting less harmful symptoms for disturbing ones; planning activities; manipulating family and other environmental factors; utilizing information and instruction; assisting the person in acquiring new skills and hobbies; recreation, work and play. Many clients must have an adequate parental surrogate, deeply interested in their welfare, before they can face disturbing conflicts. Without such support they break off before the therapeutic process is well under way. This is the only therapy needed by many clients in brief periods of unusual stress, or by the chronically ill or deprived who must have a more or less permanent professional friend from whom to draw emotional sustenance.

The use of reassurance and support is justified for many reasons in working with certain clients, but the emphasis should be upon its conscious use, based upon the immediate and long-range needs of the client, rather than upon the therapist's need to give reassurance. Alexander [28] contended that the one constant in all healing is the "anaclitic" or supportive element, whether or not the therapist is aware of it or approves.

This *survey of methods* demonstrates that increasingly any one narrow approach has proved to be inadequate for the variety of cases confronting the average psychotherapist or counselor. Gradually psychotherapists, and especially marriage counselors, are learning that there are many ways of being helpful to people, ways that depend both upon the counselor and upon the client for their effectiveness. The needs of clients are so varied that a frankly experimental approach may be indicated with each individual, based upon an evolving diagnostic understanding. In the process of training, the counselor should be exposed to as many approaches to human problems as possible. This may make for a period of artificiality or mechanical counseling but, in the long run, it enrichens the possibilities of creative counseling relationships. Having had rich and varied experiences in training and in living, he becomes able to respond spontaneously in terms of the needs of a client at a particular time. It may be at this latter stage only that one sees the difference between the mechanics and the art of counseling.

[28] Alexander, Franz, in a discussion at Veterans Administration Clinic, Detroit, Michigan, May 8, 1957, "What We Know About Psychotherapy"; Sechehaye, Marguerite, *Symbolic Realization*, New York: International Universities Press, 1951; Ellis, *op. cit.*; and Harper, *op. cit.*

Pre-marital counseling, to a greater degree than many forms of counseling, calls for a highly varied approach, geared to the needs and capabilities of the particular individual and couple.

C. OTHER FIELDS OF KNOWLEDGE AND RESOURCES

I. Human Development

The marriage counselor must have a basic orientation to human development theory if he is to understand the motivations of behavior and of relationships. Such knowledge can be gained from many courses of study. such as: child development, adolescent psychology, mental hygiene, developmental psychology, personality development, and dynamic psychology, some of which have already been reviewed.

It would be impossible to work in this field today without frequent reference to the work of *Freud*, especially his theory of psychosexual development. His dynamic concepts of id, ego, and superego, and the topographical concepts of conscious, pre-conscious and unconscious, have permeated most of the developmental literature for the past several decades. Suttie's view of personality beginnings contrasts sharply with Freud's view of the origin of love. Hall and Lindzey have edited an excellent book, *Theories of Personality*, in which some thirteen theories are discussed in a succinct manner, with emphasis upon human development.[29]

Marriage counseling calls for familiarity with all the personal problems which can arise from needs, fear, worry and anxiety, as well as exaggerated feelings of pride and adequacy. Of particular importance is the role of feeling and emotion in all these problems from the cradle to the grave, because emotional stress interferes with the exercise of all other functions.[30]

The startling thing is that a student may come through all of the academic material to be found in the behavioral sciences and yet emerge with a fragmented picture of human personality, which prevents him from seeing whole persons and whole relationships. Many clinical settings enable the student to see more or less one category of human beings, or stage of development. It may be pathological children housed with other pathological children, alcoholics along with other alcoholics, or mental patients with other mentally sick people. Few training centers provide a balanced caseload from infancy through old age. Scarcer still in training centers are

[29] Hall, Calvin S., and Gardner Lindzey, *Theories of Personality*, New York: Wiley, 1957.

[30] Miller, Daniel R. and Guy E. Swanson, *Inner Conflict and Defense*, New York: Henry Holt, 1960.

opportunities for understanding so-called normal people. It is difficult indeed to find clinical personnel who have had intensive experience with healthy children. White has said it well: "The searching eye of scientific research has barely glanced at everyday lives in progress, to say nothing of lives marked by unusual happiness or major social contributions." [31]

The marriage counselor must make every effort to keep up with the rapidly evolving body of literature centering around human development in order to see whole persons from the longitudinal point of view, but there is no substitute for a study of and experience with "living human documents." Small children can demonstrate the basic facts of life, older people show how a human being can take it when life has done its worst, and the mentally sick reveal the strivings for health of those who have been temporarily wrecked by life.

In such a study of human development and behavior one will find enough commonality among people, especially within a given culture, to provide valuable insight into whatever behavior is presented later to the counselor. But he must also learn enough about the unique individuality of every person to discourage the writing of uniform prescriptions for personal or marital difficulties or happiness. Such a study should lead him also to an appreciation of the tremendous strengths for growth and health inherent within the human being, which must be tapped by the counseling process.

The marriage counselor should be oriented to the fact that each child has a *built-in calendar* of physiological, social, and emotional development. This will unfold in its own time and plan if given a reasonably gratifying and stimulating environment of emotional security and love. Theoretical systems can be of help in understanding a child, but in the last analysis each child is his own best "textbook." If parents and other adults can "read" him, his needs will become evident and lead to fulfillment and growth. The marriage counselor, understanding the ABC's of personality in the child, must go further in learning to "read" the complicated system that comprises each separate adult.

II. Socio-Cultural Data and Marriage Counseling

Personality and Culture. Historically, there has been a cycle in the study of socio-cultural data and their inter-relationship with the development and function of personality. One of the earliest descriptive phrases, "culture and personality," stressed culture as a process or realm distinct from personality.

[31] White, Robert W., *Lives in Progress: A Study of the Natural Growth of Personality,* New York: Dryden Press, 1952; Berelson, Bernard and Gary A. Steiner, *Human Behavior: An Inventory of Scientific Findings,* New York: Harcourt, Brace and World, 1964.

This gave way in time, under the impetus of interdisciplinary study, to the notion of "personality *in* culture." This in turn has yielded to an emphasis upon the inseparable inter-relationship of personality and culture. Culture, according to Honigmann, is a short way of describing such phenomena as (1) socially standardized behavior—actions, thoughts, feelings—of some enduring group; (2) the material products of, or aids to, the behaviors of that group; and (3) an all-embracing meaning which binds these together into a kind of system or whole.[32]

On the one hand, violence is done if in the process of studying man he is separated from the culture which has produced him. Most modern sociologists and social psychologists have argued that society cannot be anything over and above the individual minds that compose it. On the other hand, many cultural anthropologists contend that all the laws of individual psychology are inadequate to explain the facts found in various cultures. To be sure, "culture" is an abstract way of describing behavior; and yet, it does have a form, pattern, or structure which can be described and demonstrated. Benedict felt justified in referring to culture as an organic whole. The sum of all the persons in a group "make up a culture beyond and above what those individuals have willed and created." She did not mean by this some super-organic whole, since everything in a culture once was produced by persons. She was making a place for time-binding tradition, for history, which is by no means limited to a set of facts that can be discovered by introspection. This history included the process of acceptance or rejection of traits of a culture.[33]

Culture and personality are inseparably related. Culture provides raw material from which the individual builds his life, and makes it possible for him to have certain experiences in, by, and through which he can grow. To this extent he becomes a product of his group.

At any one stage of development an individual is the product of what he was born with, what has happened to him and with him, and what he has done with, or in reaction to, these experiences. It is within the latter realm, the ability to do something about what happens to him, even to choose what may happen, that many distinctly human characteristics are to be found.

To begin to understand human potential necessitates consideration of all available data on a variety of cultures. The cultural pattern of any civilization makes use of only certain segments of "the great arc of potential human

[32] Honigmann, John J., *Culture and Personality*, New York: Harper and Brothers, 1954; See also: Stoodley, G. H., editor, *Society and Self*, Glencoe: Free Press, 1962.
[33] Benedict, Ruth, *Patterns of Culture*, Boston: Houghton Mifflin, 1934.

purposes and motivations," the great arc along which all the possible human behaviors are distributed. This accounts in part for the fact that no culture has been able to eradicate the temperamental differences of its members. Individuals are not cultural automatons mechanically carrying out a civilization's decrees.

Those who fall in the arc of behavior not capitalized upon by their culture are likely to be considered disoriented or abnormal. Yet, the great changes in the world's history have been set into operation by those individuals or groups who either had to or dared to be different. All cultures seem to have some people who are striving constantly for progress, or at least for change. But even in these cases there had to be something within the cultural situation which permitted them, although opposed, so to act. To be true to culture and to personality, their mutual reinforcement must be stressed.

Outstanding contributions to the understanding of individual and group variations in the great family of man are available throughout recorded history, in the writings of the great religions and philosophies, and in all kinds of literature, sacred and profane. Modern scholars have begun to discover the great potential of collections of folklore. The classical writings of Dostoevski, Chekhov, Ibsen, Shakespeare, Kierkegaard, Bunyan, and St. Augustine are pregnant with insight.

Research from the standpoint of the cultural anthropologist can reveal to the marriage counselor the interrelationship of culture and personality; clarify tendencies to imitativeness in living out roles; sharpen insight into sub-cultural influences within one's own society; indicate something of the degree to which an individual may modify his culture or at least go contrary to its main streams; and underline the selectivity and meaningfulness of varying ways of life, including tendencies to health and illness. The potential for relatedness or for antagonism within a marriage relationship can be clarified only as each spouse separately, and the couple together, are seen within their cultural milieu. This includes the ways in which they are in harmony with, or clash with their culture. Especially helpful to the marriage counselor are such authors as Mead, Benedict, Kluckholn, Opler, and Honigmann.[34]

[34] Benedict, *op. cit.*; Honigmann, *op. cit.*; Mead, Margaret, *Male and Female, A Study of the Sexes in a Changing World*, New York: W. Morrow, 1949; Kluckholn, Clyde and Henry A. Murray, editors, *Personality in Nature, Society and Culture*, 2nd ed. New York: Knopf, 1953; Opler, Marvin K., editor, *Culture and Mental Health*, New York: Macmillan Co., 1959; Farber, Seymour H. and Roger H. L. Wilson, *The Potential of Woman*, New York: McGraw Hill Book Company, 1963 (an excellent resource).

The American Scene. The marriage counselor must be familiar with the different pressures in America which impinge upon the individual and the family, varying with the social class or sub-class, color, and the ethnic group to which he or a client belongs.

If a small baby is viewed as "potential with an urge to self-realization," it is group membership which gives a chance for the personality to develop. The family, peer group, working group, community, and nation are groups within which individuals transmit cultural expectations to the younger members, and so channelize or give direction to human behavior. So well established are some of these cultural expectations that the clinician may predict certain behavior if he knows the group from which a person has come.

The American cultural scene is complicated by its melting-pot nature. Such a mixture produces an immeasurable choice of expressions of individual needs in terms of small groups or of individuals. In spite of this, there are a number of common traits running through American culture in general, some of which are healthy and some unhealthy. The fact that a practice or institution is maintained in a culture does not mean that consistently it is helpful and healthy.

III. The Family

The point at which the many faceted cultural forces converge upon the family is a special domain for the marriage counselor. In brief, the last few decades have seen a major process of evolution and revolution in the American family scene. Some of the social changes which have affected the family are: the divisions of labor, brought about by specialization of the machine age, especially as this lured women from the home; tremendous elaboration of the desired standard of living, with a "things" based status and the development of installment buying; urbanized population; mobility both physical and social; increased amount of leisure, still increasing because of automation; wide acceptance of the limitation of reproduction; the gradual equalization of the sexes in every area of life; the elevation of the concept of love, including emotional satisfactions expected from marriage; the gradual assumption of family responsibilities by social groups and government; the intensive allegiance to the doctrine of individuality, countered by the stifling, overpowering forces for conformity in many areas of present day living.

More recently determined values centering around the economic, status-conferring, reproductive, socializing, affection-response, and security-giving functions of marriage are threatening the historical principles of marriage in America; namely, monogamy, permanence, fidelity, and love. On the other hand, marriage with its multi-dimensional aspects continues to provide the framework in which most adults seek to fulfill their principal drives and needs. The applicability of all this to a particular family is illustrated throughout this book, but Chapter 2 on marital interaction is directly pertinent.

The last two decades have seen a deluge of books on the family. The pre-marital counselor should be thoroughly familiar with this field of literature. Among the excellent volumes with which he might begin such a life-long study are: Waller and Hill's *The Family*; Le Master's *Modern Courtship and Marriage*; Duvall's *Family Development*; Bee's *Marriage and Family Relations*; the Mace's *Marriage East and West*; Ellis and Harper's *Creative Marriage*; Truxal and Merrill's *Marriage and the Family in American Culture*; Bell and Vogel's *A Modern Introduction to the Family*; Vincent's *Unmarried Mothers*; Ackerman's *The Psychodynamics of the Family*; Eisenstein's *Neurotic Interaction in Marriage*; Grotjahn's *Psychoanalysis and the Family Neurosis*; and Liebman's *Emotional Forces in the Family*. The best aid in keeping up with modern research in the area of marriage and the family is the journal *Marriage and the Family*.[35]

Deserving separate attention for purposes of this text is the concept of *family life cycle*. The life cycle of the individual has been a central concept in personality related literature for decades. Along with the increasing awareness that to know a person is to view him in relation to his family, has come the concept of the life cycle of the family. Glick [36] set the pace by pointing out that, within the life cycle of a given family, a multitude of

---

[35] Waller, Willard and Reuben Hill, *The Family*, New York: Dryden Press, rev. ed., 1951; Duvall, Evelyn M., *Family Development*, Philadelphia: J. B. Lippincott, 1957; Bee, Lawrence, *Marriage and Family Relations*, New York: Harper and Brothers, 1959; Mace, David and Vera Mace, *Marriage East and West*, Garden City: Doubleday and Co., 1961; Ellis, Albert and Robert Harper, *Creative Marriage*, New York: Lyle Stuart, 1961; Truxal, Andrew G., and Francis E. Merrill, *Marriage and the Family in American Culture*, New York: Prentice-Hall, Inc., 1953; Bell, Norman W. and Ezra F. Vogel, editors, *A Modern Introduction to the Family*, Glencoe: Free Press, 1960; Vincent, Clark, *Unmarried Mothers*, Glencoe, Ill.: Free Press, 1961; Ackerman, Nathan, *The Psychodynamics of the Family*, New York: Basic Books, 1958; Eisenstein, Victor W., editor, *Neurotic Interaction in Marriage*, New York: Basic Books, 1956; Grotjahn, Martin, *Psychoanalysis and The Family Neurosis*, New York: W. W. Norton and Co., 1961; Liebman, Samuel, editor, *Emotional Forces in The Family*, Philadelphia: J. B. Lippincott Co., 1959; *Marriage and The Family*, National Council on Family Relations, 1219 University Avenue, S. E., Minneapolis 14, Minnesota.

[36] Glick, Paul C., "The Life Cycle of the Family," *Marriage and Family Living*, XVII, 1, 1955.

demographic and economic changes take place which require continuous readjustments of the habits and values of the family members. The cyclical changes in age at marriage, size of completed family, and length of life greatly affect the patterns of family formation, development, and dissolution from generation to generation.

Stages in the Family Life Cycle

Duval divided the life cycle of American families into eight stages, denoted by (1) number of persons in the family, (2) age of the oldest child, (3) school placement of the oldest child, and (4) functions and statuses of families prior to children and after they leave the home. The stages are: [37]

Stage I.   Beginning Families (married couple without children).

Stage II.   Childbearing Families (oldest child, birth to thirty months).

Stage III.   Families with preschool children (oldest child, two and one-half to six years).

Stage IV.   Families with school children (oldest child six to thirteen).

Stage V.   Families with teen-agers (oldest child thirteen to nineteen).

Stage VI.   Families as launching centers (first child gone to last child's leaving home).

Stage VII.   Families in the middle years (empty nest to retirement).

Stage VIII.   Aging families (retirement to death of one or both spouses).

This schema is an aid to understanding the real life way in which a family "flows on from one phase to another without pause or break." The family life cycle and each of the stages are cyclical in nature, having no beginning or ending. As marriage age lowers and birth of children occurs earlier in marriage, Americans are increasingly able to see the cycle begin a second and even a third time before they die.

Duval adapted the "developmental task" concept of Havighurst [38] to the arena of the cyclical family. A developmental task ". . . arises at or about a certain period in the life of an individual, successful achievement of which leads to his happiness and to success with later tasks, while failure leads to unhappiness in the individual, disapproval by the society, and difficulty with other tasks." She saw a developmental task as an effort of an

[37] Duval, Evelyn Millis, *Family Development*, Philadelphia/New York: Copyright © 1962, 1957 by J.B. Lippincott Company. Pages 5-21.
[38] Duval, *Ibid*; Havighurst, Robert J., *Human Development and Education*, New York: Longman, Green and Co., 1953, p. 2.

individual to narrow the discrepancy between the present behavior and what he knows he might achieve. Operationally, assumption of an individual task consists of these four steps: (1) Perception of new possibilities; (2) identity formation in the new direction; (3) coping with conflicting demands; and, (4) motivation sufficient to assume the task. Certainly each of these steps are immediately pertinent to the engaged couple as they approach marriage.

"Family developmental tasks," said Duval, "are those responsibilities for survival, continuity, and growth assumed by the family as a whole as it lives out its own unique history." She listed nine central, never completed, developmental tasks of a family, seen in establishing and maintaining the following: [39]

1. A home to call its own
2. Satisfactory ways of getting and spending money
3. Mutually acceptable patterns of who does what
4. A continuity of mutually satisfying sex relationships
5. Open systems of intellectual and emotional communication
6. Workable relationships with relatives
7. Ways of interacting with associates, friends and community organizations
8. Competency in bearing and rearing children
9. A workable philosophy of life

These tasks are undertaken in an endless variety of ways as each family lives out its life cycle in a unique fashion. Individual efforts to live out the developmental tasks provide numerous opportunities for both meaningful and harmful interaction within the family unit.

Hess and Handel [40] took a slightly different socio-psychological approach in their case studies of five families. They focused upon "the interior of the family," upon individual personalities in interplay with one another, highlighting the way in which "individual uniqueness is transformed into family uniqueness." They listed six problems, the solution of which gives a family its particular structure:

1. Establishing a pattern of separateness and connectedness
2. Establishing a satisfactory congruence of images through the exchange of suitable testimony
3. Evolving definitions of male and female and of older and younger
4. Evolving modes of interaction into central family concerns or themes

[39] Duval, op. cit.
[40] Hess, Robert D. and Handel. Family Worlds: A Psychosocial Approach to Family Life. Chicago: University of Chicago Press, 1959.

5. Establishing the boundaries of the family's world of experience

6. Dealing with significant biosocial issues of family concerns or themes
They believed that each family develops a central "theme," whether consciously or explicitly, which is the guiding motif of life, giving direction to its evolution and function. Just as an individual, to be healthy, must evolve a meaningful philosophy of life, so a family must have its Weltanschauung.

Determining the applicability of all this theoretical material to a particular family is the intent of this text, as well as the goal of pre-marital counseling in general. Chapters 5 and 7 are most fundamentally pertinent.

D. MARITAL BREAKDOWN AND REMARRIAGE

No discussion of the nature of modern marriage can end without taking into account the extent of marital breakdown and the success or failure of remarriages.

I. The Extent and Kinds of Problems [41]

One way to see what is wrong with marriage is to look at what is wrong with people. The United States continues its trend toward higher rates of mental illness, alcoholism, crime, and psychogenic illnesses. To whatever extent the family is responsible for personality development and function, it must accept responsibility for this disturbing picture.

As the marriage ideal moves closer to the Hebrew-Christian-Humanitarian concept of equality, serious conflict becomes inevitable. It is impossible to compile the total picture of destructive marital conflicts, and difficult to get even a representative sample. Divorce and separation statistics give a sampling of the end results, and the ill health picture presented above, plus pre-marital pregnancies, venereal disease and abortion serve also as end products or symptoms.

Certainly serious conflict causes more people to seek help with their marriages than available resources can serve. In metropolitan centers the waiting lists at available services run into thousands with delays of three months to a year for the first interview. Often when the intake is completed, applicants are then placed on a three months to a year waiting list for service. Most private practitioners of marriage counseling have more clients than they can handle, and of course thousands cannot afford the cost of private care.

The list of marriage complaints brought to the marriage counselor varies with the socioeconomic, educational, ethnic, and other characteristics of the

[41] This material first appeared in similar form as: Rutledge, Aaron L., "Marriage Problems and Divorce," *Children and Youth in the 1960's*, White House Conference on Children and Youth, 1960, pp. 219-232.

population being served, along with the particular point of disagreement at the moment. Not so well recognized is the role of the counselor or the type of agency in shaping the statement of the problem. The same couple seeking help often state their problem differently if talking to a priest, a psychiatrist, a marriage counselor, a child guidance clinic, or family service. Often, with or without being aware of it, the person in trouble calls his problem by the name which he feels will appeal to the particular professional helper.

In endless variety, marriage problems are stated as: just quarreling, finances, sexual incompatibility, irresponsibility, alcoholism, gambling, in-laws, religion, general incompatibility, or the children. Increasingly, Child Guidance Clinics are finding that the central difficulty lies in the marital relationship rather than in the child. Only a careful study of each case will reveal which is problem, which is only symptom, and which was only symptom at first but then became additional problems.

Some of the marriage clients are emotionally crippled and are having weaning difficulties with parents or with the mate. Some get caught up in a vicious cycle of feeling rejected, rejecting, and being rejected. Many lack the basic skills of sharing and communicating, or communication has been blocked and distorted until the total relationship is involved in the problem. Problem-solving skills are absent or blocked. Often real shocks have occurred—infidelity, poverty, desertion, divorce, etc.—when they come for help. Even here, feeling and attitude may be much more significant than facts about their problems, because feelings determine action or cause tension and prevent action, as well as interfering with the working through of matters of mutual concern. Characteristic of most people at the point of asking for help, down underneath the hurt and the bitterness, is a feeling of intolerable loneliness, often approaching despair.

II. The Termination of Marriage

Divorce Statistics. Although about 10 million of the Americans living today have been divorced, the percentage of couples remaining married has increased during the last few years. In 1948, there was approximately 1 divorce for every 2.5 marriages. In 1960, there were approximately 1,523,-000 marriages and 393,388 divorces and annulments, a ratio of 1 divorce to 3.9 marriages. About 1 marriage in 4 was a remarriage for one or both parties.[42]

[42] Vital Statistics of the U.S., "Marriages": 1960, Volume III, Sections 1, 2 & 7 *National Vital Statistics Division,* Vital Statistics of the U.S., "Divorces," 1960, Volume III, Sections 3, 4 & 7, *National Vital Statistics Division.*

The higher divorce rates are found among those who at marriage: are still in the teens, have only grade school education (grammar school graduates are twice as likely to divorce as college graduates), have low income, and were formerly married. The median duration of all marriages which ended in divorce in 1960 was 7.2, with more than one third occurring after a duration of less than five years.

The tendency to marry at an earlier age has a direct bearing on the divorce rate. The median age of first marriage for men in 1960 was 23.1 and 20.1 for women.[43] The proportion of first marriages for men under 20 increased from 11 percent in 1951 to 17 percent in 1960 while for brides the percentage increase was from 39 to 49.

A variety of studies indicate that more than a third of the girls in teenage marriages are pregnant at marriage and that an unusually high proportion of the total divorces are from this population. Approximately a third of the remarriages of divorced people end in divorce, usually an early one.

Misuse of Statistics. The divorce and annulment statistics can serve an escapist function for the public and for social scientists. Divorce is a product; interest here is focusing on the end result, and only a part of the end result at that. Census reports indicate that more than twice as many adults are maintaining separate residences as the number of divorced people reported. There is no reliable breakdown as to why these people are living separately. The Armed Forces account for part of this number and distant employment for others. But there is no way of dodging the fact that a rather large percentage represent mutual separations, legal separations, and desertions. There is some evidence that in 1948, when specialists were so concerned about one marriage out of each two and a half ending in divorce, the total of married couples who separated exceeded 50 percent. Today when the divorce rate is less there is reason to believe that the separation rate follows about the same relevant percentage. Another block of broken homes is due to the health of one of the couple. Still more children are receiving Aid to Dependent Children because of the death of the father than for any other reason, although other causes are steadily increasing.[44] The divorce rate is slowly dropping, but a larger number of children are involved because of several interrelated factors: couples are having more children and grouping them in the first five to seven years of marriage; the median duration of marriage ending in divorce is 7.2 years.

[43] *Ibid.*

[44] White House Conference on Children and Youth, *Children in a Changing World,* 1960, Chart 17.

Of the 25.8 million families with children under 18 in 1958, 2.8 million (about 11 percent) were 1 parent homes, broken by death, divorce, separation or desertion. In 1960 56.1 of those divorcing had children.[45]

By adding to this picture the thousands of couples that have just as serious conflict but do not separate, and the effect upon the personalities of adults and children, only then does the researcher get a glimpse of the true nature of this colossal problem.

III. Divorce Laws and Proceedings

There are fifty sets of marriage and divorce laws, one for each state, with many variations of interpretation and procedure in the local courts.[46] These laws contain elements of Roman law, law of the Ecclesiastical Courts of England, Catholic Canon law, Common Law, and the fluctuating laws of the frontier, all geared by intent to the protection of marriage. The primary variations in marriage laws have to do with ages for marriage with and without parental permission, waiting periods, and exclusion of people from marrying because of mixed race or undesignated illness, property and child custody rights, and conditions of remarriage. The early established grounds for divorce usually attempted to provide the absolute minimum of escape from marriage dictated by the particular pressures of the day. With the American philosophy of individual rights challenging the limited grounds for divorce, the laws have been distorted, aborted, and turned against each other to the point of tragicomedy. The public has decided to have its way in spite of the hodge-podge laws, or perhaps because of them, and tolerates endless violations of the law.

The Residence Farce. Laws and rulings, including those of Supreme Courts, are so confused that, depending on the state he lives in, a man or woman can be married, single, or adulterous; a child legitimate or illegitimate. Some states have deliberately catered to "marriage by flight" into adjoining states, and to divorce based on farcical residential requirements. A few years ago 1 divorce lawyer in a small Florida city handled 10,000 divorces in 1 year from New York alone through collaboration with New York lawyers.

States vary from one ground for divorce to many, and it is difficult to tell which system engenders the most insult to law and to marriage. When adultery is the only ground, then "adultery packages" tend to be bought and

---

[45] *Ibid.*, Chart 17; Also "Divorces," Vital Statistics, *op. cit.*

[46] Pilpel, Harriet F. and Zavin, Theodora, *Your Marriage And The Law*, New York: Rinehart, 1952.

sold on the market, or the gentlemanly thing may be done by one party admitting guilt which may be nonexistent. Others take residence, legal or contrived, in another state and start proceedings.

Divorce by Duel. The legal heritage says that the court serves as an arena where adversaries fight out their case in order for right to "win." In fact one must be found to be all wrong and the other innocent in order to obtain a divorce. Accusations and the faulty testimony of guilt are commonplace. This insistence on a duel often causes a couple to cease all efforts to reconcile once they enter into the legal struggle. In spite of these barriers to divorce in some states, other courts grant divorces almost assembly line fashion with "mental cruelty" and "incompatibility" covering dozens of grosser sounding offenses and some that could be stated in much milder form.

Two other methods of breaking up a marriage are *annulment* and *legal separation.* In annulment the marriage is declared never to have existed. In some states, where divorce grounds are limited, annulments may exceed divorces. Legal separation prevents the couple from living together, and at the same time forbids intimate relations with others. Children born during this time may be illegitimate. The advantage of legal separation is that a financial arrangement usually is included which protects the children in the absence of the father. A separate maintenance plan is often used instead which permits the couple to come and go at will in the home, and includes a financial arrangement.

Collusion—mutual agreement to divorce—is against the law; yet in most cases both parties want a divorce. This leads to legal shadow boxing, with one outstanding judge claiming that collusion exists in 95 percent of cases. Perhaps the most vicious laws are those pertaining to "*condonation.*" Lawyers must warn clients against having anything further to do with each other once they have filed for divorce. To relate to each other, have sex relations, spend time in the home or a hotel together, etc., can be interpreted as forgiveness and "condonation" of past faults. When this label is applied, the offended has to wait until the partner becomes guilty again and refile a complaint. This certainly works against reconciliation of marital difficulties.

Perhaps most of the couples who actually get into court will continue to divorce, but the nature of divorce proceedings under the law is such as to make it a humiliating and punitive experience. Vengeance is encouraged in such an environment. The primary ways of striking back are through property settlements and the custody of children.

In 1948 an American Bar Association Committee declared: "Our divorce laws are a mess, they are rotten: they have totally failed to accomplish their declared objective; they aggravate a condition that is already cancerous." The committee added that lawyers are ashamed of their enforced double-talk, judges are bitter about their hopelessness, and other professional people have unconcealed scorn for the travesty on justice.

The movement for uniform divorce laws or a Federal divorce law has gotten nowhere. More recently the emphasis has been for a completely new legal system which would make divorce "neither easier nor harder, but sensible and salutary." "Therapeutic" is another term that has been applied.[47] It would enable the court to do what is best for a family (all members being considered) and hence best for society. Once it has been determined that a marriage is unquestionably dead, says Alexander, "There is no human reason why the court should not be able to perform the necessary operation quietly and privately and mercifully, much as the surgeon operates on a person." Until the fact is determined, however, the newly advocated system would see the case treated something as follows:

(1) Application made for divorce
(2) Private diagnostic investigation by specialists
(3) Special help for emotional problems and for marriage problems
(4) Economic advising when indicated
(5) Report made to judge, successful or not
(6) Divorce granted only if treatment fails and the case is hopeless
(7) Financial settlement for adults and children based on real needs and resources

In the absence of such ideal provisions some "domestic relations courts" or "family courts" have been established. A few states have passed laws strongly suggesting or making counseling mandatory. If judged on the basis of divorce proceedings which are dropped as a result of counseling, these efforts will probably be considered a failure. If the effort is seen as an investment in the growth of two hurt adults and the resultant changes for the children, then they can hardly fail. The greatest work of these court-related counseling centers is being done with the thousands of people who come to them for help before they ever file for divorce.

IV. What Happens to the Divorced Person?

The pre-marital counselor should be alert to the needs of the divorced. In the discussion of marital conflict, loneliness was pointed out as the most painful part of the experience. After studying 425 divorced women in

[47] Alexander, Paul, "Divorce Without 'Guilt' or 'Sin' ", *New York Times*, 1951.

Detroit, Wittels [48] declared that "the feeling of loneliness turned out to be the most universal and poignant problem of all." There may be release from abuse, relaxation after turmoil, but this can be corroded by the persistence of loneliness, which may be even worse for one who has just lost children in the divorce settlement.

The general impression is that society is increasingly tolerant of divorce, but the majority of Wittels' subjects were made to feel like "strange and alien creatures." They found that a large number of people, even those without religious bias against divorce, looked askance at divorcees as persons. More than 80 percent of the women had to go to work, as well as often begging and battling for what they had been awarded from the former husband. Many must turn to Aid to Dependent Children or other forms of charity to support their children. Former husbands sometimes abscond to escape the financial burden that prevents the former standard of living, or to avoid the periodic emotional struggles associated with seeing the children. Others stick it out only to find that the financial arrangement prevents their remarriage unless the second wife helps support the first wife and the children.

Remarriage. The general assumption, reenforced by pilot research, has been that the divorced person is likely to be misunderstood, displaced, and unhappy; that the woman is likely to have particular difficulty finding a mate if she has children, and that in general the divorced person is a poor bet for marital success. Some of the studies indicate a high mortality rate for remarriages and a high rate of dissatisfaction with the new marriages that last. This area deserves further examination.

The median duration for a marriage ending in divorce is 5.7 years. It can be predicted that 75 percent of the people who receive a divorce each year will remarry within five years, and eventually 87 percent of them remarry. Of the approximately 10 million people in the United States who have been divorced, only about a million and a third are now unmarried.

In the past decade two books have appeared which are significant attempts to understand the whole area of divorce: Goode's *After Divorce* [49] and Bernard's *Remarriage*. In 1948 Goode selected 425 Detroit women aged 20-38, divided into four groups, who had been divorced 2 months, 8

[48] Wittels, David G. Five articles in *The Saturday Evening Post*, "The Post Reports on Divorce," Jan. 21 and 28, Feb. 4, 11, and 18, 1950.

[49] Goode, William J., *After Divorce*, Glencoe, Ill.: The Free Press, 1956; Bernard, Jessie, *Remarriage, A Study of Marriage*, New York; Dryden Press, 1956.

months, 14 months, and 26 months. They were studied by the question-naire method. Fifty-three percent of those divorced 26 months had remarried. Goode's findings challenged practically every assumption about the predicament of the divorced person. Overwhelmingly his subjects claimed that they were happier in their second marriage than in the first: 87 percent claimed to have a better life, 8 percent a little better—a total of 95 percent improved. Most of their families had been understanding and accepting of the new mate; they were better off financially, etc.

How can the earlier assumptions and research which stress the plight of the divorced be reconciled with the findings of these two studies on divorce and remarriage? Goode's conclusions may be challenged to a degree because of the doubtful value of the questionnaire method in eliciting the facts. There is a strong indication that women who have remarried would almost have to believe, if they planned on sticking it out, that the second marriage was better than the first. He admittedly takes as his basic gauge the fact that they say they are happier, and he admits that the nature of his sample meant that these remarriages had been of relatively short duration. Bernard's study is based more on upper-middle-class remarriages which have already lasted for some appreciable time and may not be at all typical of the population as a whole, and of course she does not claim them to be. She does infer that the study probably portrays quite clearly the success of a broad section of remarriages.

On the other hand, there is no reason to question, once you accept the basis for definition of success, that the studies of Goode and Bernard do portray relatively high success levels in the marriages studied. However, if other statistics hold true, about a third of those in Goode's group will eventually divorce, perhaps in a median of 5.7 years. This places a question mark around the validity of the claims to happiness of that portion of the sample, except that they may be happier than in the first marriage and still divorce. One would be glad to know that even two-thirds of those who remarry are appreciably happier than they were before.

The general facts seem to be that relatively soon after remarriage about a third of the divorced—sometimes neurotic, sometimes psychotic, sometimes just immature—find themselves just as unhappy as before and divorce rather quickly. Bernard recognizes that this improves the happiness rate in her group appreciably because she studied those that had survived beyond this crisis stage. In essence she was studying successful remarriage, not total remarriage. Neither of the books necessarily challenges the contention of Wittels and the testimony of thousands of divorcees that there were inconveniences, pain, misunderstanding, and loneliness involved in getting a divorce. Bernard's study paints a rather glowing picture of the divorce-remarried person but this does not rule out problems either.

In a word, about a third of the divorced people who remarry tend to repeat and to carry over the same or more complicated personality and relationship problems into their second marriage. About two-thirds tend to learn from the experience with or without professional help, tend to grow a bit and to become more skillful in relating. In effect then, for many people marriage is on a trial basis for at least one time. Recently a judge, who admitted he belonged to a church that forbids divorce, said: "We may as well get our heads out of the sand and admit the truth. Until we learn how to prepare young people, and that quite early, for the serious responsibilities of marriage, we have to be willing to accept trial marriage for one or more times until they can gain the knowhow of building a successful home."

Implications. One can well ask in the light of all this, why not make divorces easy? Why not make remarriage easy? Admittedly one of the major scars on the culture is the chaotic divorce proceedings picture, and it should be cleared up at both the punitive level and at the assembly line level. Many of the divorce cases reaching the courts will proceed regardless of counseling, although others will be stopped. There is every reason to believe that a more realistic facing up to this total picture, clarifying the laws and making the courts remedial instead of punitive or even lenient, would improve the picture. It would make it unnecessary for a tide of hate to be built up in order to justify divorce.

There is another set of factors which perhaps is more significant. By far the majority of people who divorce have within their own personalities, and between them, the basic potential that could enable them to have as good a marriage as either of them would have with any other person. If there could be enough pauses along the way toward a divorce to help them face up to this, many of these could do the same kind of growing, or even more, that is experienced in the most successful remarriages. They could find this meaningfulness within their own marriage without going through the hurt for themselves and for their children, and without putting society to the expense of the court proceedings. Closely related to this issue is a study of 200 divorced couples [50] who eventually remarried each other. Of these, 48 percent reported good adjustment, 15 percent fair adjustment. By remarrying they admitted that their divorce was a mistake and more than 50 per-

[50] Popenoe, Paul, "Remarriage of Divorcees to Each Other," *American Sociological Review*, III, October 1938, 696.

cent of them, evidently without professional help, declared that they had now been able to develop a successful marriage.

Effects of Divorce and Marital Tension Upon the Children. Putting together all estimates, about a third of a million new children a year are affected by divorce or annulment. The number who are orphaned each year is slightly higher than this. However, most divorced and bereaved parents remarry. In 1958 approximately 87 percent of families with children under 18 had two parents. An approximation of the other 13 percent was shown in the June 1955 report of the Metropolitan Life Insurance Company report, which showed 7 million children living with only 1 parent or neither parent; 4,100,000 of these with the mother; 600,000 with the father; and most of the others with relatives.

What is the effect of divorce upon the development, emotional stability, and attitudes of the child? The evidence is conflicting, the picture not entirely clear.

The basic contentions of specialists and of the public at large have been that divorce is detrimental to children in every way; it often robs them of proper financial support, warps their emotional development, leads to delinquency and illness and taints their attitudes toward marriage, home and society.

The extensive delinquency,[51] school dropout, mental illness,[52] psychogenic illness, pre-marital pregnancy, abortion and venereal disease among the children and youth of today is being documented repeatedly in the popular press and was endlessly demonstrated in the data for the 1960 White House Conference. The relationship of this to distressful homes has been documented repeatedly.

On the other hand, the overwhelming majority of the remarried parents studied by Goode felt that their children were faring better than in the previous conflicted home. Similarly, Bernard [53] found that an appreciable number of her college students who were children of these remarriages checked out at a higher level of maturity than those who had come from unbroken homes. At least this underlines the possibility that youth has the potential of turning most tragedy into a growing experience. For one two-year period, of the delinquents appearing before the courts in Detroit, a larger number have come from two-parent homes than from one-parent homes.

[51] White House Conference on Children and Youth, *op. cit.* Chart 20.
[52] *Ibid.*, Chart 35.
[53] Bernard, *op. cit.*

How can this fact be reconciled with the bulk of evidence of the destructiveness of divorce upon children?

Perhaps the best answer lies in the fact that divorce is an end product of an already broken home. Even when studies show that a relatively higher percentage of delinquent children come from divorced homes, one must recognize many other factors contributing to the disturbance. Among these would be economic conditions, community in which the child lives, etc., which were already in effect in most cases before the divorce occurred. Also the long-time marital conflict had had its effect upon them and could not be distinguished·from the final break of the divorce.

It is necessary to point out that even when the parents are responsible, their shortcomings and irresponsibility are not all due to willful neglect. They are the product of the culture, which points up a fact often forgotten. The delinquent or disturbed child is a product of his community just as much as he is a product of his family. The community operates not only through what it has made of the parents, but directly upon the child. Today, with a looser family structure, this impingement upon the emotional and social development of the child begins much earlier. By the time the child reaches adolescence it is demonstrable in many communities that the peer group is much more determinative of the actual behavior of the child than is a particular set of parents.

What is often forgotten again is the multiplicity of factors operating upon the child who may find himself in a seriously disturbed or broken home. Along with such community determining factors as the lower income group having their delinquency or illness reported more often, there are the forces of deprivation of the basic necessities of life due to low income and the failure to attain preventive treatment because it cannot be afforded or because the need is not perceived. Another factor, seldom mentioned in the literature, is the excess of stimulation of experiences for which there are no guidelines or integrating principles, common in poverty ridden, overcrowded settings. In attempting to determine the effect of divorce on children, stressful homes and stressful communities are one and inseparable.

One of the effects of divorce upon children that has not been researched and cannot be taken lightly is the possible cumulative effect due to example. To what extent does the fact that mother and father were divorced give an emotional set toward divorce as the solution for early conflicts in their own marriage?

The complicated and multifaceted subject of marital breakdown, and the welfare of children by previous marriages, come sharply into focus when the person decides to remarry. How can the marriage counselor assist the couple in learning from the past and in growing a more meaningful relationship this time?

Chapter 10

PREREQUISITE KNOWLEDGE AND RESOURCES - II

E. RELIGION

The average pre-marital counselor will have had little definitive training in theology, philosophy and comparative religions. These fields have not been organized and presented in succinct form for use of the scientist. For that reason more attention must be given to religion and the family in this text.

As the psychological sciences developed in America, various forces came to bear to separate the twin children of philosophy—psychology and religion. Sibling rivalries developed and the adolescent psychological science began to rebel against its parental figures. Bigoted attacks upon science as such were made by misguided religious leaders; which, in many cases, was a displacement of the fear of change. Likewise, for a few decades there was a marked tendency for behavioral scientists to ignore things religious and to discount even the scientifically based endeavors of religious leaders. Even now, in the eyes of many modern intelligentsia, no man can be religious and at the same time scientific, for to them the presuppositions of religion and of science are at variance one with the other. Many of these thinkers have come to worship at the shrine of some particular "science" and give to it the same unthinking devotion which formerly characterized the allegiance to accepted religious dogma which they criticize. Others, who want to hold on to their religious orientation while pursuing the behavioral sciences, close the two realms off into logic-tight compartments, thus making impossible an integrated spontaneous life.

Marriage counseling has been influenced by this antipathy, but today the picture is changing. Marriage counseling by its very nature calls for a total approach that takes into account every area of each of the lives involved, and often demands the individual and combined resources of many disciplines both religious and scientific. The great religions like Judaism and Christianity would readily join Freud in his attack upon the "legalizing" of religion, and the distortions of genuine religious insight which are set up falsely as revelations of divinity. They would label as sin and sickness what Freud condemned as religion.

A new science, the psychology of religion, is developing rapidly today. Such outstanding psychiatrists and psychoanalysts as Booth, Gayle, Sadler, der Horst, Frankl, Kubie, Jung, White, Suttie, de Forest, Blanton, Loomis and Menninger are calling for reconsideration of the spiritual side of man and for closer cooperation of science and religion in order to avoid errors of the past, to penetrate barriers of present ignorance, and to enlarge areas of usefulness.

This movement toward cooperative endeavor among the "helping" groups from science and from religion is of the utmost significance to marriage and pre-marital counseling.

I. Religious Information and Attitudes

For many people today religion is the most difficult topic to discuss. When the counselor also has this difficulty a vital area of life may be neglected. He may argue that this is the province of the minister and priest and that all such questions should be referred. Of course the clergy should be used as consultants but this does not excuse the marriage counselor from being intelligently informed about major faiths in general, beliefs and practices related specifically to the family, and the value of religion in individual and family life as distinguished from the pathological uses of religious dogma.

The engaged couple should be led to explore the religious denomination of each, with particular attention to forms of worship, attitude toward control of conception and other sexual practices, child rearing, attitude toward family background, and the unique cultural components of the particular faith. Other topics of interest, particularly in pre-marital counseling, will be the intensity of religious interests of each, comparisons of key ideas and beliefs, attitudes toward religious participation, religious ritual expected in the family, importance of the development of an individual faith, religion and democratic living, and family experience and values. Increasingly the need for counseling is arising around mixed marriages. Most resource literature is quite biased, but notable exceptions are Pike's *If You Marry Outside Your Faith* and *One Marriage, Two Faiths* by Bossard and Boll. The Roman Catholic point of view is set forth by Kelly in *The Catholic Marriage Manual*.[1]

---

[1] Pike, James A., *If You Marry Outside Your Faith; Counsel On Mixed Marriage*, New York: Harper and Brother, 1954; Bossard, James H. S. and Eleanor Boll, *One Marriage, Two Faiths*, New York: Ronald Press, 1957; Kelly, George A., *The Catholic Marriage Manual*, New York: Random House, 1958.

The most obvious factors creating friction in mixed religion marriages center around: The pressures of mixing representatives of minority and majority groups of the culture, which calls forth all the problems that prejudice can create; and differences in the stand taken on certain vital issues. Catholics condemn control of conception except through "natural" means; but most Protestant churches teach its value and others tolerate it. Protestants and Jews discourage divorce, but Catholics usually forbid it.[2] There are basic differences in such areas as authority in the family, the use of alcohol, and in dietary ritual. Some of these differences are just as pronounced in sub-groups within the major divisions of religious faith.

It is obvious that interfaith marriage is on the increase in defiance of discouragement by major religous groups. The marriage counselor must help couples in the search for meaningfulness within mixed marriages. The pre-marital counselor has an opportunity to help engaged couples count the cost of mixed marriage and to develop working approaches to what often is a difficult situation.

Couples who are having difficulty around religion, or individuals with an inadequate philosophy of life, have a right to expect mature guidance from their counselor or doctor, or referral to someone whom they can utilize effectively. Such questions as the following demand attention: How do you distinguish between healthy and unhealthy religion? What is the nature of man? What is the relation between mental health principles and the basic religious tenets? Are salvation and self-acceptance synonymous? What is the place of value in life? What relationship is there between the religious concepts of equality and the democratic concept of family life? How does family living fit one for life in an ever-enlarging family, beginning with playmates and school mates; continuing through an array of friendships and acquaintances, marriage, parenthood; and extending to the greater groups of community, country, and the family of mankind? [3]

II. A Frame of Reference

The counselor is called upon from at least three directions to be aware of basic philosophies or frames of reference. He must be in tune with the client, with the spouse or prospective mate, and find a meaningful philosophy of life for himself.

[2] See Emerson, James G., *Divorce, The Church, And Remarriage*, Philadelphia: Westminster Press, 1961.

[3] Rutledge, Aaron L. "The Perpetuation of Non-value," *Mental Hygiene*, Vol. 42, No. 1, January 1959, pp. 64-70.

There is a striking parallel between the traditional religious and philosophical concepts of how man attains salvation, or religious acceptance and fulfillment, and the major psychological concepts and methods of attaining health and adjustment. These are: The way of self-rejection, the legalistic or regulation way, and the developmental approach. Particularly helpful in this connection is Bonthius' *Christian Paths to Self-Acceptance*.[4]

The Self-Rejection Approach. According to the theory of self-rejection—found in Augustine, Luther, Calvin, Fox, Bunyan, the Puritans, especially in the Reformation—man is born evil and destructive. *The Larger Westminster Catechism* states that man is made "opposite unto all that is spiritually good, and wholly inclined to all evil, and that continually." This view of total depravity of man has afforded to the theologian the same scapegoat as the term "constitutional" to the physician and psychologist. If man were born that way, what can science or religion be expected to do about it except to subdue self and basic desires? Other self-rejectionist views are rationalizations of this basic theory, elminating the more objectionable aspects.

The efforts of man to negate or to destroy himself in order to prove acceptable to God are endless—all the way from doing without nourishment, to a life of poverty and seclusion, or of martyrdom, to the torture of the penitents, to self-destruction through psychogenic illness, or more direct means. Adherents of this view have found and continue to find prooftext justification for such an approach in holy writ of many faiths.

The Legalistic Approach. The legalistic or regulatory approach to life holds that religion is a divine law which must be kept to gain eternal reward, or which, if broken, brings the wrath of God. God is the supreme law-giver, sin is disobedience to the law, and salvation consists of being pardoned and rewarded. This view roots also in the doctrine of original sin, or some of its variations. In fact, many of the Christian fathers fit into this view, the self-rejectionist view, or spill over into both views. A commonly held modification of the theory of total depravity is that man is both good and evil, with his goodness due to a direct gift from God, not to inherent nature.

The way to acceptance in this view is through regulation by others and by self in order to inhibit desires and restrain destructive or selfish impulses. Jung has pointed out the supportive structure of the Roman Catholic Church in maintaining its people within the context of a regulatory way of life, and to the resultant anxiety when some Protestants hold to a similar view but leave man alone as his own representative before God.

[4] Bonthius, Robert H., *Christian Paths to Self-Acceptance*, New York: King's Crown Press, 1948.

These viewpoints can be seen also in scientific efforts to effect the best for man, including health. Zilboorg says that Freud found himself studying man in the state of sin, burdened with "the precipitate of the Oedipus Complex—man's perennial, unconscious sense of guilt." To Freud life and death (Eros and Thanatos) were the basic instincts but even the "Eros" drives were anti-social; group life and civilization were dependent upon inhibition and regulation. Love came about only as a sublimation of inhibited sexuality.

In America the "good and bad" philosophy of man came to scientific fruition in the concepts of "love against hate," with health or peace of mind tending to be equated with the delicate balance between these two forces within the personality. Watson's "Behaviorism" was a glaring example of the belief that man must be regulated, conditioned, and controlled, if anything constructive is to come from him. This odd mixture of Pavlovian animal psychology and the philosophy of the destructive nature of man continues to raise its head occasionally as the essence of human learning. This, in spite of the easily demonstrated fact that even in animals conditioned reflex training disappears in the absence of repeated practice.

The Developmental Approach. According to the belief of many present day members of various religious faiths, a child is born neither good nor evil, since these terms connote responsibility for his state. Rather, he is born as *potential with a push*. The "push" is an important element. By this is meant the innate tendency to grow, develop, and mature physically, intellectually, emotionally or spiritually, and socially; not as separate parts, but as one organism. The Bible puts it: ". . . in wisdom, in stature, and in favor with God and man." The "Christian Nurture" theory of evangelical Christianity contends that every child should be permitted to grow in such a healthy manner that there will never be a time when he does not think of himself as being a child of God.This is referred to in the Hebrew-Christian tradition as imago dei; created in the image of God, with god-like potential for growth, creativity, and relatedness. The translators of the King James Version, already influenced by the philosophy of the sinful nature of man, could only permit the Bible to describe man as created "a little lower than the angels"; not, "a little less than divine."

The heart of the psychological and of the religious approach is to be found in the developmental process. Man is born whole; the accent is on the whole organism. Man is not an accretion of parts and functions, but rather, from conception on, a whole out of which parts and functions emerge. The basic process of all growth and maturation has two components—differentiation and integration. From the formless blob of protoplasm *as a whole* comes the first throb of movement. From this emerges, through an innately guided process of differentiation, legs and livers, and other organs and appendages. But if the integrative side of the process does not keep pace, malformation and cancerous growths result.

Very early in the development of self the expectations of others begin to influence growth. Since these influences often are contrary to each other but equally demanding, and often carry the price-tag of parental and social acceptance, the self cannot continue to develop as an integrated whole. If the self cannot continue to integrate, the tendency to wholeness or containedness brings about an artificial closure or integration of one or more of these parts which, as self-images, dominate the life and development of the individual. If one of these partial self-images is ascendant, a one-sided neurosis or dominating psychosis results. In either case, in the absence of oneness, there is a multiple of diverse parts. As these become concretized, the older child or adult is seen as a multiple of selves with real self-hood lost, whether one is thinking in terms of religion or of science, or both. The internal struggle is felt as isolation, guilt, and anxiety, and most of life's energies are consumed just to contain the isolated selves and effect an illusion of unity. As growth asserts itself, often one self image is blown up as a dominating force in life. The Bible speaks of this as "false-pride," or a "state of sin," false virtue, etc. Horney [5] called this neurotic self "the proud self" in contradistinction to the real self. It is the pride that "goeth before destruction," the haughty spirit that leads to a fall; the house built upon sand rather than grown out of the basic rock of self.

The great religions, especially the Hebrew-Christian tradition, have held that the ingredient necessary to emotional and spiritual healing is love, found in its essence in the Supreme Power, in whose likeness man is made. Modern psychotherapy is rediscovering the power of love, variously described, in healing, just as it holds that deprivation of love or hurt through love warps and fragmentizes the self.

The rediscovery of self has been called "being saved," conversion, attaining salvation, and rebirth by religion, and reintegration, healing, self-realization, and maturity by psychotherapsts, to use just a few of the many descriptive concepts. From this point of view:

"The rediscovery of self demonstrates clearly that 'the Kingdom of God is within you,' just as are the barriers to its coming. The greatest

[5] Horney, Karen, *Neurosis and Human Growth, The Struggle Toward Self Realization*, New York: W. W. Norton and Co., 1950.

reconciliation is with oneself; with the *Imago Dei* in religious language. I can love others only as I love myself, forgive only as I forgive myself; serve as I serve myself—for they are *my* others now. . . .
When I am at one with myself I relate spontaneously to *my* family, *my* neighbors, *my* country, *my* world, and *my* God. I can truly experience the fellowship of all who similarly 'live' themselves." [6]

Within these three basic views of how man realizes true self-hood, with many variations to be sure, the marriage counselor will find his clients, whether or not the philosophy is articulated. Basic differences in these convictions of a husband and wife often underlie and stimulate some of the most destructive marital strife.

F. MEDICAL AND PSYCHIATRIC ORIENTATION

The average marriage counselor is not a medical doctor, but he is constantly called upon to make intelligent use of the medical profession. This requires a quite thorough orientation to medical and psychiatric principles and practices. He will need to know the various medical specialties, their areas of interest, how to choose between the professions in order to save steps and facilitate care, the relative effectiveness of specialists in dealing with specific problems, the fees expected, and the schedules and case loads adhered to.

Special study should focus upon the significance of a medical examination, including efforts to differentiate between primarily psychogenic illnesses and those thought to be specifically physiological in origin, along with an awareness of their usual ways of being interrelated in both causation and symptomatology. Constantly he will hear about or make use of the results of a basal metabolism rate (BMR), a gastrointestinal (GI) series, electroencephalogram (EEG), electrocardiogram (EKG), blood tests, oil tests and air tests to determine whether fallopian tubes are open, cystoscopic examinations, air studies of the brain, tests for pregnancy, for cancer, and a variety of tests for toxic conditions. He will need to know about the illnesses or conditions that interfere with sex life or other activities; such as, thyroid conditions, anemia, heart defects, diabetes, hypoglycemia, paralysis, deafness, menopause, sterility, tumors, frigidity, impotence, abortion, and various glandular malfunctions. Invaluable aid is found in the *MEDICAL DICTIONARY AND HEALTH MANUAL*, available in paperback.[7]

[6] Rutledge, Aaron L., "The Psychological Sciences and Religion," unpublished manuscript.
[7] Rothenberg, Robert E., *Medical Dictionary and Health Manual*, New York: New American Library, 1962.

The best possible general knowledge of medical facts cannot take the place of personal acquaintance and a working relationship with one or more physicians who will orient the counselor to the field of medical practice. Together, the counselor and the physician can discover the intricate manner in which many physical problems and marital difficulties are interrelated.

"Female" difficulties are notorious for their emotional involvements, and for their role in marital conflict. An excellent book in this field is *Psychosomatic Gynecology* by Kroger and Freed.[8] Today the odds are that one of a couple in serious trouble is taking some kind of drug such as the energizers or tranquilizers. Unless the counselor is aware of this he may be treating drugs rather than persons.

The psychiatrist and other skilled diagnosticians and psychotherapists will be invaluable both for diagnosis and referral of those who have serious emotional illnesses, and as an aid to the less skilled counselor in working out his own involvement in certain sticky cases. *Mental Illness, A Guide For The Family* by Stern and Hamilton is a helpful volume, as is Southard's *The Family and Mental Illness,* and *Action For Mental Health,* report of the Joint Commission on Mental Illness and Health.[9]

To guide him in difficult cases and to aid referral, the pre-marital counselor should be as well oriented as possible in behavioral dynamics, including the normal, the pathological, and the neurotic. It is not necessary to place diagnostic tags upon clients. In fact, modern psychiatric and psychological practice is leaning further from labeling patients with classical diagnostic terms. However, familiarity with the broad descriptive symptom syndromes upon which diagnosis of mental illness is based is one way for the counselor to alert himself to danger signals. In addition to the broad organic and functional manifestations, the counselor will deal regularly with sociopaths and other personality disorders, alcoholism, addiction, criminality, sado-masochism, and other troublesome symptoms. Courses in abnormal psychology are helpful but there is no substitute for some training in a mental hospital or mental hygiene clinic. Diagnostic manuals and dictionaries can guide the novice.[10]

[8] Kroger, William S., and S. Charles Freed, *Psychosomatic Gynecology*, Glencoe: The Free Press, 1956.

[9] Stern, Edith M., and Samuel W. Hamilton, *Mental Illness, A Guide For The Family,* New York: Commonwealth Fund, 1942; Southard, Samuel, *The Family and Mental Illness,* Philadelphia: Westminster Press, 1957; Joint Commission on Mental Illness and Health, *Action For Mental Health,* New York: Basic Books, 1961.

[10] *Diagnostic and Statistical Manual, Mental Disorders,* Washington: American Psychiatric Association, 1962; English, Horace B., and Ava C. English, *A Comprehensive Dictionary of Psychological and Psychoanalytical Terms,* New York: Longmans, Green and Company, 1958.

G. GENETICS

One of the most confusing areas for the marriage counselor, and anyone else, is the field of human genetics. People are cautioned that only the qualified geneticist should be consulted, regardless of whether his original background was biology, medicine, psychiatry, or psychology. And this is well taken, except that even the most outstanding publications on genetics manifest such disagreement as to make use of their data almost impossible. A further reason for hesitancy in consulting the geneticist is the frequent tendency to continue attributing to heredity traits long since demonstrated to be of emotional or social origin. They tend to perpetuate the age-old battle of either/or; either learned or totally due to heredity; the quite primitive rationale that if an illness or trait repeats itself in succeeding generations of a family, ipso facto it is inherited. This often is taught in complete isolation from what is known of the effects of such factors as prolonged conflict and tension; inconsistent, overprotective, or rejecting child rearing practices; the "catching" nature of emotional disturbances when lived with daily from the earliest hours of life; and the influence of community and peers in stimulating reactions and patternizing behavior, as well as a variety of prenatal influences. The picture becomes even more complicated as genetics claim the services of the biochemist and molecular physicist, although the future may be much brighter because of their interest in genetics.

Much genetic literature is concerned with abnormalities attributed to heredity for many generations, in addition to constantly adding new ones. Presently it is possible to add up more than 400 abnormalities of human beings which are being attributed by genetic literature to transmission through the genes and chromosomes. Such a battery of illnesses are encompassed in this array that hardly a family anywhere could be free of genetic "taints." This fact in itself does not invalidate these claims of the geneticist, but the impossibility of advising an engaged couple with any degree of authority becomes obvious.

Chief among the diseases and conditions still being attributed to heredity by geneticists are the major mental illnesses (schizophrenia and manic-depressive psychosis), diabetes, thyroid disease, hypertension, coronary diseases, epilepsy, mental deficiency, certain hearing defects, hair lip and cleft palate, muscular dystrophy, fibrocystic disease of the pancreas. There is a gradual lessening of claims that epilepsy and mental deficiency are accounted for by heredity. It has now become evident that "epilepsy," since recorded history, has been a catch-all diagnosis of a wide collection of convulsive disorders due to a great variety of demonstrable causes. Geneticists still tend to attribute to heredity all those cases which cannot be explained currently by other conditions.

Once mental deficiency was attributed almost entirely to heredity. Geneticists now are beginning to recognize that more than 75 possible reasons for mental deficiency have been documented. More than two thirds of all present cases of mental deficiency or retardation can be traced to other than gene transmitted causes. Among these are prenatal injuries due to high temperature of mother with such illnesses as "German measles," influenza, or other virus, drugs, or the deprivation of oxygen at crucial stages of foetal development; injuries at birth due to prolonged labor, forceps, drugs; early postnatal conditions such as deprivation of oxygen or too much oxygen; early childhood infections such as the encephalitis, high temperatures from childhood diseases, neoplasms, injuries, etc. Many of these brain injuries are also related to convulsive disorders. It is entirely possible that as medical and psychological sciences proceed additional causes of both epilepsy and mental deficiency will become evident, reducing even more the total that could be attributed to heredity.

Some of the non-hereditary causes of epilepsy and mental deficiency also are related to such anomalies as hair lip or club feet. It is now possible to create these conditions "on order" in animal experiments by interfering with the oxygen supply, injecting drugs, or exposing to radiation, among other methods, at specific times in the development of the foetus.

Anderson,[11] among others, believed that diabetes is the most common of the major hereditary diseases of man, since about one person in every sixty-five is either a diabetic or will become one at some time during his life. Again, it may be that "diabetes" describes a variety of disease anomalies with similar symptoms, the specific causes of which will in time be ferreted out by medical and psychological sciences.

A most exciting scientific break-through of the past decade has occurred in the search for the *secret of life* itself. The role of chromosomes in hereditary transmission has long been known, with some relatively sound hypothesizing about the function of the accompanying genes. Now scientists have narrowed the secret core of life to the desoxyribonucleic acid, dubbed DNA, present in the genes of all living things. Bacteria, plants, animals, and man resemble forbears because of the DNA which is inherited. A human fertilized egg is thought to have 1/10th of a trillionth of an ounce of DNA,

[11] Anderson, Ray C. "The Influence of Heredity on Family Health," *Marriage and Family Living*, XIX, No. 2, May 1957, pp. 136-141.

but encoded therein are the hereditary instructions which direct the construction of a body resembling the stock from which it descended. The DNA of all known creatures are thought to contain a basic four part code, demonstrating the one-ness of the living world. There is striking diversity, however, because each giant DNA molecule is actually a long thread containing hundreds of thousands of "letters" which can combine infinitely to produce even more varieties.

This mysterious substance has the power to direct the manufacture of more of itself as new cells are to be formed. Another function is to direct the construction of the cell's machinery, a process in which new molecules form alongside the DNA threads, and then move away carrying inherited information which directs the character of its growth. Scientists even believe that at some time in the future man may be able to have control over some of the activities of the DNA threads of his own reproductive cells. Already, a great deal is known about DNA of the fruit fly, an insect which happens to have such large DNA threads as to make them readily available for study through microphotography. Even the specific "nodules" on the threads which control the development of a variety of bodily organs are codified. As an example, by removing one such speck from the thread of DNA the offspring will not have eyes.[12]

In spite of these exciting developments, Masserman concluded that:
"All in all, genetic studies have shown that while certain defects in the helical templates of desoxyribonucleic acid in our genes (and consequent disturbances in protoplasmic ribonucleic acid) may transmit epilepsy and certain other errors in neural metabolism, there is no reliable evidence for definite hereditary factors in behavioral abberrations less directly dependent on somatic and neurologic functions. Rather, controlled genetic-environmental studies (C. S. Rosenberg) indicate strongly that parents influence their children's patterns of behavior less by genes than by the nature of parental care, precept and example." [13]

Subsequent research may well discover that prenatal conditioning, reinforced by early parental handling, is one of the major factors in many of the glandular related illnesses, such as hypertension, thyroid difficulties, the cyclical manic-depressive syndromes, and perhaps diseases of other parts of

[12] Most of this material was obtained from a film prepared by Bell Telephone Laboratories in collaboration with many specialists.
[13] Masserman, Jules H., *Principles of Dynamic Psychiatry*, Philadelphia: W. W. Norton and Co., 1960, pp. 10-11; permission of the publisher.

the anatomy which are glandularly influenced indirectly through the central nervous system. The old wives tales of folklore usually contain an element of truth. The scientifically validated truth in the fallacious concept of a mother "marking" her child rests in the manner in which the hormonal production influences the foetus. The baby is well protected from external injury and from much illness present in the mother. Alcohol, nicotine and drugs get through the placenta but in small quantities. But hormonal elements are so small as to pass into the baby's blood stream with relative ease. Much of what has been thought of as innate temperament no doubt is conditioned in this manner. The anxiety of mother, among other factors, sets her hormonal pattern. This stimulus in turn acts on the endocrine system of the foetus. Much of such conditioning contributes to the variety of personality development which is considered normal. If a particular maternal hormonal blend persists long enough, and is severe enough, it may push the basic patterning of the child's endocrine system into a form that may set the stage for some subsequent development such as emotional imbalance (i.e. manic-depressive psychosis) or for a physiological disturbance such as hypertension, or heart disease.

The issue has been labored here, perhaps creating added confusion, but hoping to provide caution and a few guide lines for examining this critical area for any couple contemplating marriage and parenthood. One of the better handbooks is Montagu's *Human Heredity* [14] which includes a list of genetic clinics.

The tremendous implications of heredity in producing the unique individual should not be overlooked by preoccupation with possible genetically determined diseases. The twenty-three pairs of chromosomes and the estimated 5,000 to 20,000 genes transmit the basic physical characteristics that make up the distinctly individual appearance. These include basic body formation (although nutrition has much to do with size), whether endomorphic, mesomorphic, or ectomorphic; the tint of the skin, color of eyes and hair; skin blemishes such as freckles and moles; and the basic organic structure including the central nervous system, with which the individual maintains and expresses himself. These basic beginning tools of living and relating, what happens to the person, and what he does with both, all inter-

[14] Montagu, Ashley, *Human Heredity*, New York: Mentor Books, 1960, see p. 320; Hammons, Helen M., editor, *Heredity Counseling*, New York: Paul B. Hoeber, Inc., 1959; Rife, David C., *Heredity and Human Nature*, New York: Vantage Press, 1960. Roberts, J., and A. Fraser, *Introduction to Medical Genetics*, New York: Oxford University Press, 1959; Winchester, A. M., *Heredity: An Introduction to Genetics*, New York: Barnes and Noble, 1961.

act to produce the individual with whom you are planning counseling or the two individuals who make up the marriage in stress.

This means that, due to both heredity and other factors, certain characteristics of each individual are as they are, and relatively little can be done to change them beyond cosmetic and surgical aids. Unless each of the couple can learn to appreciate and accept the mate as he is in these unchanging areas, he is not going to become able to grow and change in psychological areas. Such can be the goals of pre-marital counseling.

H. LEGAL ORIENTATION

The marriage counselor usually will lean over backwards to avoid giving legal advice, but he should know how lawyers function and how to work cooperatively with them around family difficulties. Also, he needs to be aware of laws pertaining to sex behavior, marriage, children and property in order to know when and how to refer clients for legal assistance. Kings' *Your Legal Adviser, A Layman's Handbook of Law*, serves well as an orientation in this area. A more sophisticated volume is Spellman's *Successful Management of Matrimonial Cases*.[15] The Legal Aid Society in any larger city is a helpful resource.

I. ECONOMICS AND WORK

It is no more the duty of a marriage counselor to make financial plans for a couple than it is for him to *do* other things for them. Rather, the function is to clarify facts, feelings, and figures, and bring to light unconscious motivations, to the end that they may make their own decisions and thereby grow into more effective people. Nevertheless, the marriage counselor does need to be familiar in general with economic problems in order to evaluate properly the concern manifested by the individual or the couple. He must be able to determine reality from unreality if he is to be of the most help.

I. An Overview of Finances

The jokesters have it that "money may not be the greatest thing in the world but it can buy it." Certainly, money is not the most important thing in family life but it is closely related to every other aspect of living. As a new couple or a couple already married re-examine finances, some vital areas

[15] King, Samuel J., *Your Legal Adviser, A Layman's Handbook of Law*, New York: Permabooks, 1955; Spellman, Howard A., *Successful Management of Matrimonial Cases*, New York: Prentice-Hall, 1954.

need to be considered. The time has passed when a woman can be married for years and say, "I don't know how much my husband makes." Regardless of the particular form of family life to which they are pledged, both members of the partnership need to know the "score" before and after marriage. Failure to interact meaningfully in this realm can bring chaos to a marriage, or a smooth, working arrangement can bring a sense of accomplishment and peace of mind.

Income. How much of a nest-egg do they have? What is the income of the man now? Probability of increase, and how much? Will the woman work? For how long? What is her income? Probability of raise? Are the parents subsidizing the marriage? What amount? His parents? Her parents? For how long, and is this advisable? Will it cause the new family to feel inadequate, or maintain their dependency rather than their having to become independent and self-sufficient? Does this obligate the young couple emotionally to either set of parents, or give the parents a feeling of justifiable interference and guidance of the new home?

Who spends the money? Will he be the treasurer, or will she? Will a separate or joint account be used? Will they share the responsibility of spending and how? Have they given ample attention to budgeting, making use of available aids?

Many American youth have been made so "standard of living" conscious, so dependent upon possession as a means of status, that each may be inclined to insist upon beginning at the same level of "this world's goods" attained in their parental home only after years of struggle. The tragedy is that this can be done, but usually in only one way, *installment buying.* With its waste and carrying charges and encouragement to live beyond one's income, this is the distinctly American curse upon young families. The situation is intensified by the use of psychological knowledge of human weaknesses to reinforce consumer advertising. By the end of their first year of marriage, many couples have contracted for their total income for years to come, paying twice or three times the value in carrying charges on furnishings which will be worn out before the bills are paid. "No debts! No credit! Home-life ceases to be free and beautiful as soon as it is founded on borrowing and debts." How strange those words sound in the midst of present-day buying habits!

Facing reality, it is assumed that a modern couple will insist upon certain basic items to begin the new home. Such a list of necessities should be compiled carefully, then cut in half, and if cash is not available, the total amount borrowed from a bank at not more than 6 per cent interest. Many stores grant discounts up to 25 per cent on cash orders on large items. Even at only a 6 per cent discount, the interest is abolished, carrying charges avoided, and payments are made at one place. Other furnishings can then be planned for, and the couple can have the indescribable pleasure of wanting something, saving for it with anticipation, purchasing it for cash, and knowing "it is ours." Installment buying can be one of the most destructive factors in family life, with couples coming unconsciously to despise each other as the reason for the collectors' notices or appearances at the door. *Living within one's income is a cardinal principal of marital happiness!*

Budgeting. Whether a budget contributes to marital happiness, or causes the misery of a self-imposed strait jacket, will depend upon its adjustability to the needs of individuals and of the family month by month and year by year. Perhaps the ideal is attained when each member of the family understands so well how much money there is and how long it must last that budgeting becomes almost automatic, rather than something on paper to be rigidly followed. Many young couples, after the most intensive planning, simply must resort to buying the bare essentials each week, then apportioning the remainder here and there until they get established. The suggested list of percentages of income may provide something for comparison in taking a look at the management of money. This is not based on anybody's averages, but rather a working estimate:

Housing: (rent, utilities, telephone, taxes, insurance, upkeep)
    25-35 per cent.

Food: 20-25 per cent.
Clothing: (purchase, repair, cleaning, and laundry) 10-15 per cent.
Savings: (bonds, investments, insurance, retirement) 5-15 per cent.
General: (education, doctors, dentists, transportation, income taxes)
    20-25 per cent.

Contributions: (church, charity, cultural endeavors) 5-10 per cent.

Equal sharing in all planning and spending calls for the greatest maturity, and by necessity this will not be the plan for the family if one of the couple cannot handle money. Even then it seems desirable to grow toward having one place—bank account, coffee can, or sock—where the money is jointly controlled and dispatched. Later there can be a division of duties, of kinds of bills to be paid by each on the basis of convenience and skill, with each being fully aware of all expenditures. *If both work*, it seems wise to put the two incomes into a family plan, creating the feeling of "our income," rather than his against hers. When wives cease working, they tend to have that "without income" feeling of dependency and insecurity. Having had only one account helps her to continue feeling, regardless of whether she works in or out of the home, that "this is our income." The idea of many couples is that she will work "until we can afford for her to quit and have children." If they begin at a standard of living based on both incomes, dropping down to one salary may appear almost impossible. One remedy may be to put the amount of one salary on debts and into savings and not incorporate it into the regular financing of the family. A welcome sense of freedom from a budget or spending plan can be had if each has a small amount per week to be spent or saved without explanation. This avoids asking for money and permits buying of gifts and little luxuries without the feeling of imposing on the family living expenses.

A family finance diary. Kiplinger [16] has discussed the value of knowing the facts about one's finances. He provides a "cash forecast" chart with space for an estimate, and a column for what turns out to be the actual cash on hand, receipts, fixed payments, variable payments, total payments, and a final recapitulation for each month of the year. It is essential to look at an entire year, since heavy payments like taxes or insurance may fall due only once a year and heating bills will be much higher for certain months. The next step is to set up an estimated spending plan for the coming year, comparing with the old, as necessary or desirable modifications are made. Subsequent steps are simply to make once a month accounting, using the "actual" column, of what is spent each month. This is the best way of growing a workable financial plan for a family and avoiding over-commitments. By adding up assets and subtracting liabilities each quarter, the second part of this chart, "net worth forecast" for each quarter of the year, can be useful.

Shopping. Many modern young families subscribe to either *"Consumer Reports"* or *"Consumer Bulletin."* Household Finance Corporation publishes a series of 12 booklets in the field of money management. A list of

[16] Kiplinger, *Family Success Book, Changing Times,* The *Kiplinger Magazine,* Washington, D.C., 1959.

these is available along with a free money management program folder from that office.[17]

Kiplinger [18] becomes specific about buying such items as meat, suits, air conditioners, washing machines, sewing machines, power mowers, automobiles, houses, life insurance, etc. This booklet is a "primer of spending," as it outlines ten ways to stretch a dollar:

(1) *Guard against "habit spending."* Question every dollar that goes out; keep an open mind; are you spending by habit, because other people do, because your family has always spent in that way, because you haven't stopped to think? The more established a family becomes, the more likely it is to develop such spending patterns, and all of them may not be economical. Check your income tax, insurance dollars, vacation spending, shelter expense, debt payments, savings program—remembering that very few expenses are absolutely untouchable. The more you challenge every expense, the less likely it is that you will be the victim of habit spending.

(2) *Plan ahead.* During the average couple's lifetime, the man and the woman will operate a partnership, making pertinent purchases up to $300,000. You won't buy well unless you plan ahead on such things as groceries, seasonal produce, seasonal sales.

(3) *Compare, compare.* Shopping means "to visit shops for purchasing or inspecting goods." Why not study your shopping habits carefully, listing in a book the items you buy frequently: favorite foods, shoes, socks, cleaning supplies, handkerchiefs, etc. By keeping the last price paid for that item you may see if you can beat it the next time. By listing the purchases you plan to make ahead of time, you can be alert to good purchasing opportunities and can shop from store to store for the same brand items.

(4) *Learn quality.* Be a label reader; learn cheap brands and quality brands and know what you are buying.

(5) *Don't over-buy.* A common fault is to buy quality that is not necessary, as in clothes that children will outgrow, decorative items that

[17] *Consumer Reports*, published monthly by Consumer's Union, Mt. Vernon, New York. $5.00 a year; *Consumer Bulletin*, published monthly by Consumer's Research, Inc., Washington; New Jersey $5.00 a year; and Money Management Institute, Household Finance Corporation, Prudential Plaza, Chicago, Illinois. National Consumer Finance Association, Washington 30, D.C., provides some helpful booklets on "Money and Your Marriage." See also Black, Hillel, *Buy Now Pay Later*, New York: Wm. Morrow and Co., 1961.

[18] Kiplinger, *op. cit.*; permission of the publisher.

will not be kept, or silver that will not be used. This is another area where habit buying or tradition can cost money.

(6) *Buy more—Buy cheaper.* Why not use the bargain rate for two or three items on things that you use regularly? Some neighbors save a lot of money by sharing the cost of such items as expensive equipment and cleaning supplies.

(7) *Keep a cash reserve.* You find an item that you really need and it is on sale at half price; bargain money is the answer. The use of charge accounts eat up savings in a hurry, and you tend to shop at the same place and not to take advantage of such savings.

(8) *Do it yourself.* One of the greatest fads of the day is to do things that in the past were paid for by most people. Careless do-it-yourself projects can cost money, but one who knows what he can do, and carefully learns to do other things, can avoid spending a lot of money for labor that he could do himself with fun and profit.

(9) *Beware of false economy.* It is foolish and unprofitable to go to extremes in saving money that will lead to worn-out appliances, or by scrimping so desperately that one has to let off steam by spending foolishly. One of the most deceptive things in modern buying is a sale or a discount house that tempts one into buying at a bargain that which he could easily do without.

(10) *Keep your sense of values.* Don't carry dollar stretching to a grim and unpleasant extreme. The purpose of dollar stretching is to make life more pleasant, to make money buy a better standard of living. Scrimping to the point of feeling surly and disgruntled is poor economy. It is important to hang on to a sense of value, putting things in proper proportion.

Savings. Saving can be accomplished by most people only if made a matter of routine or habit. Couples can set reasonable minimal goals and then strive to surpass them. Although a small reserve in the checking account is desirable, a separate fund, postal saving, or government bond, are more likely to last than a bank account which is all too accessible. Some people are so miserly that they fail to enjoy their income here and now, whereas others never save. Emergencies send the latter rushing to loan companies which charge terrific rates of interest. The pleasures and sense of security from regular saving cannot be overestimated. Saving for household furnishings, a vacation, a home, a baby, an education, and a backlog of security in case of sickness or other emergency, can be a vital part of family living. It should be remembered that equity in a house, insurance, and retirement payments are all forms of saving.

Insurance. One of the responsibilities of every family is to take some thought for tomorrow and possible emergencies. A *will* which provides for the care of a wife and children in case of death of the husband is a vital part of such planning. Insurance is a combination of savings and protection. People tend to run to one extreme or the other, either providing very little insurance at all or becoming "insurance poor." Entering the realm of insurance is a confusing adventure indeed for the uninitiated. This is an area in which even the experts choose sides. Mehr and Osler have written a valuable work entitled *Modern Life Insurance.*[19]

It is a good idea to secure the services of a reputable agency in formulating a master plan for the insurance on a family. It can be started with minimum protection and added to throughout the income producing years. Such a master plan will avoid the expense of giving up policies taken ill-advisedly which do not fit into the later plans. Many of the major life insurance companies provide such service free of charge and without any obligation to purchase. Beneficiaries of policies held until the time of marriage will need to be changed by the young couple.

Personal insurance is of several types: Coverage in case of death of the insured, usually the breadwinner; income for the family in case of death; annuities and social security, paying income for life after a certain age; and hospitalization insurance, medical and/or surgical, which is offered by many employers at group insurance rates. Few couples can afford to be without thorough medical coverage today.

Educational insurance must be paid up within a few years, and is payable when the child reaches college age. These policies amount essentially to savings, plus the interest thereon and the fact that the policy would be paid in the case of death of the insurer.

Property insurance usually consists of that on a home and its furnishings, and perhaps liability for accidents occurring on the premises. People tend to insure homes for less than their replacement value in case of fire or storm. They overlook the fact that most policies do not automatically cover the furnishings. Most people overlook the fact that an insurance policy would not cover the total cost of a home should there be a fire; paying only a percentage of the total, taking into account the items and nature of the

[19] Mehr, Robert I. and Robert I. and Robert W. Osler, *Modern Life Insurance,* New York: Macmillan Company.

damage. An important adjunct to property insurance plan is a policy on the life of the breadwinner in the amount of any loans on the house, which would pay off in case of death or permanent disability. These policies reduce as the payments on a loan are made, keeping the monthly cost of insurance at a minimum, well worth the security afforded.

Automobile insurance is a necessity today, not only to repair or replace a car, but to provide security in case of a lawsuit resulting from an accident and to provide medical care for injuries to others. Some states require such insurance or a cash bond of a certain amount for automobile owners. With the amount involved in such lawsuits soaring, not having liability insurance is an invitation to lose one's home or other possessions.

Annuities are essentially savings policies, plus interest, plus the fact that they would pay off in case of death. Hence they are expensive and can be thought of by most couples only after other essentials are provided.

On stocks and bonds,[20] authorities make the following recommendations:

(1) When buying stocks don't use money you might be needing for something else. Have adequate life insurance and a cash fund for emergencies. Don't count on stocks to tide you over sickness or loss of job.

(2) Don't try to trade in and out of the market. No one can forecast month to month fluctuations. Stay with your investments as long as they hold promise, buying for the long pull.

(3) Don't jump in all at once. Invest a fixed number of dollars at regular intervals. This means that you will buy some purchases at high, low, and intermediate levels, thus acquiring at an average cost.

(4) Diversify. Spread your money along at least five or six good quality industries as you go along. By buying shares in an investment company you get diversification automatically.

The job and the family

A reasonable income is vital to the family, but that the job should bring personal satisfaction and enhancement of the emotional environment of the family is of even greater importance. A family can be threatened if the job is so demanding or conflicting that the worker is on edge, tense, and hard to live with. Likewise, the family can be threatened if the job calls for one parent to be away for long periods, and equally so when one parent is too tired, preoccupied, or tense, to relate to the mate or to the children. The

[20] See *Consumer Reports* and Kiplinger's publications.

happiness of many families is threatened by an extra shift when the bread-winner works, or the wife works, to provide an additional automobile or a more expensive social life.

Income is significant, but overshadowed by far by attitudes toward work. In Chapter 3 it was pointed out that a mark of individual maturity is the ability to gain major satisfaction from the actual doing of a job, not upon the financial and status rewards.

High- and low-job satisfaction

In order to compare the attitudes about the father's job in families of high- and low-job satisfaction, Dyer [21] interviewed 87 families. The top and bottom thirds of the sample were labelled "satisfied" and "less satisfied," respectively; and the comparisons were made of responses to items concerning feelings of satisfaction. He found the following differences by family members:

(1) Father. The less satisfied father felt that his wife and children were not satisfied with his job, and that the family members were not satisfied with the prestige level of his job. His work was more often the cause of family disagreement and he less often wanted to see his children follow his line of work.

(2) Mother. The father's occupation affected the relationship of the mother both within and outside the family. The less satisfied wife had more feelings of dissatisfaction in her relations outside the family, apparently stemming from the less desirable nature of his job. She made more negative responses regarding in-family factors as a result of influences the job had on the father and the family. Likewise, she did not want to see her children follow the father's line of work.

(3) Children. Less satisfied children responded more negatively to both in-family and out-family items. They were not proud of the father's job, it was not as good as the jobs of their friends' fathers, or they wished he would change jobs. Within the family, the children mentioned most often dissatisfaction with aspects of the job which adversely affected the father.

Level of aspiration and achievement

Several times in this book thus far the innate drive of a child to develop and to fulfill his capacities has been emphasized. This need for self-fulfillment becomes modified immeasurably by both external and internal factors

[21] Dyer, William G. "A Comparison of Families of High- and Low-Job Satisfaction." *Marriage and Family Living*, Vol. 18, 1, 1956, pp. 58.

as development proceeds. Dynes, Clarke, and Denitz [22] in a study of 153 males and 197 females found that unsatisfactory interpersonal relationships in the family of orientation were significantly related to high aspirational levels and satisfactory relationships were related to lower aspirational level. This in isolation might indicate that, as people develop who are "happy" in their family and social situation, levels of aspiration may be lowered.

Another factor operating to modify aspirational and achievement drives was the operation of various ego defense mechanisms, power drives, and social class differences in values.

Winterbottom [23] found that mothers of children with high achievement motivation differ from mothers of children who have low motivation in: (1) making more demands at earlier ages, particularly for evidence of independence, maturity, and achievement; and (2) giving more frequent and intense rewards for fulfilling demands. McClelland et al [24] have also said that high motivation to achieve is related to the child's being urged to obtain, and rewarded for achieving independence and mastery, accompanied by fewer restrictions after mastery has been attained.

Much has been written about the relatively lower drive toward attainment and achievement in the lower socio-economic class. The tendency is to do what the child sees the adult doing, somewhat fatalistically taking his place in life. The natural achievement drive is likely to take on a rather low level of aspiration such as "being the best damned welder in Tennessee." Such observations obviously are true to a marked degree and yet there are major and frequent exceptions. Lower class frequently accept some of the ideals held by the middle and upper classes, making for constant movement upward for the more ambitious youth in the lower socio-economic strata. The power motive, as evidenced in the authority of other people found in the professions and in politics, has helped to account for the large number of leaders in the United States who originated in the lower socio-economic class.

The middle class begins to stress achievement by the time the baby is born. This has been countered somewhat by the tremendous emphasis upon permissiveness in child rearing, but at the same time achievement is stim-

[22] Dynes, Russell R., Alfred C. Clarke, and Simon Denitz. "Levels of Occupational Aspiration: Some Aspects of Family Experience as a Variable." *American Sociological Review*, XXI, 2, April 1956, pp. 212-215.

[23] Winterbottom, M. "The Relationship of Childhood Training in Independence to Achievement Motivation," University of Michigan Ph.D. dissertation, 1953.

[24] McClelland, D., S. Atkinson, R. Clark, and E. Lowell. *The Achievement Motive,* New York: Appleton-Century Crafts. 1953.

ulated by giving him warm recognition for attainment. In the pre-school period, the tendency is to make demands upon the child in terms of early toilet training, concern about cleanliness, control of feelings, etc. Parents are proud of signs of brightness in their children and often lavish rewards for intellectual attainment at this early age. This is speeded up when the children begin formal schooling and a great deal of parental attention focuses on this activity. Many of the reading and learning problems of the middle class child may be related directly to undue pushing on the part of his highly aspiring parents and teachers. From the time the child enters school, much of his reward and punishment seems to center around school performance. Middle class children are more likely to be taught not only to believe in "success" but also to be willing to take those steps that make achievement possible: in short, to embrace the achievement value system which states that, given the willingness to work hard, plan, and make the proper sacrifices, an individual should be able to manipulate his environment so as to insure eventual monetary and status success. Herein originate some of the most highly neurotic strivings of this culture.

Central Life Interests of Industrial Workers

Displacement of value from the job to what it can buy is by no means restricted to the middle class, according to Dubin.[25] There is a good deal of indication that a man's job has been his central life interest for much of recorded history. This impression has been reinforced by biographical and autobiographical studies, by the guilds and other organizations which have grown up around man's work through the years, and by the fact that man spends so much of his time in a particular endeavor. Dubin completed questionnaires on 491 workers and intensive recorded interviews with a sample of 120 employees in three midwestern plants. His findings indicate conclusively that for almost three out of every four industrial workers studied, work and the place of work were not central life issues. Not only was the place of work relatively unimportant as a place of preferred primary human relationships, but it could not even evoke significant sentiments and emotions in the employees. Deliberate efforts on the part of management to make it so seemed to be relatively ineffectual, except for that small group who see the job environment as their most likely source of desired informal group life.

[25] Dubin, Robert, "Industrial Workers' Worlds: A Study of the 'Central Life Interests' of Industrial Workers." *Social Problems* III, 3, January 1956, pp. 131-142.

Factory work was viewed by the vast majority of the sample as a means to an end, a way of acquiring income for life in the community. There is no doubt a great loss in meaningfulness in living as the assembly line job ceases to be a source of personal satisfaction, pride, satisfying human associations, and of pleasure in expressing the instinct of workmanship. However, there may be gains to whatever extent the central life interests of the employees may be refocused upon the family itself in terms of developing meaningful relationships in the home, in leisure activities, and in community participation.

II. Psychoneurosis and Economic Life

The symbolic meanings attached to money have been amply described in psychoanalytic literature and demonstrated in clinical practice. Leavy and Friedman [26] have investigated how economic activities and emotional conditions may have interacted or be interacting in those who come for psychotherapeutic help. They asked: "How do the activities and changes of economic life affect the development of emotional illness or health, and how does emotional illness or health affect the economic life?" They found that economic attitudes affect values adopted and developed by the children, and these attitudes, as well as the adaptive capacities in general, are subjected to such influences as the experience of poverty or of economic change in either an upward or a downward direction.

One generalization from this study is that economic life can be shown to have great significance as a determinant of neurosis. What persons do to earn a living, what kind of experiences they have as a result of parental problems of earning, and the kind of economic mores of a community which have been imposed on them, all constitute definable elements in the development of neurosis. They found that the major economic issues in the lives of patients could be subsumed under security, work, and competition. The finer type of scrutiny permitted by the favorable conditions of psychoanalytic psychology sharpens the view of the interweaving of economic factors with conflicts within the individual. At least two factors are involved in the generating of neurotic behavior by economic insecurity, according to these authors: (1) not only is the threat to subsistence of serious consequence, but (2) so is the threat to self-esteem. The individual being defeated in his attempt to live up to the expectations of himself resulted in greater or lesser degrees of neurotic behavior.

[26] Leavy, Stanley A., and Lawrence Z. Friedman. "Psychoneurosis and Economic Life." *Social Problems*, IV, 1, July 1956, pp. 55-56.

They found a psychological correspondence between economic insecurity and loss of love. For instance, employment may provide a demonstrable release for energies which are themselves directed by neurotic conflict and may provide a screen of acceptability for compulsive over-activity. On the other hand, these authors found that stress generated in the work situation, although perhaps precipitated by personal conflict, became an added cause of neurotic development. Economic competition operated as a pathogenic agency in several ways. Unmanageable hostility is liberated; culturally prescribed standards of success and prestige presented goals impossible of achievement, augmenting already existing conflicts; economic life offered a continuing arena for the competitive struggles originating in childhood. They found that the obligation to compete, like economic insecurity, had a double function: (1) it was a direct threat, with failure endangering subsistence, and (2), it was more involved as a social force, invoking the individual's allegiance to pursuit of a value not open to criticism.

Yes, attitudes toward finances are vital factors either in effecting a healthy way of family living, or likewise, they both contribute to and result in a neurotic use of the job and the income. There is no more effective shortcut to the revelation of the major value system of an individual than a discussion in depth of money and the job.

J.   SEXOLOGY

Sexology is a vital area of knowledge for the pre-marital counselor; so important that it has been treated in detail in Chapters 8, 11 and 12.

Chapter 11

SEX EXPERIENCE
AND SEXUAL PROBLEMS

A. SEX EDUCATION

The most lasting and effective sex education is that which occurs so naturally and spontaneously in the attitudes and discussions of the family, church and school that it does not call undue attention to itself. This is where attitudes are learned which determine how facts, including one's own body, can be utilized in adult sex expression. Experience with peers becomes likewise crucial. If the "sex environment" is comfortable and healthy, the attitudes serve the individual well throughout life; if erroneous and un-healthy, he must work overtime at correcting the emotional and factual conditioning or pay a lifelong penalty in lack of satisfaction and in misery.

Most individuals experience enough mal-healthy attitudes and trauma around sex to require specific corrective experiences of an educational, if not therapeutic, nature. Even the youth who has been most enlightened during the early years could profit from more specific sex education and reeducation as he enters puberty and proceeds to a marriageable age. Hope-fully, such education can be in the larger context of the whole of life, not discrete subject matter divorced from total reality. A family life course, or pre-marital counseling, can provide an excellent environment in which to analyze the past and present attitudes, learn new ones, and reintegrate per-sonality.

I. The Sex Educator

The Harpers [1] have suggested: Because of greater ignorance and its present emotionally charged nature, more instruction is needed on sex than any other aspect of family life; family life educators should be recruited from the most mature, the best integrated, and the most emotionally self-understanding teachers, especially in the area of sex; they should be en-

[1] Harper, Robert A. and Frances R. Harper, "Are Educators Afraid of Sex?", *Marriage and Family Living*, XIX, 3, 1957.

couraged to proceed fearlessly and honestly with a free discussion approach in the public schools; and there is no effective general alternative to the schools as the means of sexually educating the children of today.

It does seem logical that a saner, less timid approach to the total role of sex in life would produce healthier human behavior. The truth should make one free for responsible living. Whether it be the parent, educator, physician, clergyman, or counselor, and whether the approach be to children and youth or to parents and the public, there is no substitute for the authority that comes from personal understanding and inner security in what one is doing as a professional. If the doctor or counselor is in doubt, his patient is left anxious. If the professor is concerned as to whether he has a right to teach, or has not thought through the inner meaning of the subject matter to himself, his doubt will be conveyed to youth.

Yet youth wants to know, and will persist in knowing. Most of what is known about sex as fact has been heard by most before they reach adulthood. Yet, one fact is heard along with dozens of other assertions which claim to be true. The task is not so simple as memorization of fact. It requires the learning and relearning of basic attitudes, the formulation and reformulation of value systems, which can come only from painstaking self examination and careful, responsible application of what each evolves as meaningful in the context of the kind of life, individual and familial, he wants for himself.

II. The Questions of Youth

Stokes [2] has reported some pioneering work as a marriage counselor and psychiatrist in cooperating with churches in the sex education of junior high school youth, which is significant for several reasons. First, it suggests the workability of such projects, especially with joint religious and scientific backing; it highlights the basic concerns of high school youth; and, since most engaged youth have just emerged from this stage of development, it may assist the counselor in reactivating some of their concerns and the situations which went into forming their present attitudes.

After meeting with parents to tell them of the frank approach to be employed, Stokes talked with the youth in general about sex education. They then asked questions verbally and in writing which took several sessions to answer. Here are the questions asked, except for deletion of repetitions:

[2] Stokes, Walter, "A Pioneering Study in the Sex Education of Children," paper presented to the 1959 annual meeting of American Association of Marriage Counselors, in New York City.

1. Where did you obtain the necessary information for these talks?
2. Are you married?
3. Do you believe in sex education in high schools? Coeducational education? Why?
4. What is *your opinion* on "going steady" in reference to marriage later on in life? I mean "going steady" as opposed to dating a variety of people.
5. How can you tell when you are ready for marriage and whether you are "in love" enough to merit marriage?
6. Do you think physical desirability is an important factor of sex?
7. What do you think of the stress placed on the bosom by teenage girls?
8. Am I correct in getting the impression that you put an equal amount of weight on the emotional and physical sides of sex? If so, is this because you feel they are equally important and independent? If no, do you feel either one is more important than the other?
9. What do you think about the two or three dollar books on sex that are advertised in men's magazines?
10. What are your personal feelings about the movie "Cat on a Hot Tin Roof?"
11. What is your opinion of marriage involving persons of different race or religion?
12. Do you denounce polygamy?
13. What percentage of your patients "fall out of love?"
14. Does divorce solve a bad marriage? Don't most persons who divorce once go on and have several divorces?
15. Do you think there are physiological reasons for sterility?
16. Is syphilis handed down to children? If so, how will it affect them mentally and physically?
17. Is syphilis transmitted by saliva in kissing?
18. Do you consider abortion wrong? If so, why?
19. What about "Spanish fly?"
20. I feel we should define masturbation because many young people do not know what it is and are afraid to discuss it. I know what it is but I'm afraid to discuss it.
21. Please discuss masturbation fully. Does it include an ejaculation or emission? Is this harmful? Does it stunt normal body growth? Is it harmful in excess? Should it be controlled? What is the best way to control it?

22. Do you feel that masturbation is normal? When might it be normal and when not normal?

23. Does masturbation affect sex development? That is, would a person who masturbates at a young age develop sexually sooner than one who doesn't? Also does masturbation affect the frequency of pimples and does it therefore possibly affect growth rate and sexual development?

24. Some people masturbate to a great extent; is it possible for a boy to masturbate so much that he will "run out of seed" by the age of marriage?

25. What about the mental damage of masturbation in causing an unsatisfiable desire?

26. Does intercourse control masturbation?

27. Does masturbation lead to homosexuality?

28. Why is homosexuality such a topic for concern and conversation today?

29. What does it mean if a male has homosexual urges?

30. Isn't it true that a homosexual can take part in a normal sex relationship?

31. Do you find any justification for laws against homosexuality?

32. If homosexuality is not harmful, how would you lead one of your own sex on or become acquainted with people of the same feelings?

33. Are sex relations with brothers or sisters (depending on one's own sex) abnormal or wrong?

34. Do you know any instances of sodomy?

35. Do you think that rape should be a capital crime, classed with murder?

36. What about rape? Could an M.D. perform an abortion?

37. How would you do away with prostitution?

38. Do you think it is wrong to pet? If so, why? If not, why?

39. I feel you shouldn't kiss a boy unless you really like him a lot. Many people consider this old-fashioned today. I'd like to know how the boys feel about it.

40. Should a person persist in petting if the partner is not willing?

41. When you condone "leading on" do you take into account the fact that this person may cause moral worries in the other party?

42. Why should the boys care if they "go too far," for they have nothing to worry about?

43. Is it possible for a human being *not* to enjoy intercourse?
44. What is the meaning of being frigid?
45. I have read that in the Victorian Era it was understood that a married woman was to exhibit no enjoyment of intercourse. What is the truly modern aproach?
46. Is there lack of enjoyment in the use of a contraceptive?
47. Would you explain the best method of contraception, explaining that period when a girl is not likely to get pregnant and why?
48. Please explain the best method of breaking a girl's maidenhead?
49. Do you advocate the first-night routine as written by Havelock Ellis?
50. In marriage will intercourse come naturally?
51. Physiologically, who usually has more control of their sex desires at all stages of sexual behavior, from none at all to just before intercourse, the male or female?
52. There is a strong force which won't let me "go all the way." I'm not sure what it is. I've been brought up that way but that's not the only reason. I've been told many times but I'd like to know the best reason not to (aside from having a baby: I'm not that dumb!).
53. What about pre-marriage sex? To what extent?
54. What are your views on pre-marital intercourse, emotionally and ethically?
55. Why would it be wrong to go all the way?
56. Do pre-marital relationships necessarily mean an unhappy marriage? Does it depend on whether it is the man you marry?
57. Why shouldn't teenagers indulge in sexual intercourse with proper precautions like prophylactics?
58. How can you tell when a girl is sexually aroused?
59. Should we resign ourselves to the fact that we can't have "fun" until after marriage or is there some *safe* release other than such frowned-upon things as homosexuality or intimate affairs with the opposite sex?
60. Do you think that there is much of a chance of our "progressing" into an immoral society such as in Aldous Huxley's *Brave New World*?
61. Would you say that this statement by Bertrand Russell is factual? "The more timid of the young do not go so far as complete sexual relations, but content themselves with producing prolonged states of sexual excitement without satisfaction, which is nervously debilitating and calculated to make the full enjoyment of sex at a later

date difficult or impossible." More specifically, could this result actually follow from the situation described?

62. All through the ages society has changed. Now, in some countries, intercourse with girl friends and dates is not considered indecent. Do you think it is wrong, considering society does change, that teenagers now alter the way things are done? With proper precautions, why should this be considered wrong if society is constantly changing?

63. What should a parent do if he comes across his children having intercourse?

III. The Language of Sex

There are many indications that the youth in the project described above were quite sophisticated. Children from less educated families ask the same questions but in much more common language. The counselor must learn to be comfortable with the variety of sexual terminology which is common to the people with whom he works. Tension about the language is taken by the youth as discomfort with the subject of sex. Indeed, there can be integrating and healing value in encouraging engaged youth to use both correct and common terminology in discussing sexual interests.

Common expressions for anatomical and behavioral terminology may be used more frequently than correct terminology. This is only a suggestive list of sexual slang:

Correct Term	*Slang Term*
penis, phallus	dick, prick, peter, cock, shaft,
glans penis	thing, pecker, privates
	head
prepuce	foreskin
scrotum	cod, codsack
testes (testicles) gonads	nuts, balls, marbles
vulva, vagina	cock, pussy, ass, thing, twat, cunt, "some," shame, tail, piece, hole, privates, the well, the cave
	privates, the well, the cave
labia minora	
labia majora	lips

sexual intercourse coitus	fuck, screw, take, crawl, make, lay, do it, have, have sex, make love, get a
sexual congress sex relations copulate	piece (slice) of . . . shack up, sleep with, rape, live with, fool with, plank, ride ride
orgasm ejaculation	to come, go, off, finished, spent, through, climax, blow
masturbate	jack off, beat the meat, fuck off, handle self, touch off, satisfy self, self-stimulation, finger fuck, genital caressing, "abusing," play with
nocturnal emission	wet dream, mess the sheets, starch the sheets, spread the egg
fellatio oral genital cunnilingus stimulation	suck off, cock sucking, frenching, kiss vulva (penis), love with mouth, muff dive, 69, kiss off
sodomy (anal coitus)	"corn hole," ass fuck, bugging, Greeking

The homosexual world has a language all its own, which will slowly become familiar to the experienced counselor.

B. VARIETIES OF SEX EXPERIENCE

Many handicaps must be overcome in the search for knowledge and fulfillment in the sexual realm. In the midst of the confusing ideation of double and triple standards freely and compulsively peddled, the average child and youth is forced to educate himself sexually through his own experience. Being on one's own might not be so devastating except that he must have these experiences in isolation or with individuals or small groups under surreptitious circumstances. Several consequences are notable. Some gradually evolve quite healthy attitudes toward their sexual nature and behavior. But many others are hurt and crippled for the remainder of life, either by failing to develop or maldeveloping sexual attitudes and capacities. Some of the greatest residual damage is evident in impotence, frigidity and an endless variety of neurotic sexual behavior. Notorious in marriage is the condition that makes it seem necessary to separate sex satisfaction from love to the extent that these experiences must be with separate partners. Many people can enjoy sex only under forbidden conditions. Even the fairly healthy often are unnecessarily encumbered by the load of guilt, shame and anxiety that attend sexual functioning.

Forced into the realm of the isolated and surreptitious to satisfy curiosity and accumulate the experience necessary to fulfillment as sexual beings, many youth are left with an incapacitating morbidity. To this load of guilt often is added the fear of the abormal or perverted. An amazing amount of the crippling anxiety found in high school and college youths can be traced to such guilt and moribund fears. The belief that no one else—at least no one who is healthy and respectable—has had such urges or experiences, fanned by community attitudes, can drive one to distraction.

There is no commonly known normative frame of reference within which one can evaluate his unusual experiences. The sexual behavior of his peers is under similarly secretive circumstances and is likely to be thought of as perverted, or at least as taboo. As adults, who have repressed their own early erotic experiences, are exposed to bits of youthful sexuality, they begin to fear the illness, perversion, or disrepute into which the child might be led. This anxiety is all the more vicious when the adult cannot permit himself to recall or experience in his own fantasy what the great fear might be. Tremendous therapeutic and corrective value would accrue if such adults could come to know this unspeakable worry, which often goes far beyond the possibility of undesired pregnancies or venereal infections.

An illustration might serve the dual purpose of putting these fears into conscious expression and demonstrating some of the orgiastic results of sexual mal-education, whether by repression or by the tense and compulsive teaching of sexual experience by parents.

A client who was periodically impotent, with a long time fear of homosexuality, was invited to a party "for professional people." Two men, with several convictions for such offenses as dispensing pornography, indecent exposure, and molesting, arranged these parties, either on a small scale or on a large scale basis. In a single night the client saw acted out most of his own repressed urges, fears and fantasied sexual expressions, except that simple and direct one to one heterosexual intercourse was missing. There was fellatio and cunnilingus, male-male, female-female, and male-female. Every bodily orifice—mouth, ears, nostrils, anus, arm pits and such unimaginative things as hands—were used for copulation or ejaculation. A "cake walk" was set up with the men waiting in line to urinate in a woman. One man who only observed other activities got his "kicks" from defecating in a vagina. Some women had coitus with one man orally, another analy, and another vaginally alternately and then simultaneously. Occasionally this sexual acrostic was made more complicated by an additional male having anal contact or receiving oral contact with one of the males protruding from the pile, and by the licking and sniffing of a couple of domestic pets that had been brought along to add interest. Other on-lookers contributed by spankings, electric vibrators, or cigarette burns.

To a greater or lesser degree, this scene contains the unspeakable worry of many adults for their children, and of youth who, in isolation, equate their own behavior with the perverted or abnormal. They know that such orgies of sexuality appeal primarily to those whose sex education and development was botched in some way.

However, adults are unfair, and youths are too critical of themselves, if occasional bits of experiences, similar to some of this behavior, are equated with perversion and ill health. In all probability these early experiences, had in the search for sexual knowledge and self-identity, would be outgrown and replaced with an adequate adult sexual life if unacceptance and fear were not perpetuated in their own feelings and by the attitudes of adults, whether parents or leaders in education, religion, medicine or the law.

Many of the better educated adults, who should be most helpful to their children, are so afraid of sexuality that they dare not discuss or even recall their own childhood experiences or admit those of present day youth. Others rebel blindly against such strictures in their own childhood and seek to teach their children direct sex expression long before the child is able to understand or cope with this in a healthy manner. Clinicians are now seeing the same kind of sexual neuroses among these "liberated" children as among the families where sexuality is repressed and tabooed.

Operating on the general philosophy that "you shall know the truth and the truth shall make you free," a wider general knowledge of the endless variety of sexual experiences common to growing youth can relieve crippling anxiety in them and in their elders. Freed of such morbid preoccupation, young people are more able to learn from past experiences, evaluate and accept responsibility for present behavior and for a healthy way of heterosexual life. Similarly freed, adults enjoy a happier sex life themselves, and thus become available as relaxed and comfortable sources of knowledge and attitudes in the affectional and sexual areas.

So, for the sake of conflicted youth and adults, and as an aid to the pre-marital counselor, the sexual experiences of growing young people will now be reviewed.

I. The Dilemma of Youth

As in many other areas of life, conflicting systems of values and ideals are held up to youth in the area of sex. In middle class America girls are to be glamorous and sexy, and yet not participate in sex behavior. They are told to give sex to be accepted and that they will be rejected (as wives) if they do. Boys and men are to be attractive and desirable and always on the make for a willing female, and yet, in terms of religion and as reared in many homes, they are expected to be as chaste as are the girls. Is it any wonder that youth get mixed up? If they become sexual profligates, they set into operation forces that can destroy their own peace of mind and drastically affect the type of family life they desire. If they try to remain virginal, the methods of control may interfere with later sexual expression in marriage.

Take the illustration of a young adult male in this culture, who tries to meet expectations of his family and church and the law that he remain sexually continent until marriage. He is in quite a dilemma; a dilemma which, if not created by, certainly is contributed to by the contradictions in cultural emphasis. For the moment, it may be well to forget the rightness or wrongness of sexual behavior and consider the facts of what has happened to a hypothetical young man of 30.[3] First, let it be clear that this material is relevant to as many women as men. There are more similarities than dissimilarities in the sex needs of men and women. This young man is expected to have a late marriage, for educational and financial reasons, or because he has to enter the armed forces, as well as to permit him to mature emotionally for the responsibility of marriage. He is urged to develop into and assume responsibility for heterosexuality, yet he is to remain abstinent until marriage. But then he is not to get married until he has

[3] Rutledge, Aaron L., "Sexual Containment for the Unmarried," *Pastoral Psychology*, April 1959.

passed the period when his sexual urges are at the peak, say seventeen to twenty years of age.

Until marriage, society labels him a criminal if he participates in sexual activity and it becomes known. The same society subjects him to every possible sexual stimulation via radio, movies, television, magazines, and books from the time he is amenable to such communications. Along with this intensive sexual stimulation often goes the inference that he is not a man unless he pursues women sexually. Thus, society puts him in the same position as does the girl who pets with him until he is wild with passion but says "no" or slaps his face if he attempts intercourse. He is urged on toward sexual maturity and sexual behavior but then refused the experience unless he is willing to disobey, incurring either a punitive wrath or the resultant guilt feelings.

II. Varieties of Sex Experience

The problem can best be approached developmentally. Sexual need emerges as a part of the natural development of the human being. A child becomes aware of sex at an early age and it becomes a pressing need as maturing progresses. *Energy* set into operation by sex urges can be utilized in many ways, including study, art, recreation, religion and other creative endeavors. *Sex need* per se can be directed into only a few channels, however: autosexual, homosexual, animal-sexual, and heterosexual.

An outline of some of the sexual experiences boys and girls may have in the process of growing up will serve to reorient the counselor. Little is to be gained for the individual by statistical analysis.[4] Let it suffice for now to say that every type of experience mentioned has been revealed repeatedly in counseling and psychotherapy as part of high school and college students' sexual heritage. Some would immediately reply, "See, these were abnormal people who had to have therapy." In many cases they were emotionally disturbed or stunted in their personality development, but this does not necessarily mean that their "unusual" experiences were the result of illness or causative of illness in themselves. Furthermore, many of the youths involved were quite healthy but were seeking to clear up certain points on which they were anxious prior to marriage. In addition the author

---

[4] For the best studies, see, Kinsey, A. C., Pomeroy, W. B., and Martin, C. E., *Sexual Behavior in the Human Male*, Philadelphia: W. B. Saunders, 1948; Kinsey, A. C. et al. *Sexual Behavior in the Human Female*, Philadelphia: W. B. Saunders, 1953; and Gebbard, Paul H., Pomeroy, Wardell B., Martin, Clyde E., and Christensen, Cornelia V., *Pregnancy, Birth and Abortion*, New York: Harper and Brothers, 1958.

and colleagues have interviewed large numbers of people who were demonstrably healthy, and who revealed similar varieties of sexual experiences. The differences in experience of the healthy and unhealthy personalities were not in kind but in frequency, compulsivity, exclusivity, the total meaning of the experiences, and subsequent attitudes. This does not mean necessarily that every one *should* have had a battery of similar practices, or should *not* have had some such experiences. The desire at this point is not to focus so much on the health or unhealth of the experiences but to see them as just experiences and to be aware of reactions of the individual and of others. Questions of health will have to be applied largely at the level of what has been done about and with the experiences by the individual.

1. Autosexual Behavior

Masturbation either by hand or object is the first direct physical expression of sex for most boys and girls. In early childhood this was pleasurable although it did not lead to orgasm, as more commonly occurs at puberty. Masturbation may have been accompanied by any or all such attitudes as: it just feels good, blocking out all sexual concern and merely thinking of releasing physical tension, unconscious of the fact that masturbation is occurring until orgasm occurs, heterosexual fantasy about the opposite sex in general or a desired mate in particular, or homosexual fantasy.

If a boy or girl practices masturbation, what kinds of attitudes will be encountered in the immediate environment and in the rest of this culture? Autosexuality, finding expression in preoccupation with masturbating, is condemned by some specialists in religion and in science. Yet it is almost universal at varying stages of the development of youth, and in adulthood in the absence of other sexual satisfaction. Nevertheless, it is often guilt laden and discouraged by the still common erroneous belief that it results in insanity, epilepsy, draining off the brain power, impotence, or general debility.

Recognizing the practical necessity of some sort of release from sexual tension, other leaders in both science and religion have half-heartedly approved masturbation as the least harmful substitute, but even then usually with reservation, because of its "self-centeredness" and possible "habituation to the exclusion of heterosexuality."

The most usual forms of masturbation in boys are direct stimulation of the erect penis to the point of ejaculation. This may be done by copulating with the bedclothes, a doll, or any hollow or notched object that will permit penetration or friction with movement. The girl most often masturbates by caressing the clitoris or vaginal lips directly, or by massaging the whole pubic region. In some cases this is accomplished by breast and nipple stimulation. There are perhaps more non-direct ways of masturbation with girls, both consciously and unconsciously applied, than with boys. They may rub against tables, beds, or the floor. Some can squeeze and rub the thighs together to the point of inducing sexual pleasure and orgasm. Girls for whom direct masturbation is denied can become quite adept at finding substitutes which even they do not recognize for what it is.

Sometimes it is the extra "frills" or variations of masturbation that cause anxiety. Genital movement may be accompanied by stimulation of other parts of the body such as lips, ear lobes, or anus, or other parts of the body may give erotic pleasure apart from any genital contact. Some of these contacts may be manual and others orally applied. Usually fingers alone are used, but occasionally objects may be inserted in the anus, mouth or urethra as an accompanying stimulation.

In order to keep emotional and aesthetic reactions in the open and deal with them, perhaps it is important to pause occasionally to recognize where there is possibility of physical injury. Some objects can be inserted past the sphincter muscles and require medical assistance to remove from the anus. The anus is not naturally lubricated for such use and can be irritated, leading to infection and a good deal of misery. Sharp objects could perforate the thin intestinal walls if forcefully inserted. Some boys and girls insert objects into the urethra, a canal that is too small for such use. Toothpicks, matches, and birthday candles have been inserted; but there is risk of irritation, and in a few cases the object has slipped in too far to be extracted and even into the bladder. Girls also may use various objects to stimulate the genitals, whether applied to the clitoris, labia, or into the vaginal canal. A modern mechanical aid which has been widely adopted to masturbatory use is the electric vibrator. A few years ago several companies advertised a "vibrating finger" for dental massage. One senator decried the use of scientific talent to manufacture for lazy people such unnecessary items as a "power tooth brush." He seemed unaware of the uses for which the gadget was really intended, as indicated by the "true story" and "love story" magazines where they were first advertised.

Many girls, although continuing to use such objects as hair pins, fountain pens, pencils, and drink bottles, are bothered by fears of objects getting "lost" in the vagina. Contrary to what is true with the urethra and anus, any large object can be easily removed from the vagina. If smaller objects are dropped into the vaginal tract, particularly if the hymen is intact, medical dilation often is required for removal. By and large, fingers are best for self-stimulation—they do not irritate or puncture, cannot be inserted in places which are too small for such use, and they are not detachable.

What would be a sensible mental health approach to masturbation? Perhaps self-stimulation can best be summed up as completely normal in the absence of other direct sex expression. Under what conditions, then, should a counselor or psychotherapist be consulted? Concern would be registered only if the fantasy around masturbation showed unhealthy components as a pattern, or if the practice resulted in undue guilt reactions, was associated with fetishes, or took on a compulsive quality.

Some boys and girls have been conditioned from babyhood to feel deeply guilty about self-stimulation. Such an attitude likely may carry over to other forms of sex interest or expression, creating a disturbing guilt problem. The anxiety growing out of this may bring sexual incapacitation, or, in reverse, the tension may stimulate sex needs out of natural proportion. This can lead to compulsive or uncontrolled masturbation, which can have a variety of meanings. The person may have learned that the one sure way of gaining some immediate and complete relief from unbearable tension is through orgasm. At the same time, internalized conflicts are creating an undue amount of anxiety and tension. Guilt over masturbation becomes a primary stimulant to that anxiety and the result is cyclical. Conflict leads to anxiety, which produces energy to cope with the anxiety; the anxiety, not being conscious and out in the open so it can be handled, is not resolved; tension builds up so that the person almost automatically and uncontrollably turns to masturbation in order to find some momentary relief through orgasm. This is why compulsive masturbation has little to do with sexual need as such. Rather than the counselor being concerned about masturbation, the person should be given help with his emotional problems, after which masturbation will take care of itself in a more casual manner.

Another basis of compulsive masturbation can be seen symbolically in the substitution of the hand for the mother who has rejected or abandoned the child. Some of this self-caressing is natural in the long transition from a symbiotic relation to mother to a more self sufficient existence. It becomes a problem when the need for attention, which is not met otherwise, becomes insatiable. The masturbatory act can become both self-indulgent "crime" and its painful punishment when guilt is added to this constellation of need and meaning. Accumulation of guilt around this can result in the vicious cycle described above.

Some specialists are concerned lest this preoccupation with masturbation condition the young person away from ultimate heterosexual adjustment. Again, it is doubtful that compulsive masturbation is cause, but rather has become effect already. Such a preoccupation says that the personality has been stunted and has failed to grow through some of the natural stages of development, which bring desire and ability to relate to others. These extreme symptoms are bases for counseling and psychotherapy and do not justify labeling masturbation, as such, a pathological condition, or even as unhealthy.[5]

2. Homosexual Behavior

Homosexual expression, varying from mutual masturbation per manual or interfemoral stimulation to oral-oral, oral-genital, anal-genital and genital-genital contact has been experienced by many young people in the search for satisfaction and for sexual identity. Disregarding many of the disadvantages, including the possibility of ostracism, arrest, blackmail, and the possible conditioning against ultimate heterosexuality, fearful youth might feel there were certain advantages in homosexual expression. These would include no risk of pregnancy, less or no more expensive, the belief (although erroneous) that there is less danger of veneral infection, and little danger of being pressured into a marriage for which one does not want to assume the responsibility. Isolated experiences on the other hand, have little if any permanent effect, except through attitudes of guilt and fear.

But what are the official attitudes here? Homosexuality is considered a crime by the law, a sin by many religious groups, an illness or symptom of illness by much of modern medicine, and an indication of behavior fixated at a childhood level of development by much of the social and behavioral sciences. In spite of the unconstitutionality of entrapment, society's super-ego, the vice squad, repeatedly resorts to illegal means of detecting and arresting suspected homosexuals.

Many youths experience homosexual contacts occasionally in the process of growing up, although these experiences have more fascination at puberty and beyond if heterosexual interests are threatening. It may take the form of mutual bodily exploration or masturbation for either boys or girls. For

[5] See, Dearborn, Lester, select bibliography on Autoroticism, in *The Encyclopedia of Sexual Behavior*, edited by Albert Ellis and Albert Abarbanel, Vol. I, New York: Hawthorne Books, 1961, pp. 204-215.

boys it may mean kissing any part of the body, or fellatio as one does a "blow job" or a "suck off" for the other. One may use any available place on the body—arm pits, thighs, anus or crotch—for copulation, with one or both actively involved. Objects may or may not be used for added stimulation. Girls may find that their genitals are not so versatile in stimulating the partner of the same sex, but they can massage genitals with genitals and experience any of the oral contacts of cunnilingus, kissing of breasts, and any variety of kissing and caressing. Any or all of these experiences may be had with other children in growing to adulthood.

Of particular concern to most parents is the fact that confirmed homosexuals or other adults instigate these practices with children. In all detected incidents the adult is held responsible even if, as often happens in the search for sexual knowledge, the child seeks out and seduces the adult.

Over and above the issue of children being exploited by adults, the mental health expert will be more concerned with the particular meaning of isolated experiences, the guilt or lack of guilt, the possible habituation or patternization, and the exclusive or escapist nature of the experiences. He will help the youth consolidate the learning involved in the experience and integrate it into an ongoing heterosexual identification.

Contrary to much of the emphasis in both popular and professional literature, early detected homosexual problems are as amenable to psychotherapy as other emotionally based and environmentally re-enforced symptoms. Much of homosexual urges have more to do with unfulfilled childish longings for attention and self-identity, and the need to strike back when they are missing, than with sexuality per se. Confirmed homosexuality which one does not wish to change should be viewed as a neurotic adjustment to some kind of emotional stunting or crippling, but occasional experiences are almost "common to man" and should not necessarily be viewed as homosexuality.[6]

3. Sexual Contacts With Animals

As many have done from earliest recorded history, some of today's youth have resorted to animal contacts as a part of their struggle for sex

[6] For a first hand account of male homoeroticism, see Cory, Donald Webster, *The Homosexual in America: A Subjective Approach*, New York: Greenberg, 1951; 2nd ed., New York: Castle Books, 1960. For a subjective female approach, see Aldrich, Ann, *We Walk Alone*, New York: Fawcett Publications, Inc., 1955; For a professional analysis, see: Berg, Charles, and Clifford Allen. *The Problem of Homosexuality*, New York: Citadel Press, 1958; Henry, G. W., *Sex Variants: A Study of Homosexual Patterns*, New York: Paul B. Hoeber, Inc., 1941.

identity, for sex release, and the satisfaction of curiosity. The occurrence of this type of experience may be determined more by opportunity than by other factors. For instance, a city boy does not have the opportunity to cohabit with the more cooperative kind of farm animals, such as cows, sheep and horses. Animal contact may vary, including just getting excited watching animals, sex play with or masturbation of the animal and direct coitus. Many have permitted a dog or cat to excite them by licking the genitals as a part of masturbation or as a substitute for it.

Although against the law of most states and religions—labeled variously as bestiality, crime against nature, etc.—these experiences should be viewed from a mental health vantage in about the same way as masturbation. If sadistic mistreatment of the animal is a component, or the practice is exclusive or compulsive, then one must treat it as a symptom of other difficulties.

4. Heterosexual Behavior

In the *heterosexual* realm youth may have experienced sexual pleasure in endless variations.[7] There is the relaxed comfort and the excited glow of being with a considerate person which may have little to do with his gender, or it may be heightened because opposite sexes are involved.

Statistics indicate that for the group of young people who delay marriage until after college "petting" and "necking" become more important before marriage than does heterosexual intercourse. Often dating relationships are accompanied by intensive petting and stimulation as a form of sexual pleasure. This pleasure turns into pain when the sexual need reaches the point that any further stimulation calls for complete but forbidden satisfaction, rather than merely cessation. Many generalized anxiety states are due to this combination of factors. Such experiences may or may not be followed by masturbation for release when alone. Others may occasionally or regularly stimulate each other until one or both have an orgasm, yet short of contact with the genitals except perhaps through the clothes (sometimes called "dry intercourse").

Out of consideration for or obligation to the one whose needs have been aroused, one may masturbate the other to orgasm. Some men and women practice oral-genital contact as a means of satisfaction which avoids coitus.

[7] For excellent recent analyses of the variety and incidence of pre-marital sexual experiences, see: Ehrmann, Winston, *Pre-marital Dating Behavior*, New York: 1959; Reiss, Ira L., *Pre-marital Sexual Standards in America*, Glencoe: The Free Press, 1960; and Kirkendal, Lester, *Pre-marital Intercourse and Interpersonal Relations,* Stanford University Press, 1961.

When looked at from any moral or legal standpoint, one may be hard put to demonstrate why these methods are any less "immoral" than direct sexual intercourse. Practically, they do run less risk of resulting in pregnancy, which might call for abortion or a forced marriage.

Direct heterosexual experiences are attempted by many youths before they have the physical prowess to complete the act. Maids, siblings, sexually frustrated relatives and neighbors may attempt to teach a boy or girl direct sex expression. Many youths make their first direct sexual attempt with someone in this category. Other boys are initiated by prostitutes and girls often by older and more aggressive male dates. Contrary to many opinions, children themselves often solicit or seduce the older person into such experiences. Many other youths who have had coitus have done so only as a part of a steady relationship in which they felt love and affection, even if superficial and short lived. Others, both boys and girls, have insisted on limiting coitus to the engaged lover whom they plan to marry shortly. And, too, many college age youths are virgins and plan to remain so until marriage.[8] The meaning of such experiences, including abstinence, is unique to each person.

In spite of the tremendous sexual stimulation focused upon youth through communication media, the culture focuses other powerful forces on preventing sexual intercourse. Religion generally urges chastity before marriage. Parents, at least from the middle and upper class, generally discourage and severely punish pre-marital coitus, especially for the girls. The tendency of the law is to treat youths of all ages as delinquents or criminals if detected in sexual acts. Although generally conceded to have a bit more freedom for sexual expression, the boy, if caught, tends to be punished more severely by the law. Many a 17 year old has gone to prison for "contributing to the delinquency of a minor," although the girl was in fact the aggressor or equally as willing as he to participate.

The consequences of non-marital coitus vary from "just for fun," to disturbing guilt, social ostracism, or a jail sentence. Old wives' tales have it that the girls and women must do the suffering while the men simply have fun. Clinical experience reveals as many seriously anxious males as females in regard to illicit coitus. Some regularly use contraceptives; some never have learned about them; others refrain for religious reasons, although they go ahead with coitus; and others irresponsibly refuse to practice contraception or to take any responsibility for the consequence of their sex expression. In spite of prophylactics the highest known rate of venereal in-

---

[8] For a good discussion of the relationship aspects of pre-marital sex, see Kirkendal, *op. cit.*

fection among teenagers in history is reported by the American Social Health Association. In spite of antibiotics, there is a high incidence of residual venereal infection among those who are inadequately treated.

Many of the lower socio-economic youth tend to follow a somewhat routine pattern that is more natural and yet has its own liabilities. The more responsible of these groups, having reached puberty and adolescence, date a while, begin to have intercourse regularly, and get married when pregnant or when the parents feel it is time to make it "right." The less responsible of the lower socio-economic group account for much of the high rate of children born out of wedlock. In thousands of these cases the girl and her family assume responsibility for the child. An appreciable number of middle-class youths have been pregnant (or impregnated someone); however, this is more likely to be followed by either marriage, an abortion or an adoption of the baby. The abortion may have been medically performed, but often it was done by a quack under emotion laden circumstances and unsanitary physical conditions. Some have been sterilized in the process. There may have been a marriage "to give the baby a name" and "to make an honest woman of her." In general pregnancy is a poor reason for marriage, in the absence of a relationship that has already been well tested. In some cases the girl has reared the baby, with or without parental assistance. More generally in middle-class families the child is placed in an adoptive or foster care home.

There is little wonder that many young people get lost in the no man's land between "sex is all that matters in the world, and we will stimulate you all we can," and "one must block out sexual interest until he is married." They are lost in the dilemma of their needs and the conflicting expectations of society in general and/or their religion in particular; often emotionally deprived and crippled; plagued by the fear of disease, guilt before God or the law, and pregnancy; torn between responsibility to marry and the desire for an education and to become established in a career. All of this, including a fear based abstinence, can mitigate later against the ability to be successful in adult heterosexuality in marriage.

III. Compromises

With all of this dilemma it is easy to *say* that the ideal solution to the sex problem, both from the standpoint of religion and the law, would be to resist the pressure of major sex needs and the stimulation of environment and remain totally continent; but it is not so easy to *practice* without serious consequences in later marital adjustment. The person who grows to adulthood, and remains continent, may succeed in one of several ways.

As did Origen, he may castrate himself, although few would recommend this today. Emotional castration is much more common, brought about by blocking out sexual interest from consciousness. It is conceivable that one could go on feeling sex needs and yet stubbornly refuse to accept direct sexual stimulation from others or from himself. Some of these consume the majority of their psychic energy fighting and controlling sex expression. It is more likely, however, that such blocking out can succeed only via repression of the entire awareness of sexual needs. Clinical literature is filled with evidence of the symptoms, both in terms of behavior and of illness, which can be associated with such repression. Usually, to be successful repression must be accompanied by the absence of close association with people of the opposite sex and perhaps also from the same sex.

This means that all the intricacies of learning to get along with the other sex is absent from the development of the young person. It has been demonstrated conclusively that, having blocked out all sexual urges for thirty years, one does not have these restored in a healthy form by a marriage ceremony. Clinical experience is replete with despairing young people who, having maintained themselves as virgins through complete repression of sexuality, were unable to relate well sexually when married. From a religious viewpoint, it is an interesting commentary on this whole problem that the young person who has disregarded some of the limitations on sexual expression may have a better chance at sexual happiness within marriage than the one who has, in trying to follow the edicts of church and the law, blocked out the area entirely through repression. On the other hand, much has been written about the detrimental effect upon marriage of pre-marital sexual exploitation.

Kinsey has shown that those in his study who had sexual stimulation to the point of orgasm before marriage had orgasm more frequently and more satisfactorily after marriage. He was willing to concede, however, that these individuals might have had more pre-marital orgasm because they were naturally more responsive people and the naturalness of this responsiveness carried over after marriage.

Sexual license throughout the developmental scale has failed to bring healthy married life. Some form of sexual control seems necessary to civilized living, and the mature guidance and acceptance of responsibility for one's sex needs is a fundamental expectation in the Hebrew-Christian religious tradition and of many other humanitarian approaches. One of the unsolved dilemmas of churches and of parents and other educators today is how to rear youth to adulthood who are, at the same time, virgins and yet fully capable of spontaneous sexual and affectional expression in marriage.

Some youth seem to have a minimum of sex drive and for them this is not such a problem (it may be quite a problem when they marry); but for others the press of sex needs is relentless. All too often, youth, feeling that it is "better to marry than to burn," rushes into marriage to solve the dilemma, only to find lack of readiness to accept its responsibilities or even to enjoy its blessings. Others, wisely avoiding marriage, have little help from professional people in guiding their sex needs.

Some of the unused or excessive energy resulting from sexual need may be utilized through sublimation in various other activities, including art, literature and athletics. A certain amount of relaxation is brought about when this energy is drained off, relieving tensions and leaving a natural tiredness in the place of the previously felt tightness. This does not mean, however, that the expenditure of energy in calisthenics can be equated with sex expression and orgasm. When this works routinely to the exclusion of all sexual interests, it is probable than an unhealthy degree of sex repression already has occurred. The healthier the adolescent or young adult the greater the probability that, in spite of a very active life in sports, work, and other interests, periodically he is going to have an intensive sense of sexual need.

Many young people, having given careful thought to the gamut of experiences outlined above, have concluded that the best solution to the religio-cultural-health dilemma is as follows: to cultivate healthy interaction with the opposite sex, accompanied by the kind of physical contacts found in recreation, dancing, etc.; consciously and deliberately to postpone sexual intercourse until married or until engaged to be married; to intensify gradually sexual stimulation, such as petting, as one grows up, rather than jumping into it too fast, and thus avoiding getting oneself on the horn of the dilemma of need and prohibition; to masturbate when sex needs become great enough to demand relief, but consciously recognize that it is a substitute for the satisfaction for which one is gradually maturing; to spend the time just before marriage in working out any conflicts about heterosexual expression which has grown out of this struggle to handle sex, including getting counseling or even intensive psychotherapy if it is indicated; and then to realize that it is going to take some time within marrage to find a "conflict free" heterosexual meaningfulness. Many of the most aware parents, as well as religious and educational leaders, are coming to this position likewise, and are supporting their youth in this "most acceptable under the circumstances" solution.

Faced with the dilemma of seeing methods which were aimed at maintaining virginity backfire in later sexual inabilities, or seeing youth rebel to the point of getting hurt by pregnancy, disease, public opinion, and the law, some adults are advocating complete sex education for their children, including the know-how and responsibility for using adequate contraception. They feel that this knowledge, shared in a comfortable and accepting manner, will be of primary value later in marriage; that accepting contraception as a part of early education will avoid guilt reactions that interfere when it becomes necessary in marriage. They believe that this attitude of helpfulness in the search for sexual knowledge will take away the compulsiveness and clumsiness of having to discover under secretive circumstances. Many are convinced that this will reduce the incidence of overt sex experiences in adolescence and guarantee less emotional disturbance when it does occur. Some are not particularly concerned so long as the girl doesn't get pregnant and may follow through with an abortion if she does. The concept of responsibility in many such parents sets itself against the idea of exploitation of another, and emphasizes the value of sex within meaningful relationships. At the same time the boy is taught to be responsible for his sperm and the girl for her eggs. All of this is likely to be presented in the context of a future adult marriage in which complete self-fulfillment is a major value.

Others among the most enlightened adults, equally as thoughtful and as committed to the meaningfulness of life for youth, accepting the philosophy of careful and complete sex education, continue to believe that chastity before marriage is a primary value for society and for youth. They insist that youth can be helped to maintain this goal and remain essentially healthy human beings. They see the hurts of pre-marital coitus in this culture as more than offsetting the positive lessons to be learned. They rely on a growing understanding of sexual nature and function to make it possible for youth to guide their own development without repression or warping of their sexual future. Most of those who fit into this category are very tolerant of masturbation, and some encourage it, as a temporary substitute. They reinforce the factual and attitudinal education within their value system with responsibility rather than fear; depend upon inbuilt self-guidance in youth rather than terror of detection and punishment. Responsibility is viewed in terms of the whole of life, including societal welfare, rather than in terms of immediate pleasure only.[9]

Another dilemma is posed by the single, widowed or divorced adult who desires a heterosexual life. Some are quite successful in living an adequate and comfortable life without sexual intercourse. They should be accepted as they are; neither frowned at nor revered. Some desire this way of life but cannot reach it or do so at almost unbearable cost in energy and feelings of deprivation. Others have a different value system, based exclusively upon satisfaction of the moment. There are still other single people, however, who have spent great efforts in evolving for themselves an ethic which integrates heterosexual satisfaction as a part of their total life. The concept of "ethic" is used because they have taken into account such factors as respect for the individual, relationships of trust and respect, and responsibility in developing their own hierarchy of values.

Admittedly, much of the unmarried heterosexual intercourse of today is at an immature and irresponsible level, also lending itself to exploitation of one or both personalities. Nevertheless, counselors are finding young adults who have developed what they believe to be a responsible philosophy of sexual intercourse outside of marriage. Although perhaps still tinged with guilt, this compromise enables them to handle both their needs and their conscience with some degree of satisfaction. As an example, take a young person who is "mature enough to know that he is not mature enough" for marriage and its responsibilities. Suppose he has intercourse only with women who have arrived at a similar position. This quite easily lends itself to rationalization, self-deception, and resultant hurt to one or both. But there are increasing instances when adults carefully count the cost, weigh every factor in terms of what they consider to be the very basic elements of their faith, and still arrive at a position justifying sexual intercourse under the circumstances. Having accepted their basic needs, including the need to be near someone of the opposite sex, and having established the inadvisability of marriage in the near future, they limit their sexual expression to one whom they like or love and who has the same kinds of feelings and is quite willing to participate. They feel they can share sex and affection with each other without hurt, or are willing to accept the responsibility for the hurt involved. Often they count the cost of children who might be born of such a relationship and avoid this by contraception or sterilization. They too, have

[9] Frank, Lawrence, *The Conduct of Sex, Biology and Ethics of Sex and Parenthood in Modern Life,* New York: Wm. Morrow & Co., 1960.

a right to acceptance which need not infer censure or adulation. It is their way to self fulfillment.

Fortunate indeed is the person whose sexual upbringing has been consistently sound, leading to conscious self-determination of his sexual experience in the Babel of confusion of sex ethics. Most have had a mixture of healthy and unhealthy upbringing and must do some further learning prior to and as a part of marriage. In order to stimulate self examination and growth the therapist should be aware of this representative sampling of sex related experiences which may or may not be found in the history of any particular person. They are his, to repeat blindly and impulsively, or to learn from and give direction toward more responsible fulfillment as a sexual being.[10]

C. SEXUAL PATHOLOGY

What is healthy sex expression, and what is unhealthy? Probably in no other area of life does so much lack of clarity exist. Certainly much of what has been labeled as perversions in the past is common practice in thousands of meaningful marriages. The most that can be said in general is that sex expressions are unhealthy to the extent to which they violate the personality of the mate, exclude other healthy practices, become fixated, ritualistic, fetishistic, or compulsive, or are detrimental to total self-fulfillment as a psycho-social-sexual being.

The counselor must be aware of the more neurotic or immature types of sex experience if he is to prognosticate the possible health of an engaged couple's sex life and guide them into total readiness for marriage.

I. Types of Sex Pathology [11]

Sexual experiences may be viewed in terms of the object or direction toward which the sex drive is aimed, the underlying meaning, and the level of maturity portrayed. The following terms should not be applied when describing isolated experiences of youth, but do describe sexual pathology when the above criteria of ill health are present.

Certain varieties of sexual experience may be looked at in terms of *the object or direction* toward which the sex drive is aimed. Many people whose sex drives are heterosexually directed may have problems in that they must change sex partners frequently, or attach them to persons who have some

---

[10] Mace, David R. and Stokes, Walter R., "Sex Ethics, Sex Acts, and Human Need: a dialogue *Pastoral Psychology*, 12, 117 & 118, 1961.

[11] Ellis and Abarbanel, *op. cit.*, Vols. I and II.

peculiar appearance or character trait, or to individuals who are much younger or older than they.

Narcissism, in its narrowest sense, is defined as the love of and sexual desire for one's own body or one's own self. In extreme, it describes the self-worshiping type of sexuality, not the usual self-satisfaction through either masturbation or coitus. Narcissism of one or both mates is a major factor in many disturbed marriage relationships.

Fetishism is a condition in which an individual is sexually stimulated by or uses inanimate objects for sexual practices in a compulsive or ritualistic manner. This may be some article of clothing belonging to the opposite sex, or it may be an object such as hair, fur, or silk which has been retained from childhood. It may also take the form of eroticization of parts of the anatomy not commonly the center of sexual stimulation.

Pedophilia describes the sexual desire for children. This may be attraction to children of any age and may be directed toward a child of the opposite or the same sex. People often mistake the pederast for a sadist, but usually when murder follows a sexual act with a child it is the result of a panic in which the person is trying to cover up evidence, rather than getting any particular pleasure out of killing the partner.

Bestiality or zoorasty is sexual expression of a human being with an animal.

Necrophilia is sexual attraction to a corpse.

Homosexuality is that condition where the sex desire is directed in large measure or in totality toward a person of the same sex. The term lesbianism is used to describe sexual practices of female partners. Most adolescent children of both sexes have tendencies in this direction, but in an adult it represents a stunting of or misdirection of the natural sexual drives.

Another way of looking at sexual variance is in terms of disturbances in the *methods* of sexual behavior.

Exhibitionism represents a desire to surprise, offend, or shock the other person by revealing the genitalia. Most exhibitionists are disappointed and lose sexual interest if the person to whom they show themselves is casual or pays no attention. Many others will cease their act and run even when interest is shown. Adults get disturbed if this happens to children, and yet there is reason to believe that the disturbance of the parents has more effect upon the child than the act of exhibiting by the other adult. Of significance is the fact that some individuals, not true exhibitionists, exhibit themselves to children as a way to enlist them in further sexual acts.

Voyeurism (peeping Toms) is motivated by the desire to see the unclothed or partially unclothed sexual object. Many times this must be accomplished without the person's knowing he is being observed or else it does not have attraction. Some who do not need the element of surprise can gratify their sex needs for stimulation in burlesque shows, pornographic pictures, magazines or at the public beaches. The true voyeur has little interest, however, in acceptable viewing of nakedness.

Both he and the exhibitionist are likely to become very bitter when arrested, because they cannot see that they have hurt anybody except themselves.

Sadism, in its narrowest sense, is obtaining sexual pleasure through hurting another person. An element of sadism is to be found in most people at some time or another, it seems, but in its pronounced form it can represent serious personality disturbance. This is particularly true of the person who can gain release from sexual tension only through inflicting pain or injury. Sometimes repressed sadistic urges break loose under the influence of drugs or alcohol.

Masochism, the other side of the sadistic coin, is the desire, in order to obtain or increase sexual pleasure, to be hurt by the sexual partner. Sado-masochistic problems are frequently encountered in marriage counseling.

Molesting is a legal term applied to several kinds of sexual acts, including exhibitionism, sexual comments to minors or adults in public places, or any uninvited attempts to gain sexual communication with another.

The *frotteur* gets sexual pleasure from rubbing against various parts of people's anatomy, for instance, in a bus or eating place.

Transvestism is the expression of one's sexual need through the wearing of clothes of the opposite sex. This may be continuous, as one lives out the sex role opposite to his biological make-up. Or, it may occur only during masturbation or sexual fantasy.

Pyromania is the obtaining of sexual satisfaction through watching a burning building, and is involved in many cases of arson.

Kleptomania may have other meanings but it quite often is a means of gaining sexual satisfaction from stealing. The individual may or may not experience an orgasm as he takes the forbidden object, which may or may not have symbolic significance.

Nymphomania is the term applied to a frigid woman who cannot attain sexual satisfaction, but pursues either heterosexual or homosexual behavior endlessly in an effort to satisfy her insatiable appetite.

Masturbation is any form of pressure or manipulation of the sex organs for pleasure or for release of tension.

Tribidism or sapphism is the mutual friction of genitals of two people of the same sex. This may be accompanied by other methods of sexual stimulation, and is most often found among practicing Lesbians.

Pederasty is coitus through the anus of a small boy, purportedly a form of sex expression popular in ancient Greece.

Oniomania is sexual satisfaction through purchasing items and is a fairly common narcissistic expression among unhappy people.

Sodomy is anal intercourse whether male with male or male with female, in its strictest sense. However, in the laws of some states many kinds of sexual variations are described as sodomy. Occasional anal stimulation is a part of sexual practice among some well adjusted heterosexual couples.

Fellatio is sex expression through oral contact with the penis, whether it is practiced by one man with another or by a woman with a man. It is a common form of sex expression among some homosexuals, and has been known to be quite popular in certain houses of prostitution. On the other hand, when incorporated into love making within heterosexual relationships, it is a legitimate part of sexual expression.

Cunnilingus is sexual expression through oral contact with the female genitals. It may include penetration by the tongue, or simply the caressing of the clitoris and labia with the tongue and lips. It is one of the chief forms of sexual expression in the homosexual group, but it is incorporated meaningfully in many marriage relationships.

Coitus interruptus is the termination of the sex act, or withdrawal of the penis, prior to ejaculation. It is one of the most popular, although one of the most ineffective, methods of birth control. When insisted upon by either the male or female for psychological reasons, it is symptomatic of a basic emotional problem.

Some of these sex expressions immediately are labeled as undesirable because the rights of others are violated. It is not easy to determine when other expressions are serving a wholesome function of providing variety and when they represent fixations or regressions of behavior.

Chapter 12

SEX AND MARRIAGE

An increasing amount of marriage counseling time is devoted to acute and chronic sexual problems. The chronological development of an individual, along with the psychosexual mechanisms of response, are so complicated in themselves, and so interrelated with a complex of cultural and relationship factors, that treatment of sex problems in isolation is futile. Adequate sexual functioning is an expression of total personality within total relationship to another. However, for learning purposes, a variety of sex problems and sex phenomena must be isolated for study.

Sexual preparation for marriage is treated in greater detail in this book than other areas of life for a variety of reasons. It is a topic of primary interest to people approaching marriage, and thus becomes a hub from which many other interests can branch forth like spokes in the wheel of life. Sexual function is so close to the psycho-physio-sociodynamics of the total person that both healthy and unhealthy attitudes toward life in general are found in prototypical form as sexual preparation proceeds. The needs of the counselor also call for a special emphasis on sex in any text on pre-marital counseling. Often his attitudes need reconditioning, his feelings desensitized, and then resensitized before he can relate comfortably with youth or adults in regard to their sexual concerns. He must develop professional skill in this area as well as many others. Hardly a graduate school in the nation provides adequate training in sexology. Therefore, each counselor must develop his own frame of reference for guiding clients. Parents, pastors, educators, physicians, and counselors must learn to work together in this vital area, or they will defeat each other.

A. SEX ATTITUDES

Sex has been brought from the gutter and alley to a place in everyday conversation, and yet the average youth may find himself more lacking in facts and healthy attitudes than was his grandmother. He talks about sex, but he does not comprehend it; he accepts the concept of sex, but not sex; or he accepts sex, but cannot integrate it with love and affection or live it out in a responsible manner.

A part of sexual preparation for marriage is instructional, and yet, even the best information imparted didactically may be merely superimposed upon lifelong ways of thinking and feeling; added as it were, from the eyes up. Some couples, when questioned, can give beautiful intellectual answers; thus, the novice counselor or physician may be blinded to deep-seated problems. Intellectually both of the couple may be adequate, but in love they respond emotionally, and the healthier concepts have never penetrated their emotional structure. More often both are true; the engaged couple does not know enough facts and has not had opportunity to re-work harmful attitudes accumulated throughout life. Merely to instruct them leads to a false sense of security, a perfect set-up for frustration in marriage.

When a counselor begins to work with a client, or a pair of clients, it is not sufficient to consider the ethical position or his own position on sexual matters. The client's practices and beliefs, those of the communities in which he has functioned, and the inconsistencies in teaching and feeling in both himself and the community—these are the subject matter of counseling. Unless the counselor can feel and perceive the meaning of what the client has experienced sexually, (See Chapter 11) his efforts to help will be stymied. Sensing the counselor's inadequacies in this field, many youth, who are approaching marriage with grave confusion about sex, persist in not discussing it. Or, the counselor who is uncomfortable may minimize the pain to himself by taking over the sexual discussion, changing it into a lecture on the ideal or what ought to be from a scientific viewpoint.

The counseling process should provide opportunity for each of the couple to talk out sexual fears, misbeliefs and doubts, as well as positive feelings, with the counselor and with each other. This opens for discussion the entire area of man-woman relations. Talking out older unwholesome feelings as many times as necessary will have great therapeutic value, freeing the mind and emotions of hurtful concepts, experiences and anxieties. With the door of receptivity still open, healthy sexual attitudes and facts can be implanted through suggestion, instruction, reading and observing. There must be time for these new ideas to incubate. Frequent use of them in the counseling situation, and between the couple, speed up the process of assimilation, and then these healthier attitudes can begin to emerge spontaneously. This can be a slow process, and many older ideas and feelings will reassert themselves and must be dealt with again. That is sufficient reason for beginning the discussion of sex and affection early in the process of pre-marital counseling, as well as teaching them a way of working together on these problems long after they are married.

In no area of life is there such a hodgepodge of teaching, mores, laws, and practices. Contradiction and inconsistency is the rule, with only a few factors common to great numbers of people in this culture—sex need, fear, and guilt, which result in sexual inadequacy and hurt. Many authors have portrayed the American sexual tragedy as seen in the counselor's office every day.[1]

Soon after the Kinsey studies began to appear, Hiltner[2] took a critical look at sex practices in the light of Christian sex ethics. His book will serve as one beginning point for many professional counselors as they struggle with an up-to-date sex ethic for themselves, as well as attempting to integrate sex ethics and practice. Another point of view for stimulus to growing one's own frame of reference is Ellis' *Sex Without Guilt*.[3]

B. PRE-MARITAL SEX EXPRESSION AND MARRIAGE

The popular song has it that "love and marriage . . . go together like a horse and carriage," and "you can't have one without the other." The commonly accepted ideal in this culture continues to limit sexual intercourse to those who have gained the right through marriage, but in actuality a slowly increasing percentage of youth do not wait for the wedding ceremony. Whether this is a desirable trend or a destructive one is debated in the classroom, pulpit and scientific meeting.

Ellis and Mace,[4] both marriage counselors, have done a thorough job of summing up the pro and con of pre-marital sexual intercourse, and its possible relationship to marital success.

I. PRO Pre-marital Intercourse, by Albert Ellis

(a) *Rebuttal of Objections to Pre-marital Coitus.* Here are the alleged evils of pre-marital copulation, critically appraised:

(1) *The dangers of venereal disease.* With proper use of prophylactic devices and modern antibiotics, the informed person

[1] Ellis, Albert, *The American Sexual Tragedy*, New York: Twayne Publishers, 1954; Ploscowe, Morris, *Sex and The Law*, New York: Prentice-Hall, 1951; Gebhart, Paul H. et al, *Pregnancy, Birth and Abortion*, New York: Harper & Brothers, 1958; Bergler, Edmund, *Neurotic Counterfeit Sex*, New York: Grune and Stratton, 1951; Cleckley, Hervey Milton, *The Caricature of Love*, New York: Ronald Press, 1957.

[2] Hiltner, Seward, *Sex Ethics and The Kinsey Reports*, New York: Association Press, 1953.

[3] Ellis, Albert, *Sex Without Guilt*, New York: Lyle Stuart, 1958.

[4] Ellis, Albert and David R. Mace, *Pre-marital Relations, Pro and Con*, in *Controversy Magazine*, August 1959, pps. 24-47; paraphrased here by permission.

has small chance of suffering severely from venereal infection.

(2) *Illegitimate pregnancy and abortion.* Illegitimate pregnancy and abortion are rare among those who carefully and consistently employ birth control.

(3) *Loss of reputation.* Today's youth, including the young girls, are rarely severely condemned or ostracized for their pre-marital adventures.

(4) *Guilt and anxiety.* Since pre-marital sex relations are no longer viewed as morally reprehensible or sinful by most educated and informed individuals, there need be no intrinsic guilt attached to them; many are disturbed because they are not copulating.

(5) *Emotional risks.* Taking risks is a part of the process of emotional growth and development. Youngsters who take no emotional risks are much more likely to become seriously aberrated.

(6) *Sabotage of family life.* If pre-marital affairs really destroyed family life, the human race would have long since died out.

(7) *Sex without love.* Copulation, no matter when it is indulged, normally creates and enhances love.

(8) *Sordid surroundings.* The majority of today's pre-marital acts are performed in places far more romantic and exciting than those existing during marital relations.

(9) *Lack of responsibility.* Couples who engage in any pleasant activity also obtain satisfactions without assuming the responsibilities of marriage.

(11) *Subsequent adultery.* It has never been shown that pre-marital copulators become adulterous because of pre-marital affairs; nor that adultery is inimical to marriage.

(12) *Lack of happiness in marriage.* People who have pre-marital sex relations are generally happier in marriage.

(13) *Promiscuity.* Promiscuity means indiscrimination in one's choice of sex partners, and it is the rare person who is really indiscriminate.

(14) *Unachievable ideal.* Many individuals can only tolerate marriage because they have, in practice, seen the disadvantages as well as the advantages of sex relations outside the confines of marriage.

Ellis says, "Virtually all these objections to antenuptial affairs never had too much validity in the first place or, if they were once valid, applied largely to conditions existing many decades ago."

   (b) *Benefits From Pre-Marital Coitus.* Ellis believes there are many obvious benefits to be derived from antenuptial sex relations:

      (1) *Sexual release.* Most human beings require some form of sexual release for maximum healthfulness, happiness, and efficient functioning, best gained pre-maritally through heterosexual relations.

      (2) *Psychological release.* Most individuals who are beset with serious psycho-sexual strain and conflict and tend to be obsessed with sexual thoughts and feelings can be considerably relieved by non-marital affairs.

      (3) *Sexual competence.* Pre-marital sex relations would help the relatively impotent and frigid to become more sexually competent.

      (4) *Adventure and experience.* Non-marital affairs furnish a source of sensory-esthetic-emotional experimentation and learning.

      (5) *Improved marital selection.* One or more pre-marital affairs provides the kind of knowledge and training that will best fit one to make a good marital choice.

      (6) *Prophylaxis against sexual deviation.* Pre-marital relations doubtlessly constitute the best possible prophylaxis to serious psychosexual deviations.

      (7) *Heterosexual democratization.* Widespread pre-marital affairs lead to real democracy and equality between the sexes.

      (8) *De-emphasis on pornography.* The more an individual engages in satisfactory and consistent pre-marital relations reduces interest in second-hand picturization of sex.

      (9) *Savings of time and energy.* Pre-marital affairs save time wasted in constantly seeking direct or indirect sex gratification.

    (10) *Ending of sex discrimination.* Individuals should not be discriminated against sexually merely because they are non-maritally inclined.

    (11) *Sexual varietism.* The most practical way to meet needs for sexual varietism is through pre-marital affairs.

(12) *Limiting prostitution:* Sex relations on a voluntary basis decreases prostitutional relations.

(13) *Sex is fun.* Heterosexual relations are the very best fun; and more heterosexual relations are still more fun.

The relevant question, according to Ellis, is not: *"Must* a healthy young person engage in pre-marital affairs? It is rather: May an informed and intelligent individual in our culture justifiably and guiltlessly have coitus before marriage?"

II. CON Pre-marital Intercourse, by David R. Mace

Mace says, "All kinds of conclusions *can* be arrived at, and diametrically opposite positions can be held by people who are equally sincere and who deeply respect each other's sincerity. I shall defend our traditional moral standard which has held for ages past, and still holds, that pre-marital sex relations are undesirable. I shall deal with the subject not from the standpoint of theology, but rather shall discuss the unhappiness and difficulties which arise from such relations."

In the past, the case for pre-marital chastity was based on fear—the fear of infection, of conception, and of detection. Nowadays antibiotics, birth control, and a mellowed public opinion have reduced the intensity of these fears. Because of this, it is assumed that the case for chastity has collapsed, especially when the Kinsey report reveals that large numbers of people have abandoned the traditional standards anyway. It is unfortunate that the appeal to fear was in the past so strongly relied upon, obscuring the fact that important principles are involved; however, the fears must still be reckoned with.

(a) *Three Traditional Fears. Is* there now, for those who embark upon pre-marital sexual intercourse, nothing to fear?

    (1) *Venereal disease.* The biggest increase has been in cases of latent syphillis, in which permanent damage already has been done, but grave concern is also warranted because of the sharp increase in V.D. rates among youth 11 through 19.

    (2) *Pregnancy.* What are the facts? By taking the recorded number of illegitimate births, adding the estimated number of abortions, then adding an estimated figure for pregnancies covered by "shot-gun marriages," one obtains a figure of 1,-000,000 per year. One in five of all girls who have pre-mar-

ital sex relations gets pregnant. An unmarried girl expecting a child is in a tight spot. If the boy doesn't marry her, she has two alternatives—to visit an abortionist or to have an illegitimate child. Nine out of ten of these girls choose the abortionist. Among the women of childbearing age now alive, slightly over one in every seven either has already had, or will ultimately have, a pre-marital abortion.

In the name of "fun" hundreds of thousands of new human beings are created and then, to cover up the indiscretion involved, scientifically butchered. And this is brought about not by sinister, heartless, hardened men; but by panic-stricken young girls driven to the verge of desperation. Surely no human society ever invented for its youth a more callously brutal sport than this. The inescapable truth is that practically no couple who have pre-marital sexual intercourse can be absolutely sure of avoiding pregnancy, in spite of fairly accessible contraceptive materials.

(3) *Social ostracism.* Actions that are not morally reprehensible normally gain unqualified acceptance. How many Americans today give unqualified acceptance to pre-marital intercourse? How many parents smile indulgently on the sexual adventures of their teen-age daughter, invite her paramour into their home, obligingly put their bedroom at the disposal of the young couple? Does anyone seriously suggest that any but a few girls, who get pregnant pre-maritally, go to an abortionist merely because of the practical inconvenience of continuing a pregnancy? No, the vast majority do it for one reason only—to cover up and avoid the shame and disgrace they and their families would otherwise feel.

(b) *Results of Pre-marital Intercourse.* What is pre-marital intercourse as a growing pattern doing to marriage, to the family, to society? When the first two Kinsey Reports appeared, the prevailing reaction was: "Everybody's doing it. Why shouldn't I?" However, there were other people who said: "We have wondered why it is that Americans are so unstable and inconstant in their marriage relations, and why their divorce rates are four times as high as the European average. The Kinsey data helps us to see why family life is in such a mess in the United States."

(1) *On Marriage.* Kinsey found that women who have had pre-marital intercourse are more than twice as likely as those who have not to commit adultery after marriage. To say that adultery is not damaging is sheer nonsense.

Kinsey did not say that pre-marital sex is an aid to good adjustment in later marriage. He found that women who had had orgasm from any kind of stimulation before marriage achieved orgasm more easily in the first year of married life. When Kinsey was asked personally whether he had any proof that their pre-marital experiences *caused* better marital orgasm performance, he replied negatively and admitted that these women could have been the more highly sexed both before and after marriage. There is no evidence that less highly sexed girls in general improve their chances of good sex adjustment in marriage by seeking pre-marital experience. Notice, too, that Kinsey reported on *early* sex adjustment. Eustace Chesser, in his English research, found as Kinsey did that the non-virgins adjusted more quickly to sex relations in marriage than the virgins. But oddly enough, later the virgins caught up and in the end scored higher in sex adjustment than the non-virgins! Very little is known about the relation between pre-marital sex conduct and later sex adjustment in marriage, and specialists should quit using this kind of argument.

(2) *On the family.* Sex is abused if its use is allowed to be harmful to children. Children born as a result of pre-marital conception often start out in life under less favorable conditions than those conceived in marriage. The resort of unmarried girls to abortion does violence to their natural maternal impulses and creates a concept of the unborn child as expendable in the interests of the personal pleasure of its parents; the precise opposite of true parental feeling, which is ready to renounce personal pleasure in the interests of the child. Children of marriages in a society where sexual freedom is widespread have reduced chances of family security, because such marriages are less stable than in communities where greater restrictions on sexual behavior are accepted.

Young people should not be encouraged to embark upon pre-marital intercourse. This is not based upon a wish to be hard on young people, or unreasonable, as this society has often been in the past. In fact, earlier marriages might be less strongly opposed. On the other hand, self-restraint in sexual behavior is not pernicious. A civilized society demands control of personal desires, including sexual desires. Youth is the right time to learn such lessons, and the requirement of such disciplines in the more highly developed human cultures has something to do with the level of their cultural attainment.

C. VARIETIES OF SEX EXPERIENCE AND MARRIAGE

Whether the sexual heritage brought to marriage is destructive or helpful depends largely upon the use to which it is put. If sex expression has become exploitative, rigid, exclusive, fetishistic, or compulsive, if it has become necessary to bury it from consciousness because of guilt or fear, if the memories of it bring guilt and shame, then the effect is not going to be healthy. On the other hand, much depends on the willingness and ability of the person to learn from whatever has been experienced. With the aid of premarital counseling, this learning can be used in many ways to build a healthy sex life upon the foundation of the past. Knowledge of the variety of ways of expressing sexuality can add flexibility and adaptability of each of a couple in meeting the needs of the other and it can work against tendencies toward habituation or toward placing undue limits upon the variety of marital sex experiences. Skills developed in handling one's own urges and inclinations, including solving the resultant difficulties, become invaluable in dealing with such stress when it arises within the marriage.

All too often the experiences of the past, particularly some of the more unusual ones outlined in the previous chapter, made hurtful by the burden of taboo and guilt they carry, become an inhibiting or conflicting force in married sex life. The husband is afraid the wife will be offended if he tries some of the things he has found to be meaningful. She knows a certain movement, position or act which would be fun, but steels herself against letting it emerge, fearing "what would he think?" Or, "he might wonder where I learned that." Repeatedly the marriage counselor sees cases where this double bind in a marriage relationship has existed for years. One or both lack complete satisfaction, blame it on the other, and at the same time fail to utilize the knowledge they have, with the result that the relationship is weakened. Gradually the promise of greater fulfillment with someone else, added to the stress, wrecks what could have been an increasingly meaningful marriage.

Fear of bringing the tabooed and that which is feared as abnormal into the marriage relationship causes many to repress again their early sexual fantasies which naturally arise under sexual stimulation. In order to keep these memories from arising, they resist any effort of a more relaxed mate to lead them into an interesting variety of sexual behavior.

The repressed approach can manifest itself in another slightly different form and cause unnecessary stress. For instance, a man (it is just as common in women) has a variety of sexual experiences in youth, some of which in his estimation are quite bizarre. He "forgets" this, marries and settles down to a limited but temporarily satisfying sex life with a wife of quite limited sexual experience. Under some stress his personality is shaken up a bit. This happens to many men when the wife gets pregnant, when a child is born or reaches some period of development which was crucial in the man's own psychosexual development, or when insecurity develops on the job, or he becomes partially aware of the status quo nature of their married life. With this loosening up of personality structure, some of the repressed urges or practices begin to emerge into awareness and the need to express them becomes apparent. Whether or not he consciously remembers, he now wants to try a variety of forms of behavior which are new to their shared sex life. Such dynamics can be all the more dramatic if the bizarre was largely in the realm of fantasy, now repressed, for one or both of them.

As an illustration, take the desire for any form of oral genital contact. If the husband fears too much that the wife would be upset by such a gesture, he fantasies or actually tries to fulfill the desire with someone else. If he tries to fulfill the need with the wife, her attitude can make the difference in growth or decay of the marriage. Often the woman will withdraw in terror or seek professional help "because my husband is becoming a pervert." Still others, both husbands and wives, accept the need of the moment, handling any revulsion or guilt to the best of their ability. Results are mixed. Occasionally one mate then wants only the new and exotic, even though it may be distasteful or painful or just fail to satisfy the other. One of them may seek professional help at this point. But in many cases the more bizarre, if it can be tolerated, will lose its appeal once it has been brought out of the unconscious and experienced, and especially if the anxiety-producing condition has been alleviated in the meantime, and if the pleasure or lack of pleasure in the experience can be discussed. In many cases the man and woman learn from these episodes that their sex life need not be status quo and the new found experimental attitude adds a great deal of happiness.

One of the greatest bits of professional help to be rendered to such couples is to assist them in: reworking the sexual experiences and fantasies of their youth, deciding together which they wish to try, being honest with each other in likes and dislikes, and *being willing to go the experimental mile* in pleasing each other. Other than extremely compulsive phenomena and the extremes of sadomasochism, there is no room in a healthy marriage for automatic taboos and the fear of being perverted or abnormal. There is room for respect for personal wishes and sensitivity to traumatized areas of life, but the respect of personal wishes has to be mutually applied. When a couple accept this philosophy of sex, many of the means of stimulation and satisfaction discussed in the previous chapter in terms of masturbation and homosexual practices can find endless variations as an integral part of a heterosexual life that grows in meaning through the years.

Much has been said about the incapacitating nature of guilt, particularly unrealistically based or neurotic guilt. Such destructiveness can be interrupted by skillful pre-marital counseling. Guilt, among other things, is the feeling of pain of self censure which comes when one violates that which is felt at some level to be most valued. An always present component is a sense of isolation and loneliness. Such guilt cannot be taken lightly. Indeed, many psychotherapists find that guilt waved away magically with the therapeutic wand often returns to destroy the pleasure of living in close proximity to others which has been attained in the meantime. Guilt can be handled only by first of all accepting the fact of the transgression, whether in fantasy or act. If the value concept which was violated has changed in the meantime, then that fact also must be accepted. The next step is accepting responsibility for one's own conduct, past and present. This responsibility calls for creative use of the past in evolving a value system that has relevance for the present and guidance for the future of the individual alone, and in relation to others. The truth of one's own experience and capacity, earnestly sought out and accepted, becomes the main highway to responsive and responsible adult sex fulfillment as an integral part of a whole life.[5]

D. SEXUAL PROBLEMS IN MARRIAGE

The marriage counselor, with a thorough knowledge of the mind-body relationships of total personalities, familiar with the variety of sexual experience described in Chapter 11, alert to the multifaceted meaning of sex

[5] See Calderone, Mary S. *Release From Sexual Tensions,* New York: Random House, 1960.

in human experience, coupled with a devotion to what is helpful to his clients, can serve well in guiding couples in preparation for marriage. Although pre-marital counseling is a positive process by and large, an awareness of the most common sources and types of sexual conflict common in marriage will provide many checkout points in examining and guiding a specific couple who are contemplating marriage. As with other marital difficulties, sexual problems may be the basic cause of marital disharmony, the result of it, or a combination in which cause becomes effect becomes cause.

The more common sexual problems include unequal desires or fulfillment, infidelity, impotence, frigidity or orgasm inadequacy, guilt and accusations about infidelity, contraception, sterility and sterilization, abortion, and so-called perversions. The causes of each of these symptoms may be the same or quite different; based in the neurotic difficulties of one or two crippled personalities, in organic difficulties, or relationship difficulties, including ignorance or lack of information about sex and affection. The symptoms may be due to accumulated hostility and resultant tension from lack of adequate communication or from hurtful interaction between the couple. Guilt over pre-marital or extra-marital sex, or over masturbation, are common sources of anxiety, as are fears about coitus, pregnancy and parenthood, and other inhibitions.

I. Unequal Sex Desire or Pleasure

Unequal sex desire between a husband and wife may be a matter of the basic cycle of psychic and sexual energy of each, or due to the related emotional and social situations. The peak of sexual activity for the average American male comes in the late teens or early twenties, whereas the female peak tends to be in the late twenties. Often this can mean that early in marriage his desires are more frequent than hers, which may reverse itself later on. Actually, in individual cases the cycle of need may vary from time to time in the life cycle of each of the couple, or within each month for that matter. Harmful conflict arises when there is failure of one to understand the needs of the other mate, or when the rate of desire of one is much greater than the other. This sexual conflict becomes particularly charged with emotion if the marriage relationship as a whole has been a source of unhappiness, or simply has not produced the expected happiness.

Until treatment remedies some of the basic causes, as well as in cases where treatment of the individuals is not indicated, the counseling plan must be geared to effecting understanding and cooperation in meeting each other's needs. When a couple are in love and find their relationship as a whole meaningful, added sexual satisfaction of a mate, even when one's own desires are not keen, can be a pleasure rather than a disagreeable task. A man or woman may enjoy becoming excited because of the other's needs and having intercourse or other sexual activity, although his own need was not great.[6]

The problems posed by *lack of simultaneous orgasm, premature ejaculation* and *orgasm inadequacy* are closely related. The average male ejaculates after about two to five minutes of uninterrupted coitus, whereas many women cannot climax in less than ten or more minutes of continuous stimulation. This pattern is reversed in other couples. Occasionally a couple complain about failure to have simultaneous climax, although she has one or more orgasms prior to his ejaculation. This usually means they have been made anxious by reading a book or article overemphasizing *simultaneous* orgasm when the desired emphasis should be *mutual* satisfaction. In most cases the husband, after becoming less anxious and tense, can be helped to prolong intercourse by alternately relaxing and proceeding until the wife has gained satisfaction. Simultaneous orgasm may be an ideal for some, but mutual satisfaction is the real need.

Extreme cases of premature ejaculation that do not clear up soon should be adequate reason for consulting a well-trained marriage counselor or physician, or both. There can be organic factors, as well as deep-seated psychological problems, but usually it has something to do with the tension level, conditioning, and lack of conscious control. Many men do not realize that it is possible to control ejaculation in coitus or how to go about gaining this control.

Requests for counseling because the wife's sex needs are not met are increasing. This is due in part to increased opportunity for, and the removal of stigma from, marriage counseling, but no doubt much of it is related to the new concept of equal satisfaction for the woman as a marital value and a human right, and the tremendous emphasis in popular literature upon the necessity of female orgasm. Orgasm inadequacy may be related to endocrine imbalance, general fatigue or other organic factors. More often it is related to a combination of deep-seated personality needs, relationship conflict, and lack of knowledge, skills and spontaneity in sexual intercourse.

The older sex manuals leave the impression that lack of female satisfaction is due to poor technique of the man, a statement which has been used

[6] Ellis, Albert, *The Art and Science of Love*, New York: Lyle Stuart, 1960.

repeatedly by wives to intensify the inadequacy feelings of their husbands. Of equal importance is the sexual responsibility of the woman.[7] Although orgasm ability in general tends to be more related to total responsiveness as a person, and to the total relationship of the couple, much is dependent upon knowledge and use of female anatomy, by herself as well as by the husband, in bringing sex excitement and satisfaction.[8] The normative cycle of sex response for the man and woman were discussed in Chapter 8.

II. Impotence and Frigidity

The most severe sexual problems focus around impotence and frigidity.[9] Symptoms described in the literature as frigidity range from any frequent mild difficulty in responding, through failure of the female to have a vaginal orgasm in contradistinction to a clitoral orgasm, to total vaginismus. In the male, some authorities diagnose any erection difficulty or premature ejaculation as impotence, whereas others limit the term to failure to maintain an erection to orgasm. Male and female may be grouped together at this point in terms of severity or degrees of inadequacy, according to the presence of one, several, or all of the following conditions: frequent difficulty in beginning or maintaining sexual intercourse; lack of ability to have a sexual climax, or to gain release and relaxation thereby; hypersensitivity and pain in sexual activity; lack of pleasure in sex stimulation; desire for sex relations weak or absent, or dislike for sex relations.

It is of the utmost importance that medical examination rule out or locate any organic factors in impotence and frigidity, since these may be related to general health or energy level. In the woman, dormant or inactive vaginal muscles, vaginal infection or irritation, or hormonal imbalance may be vital factors. The fear of unwanted pregnancy, tension over not being able to conceive, doubts about the husband or desire to punish him, any variety of anxieties and lack of knowledge of her role in sexual intercourse, may be related to inadequate sexual response by a woman. Similar dynamics may be at work with the impotent male.

[7] Davis, Maxine, *The Sexual Responsibility of Woman*, New York: Dial Press, 1956.

[8] Rutledge, Aaron L., *Marital Therapy*, Manuscript in preparation; Caprio, Frank S., *The Sexually Adequate Male*, New York: Citadel Press, 1952; ———— *The Sexually Adequate Female*, New York: Citadel Press, 1953; Kroger, William S. and S. Charles Freed, *Psychosomatic Gynecology*, Glencoe: Free Press, 1956.

[9] Rutledge, *op. cit.*; Caprio, *op. cit.*; Bergler, Edmund, *Neurotic Counterfeit Sex*, New York: Grune and Stratton, 1951; Kroger and Freed, *op. cit.*, Chs. 12 and 13; Cleckley, Harvey M., *The Caricature of Love*, New York: Ronald Press, 1957.

Tension growing out of a marital relationship can continue to produce impotence or milder sexual difficulties in the male even after he has been "cured" through psychotherapy, unless something can be done about the wife and the way she reacts to him and he to her. These are the impotence and frigidity cases which the psychoanalyst is prone to refer to the marriage counselor. In general, as a person becomes free from major tension— which presupposes resolution of basic anxiety producing conflicts and the elimination of such stress inducing attitudes as jealousy, envy and greed— and begins to enjoy interpersonal intimacy, satisfactory sexual feelings begin to emerge.[10] Specific sexual guidance may be necessary to overcome these difficulties when psychotherapy is nearing completion if newly discovered self knowledge is to find expression in mutual sexual satisfaction.

Until the symptoms of frigidity or impotence are replaced with sexual adequacy, temporary measures may save the marital relationship. An impotent man may still gain much satisfaction out of intensive love play, if both he and the wife are understanding and actively participate. Often such a man withdraws from show of affection because it reminds him of his "lack of manhood," or because she gets excited and he cannot satisfy her. The wife who is uninhibited enough to let herself enjoy manual and oral stimulation may be brought to orgasm or satisfactory climax by the loving husband who understands sex needs, although he is impotent.[11]

III. Infidelity

Among the major complaints brought to the marriage counselor is sexual infidelity, either actual or suspected. Traditionally man has been presented as the polygamous animal of the species, held to one woman only by law of man or of God, plus perhaps a wife who was either especially desirable or dangerous. Woman, on the other hand, has often been labeled as monogamous by nature. Gradually it becomes evident that marital practices are largely due to social conditioning rather than to inheritance, although a few higher animals are monogamous. At any rate mankind usually prides itself in certain characteristics that are different than or above the lower animals. Kinsey [12] has shown that pre-marital and extra-marital sexual experience is

[10] Fromm-Reichmann, *Principles of Intensive Psychotherapy,* Chicago: University of Chicago Press, 1950.

[11] For experimental treatment of sexual pathology, see Rutledge, *op. cit.*

[12] Kinsey, A. C., W. B. Pomeroy, and C. E. Martin, *Sexual Behavior in the Human Male,* Philadelphia, Pa.: W. B. Saunders & Co., 1948; ———— W. B. Pomeroy, Clyde E. Martin, and Paul H. Gebhart, *Sexual Behavior in The Human Female,* Philadelphia, Pa.: W. B. Saunders & Co., 1953.

quite frequent among both men and women. In literature one still hears more about "the other woman" than "the other man" but the marriage counselor must deal with each.

Many adults are not ready for the intimate life with another person which is expected in marriage. Some are prepared, but only to a carefully selected kind of partner, and modern means of dating and courtship frequently fail to bring about this type of mate selection. In some cases the couple is suited to each other early in the marriage because of the complementary needs which drew them together. Later one mate changes and the marriage loses its meaning and becomes a source of frustration. This provides a natural setting for entrance of "the other person."

Infidelity has almost as many meanings as there are couples involved. It may be an attack upon or refuge from the spouse; an attempt to prove manliness or womanliness; revolt against childish taboos; a method of working out impulses derived from earlier unresolved experiences; an act of revenge upon the other woman or man; gratification of a physical urge which has been inhibited by morals and scruples. It may take the form of adultery, promiscuous necking, flirtation or merely frequent daydreaming. The *fact* of infidelity is relatively unimportant to the stability of a marriage, in contrast to the meaning of infidelity within the relationship; its motive, the interpretation both mates put upon the act, along with their uncultured perceptions of what *should* be done about it.[13]

A slightly different type of dynamics may be operative if the mate turns to prostitutes rather than to a friend or lover. Habitual coitus with prostitutes, as Karpf [14] has pointed out, can have equally disastrous results. Often these relations carry a deprecating attitude toward the woman, an exaggerated sense of self-importance by the man, and lead to dominating demands on the wife which she cannot tolerate. Frequenting prostitutes is not conducive to control or guidance of sexual desire in accordance with mutual satisfaction of husband and wife. It tends to develop grossly self-centered attitudes, with intercourse having little more meaning than masturbation. It discourages thoughtfulness, patience, consideration, gentleness and interest in the woman's needs. Sex habits developed with the prostitute, all the way from the absence of affection to a "quickie" orgasm, are notorious for their inadequacy in marriage. Yet because the prostitute caters to the man's

---

[13] Levy, John and Ruth Monroe, *The Happy Family,* New York: A. A. Knopf, 1938, Chapter 3; Rutledge, *op. cit.*

[14] Karpf, Maurice J., "The Effects of Prostitution on Marital Sex Adjustment" in *Marriage and Family Living,* Vol. XV, No. 1, 1953, pp. 65-71.

every whim, for a price to be sure, his wife seems inadequate. Once the wife is aware of the source of some of the husband's sex knowledge and demands, she may resist many of his desires for unusual sex experiences, lest she be placed in the category of a prostitute. On the other side of the slate are those individuals with intensive experience with prostitutes who nevertheless make good sexual adjustment in marriage.

The marriage counselor's role is not to decide the right or wrong of an adulterous act, or, usually, even whether it is to be continued. He helps the clients handle the panic reactions, which often have made them sexually and emotionally impotent with each other. Then in a calmer mood he and they can get at the real meaning of the infidelity for each of them personally and for the marriage. As things clarify and as they grow in understanding, they become able to make their own choices. When both have faced squarely their involvements in the infidelity, their newly activated love may lead to mutual acceptance and the beginning of renewed marital progress.

IV. Contraception

Although the problem of controlling human fertility goes far beyond the decisions of two people as to whether to have children, when to have them and how many to have, the difficulties of some couples center in such questions. A couple who have a comfortable marriage are likely to find agreement here, or respect for each other in their disagreement. An immature man or woman may resist having children because he doesn't want to share the mate or accept the responsibility of parenthood. A narcissistic person may insist on coitus without a sense of responsibility for possible off-spring. A mature and responsible man or woman justifiably may wonder if an irresponsible mate will be adequate as a parent. Adequate parents may be undecided about their ability to provide for additional children.

Most of the serious conflict about contraception arises around who is going to use what method, anxiety about its effectiveness, and the ethical issue of rightness or wrongness. Contraception taboo, coupled with a few harmful experiences with unsuccessful methods, are woven into certain old wives' tales which become imbedded in the minds of youth as they grow up. The most vicious of these threaten the user of contraceptives with everything from sterility to cancer and impotency. Except when imbued with neurotic meaning these fears are easily erased in a counseling relationship.

Not so easily eradicated are the taboos based upon religious admonition. Quite often the troubled mate or couple are torn between two sets of values

—the right to determine one's personal and family destiny, and the obligation to have it determined by a church or some other force. Disagreement over contraception is a primary source of marital conflict when one or both of the couple believe the practice to be sinful or harmful. When the only method available to them is "rhythm," and when this does not meet their needs, thousands turn either to repression of sexuality or to extramarital sex to resolve the dilemma. This, in turn, often deteriorates a marital relationship which previously was relatively sound.

Conflict is inevitable when a person who believes that sex is a natural or a divine gift whereby man and woman are to express their love, fulfill their needs, and in general contribute to individual and marital health—a view increasingly held by Protestants and Jews—marries another person who believes that, except when used in willingness to conceive, sex is a sin. Such beliefs often are built into the personality fibers and cannot be changed with ease or violated without guilt, and resultant sexual problems. Yet under the pressures of a disagreeing mate, social and economic pressures to have no more children, and perhaps a threat to the mother's health, thousands of people of all religious faiths practice contraception. If it is forbidden they repress the idea of sin, or accept responsibility for the guilt. In other words, they set up a new hierarchy of values, deciding that one sin is greater than another, or that one responsibility takes precedence over another.

The counselor has a tremendous responsibility in such cases to clarify his role, to stimulate the greatest self-fulfillment, and yet not to encourage behavior which will result in incapacitating guilt from violation of a religiously fortified superego.

V. Sterilization

Surgical sterilization is becoming a popular form of conception prevention when couples have all the children desired. This is a simple office procedure for the man but it requires abdominal surgery for the woman. Since it does not interfere physically with sex desire or pleasure, there is much to commend this as a way of eliminating the fear around unwanted pregnancies for those who have enough children or who for various reasons should not have children. Yet it cannot be taken lightly. The emotional effects can be quite serious, particularly the guilt reactions, for those whose value system is violated thereby, and the reactions of the highly neurotic are unpredictable. Some people have become disturbed at a later date when surgery could not *restore* fertility, because circumstances made them desire additional children. Today in only a small percentage of cases can either the male or female tubes be reunited well enough to transport sperm or egg.

Occasionally severe depressive reactions occur in a sterilized or hysterectomized woman. For some it is as though they had given in to early childhood urges to destroy their femaleness and now were taking the consequences, paying the price. Some women, fearing that sterilization means loss of sexual desire or attractiveness, may simply give up as women and as human beings. Actually, the few research results available indicate that only a small percentage of hysterectomized women show depressive reactions. Melody [15] found that four percent of his patients became depressed within three months after hysterectomy; however, careful histories revealed that these women had demonstrated prior to the operation the proclivity for reacting to threat with the particular adaptive pattern of depression. Whether she reacts depressively is dependent upon her own self evaluation which in turn is related to how she perceives and symbolizes the attitude, behavior and expectations of those whose opinion she values. Such a woman may perceive any act of threat or rejection following a hysterectomy as proof that she is ejected from a valued place in life, and therefore resort to her previously selected depressive pattern.

Psychologists and psychiatrists are familiar with the type of man who unconsciously equates sterilization with castration and has increased impotency problems following surgery. Clinicians often infer that some desire for castration may underly the willingness or desire to use vasectomy as a conception prevention measure. However, independent studies by Poffenberger and by Prentiss [16] found that the men who had voluntarily chosen vasectomy as a means of birth control were above average in the absence of emotional disturbance and anxiety. On the other hand, individual cases within these two studies, along with widely reported clinical practice, would indicate that no one should obtain a vasectomy without careful consideration of all the factors involved presently and in the future.

Whether sterilization will prove to be a blessing or a source of problems will be determined by a variety of factors. Many couples find a greater free-

[15] Melody, George F. "Depressive Reactions Following Hysterectomy," *American Journal of Obstetrics and Gynecology*, Vol. 83, No. 3, pp. 410-413, February 1962.

[16] Poffenberger, Thomas and Shirley B. Poffenberger. "Vasectomy as a Preferred Method of Birth Control." *Marriage and Family Living*, Vol. 25, No. 3, August 1963. pp. 326-330; Prentiss, Robert J. et al, "Sociopsychological Characteristics of Patients Obtaining Vasectomies from Urologist," *Marriage and Family Living*, Vol. 25, No. 3, August 1963, pp. 331-335.

dom to enjoy sex life after sterilization than could be experienced so long as unwanted conception was a possibility. Other couples use it as a central point of conflict when one did not wish the operation, or suspects that the sterilized mate merely wanted protection from pregnancies in extra-marital exploits.

VI. Abortion

Abortion is a major health problem since most such operations are illegal and frequently are carried on in unsanitary and otherwise unfavorable circumstances. Several countries have legalized abortion in an attempt to solve the health problem and to reduce the birth rate. The difficulty in obtaining a medically approved abortion in America has resulted in a lucrative market for abortion parlors and lonewolf practitioners, including untrained quacks, nurses and medical doctors of questionable ethics developing a lucrative practice. Unofficial statistics indicate that more abortions are had by married women than by the single. In general, abortion is considered a crime by the law and a sin by the churches because a living, although not yet born, human organism is destroyed.

Findings of the Institute of Sex Research would indicate that many women experience abortion with no interference with their emotional health or subsequent sex enjoyment.[17] Clinical practice, however, portrays the frequent psychological suffering around abortion as seen in marital conflict about it, tension resulting from guilt, and various sexual, mental and psychosomatic symptoms which can follow. One or both of the couple may be so shaken by the experience of abortion as to cease or greatly curtail the enjoyment of sex life together. While the practice of abortion seems to be on the increase, American medical opinion generally seems to veer toward greater conservatism. Author after author in Rosen's book, *Therapeutic Abortion*,[18] gives special emphasis to the guilt complex, "psychic hangovers," and traumatic experiences, which often accompany and follow artificially induced abortion. The subsequent degree of emotional trauma may exceed by far that which would have attended continuation of the pregnancy. Unconscious sentencing of the self to a life of displeasure in all sexual relations is not infrequent.[19]

[17] Gebhart, Paul H. et al, *Pregnancy, Birth and Abortion*, New York: Harper and Brothers, 1958.

[18] Rosen, Harold, editor, *Therapeutic Abortion*, New York: The Julian Press, 1954, pp. 47-96; Kroger, *op. cit.* Chapter 7.

[19] Kroger and Freed, *Ibid*.

Obviously, some of these intense reactions would be reduced in a culture which was more accepting of abortion under clearly understood circumstances. The marriage counselor must work on a smaller scale with one woman or one couple.

VII. Sexual Variations

The varieties of sex experiences which may have been engaged in while growing up have been outlined earlier in Chapter 11. Most of these experiences, in isolation, have little if any direct bearing upon a marital relationship. However, latent or overt homosexuality may be a major factor in frigidity or impotence, and many other kinds of marital stress. The young person turns to homosexual expression as a result of such factors as: failure to resolve male-female identifications as a small child; habit, growing out of adolescent experimentation, often spurred on by segregation of the sexes in schools; fear of adult sexuality; or a combination of these. The psychodynamics of homosexual problems can be most complicated. Early homosexual expression or desire may take on added values which discourage heterosexual development, or become repressed and cause many problems in sexual adjustment. For many men and women homosexuality becomes a way of life meaningful enough to resist all efforts at change. If motivated to change, either of these causes may yield to psychotherapy, particularly if the person is young or not too fixated by habit. Marked involvement in or concern about homosexual tendencies is sufficient reason for recommending postponement of marriage until psychotherapy has brought convincing proof of change. If homosexuality roots in early childhood confusion of roles, or early gross emotional deprivation, long-term psychotherapy will be necessary.

Some individuals with intensive homosexual experience marry, have children and a meaningful home life, but they have to work hard at it. Some are almost equally interested in the sexes and keep up a homosexual liaison after marriage. When discovered by the mate or community this may lead to chaos. Sometimes a job change or even a new community is necessary for a person to avoid continued homosexual temptations when the individual chooses to stick with the marriage. Occasionally each of a couple are homosexual and their marriage serves as a somewhat satisfactory companionship and keeps down suspicion about their sexual relations with homosexual friends, but most of these liaisons seem to break up because of jealousy and other problems.

Many of the sexual expressions which are usually called perversions or aberrations in professional literature are common in marriage. If a term must be applied, a much less judgmental one is *sexual variations,* in that the practices are not the most expected forms of behavior, and yet are not abnormal in themselves. Fellatio, cunnilingus, and other forms of sexual stimulation may represent an illness or emotional stunting if practiced as ends in themselves. As preparatory to or for variety along with sexual intercourse, they are within the range of acceptable human behavior in thousands of healthy marriages. Often one or both of a couple will have major anxiety about these desires and practices. The problem will not be resolved until the practices can be mutually acceptable or one gives them up as not worth the anxiety being caused.[20]

The discussion of sexual experiences in and out of marriage should keep the marriage counselor alert in his own work with the pre-marital couple, and facilitate the task of the physician entrusted with the pre-marital physical examination.

[20] Cory, Donald Webster, "The Homosexual in America," New York; Greenberg, 1951; Aldrich, Ann, "We Walk Alone," New York: Fawcett Publications, Inc., 1955; Ellis, Albert, "The American Sexual Tragedy," New York: Twayne Publishers, 1954; Stekel, Wilhelm, "Patterns of Psychosexual Infantilism," New York: Liveright Publishing Corporation, 1952; Henry, George, "All The Sexes," New York: Rinehart, 1955; Rickles, N. K., "Exhibitionism," Philadelphia: J. B. Lippincott Co., 1950.

BIBLIOGRAPHY

Ackerman, Nathan W., "The Diagnosis of Neurotic Marital Interaction," reprinted from *Social Casework* (April, 1954), Family Service Association of America.

——, *The Psychodynamics of the Family* (New York: Basic Books, Inc., Publishers, 1958).

Alexander, Franz, "Current Views on Psychotherapy," *Psychiatry*, 16 (1953) 113-122.

—— and Ross, Helen (eds.), *Dynamic Psychiatry* (Chicago: University of Chicago Press, 1952).

Allport, Gordon W., *The Individual and his Religion; A Psychological Interpretation* (New York: Macmillan Co., 1950).

Anderson, Harold and Anderson, Gladys (eds.), *An Introduction to Projective Techniques and Other Devices for Understanding the Dynamics of Human Behavior* (New York: Prentice-Hall, Inc., 1951).

Anderson, Ray C., "The Influence of Heredity on Family Health," *Marriage and Family Living*, XIX, 2 (May, 1957), 136-141.

Angyal, Andras, *Foundations for a Science of Personality* (New York: Commonwealth Fund, 1941).

Baruch, Dorothy, *New Ways in Discipline; You and Your Child Today* (New York: Whittlesey House, 1959).

Beasley, Christine, *Democracy in the Home* (New York: Association Press, 1954).

Beauvoir, Simone de, *The Second Sex*, trans. by H. M. Parshley (New York: Alfred A. Knopf, Inc., 1952).

Beck, Samuel J., *Rorschach's Test, Vols. I and II* (New York: Grune and Stratton, Inc., 1949).

Bee, Lawrence, *Marriage and Family Relations* (New York: Harper and Brothers, 1959).

Bell, Norman W. and Vogel, Ezra F. (eds.), *A Modern Introduction to the Family* (Glencoe, Ill.: The Free Press, 1960).

Benedek, Therese, *Insight and Personality* (New York: The Ronald Press Co., 1946).

Benedict, Ruth, *Patterns of Culture* (Boston: Houghton Mifflin Co., 1934).

Berelson, Bernard and Steiner, Gary A., *Human Behavior: An Inventory of Scientific Findings* (New York: Harcourt, Brace and World, Inc., 1964).

Bergler, Edmund, *Neurotic Counterfeit Sex* (New York: Grune and Stratton, Inc., 1951).

Bernard, Jessie, *Remarriage: A Study of Marriage* (New York: Dryden Press, 1956).

Binkley, Robert C. and Binkley, Francis, *What's Right with Marriage* (Appleton-Century-Crofts, Inc., 1929).

Black, Hillel, *Buy Now, Pay Later* (New York: Wiliam Morrow and Co., 1961).

Blood, Robert O., *Anticipating Your Marriage* (Glencoe, Ill.: The Free Press, 1955).

Bonner, Hubert, *Group Dynamics* (New York: The Ronald Press Co., 1959).

Bonthius, Robert H., *Christian Paths to Self-Acceptance* (New York: King's Crown Press, 1948).

Bossard, James H. S. and Boll, Eleanor, *One Marriage, Two Faiths* (New York: The Ronald Press Co., 1957).

————, *Parent and Child* (Philadelphia: University of Pennsylvania Press, 1953).

Brammer, Lawrence M. and Shostrom, Everett L., *Therapeutic Psychology; Fundamentals of Counseling and Psychotherapy* (Englewood Cliffs, N.J.: Prentice-Hall, Inc., 1960).

Brody, Sylvia, *Patterns of Mothering; Material Influence During Infancy* (New York: International Universities Press, 1956).

Buhler, Charlotte, *Values in Psychotherapy* (Glencoe, Ill.: The Free Press, 1962).

Burgess, E. W., "The Value and Limitations of Marriage Prediction Tests," *Marriage and Family Living*, 12 (1950), 54-55.

Burton, Genevieve, "Group Counseling with Alcoholics and their Wives," *Marriage and Family Living*, 24, 1 (1962), 56-61.

Calderone, Mary S., *Abortion in the United States* (New York: Hoeber and Harper, 1958).

————, *Release from Sexual Tensions* (New York: Random House, 1961).

Caprio, Frank S., *The Sexually Adequate Male* (New York: Citadel Press, 1952).

————, *The Sexually Adequate Female* (New York: Citadel Press, 1953).

Chance, Erika, *Families in Treatment* (New York: Basic Books, Inc., Publishers, 1959).

Chaskel, Ruth, "Short-Term Counseling—A Major Family Agency Service," *Social Work Journal*, 34 (1953), 20-23.

Children in a Changing World, White House Conference on Children and Youth, 1960.

Christensen, Harold T. (ed.), *Handbook of Marriage and the Family* (Skokie, Ill.: Rand-McNally and Co., 1964).

Clark, Robert, *Six Talks on Jung's Psychology* (Pittsburgh: Boxwood Press, 1953).

Cleckley, Harvey M., *The Caricature of Love* (New York: The Ronald Press Co., 1957).

Davis, Maxine, *The Sexual Responsibility of Woman* (New York: Dial Press, 1956).

Deutsch, Helen, *The Psychology of Women, Vol. II* (New York: Grune and Stratton, Inc., 1945).

Diagnostic and Statistical Manual, Mental Disorders (Washington: American Psychiatric Association, 1962).

Dickinson, R. L. and Pierson, H. H., "The Average Sex Life of American Women," *Journal of American Medical Association*, 85, 1113-1117.

"Divorces," in *Vital Statistics of the U.S.*, III, Sections 3, 4, and 7, National Vital Statistics Division, 1960.

Doniger, Simon (ed.), *Religion and Human Behavior* (New York: Association Press, 1954).

Dubin, Robert, "Industrial Workers' Worlds: A Study of the 'Central Life Interests' of Industrial Workers," *Social Problems*, III, 3 (January 1956) 131-142.

Duval, Evelyn Millis, *Family Development* (Philadelphia/New York: Copyright 1962, 1957 by J. B. Lippincott Company).

Dyer, William G., "A Comparison of Families of High- and Low-Job Satisfaction," *Marriage and Family Living*, 18, 1 (1956).

Dynes, Russell R., Clarke, Alfred C., and Denitz, Simon, "Levels of Occupational Aspiration: Some Aspects of Family Experience as a Variable," *American Sociological Review*, XXI, 2 (April, 1956), 212-215.

Ehrenwald, Jan, *Neurosis in the Family and Patterns of Psychosocial Defense* (New York: Hoeber Medical Division, Harper and Row, Publishers, 1963).

Eisenstein, Victor W. (ed.). *Neurotic Interaction in Marriage* (New York: Basic Books, Inc., Publishers, 1956).

Ellis, Albert. *The American Sexual Tragedy* (New York: Twayne Publishers, 1954).

————, *The Art and Science of Love* (New York: Lyle Stuart, 1960)

———— and Harper, Robert, *Creative Marriage* (New York: Lyle Stuart, 1961).

———— and Harper, Robert, *A Guide to Rational Living* (Englewood Cliffs, N.J.: Prentice-Hall, Inc., 1961).

————, "New Approaches to Psychotherapy Techniques," *Journal of Clinical Psychology*, Monograph Supplement No. 11 (July, 1955).

———— and Mace, David R., "Pre-marital Relations, Pro and Con," *Controversy Magazine* (August, 1959), 24-47.

————, *Sex Without Guilt* (New York: Lyle Stuart, 1958).

Emerson, James G., *Divorce, The Church, and Remarriage* (Philadelphia: Westminster Press, 1961).

English, Horace B. and English, Ava C., *A Comprehensive Dictionary of Psychoanalytical Terms* (New York: Longmans, Green and Co., Inc., 1958).

Farber, Seymour M. and Wilson, Roger H. L. (eds.), *The Potential of Woman* (New York: McGraw-Hill Book Co., Inc., 1963).

Feldman, Frances L., *The Family in a Money World* (New York: Family Service Association of America, 1957).

Folsom, J. K., *The Famiy and Democratic Society* (New York: John Wiley and Sons, Inc. 1943).

Foote, Nelson and Cottrell, Leonard S., Jr., *Identity and Interpersonal Competence; A New Direction in Family Research* (Chicago: University of Chicago Press, 1955).

Frank, Lawrence, *The Conduct of Sex, Biology and Ethics of Sex and Parenthood in Modern Life* (New York: William Morrow and Co., 1960).

Fromm, Erich, *The Art of Loving* (New York: Harper and Row, Publishers, Inc., 1956).

Fromm-Reichmann, *Principles of Intensive Psychotherapy* (Chicago: University of Chicago Press, 1950).

Freud, Sigmund, *A General Introduction to Psychoanalysis* (New York: Liveright Publishing Corp., 1920).

————, *A General Introduction to Psychoanalysis*, trans. by Joan Riviere, rev. ed. (Garden City, N.Y.: Garden City Publishing Co., 1943).

————, *New Introductory Lectures on Psychoanalysis*, trans. by W. J. H. Sprott (New York: W. W. Norton and Co., Inc., 1933).

————, *An Outline of Psychoanalysis* (New York: W. W. Norton and Co., Inc., 1949).

Gebhart, Paul H. et al., *Pregnancy, Birth and Abortion* (New York: Harper and Brothers, 1958).

Glick, Paul C., "The Life Cycle of the Family," *Marriage and Family Living*, XVII, 1 (1955).

Goldstein, Kurt, *The Organism, A Holistic Approach to Biology* (Boston: The Beacon Press, Inc., 1963).

Goode, William J., *After Divorce* (Glencoe, Ill.: The Free Press, 1956).

Greenblat, Bernard, *A Doctor's Marital Guide for Patients* (Chicago: The Budlong Press, 1959).

Grotjahn, Martin, *Psychoanalysis and the Family Neurosis* (New York: W. W. Norton and Co., Inc., 1961).

Guttmacher, Alan F., *The Complete Book of Birth Control* (New York: Ballantine Books, 1961).

Hall, Calvin S. and Lindzey, Gardner, *Theories of Personality* (New York: John Wiley and Sons, Inc., 1957).

Hall, Robert E., "Use of Intra-Uterine Contraceptives in an Indigent Population," in *Advances in Planned Parenthood*, ed. by Aquiles J. Sobrero and Sarah Lewit (Cambridge, Mass.: Schenkman Publishing Co., Inc., 1965).

Hammons, Helen M. (ed.), *Heredity Counseling* (New York: Paul B. Hoeber, Inc., 1959).

Harper, Robert A. and Harper, Frances R., "Are Educators Afraid of Sex?", *Marriage and Family Living*, XIX, 3 (1957).

———, *Psychoanalysis and Psychotherapy: 36 Systems* (Englewood Cliffs, N.J.: Prentice-Hall, Inc., 1959).

Harrower, M., "Summary of Test Findings" in *Personality Change and Development* (New York: Grune and Stratton, Inc., 1958).

Hastings, Donald W., *Impotence and Frigidity* (Boston: Little, Brown and Co., 1963).

Hathaway, Starke R. and Meehl, Paul E., *An Atlas for the Clinical Use of the MMPI* (Minneapolis: University of Minnesota Press, 1951).

Havighurst, Robert J., *Human Development and Education* (New York: Longmans, Green and Co., Inc., 1953).

Henry, G. W., *Sex Variants: A Study of Homosexual Patterns* (New York: Paul B. Hoeber, Inc., 1941).

Hess, Robert D. and Handel, Gerald, *Family Worlds: A Psychosocial Approach to Family Life* (Chicago: University of Chicago Press, 1959).

Hiltner, Seward, *Sex Ethics and the Kinsey Reports* (New York: Association Press, 1953).

Hitschmann, E., and Bergler, E., *Frigidity in Women, Its Characteristics and Treatment*, trans. by P. L. Weil (Washington/New York: Nervous and Mental Disease Publishing Co., 1936).

Honigmann, John J., *Culture and Personality* (New York: Harper and Brothers, 1954).

Horney, Karen, *Neurosis and Human Growth, The Struggle Toward Self Realization* (New York: W. W. Norton and Co., Inc., 1950).

Jahoda, Marie, *Current Concepts of Positive Mental Health* (New York: Basic Books, Inc., Publishers, 1958).

Johnson, Virginia E. and Masters, W. H., "Intravaginal Contraceptive Study: Phase I. Anatomy," *Western Journal of Surgery, Obstetrics, and Gynecology*, 70 (1962), 202-207.

Joint Commission on Mental Illness and Health, *Action for Mental Health* (New York: Basic Books, Inc., Publishers, 1961).

Jones, Maxwell, *The Therapeutic Community* (New York: Basic Books, Inc., Publishers, 1953).

Jung, C. G., *Two Essays on Analytical Psychology* (New York: Pantheon Books, Inc., 1953).

Karpf, Maurice J. "The Effects of Prostitution on Marital Sex Adjustment," *Marriage and Family Living*, XV, 1 (1953), 65-71.

Kelly, George A., *The Catholic Marriage Manual* (New York: Random House, Inc., 1958).

King, Samuel J., *Your Legal Adviser, A Layman's Handbook of Law* (New York: Permabooks, 1955).

Kinsey, A. C., Pomeroy, W. B., Martin, Clyde E., and Gebhart, Paul H., *Sexual Behavior in the Human Female* (Philadelphia: W. B. Saunders and Co., 1953).

——, Pomeroy, W. B., and Martin, C. E., *Sexual Behavior in the Human Male* (Philadelphia: W. B. Saunders and Co., 1948).

Kiplinger, *Family Success Book* (Washington, D.C.: *Changing Times*, The Kiplinger Magazine, 1959).

Kirkendal, Lester, *Pre-marital Intercourse and Interpersonal Relations.* (Stanford: Stanford University Press, 1961).

Kleegman, S. J., "Frigidity in Women." *Quarterly Review of Surgery, Obstetrics and Gynecology*, 16 (1959), 243-248.

Kluckholn, Clyde and Murray, Henry A. (eds.), *Personality in Nature, Society and Culture*, 2nd ed. (New York: Alfred A. Knopf, Inc. 1953).

Koffka, Kurt, *Principles of Gestalt Psychology* (New York: Harcourt, Brace and Co., 1935).

Kroger, William S. and Freed, S. Charles, *Psychosomatic Gynecology* (Glencoe, Ill.: The Free Press, 1956).

Laidlaw, R. N., "The Psychiatrist as Marriage Counselor," *American Journal of Psychiatry*, 106 (1950), 732-736.

Landis, Judson T., "Length of Time Required to Achieve Adjustment in Marriage," *American Sociological Review*, XI, 6 (1946), 666-699.

Leavy, Stanley A. and Friedman, Lawrence Z., "Psychoneurosis and Economic Life," *Social Problems*, IV, 1 (July, 1956), 55-56.

LeMasters, E. E., *Modern Courtship and Marriage* (New York: Macmillan Co., 1957).

Levy, Leon H., *Psychological Interpretation* (New York: Holt, Rinehart and Winston, Inc., 1963).

Levy, John and Monroe, Ruth, *The Happy Family* (New York: Alfred A. Knopf, Inc., 1938).

Lewin, Samuel A. and Gilmore, John, *Sex Without Fear* (New York: Lear Publishers, 1950).

Liebman, Samuel (ed.), *Emotional Forces in the Family* (Philadelphia: J. B. Lippincott Co., 1959).

Lief, Harold I., "What your Doctor Probably Doesn't Know about Sex," *Harper's* 229, 1375 (December, 1964), 92-98.

Lydon, R. J., *Catholic Teaching on Marriage and Divorce* (New York: Catholic Information Society).

Mace, David R. and Mace, Vera, *Marriage East and West* (Garden City. N. Y.: Doubleday and Co., Inc., 1961).

——— and Stokes, Walter R., "Sex Ethics, Sex Acts, and Human Need: a Dialogue," *Pastoral Psychology*, 12, 117 and 118 (1961).

Malleson, Joan, "Vaginismus: Its Management and Psychogenesis," *British Journal of Medicine*, 2 (1942), 213-216.

Marriage and Family Living (Minneapolis: National Council on Family Relations).

"Marriages," in *Vital Statistics of the U.S.*, III, Sections 1, 2, and 7, National Vital Statistics Division, 1960.

Maslow, A. H., "Self-Actualizing People, A Study of Psychological Health," in *Personality Symposium. No. 1*, ed. by W. Wolff (New York: Grune and Stratton, Inc., 1950).

Masserman, Jules H., *Principles of Dynamic Psychiatry* (Philadelphia: W. B. Saunders Co., 1961).

Masters, W. H., "The Sexual Response Cycle of the Human Female: I. Gross Anatomic Considerations," *Western Journal of Surgery, Ob-*

stetrics and Gynecology, 68 (January-February, 1960), 57-72.

————, "The Sexual Response Cycle of the Human Female: II. Vaginal Lubrication," *Annals of New York Academy of Science*, 83 (1959), 301-317.

———— and Johnson, Virginia E., "The Sexual Response of the Human Male: I. Gross Anatomic Considerations," *Western Journal of Surgery, Obstetrics and Gynecology*, 71 (March-April, 1963), 85-95.

McClelland, D., Atkinson, S., Clark, R., and Lowell, E., *The Achievement Motive* (New York: Appleton-Century-Crofts, Inc., 1953).

McHugh, Gelolo, *The Sex Knowledge Inventory, Form X* (Durham, N. C.: Family Life Publications).

Mead, Margaret, *Male and Female, A Study of the Sexes in a Changing World* (New York: William Morrow and Co., 1949).

Meader, A., *Ways to Psychic Health*, trans. by Theodore Lit (New York: Charles Scribner's Sons, 1953).

Mehr, Robert I. and Osler, Robert W., *Modern Life Insurance* (New York: Macmillan Co.).

Mikesell, W. H. (ed.), *Modern Abnormal Psychology* (New York: Philosophical Library, 1950).

Miller, Daniel R. and Swanson, Guy E., *Inner Conflict and Defense* (New York: Henry Holt, 1960).

Money Management Booklets (Chicago: Household Finance Corporation).

Montagu, Ashley, *Human Heredity* (New York: Mentor Press, 1960).

Moore, Eleanor A., "Casework Skill in Marriage Counseling," *Social Casework*, 34, 253-258.

Moreno, Jacob L., *Psychodramatic Treatment of Marriage Problems* (New York: Beacon House, Inc., 1945).

————, *Who Shall Survive?*, rev. ed. (New York: Beacon House, Inc., 1953).

Morris. J. K., *Premarital Counseling: A Manual for Ministers* (Englewood Cliffs, N. J.: Prentice-Hall, Inc., 1960).

Monroe, Ruth L., *Schools of Psychoanalytic Thought: An Exposition, Critique and Attempt at Integration* (New York: Dryden Press, 1955).

Murray, Henry A., *Thematic Apperception Test* (Cambridge: Harvard University Press, 1943).

Nash. Herndon C. and Nash, Ethel M., "Remarriage and Marriage Counseling," *Journal of the American Medical Association*, 180 (May 5, 1962), 395-401.

Noyes, Arthur P., *Modern Clinical Psychiatry* (Philadelphia: W. B. Saunders Co., 1948).

Opler, Marvin K. (ed.), *Culture and Mental Health* (New York: Macmillan Co., 1959).

Parker, V. H., *The Illustrated Birth Control Manual* (New York: Cadillac Publishing Co., 1957).

Patty, William L. and Johnson, Louise Snyder, *Personality and Adjustment* (New York: McGraw-Hill Book Co., Inc., 1953).

Pennington, L. A. and Berg, Irwin A. (eds.), *An Introduction to Clinical Psychology* (New York: The Ronald Press Co., 1948).

Phillips, Helen U., *Essentials of Social Group Work Skill* (New York: Association Press, 1957).

Pike, James A., *If You Marry Outside Your Faith; Counsel on Mixed Marriages* (New York: Harper and Brothers, 1954).

Pilpel, Harriet F. and Zavin, Theodora, *Your Marriage and the Law* (New York: Holt, Rinehart and Winston, Inc., 1952).

Popenoe, Paul, "Remarriage of Divorcees to Each Other," *American Sociological Review*, III (October, 1938), 696.

Pumpian-Mindlin, E. "Considerations in the Selection of Patients for Short-Term Therapy," *American Journal of Psychotherapy*, 7 (1953), 641-653.

Raimy, Victor C. (ed.), *Training in Clinical Psychology* (New York: Prentice-Hall, Inc., 1950).

Reiss, Ira L., *Pre-marital Sexual Standards in America* (Glencoe, Ill.: The Free Press, 1960).

Retief, P. J. M.. "Physiology of Micturition and Ejaculation," *South African Medical Journal*, 24 (1950), 509-514.

Reusch, Jurgen and Bateson, Gregory, *Communications* (New York: W. W. Norton and Co., Inc., 1951).

Rice-Wray, Edris, "Investigating the Orals," in *Advances in Planned Parenthood*, ed. by Aquiles J. Sobrero and Sarah Lewit (Cambridge, Mass.: Schenkman Publishing Co., Inc., 1965).

Rife, David C., *Heredity and Human Nature* (New York: Vantage Press, 1960).

Roberts, J. and Fraser, A., *Introduction to Medical Genetics* (New York: Oxford University Press, 1959).

Rogers, Carl, *Client Centered Therapy* (Boston: Houghton-Mifflin Co., 1942).

Rorschach, H. *Psychodiagnosis*, trans. by Lemkau and B. Kronenberg (New York: Grune and Stratton, Inc., 1942).

Rosenblum, B., "The Single Interview Case," *Jewish Social Service Quarterly*, 28 (1952), 257-265.

Rothenberg, Robert E., *Medical Dictionary and Health Manual* (New York: New American Library, 1962).

Rotter, J. B., *Social Learning Theory and Clinical Psychology* (New York: Prentice-Hall, Inc., 1954).

Rutledge, Aaron L., "Marriage Problems and Divorce," *Children and Youth in the 1960's*, White House Conference on Children and Youth (1960), 219-232.

————, "The Essence of Family," *Merrill-Palmer News*, IV, 5 (October, 1961).

————, "Evidence of Strength in the Modern Family," *Journal of Home Economics*, 48, 5 (1956), 323-326.

———— and Mace, David R., "Female Orgasm Conference Proceedings," American Association of Marriage Counselors, 1963.

————, "Experimental Techniques with Marital Problems," *Merrill-Palmer Quarterly*, 4, 2 (1948), 88-89.

————, "The Future of Marriage Counseling," *Merrill-Palmer Quarterly*, I (Summer 1955), 141-147.

————, *Individual and Marriage Counseling Inventory* (Detroit: Merrill-Palmer Institute).

————, "Male and Female Roles in Marriage Counseling," *Pastoral Psychology* (October, 1962).

————, "Missing Ingredient in Marriage: Nearness," *Social Science*, 36, 1 (1961), 88-90.

————, "The Perpetuation of Non-value," *Mental Hygiene*, 42, 1 (January, 1959), 64-70.

———— and Gass, Gertrude Z., *Nineteen Negro Men; An Experiment in Manpower Retraining* (Jossey Bass Publishers, Inc., 1966).

————, "Sexual Containment for the Unmarried," *Pastoral Psychology* (April, 1959).

Sadler, W. S. and Sadler, L. K., *Living a Sane Sex Life* (Chicago: Wilcox and Follett Co., 1944).

Saul, Leon J., *Emotional Maturity* (Philadelphia: J. B. Lippincott Co., 1947).

————, "On the Value of One or Two Interviews," *Psychoanalytic Quarterly*, 20 (1951), 613-615.

Sechehaye, Marguerite, *Symbolic Realization* (New York: International Universities Press, 1951).

Segal, Sheldon J., "Fertility Control: Charted and Uncharted Horizons," in *Advances in Planned Parenthood*, ed. by Aquiles J. Sobrero and Sarah Lewit (Cambridge, Mass.: Schenkman Publishing Co., Inc., 1965).

Slavson, S. R., *The Field of Group Psychotherapy* (New York: International Universities Press, 1956).

————, *A Textbook in Analytic Group Psychotherapy* (New York: International Universities Press, 1964).

Sobrero, Aquiles J., "Planned Parenthood Clinics and Medical Research: General Aspects," in *Advances in Planned Parenthood*, ed. by Aquiles J. Sobrero and Sarah Lewit (Cambridge, Mass.: Schenkman Publishing Co., Inc., 1965).

Southard, Samuel, *The Family and Mental Illness* (Philadelphia: Westminster Press, 1957).

Spellman, Howard A., *Successful Management of Matrimonial Cases* (New York: Prentice-Hall, Inc., 1954).

Standal, Stanley W. and Corsini, Raymond J. (eds.), *Critical Incidents in Psychotherapy* (Englewood Cliffs, N. J.: Prentice-Hall, Inc., 1959).

Stern, Edith M. and Hamilton, Samuel W., *Mental Illness; A Guide for the Family* (New York: Commonwealth Fund, 1942).

Stokes, Walter, "A Pioneering Study in the Sex Education of Children," paper presented before American Association of Marriage Counselors, New York City, annual meeting 1959.

Stone, H. M. and Stone, A., *A Marriage Manual* (New York: Simon and Schuster, Inc., 1953).

Strecker, Edward, *Their Mother's Sons* (Philadelphia: J. B. Lippincott Co., 1946).

———— and Lathbury, Vincent T., *Their Mother's Daughters* (Philadelphia: J. B. Lippincott, 1956).

Sullivan, Harry Stack, *Clinical Studies in Psychiatry*, ed. by Helen S. Perry, Mary L. Gawel, and Martha Gibbon (New York: W. W. Norton and Co., 1956).

————, *The Psychiatric Interview*, ed. by Helen S. Perry and Mary Gawel (New York: W. W. Norton and Co., 1954).

Swan, R., "The Application of a Couple Analysis to the MMPI in Marriage Counseling," Ph.D. Thesis, University of Minnesota, 1953.

Terman, L. M., *Psychological Factors in Marital Happiness* (New York:

McGraw-Hill Book Co., Inc., 1938).

Thorne, F. C., "Directive Psychotherapy: Theory, Practice and Social Implications," *Journal of Clinical Psychology*, 9 (1953), 267-280.

Tietze, Christopher, "Review of Clinical Data on Intra-Uterine Devices," in *Advances in Planned Parenthood*, ed. by Aquiles J. Sobrero and Sarah Lewit (Cambridge, Mass.: Schenkman Publishing Co., Inc., 1965).

Truxal, Andrew G. and Merrill, Francis E., *Marriage and the Family in American Culture* (New York: Prentice-Hall, Inc., 1953).

Trythall, Sylvester W., "The Pre-marital Law, History and Survey of its Effectiveness in Michigan," paper presented before American College of Osteopathic Obstetrics and Gynecology, Detroit, Michigan, February 18, 1964.

Van de Velde, T. H., *Ideal Marriage* (New York: Covici Freide, 1939).

Vincent, Clark, *Unmarried Mothers* (Glencoe, Ill.: The Free Press, 1961).

Waller, Willard, *The Family*, rev. by Reuben Hill (New York: The Dryden Press, 1938).

Wechsler, David, *The Measurement of Adult Intelligence* (Baltimore: The Williams and Wilkins Co., 1944).

West, Jessamyn, *Love is Not What You Think* (New York: Harcourt, Brace and Co., 1959).

Wheeler, R. W., "Gestalt Psyhology," *Encyclopedia of Psychology*, 239-244.

———, *Readings in Phychology* (New York: Thomas Y. Crowell Co., 1939).

———, *The Science of Psychology* (New York: Thomas Y. Crowell Co., 1929).

White, Robert W., *Lives in Progress: A Study of the Natural Growth of Personality* (New York: The Dryden Press, 1952).

Winch, Robert F., *Mate Selection; A Study of Complementary Needs* (New York: Harper and Brothers, 1958),

Winchester, A. M., *Heredity: An Introduction to Genetics* (New York: Barnes and Noble, 1961).

Winnick, Louis and Shilling, Ned, *American Housing and its Use* (New York: John Wiley and Sons, Inc., 1957).

Winterbottom, M., "The Relationship of Childhood Training in Independence to Achievement Motivation," Ph.D. Thesis, University of Michigan, 1953.

Wittels, David G., "The Post Reports on Divorce," *Saturday Evening Post* (January 21, 1950; January 28, 1950; February 4, 1950; February 11, 1950; February 18, 1950).